Religion and Politics
in the Middle East

Religion and Politics in the Middle East

Identity, Ideology, Institutions, and Attitudes

SECOND EDITION

Robert D. Lee
Colorado College

WESTVIEW
PRESS

A Member of the Perseus Books Group

Westview Press was founded in 1975 in Boulder, Colorado, by notable publisher and intellectual Fred Praeger. Westview Press continues to publish scholarly titles and high-quality undergraduate- and graduate-level textbooks in core social science disciplines. With books developed, written, and edited with the needs of serious nonfiction readers, professors, and students in mind, Westview Press honors its long history of publishing books that matter.

Designed by Pauline Brown

Library of Congress Cataloging-in-Publication Data

Lee, Robert Deemer, 1941–
    Religion and politics in the Middle East : identity, ideology, institutions, and attitudes / Robert D. Lee. — Second Edition.
        pages cm
    Includes bibliographical references and index.
    ISBN 978-0-8133-4873-5 (pbk.) — ISBN 978-0-8133-4874-2 (e-book)
    1. Religion and politics—Middle East. 2. Islam and politics—Middle East. 3. Middle East—Politics and government. 4. Judaism and politics—Middle East. 5. Group identity—Middle East. 6. Political culture—Middle East. 7. Religion and state—Middle East. 8. Secularism—Middle East. I. Title.
    BL65.P7L4263 2013
    322'.10956—dc23
                                                    2012050398

10 9 8 7 6 5 4 3 2 1

Contents

Preface

I emerged from graduate school in an epoch of great hope for the discipline of comparative politics. David Easton's definition of the political system offered a basis for analyzing both democratic and authoritarian, developed and developing countries. Structural-functionalism dominated the academy. Modernization theory garnered nearly unanimous support. We argued about whether the concept of political culture paved the way toward more useful comparison or only served to emphasize those elements of a system that are unique, but we thought we knew where we were going.

As I finished a dissertation and began to teach, I saw that those ideas and schemes, however provocative, constituted a set of lenses colored differently from the older, institutional lenses but nonetheless colored. The hope for quantification contained in some of the structural-functional thinking never proved practical, at least not in the Middle East and North Africa, the area of my special interest. Detailed comparisons of structures and functions produced description more than analysis. So what if a particular political structure does not perform a particular function that the structure performs in another political system? Methods, approaches, and paradigms began to proliferate.

Some of the most persuasive and influential work on the Middle East and North Africa continued to focus on a single society at a time. However much inspired by theory, and even though their authors often referred to them as "case studies," they described a unique set of institutions functioning in a specific context. Even volumes in the Little, Brown series in comparative politics, while similar in theoretical interests, were not exercises in genuine comparison.

Alternatively, those who turned to rational choice models or political economy for theoretical inspiration neglected the unique for the general. Ronald Inglehart, who took political surveys to Europe (Eurobarometer) and then to the world as a whole (World Values Survey), claimed to show that political cultures remain unique even though his model of "human development" includes only universal propositions. According to Inglehart, all societies are headed in the same direction, though along somewhat different paths and at different speeds. The uniqueness of individual cultures gets lost in the wide-reaching comparisons.

In forty years of trying to teach comparative politics, I have struggled with a dilemma. I believe that students, like scholars, must understand some political systems in depth before they can make broad comparisons. To introduce all the countries of the Middle East and North Africa and suggest that the cultures are all similar is not satisfactory, in my view. But books on the politics of individual countries—and I have always used four countries as my base: Egypt, Israel, Turkey, and Iran—provide some depth for students but differ so much in perspective and approach that comparison is difficult. Some monographs are too complicated for beginning students. Journalistic studies, however readable, lack systemic analysis. Historical studies, however useful, do not emphasize the political dimension that I want to be the center of my course.

I have yearned for materials that would examine a subset of countries with regard to a single set of issues. In recent years, I have focused my course on the relationship between religion and politics, and I began to think about writing a book that would approach that domain and that domain alone. I yearned for a modern rendition of Donald Eugene Smith's *Religion and Political Development*, an enormously ambitious volume that set no geographical or cultural limits for itself. I admire his boldness, but the conclusions do not stand up in the wake of the religious revival that has occurred since it was written.

Would it not be possible to (1) examine the propositions Smith and others have advanced against a more modest range of examples in genuinely comparative fashion and at the same time (2) ground those examples in sufficient cultural detail so that the unique qualities of political systems do not get lost in the comparison? In other words, might it be possible to combine some of the merits of single-country monographs with an effort at comparison limited to a single-issue area, religion? Might it be possible to generate some useful comparative generalizations at a regional level? This study pursues that possibility.

It also seeks the middle ground in another respect. Smith's book was exceptional in its time, because it focused on a topic that was largely neglected: religion and politics. The infatuation of our discipline within modernization theory and the secularization hypothesis that lurked near the center of that theory caused most scholars to downplay the importance of religion. Then came the Iranian

Revolution of 1979, which brought a great turnaround. Suddenly there was an outpouring of studies on Islam and politics. From the supply of books now available on the subject, one could easily conclude that religion is the most important factor in explaining politics in the Middle East and North Africa. With its underlying contention that politics has shaped religion as much as or more than religion has shaped politics, this study seeks to pull back from that idea without dismissing the religious revival as a passing phenomenon of little consequence.

In this second edition, I have added one case study to the four included in the original book. I initially justified my selection of countries on the ground of importance, and I think the addition of Saudi Arabia conforms to that standard. Turkey, Iran, and Egypt have populations (70 to 80 million each) that give them military, economic, and political weight in the region. Israel, despite a much smaller population, qualifies by virtue of its superior military and economic strength. The oil wealth of Saudi Arabia, combined with its rapidly growing population (about 25 million), makes it a member of the club. Moreover, adding Saudi Arabia means bringing into the study a second Arab state, a state that has long identified itself with Islam and is, unlike the other states included here, a monarchy. As one who has always had a strong interest in North Africa, I regret not including Algeria, Morocco, or even Tunisia. But here is the dilemma of one who teaches comparative politics: Is it better to introduce students to a large number of countries in a more superficial way or to a smaller sample of countries in a more detailed way? I have always preferred the latter option. Brief introductions to all the states of the Middle East and North Africa are readily available.

This volume treats five countries with regard to a single issue, the relationship between religion and politics. I have added brief chronologies to help students relate my account to a broader set of events, but I have not attempted to provide detailed coverage of elections, political economy, foreign policies, social issues, or other important topics. I have chosen depth over breadth, although *depth* is, of course, a relative term. The bibliography is a student's route toward a still more thorough understanding than this volume can provide.

Acknowledgments

When a work is long in gestation, it is difficult to reconstruct all of one's debts. I delivered an early version of chapter 3 as a paper at the annual meeting of the Middle East Studies Association a few years ago. I don't remember that it stirred much discussion, but I do remember that Bill Ochsenwald encouraged me to think about writing a textbook. I am grateful for his encouragement.

I began work on this manuscript while on sabbatical leave from Colorado College, and later I received a second leave of absence that permitted me to accelerate the project. The college, where I have been happily employed since 1971, also provided research funds on several occasions to help defray travel expenses. Departmental colleagues listened with patience to elements of my argument and tolerated my occasional absence.

I am especially grateful to a friend from graduate school, Ann Lesch, recently dean of arts and sciences at the American University in Cairo, for reading the whole of the manuscript and providing excellent suggestions. (She looked at the Saudi chapter for this second edition.) Several anonymous readers also provided useful advice, much of which I have tried to follow. Libby Rittenberg, an economist who has worked in Turkey, read the Turkey chapter and provided comments and encouragement.

I did some of this work in Florence, Italy, where I shared many thoughts about religion and politics with Jean Blondel on long walks along the Arno. When he came to Colorado College in Colorado Springs as a visiting professor, we had to settle for sorties along Monument Creek. It is easy to be inspired by a friend of such accomplishment and energy.

To several scholars I have debts not fully reflected in the notes and bibliography. From Mohammed Arkoun, Mustapha Tlili, and Hamadi Redissi I have learned much about the matters I discuss in this book. Similarly, in working on this manuscript, I profited from conversations with Leonard Binder, Robert Bianchi, Eric Davis, Najib Ghadbian, Ellen Lust, and the late Iliya Harik, among others, in multiple sessions of a workshop on the *turath* (heritage) organized by Professor Binder at the University of California–Los Angeles.

Two students at Colorado College, both now alumni, made important concrete contributions to this manuscript. Elias Cohen helped with the research and drafting of the chapter on Israel, and Colin Johnson used a sharp pencil to help with both the prose and the substance of the manuscript. Other students too numerous to name have influenced my thinking by way of discussion in my classes.

At Westview, Karl Yambert showed early interest in this manuscript and offered helpful encouragement. Laura Stine, senior project editor, and Antoinette Smith, copy editor, provided invaluable help in bringing the first edition to fruition and in achieving greater consistency in the text.

In preparing a second edition, I am especially grateful to ten anonymous reviewers recruited by Westview who have used this text in their classrooms. My own experience with Colorado College students suggested the utility of adding a basic chronology for each country to counterbalance the organization of chapters in four nonchronological sections: identity, ideology, institutions, and attitudes (political culture). From the beginning, moreover, I had thought about adding Saudi Arabia to the mix of cases but had decided not to delay publication of the first edition in order to do that. Most of the ten reviewers of that edition endorsed the idea of adding chronologies and a fifth case study; they also mixed praise for the volume and reasons for its usefulness in the classroom with other suggestions for improvement. Perhaps the most important suggestion was their sense that the first two chapters of the first edition were too hefty. I have responded by trimming material from each of them and remolding them into a single chapter. From the twenty-four hypotheses advanced in the second chapter of the first edition, I have chosen to focus on nine, which I return to consider in the final chapter of the book. The consolidation of the first two chapters permitted me to add a case study of Saudi Arabia without adding to the overall length of the book. I would not, of course, pretend that these changes speak to the concerns of all the reviewers. Responsibility for the errors or weaknesses of this book remains entirely my own. I am grateful to Priscilla McGeehon, Anthony Wahl, and Carolyn Sobczak at Westview for shepherding this second edition through the press. Patricia E. Boyd deployed her formidable copyediting skills to make things easier for readers.

None of these persons bears responsibility, of course, for the errors of fact and judgment that I have surely committed despite their help, or for the inconsistencies that remain.

It is my wife of forty-five years, Susan Ashley, professor of history at Colorado College, to whom I owe the most. In Colorado and Oregon, in France and Italy, we have shared a life marked by a combination of tranquility and stimulation, teaching and research, work and play. Her energy keeps me moving both physically and mentally. I run to keep up.

Transliteration

Three of the countries included in this study speak languages written in non-Western alphabets. The fourth country, Turkey, switched to the Western alphabet in the early twentieth century but uses diacritical marks to indicate pronunciation of letters with multiple uses. Both Turkish and Persian include many words of Arabic origin, which are nonetheless pronounced or written differently in Arabic. These problems create difficulty for every Western writer, who must decide how to spell words and proper names coming from these languages. Writers must decide how to transliterate terms; readers must adapt to those decisions.

I have opted to use spellings that are common in the press, largely shorn of diacritical marks. For words that appear frequently in texts on Middle Eastern affairs, I will not use diacritics or set them off with italics. Where a word is less common and might be mistaken for other terms, I will use italics. Thus I will write ulama (rather than ulema or *ulama*). Ulema and ulama are both common spellings of the plural noun meaning "learned men, scholars of Islam." I will write Quran, rather than Koran or Coran, because Quran has become the preferred spelling in the English-speaking world. And I will write Quran rather than Qur'an or Qur'ān for the sake of simplicity. I will write Shia rather than Shiah or Shi'a, and Shii rather than Shiite. For the concept of law in Islam, I will write sharia rather than shariah or shari'a. I will write halakha rather than halaka or halakhah for the concept of Jewish religious law. I will not italicize or capitalize either sharia or halakha, on the grounds that these concepts are commonly invoked in English and capitalization should be minimized.

When words such as these appear in quotations, I will honor the spellings used in the original source.

In general, I will use Arabic versions of words rather than Persian or Turkish derivatives. Thus I will write Muhammad Ali rather than Mehmet Ali (or Muhammad 'Ali), and *tariqat* rather than *tarikat*, for Sufi orders; madrasas rather than medrese for institutions of higher religious learning. But I will violate that rule in some cases, such as ayatollah, which is the Persian title for a high-ranking member of the ulama, meaning "sign of God." The Arabic would be *ayatallah*. And I will violate it with Persian and Turkish names, such as Khomeini.

For similar reasons I will drop the use of even *ayn* and *hamza* from proper names. Thus, the cousin and son-in-law of the Prophet Muhammad, 'Ali ibn abi Talib, will be simply Ali. And the radical Islamist 'Ali Shari'ati will be Ali Shariati. Of course, such policies still involve choice. I will write Gamal abd al-Nasir rather than Gamal Abdel Nasser—both versions of that name seem broadly accepted—or Jamal 'abd al-Nasir or Jamal 'abd an-Nasir, which some Arabists might prefer.

I will write Turkish words and names as the Turks write them, diacritics included, for the same reason one uses accent marks in writing French. The Turks use ş to indicate the "sh" sound. They normally pronounce *c* as English speakers pronounce "j," but ç indicates a "ch" sound as in "child." The ğ (as in Prime Minister Erdoğan's name, for example) serves to lubricate the linkage of two vowels. Dots over vowels (as in Atatürk) have roughly the same effect on pronunciation in Turkish as they do in German.

Experienced readers will have little difficulty with these matters, but may well disagree with my choices. My hope is that readers who are inexperienced in reading texts on the Middle East will be intrigued but not confused by these problems of transliteration. My objective is a policy that permits readers to focus on the substance of my argument.

COLORADO SPRINGS
FEBRUARY 12, 2013

1

The Political
Determinants of Religion

Revolution brought change to several countries of the Middle East in the spring of 2011, but one thing that did not change is the centrality of religion to politics. Although the toppled governments in Egypt, Tunisia, and Libya, all military in origin, saw themselves as secular, they nonetheless had trumpeted their fidelity to Islam. The opposition forces that arose to seize power in Egypt and Tunisia rejected the previous regimes for their hostility to Islamist groups and Islamic principles as well as their authoritarianism. Postrevolutionary political discussions all over the region centered on the place of religion in the state. Islamists strived to show that religion does not blind them to the realities of governing; secularists denounced Islamists but insisted upon their own respect for all religious belief. What had been a simmering issue partly concealed by repression and censorship came into the open and threatened to dominate the new politics in all three of these countries. Western leaders pleased by the overthrow of dictators they had dealt with, all the while holding their noses, now found themselves worried about relations with new regimes more deeply committed to religion than their predecessors. They worried that the new regimes would relapse into authoritarianism or veer toward anti-Westernism, or both. The same sorts of fears complicated attitudes toward the civil war in Syria, where a minority-dominated, sectarian regime supported by Shii Iran faced opposition from Sunni rebels, some of them Islamists. The emergence of Turkey as a democratic, Islamist model for these Arab states reassured many and disconcerted others.

At every turn of events, religion seems to insert itself into the politics of the Middle East, but the region is not unique. One is unlikely to read about current events in any country of the world without encountering some reference to the interplay of the religious and the political. It is hard to think of any moment when this would not have been so in the history of the inhabited space that emerged in the Mediterranean area in classical times and gave birth to three great interrelated religious traditions, Judaism, Christianity, and Islam. Only in the past two or three centuries have people begun to argue that there is something inherently wrong about entangling religion and politics and to suggest that these spheres should be utterly separate. Both Western scholars of Middle Eastern languages and cultures (Orientalists) and champions of modernization theory, such as the German sociologist Max Weber, argued that there were two contrasting possibilities: a "traditional," religiously based state and a modern, secular state. But politics and religion have seldom been so thoroughly fused as the "traditional" model suggests or quite so separate as modern secularists might wish.

Five centuries before the beginning of the common era, Socrates challenged his fellow citizens to think rationally about political matters; he challenged the notion that the state should depend for its notions of justice upon the inscrutable actions and pronouncements of the gods. Accused of attacking the religion of the city, he responded obliquely that he believed in things "divine," and hence in gods, but the defense did not save him from conviction by a jury of his fellow citizens. Yet rather than run away from his death sentence, he chose to obey the laws of Athens, proclaiming that the state is "dearer than one's mother or father," because only within the confines of a state can one live under the law, and without law, the good life is not possible. How could he be sure of these things?[1] The little demon, his divine inspiration, did not stop him in his course of action. Socrates opposed the conventional religion of the city in the name of a belief in a logic itself sustained by divine inspiration.

About a thousand years later, Muhammad emerged in Arabia with a fresh religious vision and the requisite political skills to fashion a state. For many Westerners, and for many modern Islamists, Muhammad's success illustrates the ultimate oneness of religion and politics in the Islamic tradition. In twentieth-century Egypt, Islamists following Sayyid Qutb would seek to re-create that oneness by invoking the revolutionary methods of Muhammad in an effort to overcome what he called the new age of ignorance, a modern *jahiliyya*.[2] Some Westerners, reacting in part to Islamist claims, have suggested that Islam necessarily implies a politics of authoritarianism and aggressiveness. Yet Muhammad, even if he incarnated some perfect fusion of religion and politics, lived only ten years beyond the *hijra* (migration) from Mecca to Yathrib, a town that became known as Medina, the city of the Prophet. From the year 632, the new Islamic community faced the future without a prophet to guide it. The office of successor (caliph) was neither entirely religious in responsibility nor entirely political. The first caliph, Abu Bakr, told his fellow Muslims to follow him only so long as he remained faithful to God and the Prophet. "If I do well, help me, and if I do ill, correct me." He claimed no divine powers.[3] The Islamic world has struggled ever since to balance the religious and the political.

About eight hundred years after Muhammad's death in 632, Sir Thomas More died a martyr in England for his principled stand against the king. A deeply pious man, More accepted appointment by Henry VIII as lord chancellor of England but could not bring himself to bend religious conviction on behalf of his king, who wanted to divorce his wife and marry his mistress, Anne Boleyn, without papal sanction. Henry believed he could not go forward without the moral legitimacy that More's support would convey, but More saw the legitimacy of the British Crown as anchored in the law, and the law as dependent on righteousness and morality. To break with the Roman Catholic Church as the king wanted was simply wrong in More's view. Neither he nor Henry sought to separate religion from politics; it was precisely their interdependence that drove Henry to execute More.

Five hundred years later, in a political system proclaiming the separation of church and state, Martin Luther King Jr. used religious conviction as the foundation of his campaign for civil rights. Like Socrates and Sir Thomas More, he proclaimed his allegiance to absolute standards of truth and justice, which were for him a part of the Christian faith. He appealed to fellow Christians to recognize the injustice of discriminatory laws in the name of a political system founded, in his view, on the Christian precepts of truth and justice. It is hard to imagine that a secular King could have won such support in the black community, and it is hard to imagine the success of the civil rights movement without the support of white liberals, many of them acting from religious conviction.

Of the three religions so tightly related by Abrahamic revelation that they are often called the "religions of the book," Judaism seemed most disengaged from politics. In the Diaspora of Europe, Jews moved toward assimilation in nation-states dominated by Christians, keeping religion in the private sphere. Then, in the midst of the nationalist fervor of the nineteenth century, Theodor Herzl and others began to dream of a Jewish state, creating a movement that came to be known as Zionism. Although the leadership of the Zionist movement was predominantly secular, Zionism without reference to Judaism is inconceivable, and the notion of a Jewish ethnicity independent of religion—a concept embraced by the Israeli left—does not withstand close scrutiny. However, to equate Judaism with Israel and to label Israel a religious state oversimplifies a complicated matter. A purely religious state is a phenomenon just as difficult to imagine as a purely secular state.

Secular state, secularism, *état laïc, laïcité, laïcisme,* separation of church and state, religious state, Islamic state—all these terms tend to be used in ideological fashion to indicate what proponents deem a proper balance between the political and religious spheres. "The separation of church and state is a construct of political theory rather than a description of governing reality," writes N. J. Demerath III.[4] The terms continue to be used even though they do not accurately describe historical realities. On the one hand, French writers attempt to reinterpret laïcité to accommodate the modern reality of state involvement in religious organizations and education. The French government's creation of a council to represent French Muslims illustrates a lack of clarity quite inconsistent with the theoretical formulation of the secular state, the état laïc. On the other hand, although Iranians have declared that theirs is an Islamic state, their constitution contains few elements that correspond directly to Islamic concepts or practice. Debate rages inside Iran about what sorts of liberties and changes can be permitted without jeopardizing the regime's Islamic character.

All states combine religion and politics in some fashion. As Jean-Paul Willaime puts it, "Every set of political institutions is linked to a certain treatment of the religious fact."[5] When strong in organization, the religious sphere always constitutes a potential threat to the political domain because it appeals to the moral sensibilities of the nation. The political sphere, with the powers of coercion and incentive at its disposal, can make life difficult if not impossible for autonomous religious organizations, yet few states have managed to subjugate all manifestations of religion for long periods. Political stability requires "an appropriate harmony between religion and politics."[6] One might define harmony or balance as a condition in which neither the religious sphere nor the political sphere seeks radical redress in the relationship. That does not imply that the power of the two spheres is equal. The power resources of a religious establishment and a political regime are too different to be measured in terms of quantity or even quality. *Balance* merely suggests a condition, necessarily impermanent, in which neither side is explicitly seeking major change. *Settlement* would suggest the maintenance of a long-term condition of balance in a given country.

Any sort of balance depends upon the will of major actors in the two spheres, but it also depends upon the social environment in which these actors must function. Social change affects the two spheres differentially. For example, rising literacy rates increase the ability of the public to read scriptures and political propaganda, including that of religious groups. Believers who study religion in church and in school, and who learn about religions other than their own, come to think of religion as something chosen rather than given, as an object with a given set of characteristics that differentiates itself from other religions. Educated believers open the way toward change in the religious sphere; they enable, but do not necessarily force, religious elites to make new sorts of appeals to followers and demands upon them and the state. The political sphere, still dependent on old elites, may find these demands repugnant, even though by fostering education it may have triggered a transformation in the nature of religious activity. By promoting education and other welfare activities, the religious sphere may itself be able to change society in ways that threaten the power of dominant elites.

Hence, any balance between the religious and the political spheres depends upon a specific set of environmental circumstances over which each sphere has only marginal control. A relatively poor, isolated community governed by elites nominally responsible to an outside power may achieve balance by virtue of its distance from the forces of modernization and globalization. If that community comes to be absorbed into a larger one, or if indigenous forces take full control, or if the outside power introduces schools and teachers, stability may give way to instability in the relationship between religion and politics. To push social change, the state may seek to augment its autonomy from "traditionalizing forces," such as religion, and the balance may tip away from the religious. At other times, the religious sphere may become aggressive in its efforts to redress the balance and curb the ability of political elites to act without religious support.

Historic Moments

Four historical developments have had particularly heavy consequences for the relationship between religion and politics. The first is the advent of the state itself. Marcel Gauchet hypothesizes a prehistoric domain in which religion holds a monopoly on the regulation of society.[7] The foundation of the state constitutes "the first religious revolution in history," he says, because it divides the locus of social control.[8] With the state there emerges a hierarchy that requires explanation and justification. "All subsequent major spiritual and intellectual developments will arise from the contradictions between the inherited representations of the foundation, in whose name sovereignty is wielded, and the historical forms clothing its practice."[9] The state creates movement, whereas the object of religion is to "ward off movement and everything in the society that is likely to engender it. . . . The essence of religion is to be against history and against that which it imposes on us as destiny."[10]

The second historical development is the shift from oral to written traditions, which gave rise to scholarship and the development of law and theology in the "religions of the book," Judaism, Christianity, and Islam. The religious sphere augmented its capacity to function in support of politics, or in opposition to it, over vast geographic spaces and even across cultures. The law (canon law in Catholicism, the sharia in Islam, the halakha in Judaism) became a standard for right conduct and rightful rule; usually a beneficiary, the state nonetheless felt constrained. The interpreters of the law constituted a group of intellectuals capable of exercising political influence.

The third great development, the invention of the printing press, made scholarship, scripture, and law accessible to much larger numbers of people. It was no longer just a few who were in a position to compare the standards of political activity with reality. As literacy rates began to rise, there emerged new religious sects and fresh political demands. The increasingly autonomous individual demanded liberty of religion and other freedoms. The printing press made its debut in Europe about the year 1500, stimulating a push for literacy and contributing to the spread of Protestantism, but the invention found its way to the Middle East only in the nineteenth century. That fact probably helps explain why the religious ferment linked to the diffusion of the printed text in Europe came later in the Middle East and North Africa.

Finally, the printing of materials in vernacular European languages after 1500 contributed to the growth of sentiments that have come to be identified as nationalism. Groups of people, divided by historical experience or united in vast empires with other groups, came to imagine themselves as communities.[11] These communities coincided in only a few cases with existing political boundaries and in still fewer cases with the limits of religious affiliation. As the new phenomenon of the nation-state took shape in Europe and America, the old relationships between religion and politics—for example, a relationship between a multinational empire, such as the Ottoman, and a multinational religion, such as Islam—faced nationalist threat. Among late-developing European nations, Italy is an example of a place where nationalism challenged religion. Far from achieving immediate congruence between religion and state after unification in 1870, the new Italian Republic found itself at odds with the central institution of Christianity, the papacy. The Ottoman Empire faced nationalist challenges in Serbia, Greece, Egypt, and elsewhere in the Balkans. When the empire finally succumbed to European defeat in World War I, Turkish nationalists sought to build a new state without the Ottoman dynasty or its legitimating prop, the religious establishment.

Nationalism in the Middle East

As a new nation in the Middle East, one cut from the heart of a great empire, Turkey was the first to face the need to construct a new relationship between religion and politics. Having decided to accept the Anatolian peninsula as the geography of the new Turkey, the Turkish military, led by Mustafa Kemal (later called Atatürk, Father of the Turks), had little choice but to eliminate the imperial institutions that sustained the old order. And that meant attacking the Ottoman sultanate-caliphate, which had from the beginning pictured itself as a champion of mainstream (Sunni) Islam. While Mustafa Kemal invoked Islam in the name of the new Turkey, especially as he sought to rally non–Turkish speakers such as the Kurds to support the war for independence, politics dictated a revision of the relationship between Islam and the state.

Nationalism in the Middle East nonetheless differed from the European model, because new nations appeared without the widespread literacy that marked Europe in the nineteenth century. Whereas in Europe the development of national literatures had contributed to the growth of nationalism, the push toward mass literacy in the Middle East followed the development of nationalism.[12] It was result rather than cause. Thus, when Mustafa Kemal decided Turkish should no longer be written in the Arabic script but in the Western alphabet, he discombobulated the literate few but not the illiterate many. Similarly, when he acted against the religious elites (the ulama and the Sufi orders), who were compromised by their ties to the landed and military classes of the old regime, he could do so with relative impunity. In Saudi Arabia and in other states of the Middle East, such as Jordan, Morocco, and the shaykhdoms of the Persian Gulf, the political irrelevance of the masses made it relatively easy to create or sustain relationships with religious elites. Limited literacy permitted a shift toward radical secularism in Turkey as it permitted a version of religious traditionalism in Saudi Arabia and elsewhere to capture nationalist impulses and minimize at least temporarily the potential tensions between religious and political life.[13]

One place where widespread literacy conditioned nationalism from the outset was the state of Israel. There a fog enveloped the relationship between religion and politics from the start. Most Jewish immigrants to Palestine before World War II came from Eastern Europe and had the benefit of schooling within the Jewish community. Once the immigrants were in Palestine, the Zionist leadership pushed them to learn Hebrew, which solidified national identity and underscored the relationship between Zionism and scriptures. The proliferation of secular and religious groups, each with somewhat different attitudes about the proper relationship between religion and politics in a Jewish community, made it impossible to govern in the name of religion and impossible to govern without the support of deeply religious people. Mass politics as a fundamental characteristic of Zionism, as it was of European nationalism, conditioned the relationship between religion and politics from the outset.

The invention of the printing press, mass literacy, and the new mass media—radio, television, cassette recorders, the Internet—all have transformed religion and politics. When the dissident religious leader Ayatollah Khomeini succeeded in reaching the Iranian masses via taped sermons in the months before the 1979 revolution brought him to power, he effectively transformed the structure of Islam in that state. In Cairo or Riyadh, taxi drivers listening to sermons on cassette engage in a modern version of an age-old exercise, but sermons on cassette also help create a system of preacher-stars, and since it is more difficult to control the production and dissemination of cassettes than it is to monitor who is preaching in a mosque, the technology hinders state efforts to control religious discourse.[14] That the Saudi opposition finds itself reduced to using fax machines and the Internet to spread its ideas speaks both to the effectiveness and the ineffectiveness of the Saudi regime in its efforts to monopolize the religious sphere. When any Muslim with a few skills and a little money can create a Web site to "explain" Islam, the power once exercised by clergy is diminished.

Modernization Theory

Modernization theory as it was articulated in the 1950s and 1960s identified political development with secularization of the polity. A fusion of religious and political systems was said to mark *traditional society,* the term used to characterize third-world cultures prior to European intervention. The bureaucratization of the polity required the separation of religion and politics, and the creation of participatory institutions depended upon the rationalization of political culture. Religion might condition responses to modernity, but political development meant the progressive relegation of religion to the realms of civil society and private belief.

Modernization theory collapsed in the 1970s and 1980s under a withering barrage of critiques for its reification of two categories, traditional society and modern society; for its insistence on development as a linear process; for its transparent embrace of Western ideals under the guise of scientific objectivity; and for its failure to account for important aspects of both Western and non-Western history—to name a few of its most notable weaknesses. The secularization hypothesis, central to the whole body of theory, proved especially vulnerable to counterfactual critique. Religion began to reemerge as a dynamic, vital force in the politics of most Muslim countries; the civil rights movement in the United States, liberation theology in Latin America, the clash between Protestants and Catholics in Ireland, and the prominence of Christian democratic parties in several European states cast doubt on the notion that religion no longer counted in the politics of the West. The defenders of modernization theory found themselves trying to account for aberrations in implausible ways: "Yes, religion remains important in the United States, but American religion is more social than religious." Or "the Islamic revival is a mere blip on the screen, a short-term deviation from the pattern."

Modernization theory relegated religion to the dustbin of history—where Marx had already put capitalism—but like capitalism, religion did not go quietly. Religion and politics seem as thoroughly intertwined as ever, perhaps more thoroughly in some parts of the world than others, but the difference is one of degree rather than kind. Religion shapes politics, and vice versa. Under what circumstances, if any, can religion play a positive role in political development? How can the state negotiate a relationship with organized religion that serves the interests of political stability and of religious integrity? What are the possibilities for "settlement" of this relationship in a relatively durable way? Can one discern multiple versions of secularism or multiple roles for religion in political life? As one writer puts it: "We do not yet have a very good conceptual model, much less a theory, to account for the tumultuous entanglement of religion in politics all around the globe."[15]

Comparative politics necessarily presupposes a normative perspective. Aristotle founded the discipline with his effort to discern the advantages and disadvantages of different types of government. Machiavelli fashioned his notion of the ideal prince on the basis of a conviction that a strong government capable of maintaining political order is better than a weak government and that peace is a requisite of civilized life. Both Thomas Hobbes and John Locke sought to construct models of good government capable of producing not just peace but a modicum of political liberty as well. Comparisons done in the name of structural-functionalism, Marxism, civil society, and political economy—all presume judgment about desirable versus undesirable outcomes. Any comparative treatment of religion and politics must ask how the interaction of religious and political spheres affects the possibility of realizing desirable outcomes.

The notion of political development, although it emerged from modernization theory, remains useful as a shorthand for desirable political outcomes. Following Samuel Huntington and others, Thomas Ertman defines political development to include two components: the institutionalization (bureaucratization) of the state and the expansion of inclusiveness through the implementation of constitutionalism.[16] A state that is increasingly staffed by professionals, who are chosen on the basis of merit, will be capable of providing higher-quality services—defense, economic regulation, infrastructure, health, education; it will be increasingly capable of responding to emerging needs and using resources efficiently. A state based on broad participation and the guarantee of individual rights will command greater loyalty from its citizens and be capable of extracting the resources required to provide high-quality services. A state based on patrimonialism and authoritarianism will be incapable of competing with a bureaucratic, constitutional state in waging war and providing the good life for its citizens. As Ertman shows in the case of Europe, neither aspect of political development is sufficient without the other.

A study of religion and politics undertaken with political development as the norm must ask how the interaction of religion and politics affects the possibilities for bureaucratization and constitutionalism. Can organized religion, understood in the broadest sense as a set of beliefs, identities, organizations, and practices, contribute under specific conditions to political development? Does religion under some (or all) circumstances retard political development? Why does religion reinforce the strength and stability of the state under some circumstances and undermine it in others? Why under some circumstances does it devolve into sectarianism while in other contexts it becomes a foundation for compromise and construction? Under what circumstances does religion tend to disappear from the public arena, and under what conditions does it reappear?

Is any relationship between the political and religious domains more conducive than others to the emergence and maintenance of a bureaucratic-constitutional state? The secularization hypothesis suggests that such a relationship must be based on political secularism. Are other models of religious-political equilibrium conducive to political development at some stage? What might be the advantages of an official state religion?

These questions focus on religion as an independent variable and politics as a dependent variable. Scholars working from the perspective of modernization theory have asked whether Protestantism or Catholicism is more consistent with democratic development, whether Christianity or Islam poses greater obstacles to modernization, and whether citizens with strong religious beliefs are more or less inclined to vote for certain parties or policies.[17] Religion appears from this perspective to be a fixed, primordial aspect of a person's psyche and a long-term influence over the politics of a country. It is usually treated as having existed prior to the formation of political institutions and policies, a cause of politics rather than an effect. I propose to examine a set of propositions offered in this vein. The propositions are paired, one positive about the role of religion, one negative, in each of four categories: identity, ideology, institutions, and political culture. All the propositions reflect arguments found in the literature of sociology and politics, but the textual formulations, which combine and simplify ideas, are mine.

Identity

The modern doctrine of social contract proposes that states should be the creation of peoples who already have a common identity and reach agreement with each other to form a government. The French nation made revolution. The American nation revolted against the British and adopted a constitution. What the new nations showed was an incredible vigor produced by the loyalty and energy of the citizens who identified with them. Identity powers the nation-state. The question, then, of what constitutes identity with the nation becomes a much more critical issue than ever it was in the age of empire. In fact, the Ottoman Empire, which housed a panoply of religious and ethnic identities, came under pressure to acknowledge the rights and legitimacy of ethnic and religious minorities, who were increasingly hostile to an empire they began to see as outmoded.

The triumph of the nation-state, thanks largely to imperialism in the Middle East, has disrupted the relationship between religious identity and political identity virtually everywhere. There is not, and never was, any perfect correspondence between religious and political identity in the area, but it scarcely mattered in an earlier era. Now it does matter, because the new nation-states lack legitimacy. To pretend that all Syrians gathered together to make Syria a state would be preposterous. Modern Syria emerged from Ottoman control after World War I as a result of French and British decisions rather than Syrian self-determination. But the leaders of the new Turkey, like leaders in Egypt, Morocco, Iraq, Syria, and elsewhere, know that any hope of making strong, effective political entities means building an identity within the body politic. That is the foundation of any nation-state. Religious identities, on the other hand, divide states within their borders and create allegiances across borders, weakening fragile nation-states.

Hypothesis 1: A state built upon religious identity and reflecting major elements of national history may be able to construct institutions seen as indigenous in origin and capable of generating a loyalty among subjects and citizens that other governments do not enjoy.

A state that shapes its institutions to reflect religious tradition may appear more authentic and genuine than a state that keeps religion at arm's length. The Saudi and Iranian states enjoy an aura of legitimacy that comes from identifying with Islam. Whether their institutions reflect foreign influences as well, or whether their policies always adhere to Islamic law, as they say they do, is another matter. Though surely not invulnerable, both states have survived difficult times and avoided the political instability characteristic of more secular states. The Moroccan and Jordanian monarchies have also clothed themselves in Islam and have managed to survive despite what Huntington defines as "the king's dilemma": To modernize is to undercut the tradition upon which the regime depends, but not to modernize society and economy is to invite revolt from a people that sees others benefiting from better lifestyles.[18]

In the Middle East, Israel is perhaps the state that has used religion most successfully as a badge of its uniqueness and authenticity. While Judaism does not figure in the constitution, because there is no constitution, it constitutes an essential aspect of state institutions. The government honors the Sabbath, leaders let themselves be photographed participating in religious ceremonies, Yeshiva students enjoy military exemptions, and, most important, the state bases its case for legitimacy on Jewish history. The Shoa (Hebrew for the Holocaust) constitutes the most critical aspect of that history; the Yad Vashem, a memorial to the Holocaust, is where foreign leaders go first when they make official visits. It is difficult to imagine a state capable of incorporating Jewish immigrants from all over the world that does not have Judaism built into its institutions.

States of relatively recent origin, such as those of the Middle East, may have a particular need to draw on religion as a source of identity. Durkheim argued that religion had its origins in the human need for society. All societies come together to assert common values, and in that process, they create a distinction between the sacred and the profane. Religion necessarily evolves as societies expand and contract and the elements of commonality evolve. No community can be without religion, in his view. To integrate church and state makes for a stronger community in newly created societies. Separation of church and state relativizes all religion and diminishes the value of the religious bond.[19]

Hypothesis 2: Religious identities, when not congruent with a state's boundaries, may prevent the formation of strong polities capable of ensuring peace and liberty for its citizens.

This hypothesis counters the first. The champions of hypothesis 2 tend to see religious (and ethnic) identity as primordial, anchored deep within the human consciousness, hence enduring and nonnegotiable. Examples to support that notion abound: India, Northern Ireland, Belgium, Lebanon, Iraq, Sudan, Nigeria, and others. Hobbes, who saw the divisive effect of religion in seventeenth-century England, thought the Leviathan required a single religious identity focused upon the sovereign. Locke built a case for toleration, but not of Catholics or atheists, groups deemed incapable of collaborating in the construction of a liberal state. Arend Lijphart's consociational or consensus model, liberal and somewhat democratic, seemed to promise political development in states deeply divided by religion, but the collapse of Lebanon and the tribulations of Belgium have weakened the case for consociationalism.[20] Of course, there are also examples of modern states where multiple religious identities have not prevented the development of a strong constitutional state.

The hypothesis gains strength from being sharpened. An increased emphasis on religious identity as a tool for mobilizing political action may divide a state and compromise its ability to ensure peace and liberty. It may lead to sectarianism rather than to *sectorialism*, by which Avishai Margalit means that a group retains an "overriding commitment to keeping a shared framework."[21] The mobilization of the Shia in Lebanon in the early 1970s under Imam Musa al-Sadr to fight for social justice and a fair share of political influence in that country triggered resistance from the dominant Maronite Christian group. While the subsequent civil war can scarcely be regarded as a struggle between Christians and Muslims over religious doctrine, the appeal to religious identity in the Shii community elicited an analogous appeal on the part of others. Similarly, the rise of Islamism in Egypt in the 1970s and 1980s led to attacks on the Christian minority, who, suddenly embattled, began to rally as a group to fight for their place in politics. The creation of an Islamic republic in Iran jeopardized the already precarious position of minorities such as the Bahais.

Ideology

Religious ideas about authority tend to follow from political ideas, and political ideas often seek to ground themselves in religious thought. "In Georgian England, as much as in the seventeenth century, politics was a branch of theology," writes William Gibson.[22] One might say something similar about the Middle East in the twenty-first century. The political ideologies most hostile to religious authority—Marxism, especially in the Soviet interpretation, and French radicalism at the end of the nineteenth century—have not fared well. The Soviet Union collapsed without having eradicated religion, the French infatuation with laïcité diminished with the fall of the Third Republic and the rise of a Christian democratic party in that country, and Turkey backed away from its laïcisme when it moved to multiparty democracy after World War II. The flow of ideologies and analogies has been from politics to religion, not vice versa, but religion has successfully resisted ideas, such as Marxism, that threatened the existence of the religious sphere. Politics cannot dictate religious ideology, but religious actors have historically been creative in adapting religious ideas of authority to political circumstances.[23]

Modern religions have all faced the challenge of adapting to the democratic surge of the nineteenth and twentieth centuries. François Burgat echoes what many have said: "There is a fundamental antipathy between all religious dogma and the democratic idea."[24] Dogma depends upon certainty, which is anchored in revelation for all peoples of the book. Dogma does not depend on democratic decision-making to give it the stamp of truth. In their dogmatic forms and over long spans of history, Christianity, Judaism, and Islam have all been illiberal and undemocratic in their basic message. Many thousands of pages have been written to show how one or the other of these religions is or is not propitious for the emergence of modern liberalism, socialism, or democracy. But since human beings constructed the dogmas of all religions when they knew nothing of modern liberalism, socialism, or democracy, any hint of these modern ideas in ancient texts must be regarded as purely accidental. Fortunately, all three of these religions do contain elements that can and do serve in the contemporary era as tools for legitimating the evolution of religious thought in liberal and democratic directions.

Hypothesis 3: The progressive exclusion of religion from the body politic would undermine the state's legitimacy. The most fundamental principles of liberal-democratic government cannot be reduced to empirical propositions. It is impossible to show empirically that people are equal. That proposition, like others, requires a leap of faith or a normative judgment. Religion can help nurture faith in democracy.

Liberalism in Europe came from political thought deeply influenced by both classical and Christian writers, and religious dissenters were among those who pushed first and hardest for liberty. Owen Chadwick writes: "In Western Europe the ultimate claim of the liberal was religious. Liberal faith rested in origin upon the religious dissenter."[25] To be free to practice religion meant freedom to speak on other matters. When dissenters formed colonies in North America, they did so to be free to worship and free to establish ethical governments. In the Great Awakening of the eighteenth century, Jonathan Edwards and his followers invoked a new, benevolent, rational God. Fewer were the references to God as king. Instead, "biblical ideas of covenant were combined with Lockean ideas of political obligation."[26] As David Nicholls explains, religion supported the new politics and the new constitution: "The constitution was viewed by many Americans as an earthly reflection of that divine constitution according to which God rules the universe."[27]

Can a liberal polity sustain itself and its authority in the long run without reference to any standards external to its own decision-making processes? Those processes depend upon some form of majority rule to lend righteousness and moral purpose to the actions of the state. A majority authorizes a constitution, which authorizes a majority to decide what is right. Yet many would insist, with Martin Luther King, that laws approved by the majority can be unjust. For King, there was little question that the legitimacy of American government depended upon notions of justice generated in the Western tradition of political thought, itself conditioned by Christianity. To sever the link between religion and politics would deprive the political system of a critical source of its claim to do what is right.

Some have argued that liberalism faces a crisis of legitimacy precisely because it has sought to separate itself from its religious origins. The state has come to represent individual interests, whose only legitimacy lies in the wills of its citizens. Removed from its pedestal, the state must follow what its members decide is the path of virtue; it has lost the ability to chart that path.[28] The liberal state, says Ernest Fortin, is condemned by modernism to defend itself in secular terms, looks to philosophy for new foundations, but philosophy still seems more bent on destroying than on creating foundations: "Civil society depends for its stability and well-being on the attachment of its citizens to a set of laws and a corresponding way of life that are never completely rational, but that attachment is undermined by the philosopher's unswerving dedication to reason."[29]

The nation-state itself is an artificial entity. It has no intrinsic legitimacy. Whereas the early nation-states of Europe found plausibility in common language, they also looked in many cases to religion as a legitimating force. Newer states, many contrived on the drawing boards of Europe and constructed on the

European model by imperial powers, struggle to establish legitimate credentials. It is not surprising that they, too, seek to cover themselves with religious symbols, rhetoric, and ideas. They seek a grounding that secular liberalism cannot provide.

Hypothesis 4: Some religions, such as Roman Catholicism and Islam, are undemocratic in tendency. Others (varieties of Protestantism) seem to be linked to the growth of democratic institutions. Hence, some types of religion must give way or engage in reform if political development is to occur.

Nicholls argues that images of God necessarily derive from human experience. Insofar as human beings imagine God as authoritative and powerful, they invoke political analogies to describe those roles—ruler, Lord, king, master, sovereign, judge. God rules the heavens as kings and presidents rule on earth.[30] By the same token, religious understandings of God necessarily come to influence political ideology. For example, a notion of a transcendent God far removed from human affairs, oblivious to the disputes of humankind, unavailable to the prayers and entreaties of mere individuals, prime mover and final judge of human behavior, becomes one model for political authoritarianism. However, the image of a God present in the world to alleviate the suffering of humankind and guide it to better pastures, a God to be discovered in the actions of some and absent from the actions of others, may lend itself to exploitation by political authorities claiming to represent God on earth. Nicholls writes: "A God who is unambiguously immanent may too easily be used to sanctify a current political system, while a merely transcendent being, ruling over an alien world, readily provides a model, and thus a potential legitimation, for arbitrary political rule."[31]

Radically transcendent and thoroughly immanent concepts of God sustain authoritarianism, but neither mainstream Christianity nor mainstream Islam takes an extreme position on this matter. In the case of Christianity, God appeared on earth. In the case of Islam, God sent down the Quran to shepherd human beings toward a better life. Saint cultures emerged in both religions to soften the dichotomy between heaven and earth. Donald Eugene Smith rates Islam and Roman Catholicism equal in "dogmatic authority" and "directive authority" (three points each on a three-point scale) but ultimately judges Catholicism more authoritarian not because of ideology but because of organization (a hierarchical as opposed to an organic religion).[32]

Rulers in both traditions have found ample ammunition to claim divine origin, divine guidance, and divine status for their own versions of authoritarianism. Scholars have argued that the Catholic countries of Europe struggled longer and harder against authoritarian rule than did the Protestant states. Inglehart has reiterated the Weberian contention that Protestantism triggered the growth of materialism and entrepreneurship in northern Europe, and this shift in values ultimately contributed to the growth of liberal constitutional regimes in these countries. Attitudes in Catholic Europe remain somewhat more traditional and authoritarian in the survey data he analyzes.[33] Ideology slows political development by retarding the shift in values toward greater citizen confidence and competency.

The reform movement in Islam launched by Jamal al-Din al-Afghani and carried forward by Muhammad Abdu in Egypt proceeded from similar assumptions. Abdu believed that political and economic development in the Muslim world depended upon revising Islamic theology. The prevailing Sunni view held that truth came only through revelation and that Islamic law, as compiled by the scholars of the ninth and tenth centuries, followed directly from revelation. Religious authority aligned itself to support an authoritarian ruler committed to upholding Islam and to opposing any innovation, deemed heretical because one human being cannot change what God has fixed. Abdu argued that revelation itself affirmed reason, and thus modern scientific discoveries based on reason could not contradict revelation; they could not be deemed heretical innovation. For Afghani, Abdu, Rashid Rida, and others of reformist inclination, the capacity of Muslim societies to modernize depended first upon change in the ideology of Islam. They looked for inspiration to the pious ancestors (*salafi*).

Westerners joined these salafi reformers in blaming the backwardness of Muslim societies—economic, social, and political—on the dogmatic character of Islamic thought. Describing the victory of theology over philosophy in the medieval Islamic world, Orientalists portrayed a society convinced that it had established the truth and insulated itself against fresh ideas in any realm. The late representatives of the Islamic philosophical tradition, Ibn Rushd (Averroës) and Ibn Khaldun, however influential in the West, exercised little or no influence on Islamic thought. More advanced in military and bureaucratic techniques than its European contemporaries of the fourteenth and fifteenth centuries, the Ottoman Empire could not keep pace with Europe as the scientific, technological, philosophical, social, and political revolutions unfolded there. The Ottomans disdained innovation in deference to an ideology of unchanging truth founded in revelation. Such is the argument that religious ideology can obstruct political development.

Institutions

Separation of church and state remains fundamental to liberal thinking, just as the fusion of religion and politics remains an objective of Islamists. But neither fusion nor separation of religious and political institutions has proved workable. Islamists look to the Medina state, founded by Muhammad in 622 and destroyed by the first civil war (656–660) within the Islamic community, as an example of the fusion they admire. Even then a struggle over compiling the Quran under the third caliph, Uthman, suggests potential if not real divergence between the organization of religion and the organization of the state. Similarly, it may be possible to speak of John Calvin's efforts to make the city of Geneva into "one great church," but, like the Medina state, the arrangements depended largely on the presence of a single man. Muhammad's Medina and Calvin's Geneva constitute but tiny segments of Muslim and Christian history. They are scarcely typical of either tradition.

The complete separation of religious and political institutions has been fleeting and illusory, because religious institutions cannot exist apart from sovereign authority. Even if religious institutions are not explicitly a part of the state but rather constitute a part of civil society, the authority of the state creates the shell in which civil society can function. The state may decide to tolerate autonomous religious organizations or even favor them with tax benefits in exchange for support of the existing political order. It may choose not to favor any one organization over another. It may choose to treat members of all religious organizations as equal in importance to each other and to atheists and agnostics. But no more than corporations chartered by the state or benevolent associations founded in conformity with the law can religious organizations be entirely separate from the state.

The case of France shows why complete separation is not possible. The French conception of secularism (laïcité) responded to a precise set of political circumstances.[34] Champions of republican institutions at the end of the nineteenth century regarded the Roman Catholic Church, bulwark of the nobility and the monarchy in the ancien régime, as a reactionary force, hostile to liberal, democratic ways. (At the same time, the French state undertook a colonial *mission civilisatrice*, which was heavy in religious overtones.) Republicans sought to separate church and state and, especially, to take education out of "enemy" hands. A century later, after almost fifty years of the Fifth Republic, with the Church no longer an enemy, the state helps support private (Catholic) schools, permits tax deductions for religious donations, and funds cultural activities linked to religious causes. For example, it has supported museums located in churches, infrastructure for a papal visit to France, and Islamic cultural centers, which include mosques. This is the new version of laïcité. France may require more separation of political and religious institutions than do other European states, but the difference between France and the others is diminishing. (One French writer puts the other European states into three categories: (1) "absence of laïcité": Great Britain, Denmark, Greece; (2) "semi-laïcité": Germany, Belgium, Netherlands, and Luxembourg; and (3) "quasi-laïcité": Portugal, Spain, and Italy.)[35] Very attached to the concept of laïcité, the French would rather redefine it than simply acknowledge its inadequacy.

States have historically depended on religious organizations for a number of services vital to political development. In Europe the early development of state bureaucracies depended upon the literate class, composed mostly of clerics, who became clerks. The Church helped supply local leadership, community solidarity, schools, and welfare services long before states began to think about supplying these things. Effectively, the Roman Catholic Church, and eventually Protestant churches, gave the state greater capacity to provide for the needs of subjects than it would otherwise have had. Mosques, religious foundations, Sufi orders, and lay Islamic organizations perform some of these same services in the Islamic world. State takeover requires an increase in the state's bureaucratic, managerial capacities; in the absence of that capacity, takeover diminishes innovation, reduces service, and increases public dissatisfaction.

Religious organizations also help provide structure to a state in which political parties do not exist. Before the era of mass communication, the church reached more people than did any other institution. Dissident groups used religion to oppose the state, and the state did not hesitate to ask the established church for its support against these groups, or for war against heretic foreigners. In his study of Lindau, Germany, Wolfart argues that the breakup of Christianity into multiple confessions contributed to state building in early modern Europe.[36] The Catholic Church, closely tied to the French nobility, built rural support of the monarchy in the ancien régime. The Church of England, reaching across class barriers, structured the social stability of eighteenth-century England.[37] Alexis de Tocqueville saw the churches of America as the great organizational underpinning of democracy at a time when parties were just beginning to take root. Meeting with friends and neighbors, talking about the issues of the day, committing oneself to God and country, and participating in the new democracy were all possible through the churches. The role of churches in fostering political interest and activity may still hold. Recent studies show that churchgoing among African Americans correlates positively with political involvement.[38]

Hypothesis 5: Religious organizations engaged in projects promoting the common welfare—education, medical care, child care, and the like—can help generate a set of nongovernmental institutions that train citizens and open the way to a stronger, more inclusive state. They can contribute to the construction of civil society. Politicization of religion produces a pluralization of religious groups that may eventually contribute to pluralism in the political arena.

Durkheim posits that religions inherently reflect society. They grow from people's needs for social solidarity, and therefore they inevitably produce *churches*—communities of believers or disciples who profess common beliefs and follow common rites. Serving social needs is thus a primary rather than a secondary goal.[39] Religious institutions in many parts of the world have been major providers of clerical and educational services. Tocqueville noted the extent to which the churches of America helped draw people together and prepare them for full participation in democratic political life.

Vaclav Havel has done more to revive the theory of civil society than any other statesman. For him civil society comes as a response to a state that tries to dominate every aspect of social interaction so that citizens forget that they themselves can be the protagonists and animators, that they can, independently of the state, provide for many of their own needs and, from that experience, learn that the state, too, is their instrument, not their tutor. Political scientists have seized upon this notion and examined the extent to which various contemporary states nourish civil societies capable of carrying the societies eventually toward more liberal and democratic institutions. A pair of volumes on the Middle East edited by Augustus Richard Norton reflects that perspective.[40]

Islamist organizations such as the Muslim Brotherhood in Egypt and Jordan have created or reinvented a set of associations and organizations that enhance civil society.[41] The Brotherhood got its start as a community organization in Ismailia, an Egyptian city in the Sinai peninsula. As the Brotherhood spread to other cities, it sought to engage its members in constructing facilities such as mosques, schools, sports centers, and parks. It provided services, including education, to its members. With roots in the literate, modernizing, lower middle class, it created elements of a civil society that eventually became a political force. The state has nonetheless regulated, channeled, controlled, limited, and otherwise dominated the civil society.[42] Religion has strengthened civil society, and if civil society has thus far been unable to take control of the state in which it functions, it nonetheless represents a force for democracy. Robert Hefner calls it civil-democratic Islam as opposed to statist Islam.[43]

As Eickelman and Piscatori argue, it is increasingly difficult to identify Islam with a single voice and a single organization in Muslim-dominated countries.[44] Even in Saudi Arabia, where the state uses its power to maintain a unified front, dissident voices from within the ulama have made themselves heard. In the somewhat more liberal atmosphere of Hosni Mubarak's Egypt, a cacophony of voices claimed to speak for Islam: militants demanding revolution, secularists demanding a rethinking of the sharia, ulama attempting to support or influence state decisions, the Brotherhood and its multiple offshoots seeking to steer government action by undercutting the interpretations and authority of the ulama, and the state itself trying its best to flood the market with religious propaganda designed to legitimate its policies and actions. That list leaves out Coptic Christians, who have become more politicized in an effort to stave off Islamist legislation, and Muslim Sufis, who since 2011 may be inclined to join the game. Eickelman and Piscatori, among others, speculate that the de facto pluralization of Islamic institutions in Egypt and elsewhere bodes well for democratization.[45] Pluralism coupled with tolerance produces political competition.

Hypothesis 6: Organized religion, where it takes hierarchical form, may obstruct political development by resisting state efforts to develop state authority and to

*provide directly for the general welfare of citizens. Only a state in which religion
and politics are thoroughly separated can provide political development.*

Machiavelli pronounced Christianity the worst of religions for sustaining political
stability, because it was not identical in scope with any state. As a power outside
the state, the papacy had followers and opponents in every community, dividing
where it ought to have united. It did not hesitate to invite foreign intervention
in the Italian peninsula, if such action served the interests of the Church. Venice
earned the enmity of Rome for treating the papacy as just another state, driven
by interest rather than principle. The Venetian refusal to accept papal appointments led to the imposition of sanctions against one of the most advanced polities
of its day.

Roman Catholicism is more hierarchical than Islam by virtue of the priesthood and centralized management. The alliance of the Catholic Church with
the ancien régime and the Church's opposition to the French Republic through
the late nineteenth century embittered the debate in France about public schools.
The papacy set itself against the Italian Republic in the first half century of the
republic's existence, forbidding Catholics to vote or hold office. Smith treats
Islam as an "organic" religion, that is, one lacking in a distinct religious hierarchy,
but the Ottoman sultans of the Tanzimat period came to see the corps of ulama,
with its prerogatives and privileges, as separate from the will of the sovereign
and as an obstacle to reform.[46] In Egypt Muhammad Ali sought to subjugate the
ulama, perhaps because of their standing as an indigenous elite sustained by significant economic resources. To do so he sought to create hierarchy by elevating
the Shaykh al-Azhar to preeminence over other ulama.[47] Thus Islam became hierarchical in some times and places.

The separation hypothesis presumes that organized religion must move
from the public realm to the private and become a matter of individual con-
science. The theory claims that government combined with an official church
limits the freedom of citizens to practice religions of their choice. Effective,
rational government requires the services of all citizens, religious or not. Since
moral claims cannot be verified, the claims of religious organizations deserve no
more weight than the interests and claims of groups lacking the authority of God.
Constitutional, bureaucratic government depends upon the will of the people,
not the will of God. As Peter Berger puts it: "Religion mystifies institutions by

explaining them as *given* over and beyond their empirical existence in the history of society."[48] Modern government seeks to demystify itself and its processes.

Political Culture

Religion can contribute to personal and national identity. It offers ideological perspectives on the relationship of human beings to authority. It brings people together in organizations with potential and actual political influence. But above all, it constitutes a social "fact" in every country of the world. People pray. They attend services in churches, synagogues, and mosques. They participate in religious organizations. Most important, they see religion as a guide to behavior, promoting the good and fighting evil. When people everywhere invoke God in happiness and in despair, in gratefulness and in resentment, the expressions may be more automatic than calculated. The instinct to do right may lie much deeper than the commandments people remember and invoke. People who do not profess religious commitments do not behave much differently than those who do, but the actions of those without explicit commitment may reflect religious upbringing or exposure. The religious fact is a powerful element of every national culture, and governments ignore it at their peril.

In some circumstances, political culture may change more quickly than political institutions, and the result may be political instability. The U.S. antislavery movement in the middle of the nineteenth century is an example. A groundswell of public opinion against slavery propelled in part by religious belief and religious organizations transformed the public mind-set about slavery before political institutions could move against it. In other circumstances, political institutions seek to change political culture. The French and Russian revolutions produced governments bent upon transforming the way citizens understood their relationship to political authority. With propaganda and education, they sought to create a new citizenry. In postrevolutionary circumstances, the training of subjects and citizens becomes a critical issue. What are future generations to be taught about private versus public good, legitimate political authority, the relationship between law and morality, the place of religion in society, and the social mores they have come to take as defining elements of their lives? Such education must start from a notion of current attitudes, and in every country those attitudes reflect aspects of religious heritage.

Religion appears more important as a defining element of culture in some societies than in others. Many European students of Middle Eastern cultures writing in the nineteenth and twentieth centuries portrayed the region as bound up in religion, and the West as liberated from it. Survey data now suggest that the proportion of people in Egypt, Turkey, or Iran who see religion as important to their daily lives might be higher than it is in Europe but not necessarily higher than in the United States.[49] Is there any society in which religion can be ignored as a factor in shaping mass attitudes toward morality and authority? If political development means movement toward greater participation and inclusiveness, then political stability will be increasingly dependent on congruence between state policies and political culture.[50]

To perpetuate themselves, modern states seek to train inhabitants as subjects or citizens. Similarly, religious groups, whether they represent a majority or a minority of a society, must socialize their young, if they are to survive as distinct entities. For much of European and Middle Eastern history, religious organizations provided the only education available in the society, training both secular and religious leadership, usually from the noble classes. In modern times some states have assumed all responsibilities for education, including the preparation of clergy. Turkey in its first forty years of independence is an example. The idea was to teach an Islam that accepted the removal of religion from direct participation in the political sphere and distanced itself from the mysticism that enjoyed great popular appeal, especially in the rural, less modernized areas. The British sponsored such educational policies in Egypt, and the French did the same thing in Algeria. They hoped to use a modernist version of Islam to fashion loyal colonial subjects, cutting them away from the Ottoman tradition and the existing political culture.[51] Successor nationalist regimes continued these colonial policies.

In France, the question is most frequently posed in the opposite way: Can the republic survive without an educational system that is laïque? When three Muslim girls were expelled from high school for wearing head scarves in 1989, the government asked the Conseil d'État, a high administrative court, to rule on whether laïcité had been violated. The court responded that the mere wearing of head scarves did not compromise the integrity of education, if there was no effort to proselytize or otherwise disrupt the classroom, but this response, far from settling the issue, touched off controversy and an outpouring of books defending laïcité. Most of these books note that laïcité nonetheless means something quite different now than it did at the end of the nineteenth century, when re-publicans deemed that they could solidify loyalty to the republic only by taking over the educational responsibilities exercised by the Catholic Church. Teachers became—and remain—apostles of republican unity, alert to any hint of religious particularism. But the Catholic Church no longer constitutes a threat to republican unity, and the state has even subsidized private (mostly Catholic) schools since 1958. Private schools must hire teachers with credentials approved by the state and include programs of instruction approved by the state, but they may also offer additional courses and activities. Socialist efforts in the 1980s to redress the balance in favor of purer secularism failed, as did rightist efforts to move the marker in the other direction, with the authorization of charter schools, in the following decade. The explosion of the head-scarf controversy shows the continued centrality of education to the relationship between religion and political culture in France.[52]

Schools have also been at the center of the culture wars in the United States. On the one hand, if the Founders intended that separation of church and state would guarantee the autonomy of religion but not free the state from religious standards of right and wrong, public schools would not necessarily avoid teaching about religion, and government might reasonably encourage and even support religious schools. On the other hand, it is not obvious how state-funded schools should treat religion. Religious groups have protested the elimination of prayer from schools and the failure of schools to teach morality. Critics accuse schools of teaching an antireligious philosophy they call secular humanism. Teachers and school boards are afraid to include courses on comparative religion or the history of religions, which might well offend the groups most intent on promoting spirituality in the schools. Permitting and subsidizing religious schools, subject to conditions and cooperation, goes partway toward solving the problem at the risk of perpetuating discrete, autonomous religious communities, indifferent to the logic of public discourse, but it does nothing to expose the public-school student to religious history and doctrine. Surely the Founders did not imagine that the separation of church and state would mean the separation of citizens from knowledge of religion, but many contemporary Americans arrive in college without a solid understanding of Judaism or Christianity, Protestantism or Catholicism, much less Islam.

Hypothesis 7: "Rational" types of religion may trigger individual initiative, encourage the spread of education, and spur economic growth. Economic prosperity will in turn make available resources vital to the construction of a modern nation-state, and an increasingly educated, rational political culture will support liberalization and democratization.

In *The Protestant Ethic and the Spirit of Capitalism*, Weber argued that the peculiar propensities of Calvinism as a kind of worldly asceticism had triggered the development of capitalism in Western Europe.[53] The Calvinist belief in predestination seemed to deprive human beings of even the slightest control over their eternal fate. An inaccessible, omniscient God preordained the destiny of every human being, but this transcendent God also left human beings free to read the Bible and think about what one who merited salvation ought to do. Calvinists found themselves driven by inner ethical impulses to make this world and their place within it better. Success made them confident of their selection by God, and the certainty of selection gave them the confidence to be pioneers of the Industrial Revolution in Europe.

Inglehart finds support in modern survey data for an updated version of the Weberian hypothesis. Protestantism's instilled drive for achievement and education fostered economic growth in the West. Constructing an index of "achievement motivation" from interviews conducted in forty-three countries, Inglehart discovered a high correlation between the mean index for each country and the mean economic growth rate for that country between 1960 and 1990. He reasons that countries ranking high in achievement motivation tend to save and invest for the future and to act with determination to obtain their goals. "In short, growth rates are best understood as a consequence of both economic and cultural factors."[54]

Inglehart takes this argument one step further by confirming that economic development correlates positively with the emergence of liberal democracy. And he goes beyond that to assert that cultural factors, such as the level of education, push a society toward more liberal, participatory values that are, for him, a second major axis of modernity. "Rational religion," which Weber defined as religion shorn of most of its magical and mystical properties and anchored in an ethical code, thus promotes political development.

In a study of Canada and the United States, Corwin Smidt concludes: "The data reveal that religious tradition is moderately related to both social trust and civic engagement, though somewhat more strongly so in terms of civic engagement than social trust." The study shows a particularly strong relationship between religiosity and civic engagement among black Protestants in the United States. "This pattern is consistent with the findings of previous research that religious involvement, particularly among those who lack the resource of money, imparts civic skills and engenders civic involvement."[55]

Hypothesis 8: A culture steeped in religion—committed to myth, magic, and faith in God rather than faith in human effort—will be unable to produce subjects, much less citizens, of a modern state. Such a culture must be secularized—that is, rationalized—if genuine political development is to occur.

In the introduction to his book on Spinoza, Steven Smith writes: "The aim of the work as a whole is the liberation of the individual from bondage to superstition and ecclesiastical authority. Spinoza's ideal is the free or autonomous individual who uses reason to achieve mastery over the passions."[56] Political development depends upon autonomous, rational individuals.

That seems to be what Weber meant by the "disenchantment of the world," a phrase that appears as the title of a book by Gauchet, who writes: "For Weber this expression specifically meant 'the elimination of magic as a salvation technique.' I do not believe that broadening it to mean the impoverishment of the reign of the invisible distorts this meaning."[57] Gauchet sees the very birth of scriptural religion as the beginning of a relentless process of secularization. The logic of secularization lies within all the religions of the book—Judaism, Christianity, and Islam—and secularization means declining influence of religion (and the supernatural) on culture. In *Religion and Political Development*, D. E. Smith writes:

Underlying the secularization of political culture is the decline of explicitly religious values, generally throughout the society. Religiosity and piety are no longer highly valued socially. Material values rank higher than otherworldly values. . . . There is growing scepticism concerning the truth or validity of traditional religious doctrine. . . . Religious values no longer motivate importantly. . . . People do not think about religion much; it occupies a diminishing part of their consciousness. There is growing tolerance of religious values foreign to one's own culture and a growing relativism based on scepticism of all religious truth claims.[58]

Like Weber and Talcott Parsons, Smith regards secularization as fundamental to political development, a description of what has occurred in the West and a prescription for the developing world. He describes not just a decline in the influence of organized religions but, with his reference to consciousness, a decline in individual religiosity as well. Berger, who later had second thoughts about these matters, says much the same thing in *The Sacred Canopy*:

> [Secularization] affects the totality of cultural life and of ideation, and may be observed in the decline of religious contents in the arts, in philosophy, in literature, and most important of all, in the rise of science as an autonomous, thoroughly secular perspective on the world. And as there is a secularization of society and culture, so is there a secularization of consciousness.[59]

Echoes of logical positivism, a philosophical movement that began in nineteenth-century Europe and gained momentum in the twentieth century, reverberate in this and other statements of secularizing necessity. Logical positivism insists that only the empirical verification of testable hypotheses can generate truth. Science and rationality produce a truth that drives out magic and eventually every attachment to something that lies beyond empirical confirmation ("the reign of the invisible"). The ostensible objective of logical positivism is merely description, and description of the particular (as in the analysis of the secularization of Europe) becomes universal by virtue of theory. Political development, understood as the growth of bureaucracy and constitutionalism, requires secularization.

Most proponents of this perspective, from Spinoza through Weber, Durkheim, and Parsons, welcome secularization as a positive outcome, and only a few authors, such as Marcel Gauchet and Ernest Fortin, deplore it. For example, Gauchet worries that the disenchantment of the liberal state leaves it without the capacity to assert itself on behalf of the common good. Without any magic to lift it above the fray, the state becomes a mere container for the multitude of ideas and interests that percolate within it.[60] Fortin deplores secularization, and the role of churches in that process, for its impact on the loss of spirituality. Not even the separation of church and state has saved spirituality from the mundane, because churches have been more preoccupied, in his view, with membership and material standing than with the welfare of souls:

> Contrary to its stated aim, liberal democracy does breed a specific type of human being, one that is defined by an unprecedented openness to all human possibilities. What this leads to most of the time is neither Nietzschean creativity nor a noble dedication to some pregiven ideal, not a deeper religious life, nor a rich and diversified society, but easygoing indifference and mindless conformism.[61]

No one takes religion seriously, and the culprit, in Fortin's opinion, is liberal democracy.

Religion as a Dependent Variable

These eight contradictory propositions all presume that religion shapes political outcomes in some fashion, whether through identity, ideology, institutions, or political culture. In a short-term perspective, religion is an independent variable of some significance in explaining why a given political system veers in one direction or another. There is, however, a strong case to be made for religion as an effect, rather than a cause, especially from a long-term perspective. The religious makeup of a country is partly a result of geography, economics, and social structure, but it is also a product of political influence and decision.

Hypothesis 9: Politics shapes religion much more than religion shapes politics. Religion should thus be understood as a dependent variable, not a causative factor for political development.

In the grand scheme of human history, religion has been a variable. Insofar as it is a product of society, as Durkheim argued, then it logically must change as the definition of society itself evolves with the ages. Berger says, "Religion is the human enterprise by which a sacred cosmos is established."[62] Since all human enterprises change, religion must necessarily change. If religion is a search for meaning in life, in nature, and in the cosmos, then the effort has no logical end, because the object of the search is not fixed. Most religions seek to establish foundational truths that can resist the erosion of history. God is portrayed as an author of historical change who is unaffected by it, yet religions are produced by human beings whose experience and knowledge of God have necessarily occurred within history, not outside of it.

Each of the major religious traditions prominent today emerged out of previous traditions and practices, combining, reworking, and inventing elements of belief and ritual and unifying human beings who had been disparate in their practices. Each of these traditions evolved in ways that make them different today from what they were at the founding moments. Religion in the early kingdoms of ancient Egypt was quite different from what it later became. Judaism in exile became something quite different than it was in the ancient commonwealths. Christianity in Jesus's lifetime surely did not resemble what it became by virtue of Paul's work or Constantine's conversion. The Islam of the Abbasid caliphate did not resemble the Islam of the Medina state with Muhammad still alive, much less the Islam of the early Meccan period.

Political turbulence and change, more than any other factor, probably explain this historical evolution. Gauchet insists that the creation of the state—one should probably speak rather of the gradual appearance of statelike bodies—"can be regarded as the first religious revolution in history."[63] Before the state, religion alone drew the line between sacred and profane and pulled the society together, but then the state usurped the dominant place and created human beings who incarnated invisible forces. "All subsequent major spiritual and intellectual developments will arise from the contradictions between the inherited representations of the foundation, in whose name sovereignty is wielded and the historical forms clothing its practice."[64]

The historical forms change with the size of the state, the character of the state, and its place in the world. As states merge into larger ones, belief systems must themselves be integrated. If states splinter, each piece may develop systems of ritual and belief to help solidify the new entity, or scriptural, scholarly legal systems may serve to cement a group that becomes geographically dispersed. States conquer or confront defeat, and religious loyalties usually follow the will of the victor. Rulers themselves seek to enhance their personal power and solidify their regimes by invoking new beliefs and practices. They promote state religions by funding a friendly priesthood and repressing dissenters. Every religious organization must respond to the incentives and disincentives offered by the political circumstances in which it exists.

The argument for religion as a dependent variable may seem strange for several reasons. First, the great religions are relatively enduring phenomena. Many writers take religion to be a primordial, unchanging characteristic of individuals and even of states. Yet it is quite possible to write histories of the three major religions. They have all assumed different forms as they have adapted to geographic, social, economic, and political conditions. There is not a single Judaism, a single Christianity, or a single Islam—not in time and not in space. Max Weber argued that the advent of Protestantism contributed to the spirit of the new capitalism, but the emergence of Protestantism itself constituted a notable change in Christianity. Robert Wuthnow insists that the success of Protestantism in certain parts of Europe and its failure in others can in turn be explained by environmental and especially political factors.[65] What appears fixed in the case of most individuals is anything but stable and unchanging from the perspective of societies across time.

Second, to identify religion as a short-term factor suggests that it does not have long-term importance, which seems both counterintuitive and counterfactual. (Have not American politics been shaped by Protestantism? How can one understand Ireland or Italy without Catholicism? What are Turkish politics without Islam? How can one understand Israel without taking account of the religious parties?) But the short-term nature of religious influence is borne out in two observations: Religion does not account for differences in political development among nations, and politics everywhere bears traces of religious influence. That short-term forces disappear as significant factors in long-term explanation does not mean they are unimportant. It may mean, instead, that virtually everywhere religion has served positive and negative roles in political development and that those roles are much more similar than different from one country to another.

Religion threatens political stability when it channels dissent against a political regime, as it did in sixteenth- and seventeenth-century England, or as it did in the overthrow of the monarchy in Iran. In other times and places it enhances stability by spurring reform, as it did with the civil rights movement in the United States. Although the long-term influence of religion may be neutral, the short-term impact may be of critical importance to a single state's history, even though religion may not be a useful variable in explaining why a state advances more or less quickly toward bureaucratic-constitutional government.[66]

Third, it may seem strange to regard religion as a short-term variable, because survey research usually assumes that a respondent's answers to questions about religion reflect long-term proclivities, rather than fleeting political opinions. Cause necessarily precedes effect, so the assumption is that religious beliefs condition political attitudes. But respondents face questions put to them at a particular moment. Even when surveys seek out the same respondents again later in an effort to confirm the sequence of causation, the same questions do not necessarily have the same meaning at a distance of five or ten years. Hence, if a single individual's responses to questions about religion change significantly over a lifetime, the evolution might be as much a product of political attitudes as a cause of them. Questions about religious preferences, belief in God, and frequency of religious observance prove useful in predicting political attitudes in some contexts but irrelevant in others. In short, there is scarcely a clear pattern of short-term impact, much less proof that religion constitutes a long-term cause of political attitudes.

In the short run, religion may influence the course of political development, but in the long run, the shape and character of religion in a single country seems to depend more on political events and decisions than the character of the political sphere depends on religion. Near term, religion and politics appear to be mutually determining. They may evolve together in a relatively balanced relationship, neither domain anxious for revision, but once the balance tips sharply one way or the other, as a result of environmental change or changes in proclivity on either side, the search begins for a new "set of regularities" to replace the old.[67] Now religion thrusts, and politics parries, and then the momentum is reversed. The state becomes aggressive in seeking to revise the balance. In fact, the state enjoys long-term advantages in each of the domains where politics and religion interact, but this does not mean that church and state necessarily separate or that "secularization" adequately describes the interaction. Religious and political actors fashion a new balance that is path-dependent, reflecting previous iterations of the dialectical process by which it is created, but there can never be a guarantee of permanence. One would have to know the future to be able to offer such a guarantee.

Conclusion

The complicated pattern of interaction between the religious and political spheres precludes certainty about religion as either an independent or a dependent variable.

As an independent variable, religion appears to have contributed to political development as much as hindered it, but rare have been cases where religious identity has contributed to the solidification of national identity, where religious ideology has contributed systematically to the enhancement of bureaucratic and liberal-democratic institutions, where religious organizations have unambiguously favored pluralist, tolerant, constitutionalist tendencies, and where religion as a component of political culture has been favorable to these changes. To see England as such a case—and there would appear to be few other possibilities—would require overlooking moments in English history when religious conflict appeared to be a major obstacle to constitutional development. It is equally difficult to think of cases where religion has been an insuperable obstacle in each of the four domains: identity, ideology, institutions, and political culture. And the reason is not far to seek: Politics reshapes religion even as religion conditions political life.

Determined political efforts to eliminate the influence of religion or to subject religious identity, ideology, and organization to state control have been unsuccessful. The coercion required to enforce such policies may carry a country toward bureaucratic development, as in the Soviet Union, but runs counter to the other component of political development, constitutionalism. Even coercion cannot obliterate religious instincts from the political culture as a component of the norms and idioms of daily life. Once coercion disappears or diminishes, religious activity springs back. With its control of the educational establishment, the state can attempt to alter the foundation of religious power, which lies in popular beliefs and attitudes. But a state that moves toward constitutionalism cannot, without contradiction, adopt arbitrary, absolutist educational policies designed to undercut all religious understandings of the world. Rather, a state inching its way toward liberal democracy must seek its foundation in the existing political culture. It must work from existing notions of what constitutes a good person, a good society, and a good government. To change the country, it must win the support of doubters by persuading them that the values propounded in the schools and in the media are merely new versions of the values embraced in the existing political culture. Islamist movements in several countries have succeeded in pitching their proposals for the reformation of society in such terms. The problem of the state is not just to contain, absorb, or coalesce with Islamist movements but to respond as effectively as the Islamists to the political culture of the masses, their practices, and their norms. States find themselves resorting to the language of religion to compete with the Islamists for the allegiance of the masses, thereby giving religion even greater apparent importance in political life than it might otherwise have. They must teach religion in the public schools, because the public demands it and because refining the notion of citizenship means refining a political culture steeped in the language of religion. States have unwittingly contributed to the Islamic resurgence by virtue of policies designed to increase the power of the state.[68]

State schools all over the Middle East have helped make religion a matter of choice, as the Protestant Reformation made religion a matter of choice in Europe. What was given as a birthright comes to be a matter for reaffirmation, rejection, or reinterpretation. Islamism constitutes a set of choices, different in every time and place: a choice to run a business by certain principles; to dress in a way deemed appropriate for a believer; to adhere to a moral code that others seem to have abandoned; to associate primarily with those who have made similar choices; to participate in political life on behalf of those who are disadvantaged; to educate oneself about Islam; to rethink the meaning of basic scriptures; to work for the betterment of one's local community as a concrete way of implementing one's moral choices; to stay at home to tend one's children in deference to husband and patriarchal ways; to go into the workplace boldly, shielded by the protection of clothing that signifies commitment and virtue; or to undertake violent acts of political opposition. Jenny White emphasizes that Turkish Islamists embrace one or more such choices, even contradictory ones.[69] In exercising such choice, Turks engage in a process typical of the marketplace and of the liberal-democratic political arena, both grounded in personal choice. The expansion of the realm of choice is one way to define political development.[70]

In the contemporary Middle Eastern context, the expansion of choice has come in the realm of religion, but the reasons are not so much religious as political, economic, and social. More than any other factor, it is the nation-state with its need for identity and legitimacy that has created this set of choices. By using religion for its own purposes, and especially by teaching religion in its schools, it has demanded and enabled choice. The trials and tribulations of global ideologies such as Marxism and liberalism have constrained the definitions of choice in negative ways. Many choices bear burdens of foreign origin and influence. Modern technologies of communication have empowered choice by exposing options to people who thought they had none. Economic development has pulled people toward choices as both workers and consumers. Education and income continue to be primary constraints on choice.[71] All these factors vary from country to country, as does the coercive will of the state. The range of choices available at a given level of economic prosperity appears much greater in Turkey than in Saudi Arabia, for example, where a decision to oppose state religious teachings means prison.

The religious choices now available emerge from an evolving set of political and social circumstances that probably contribute more to understanding the choices than the study of religious scripture.[72] Religious identities, ideologies, and organizations have responded creatively to these national circumstances. Despite international ties among religious groups and a pattern of religious activity that seems similar in a number of countries, Islamist activity is probably most accurately seen as a broad set of responses to parallel (but not identical) political and social circumstances. Even if religion is much more a dependent than an independent variable, contemporary political leaders cannot afford to ignore it.

2

The Taming of Islam in Egypt

From that time [1800] to this, the secularization of the polity has been the most fundamental structural and ideological change in the process of political development.
—DONALD EUGENE SMITH

The term *secularization* seems inappropriate to describe what has happened in Egypt or in most of the Middle East since Smith wrote those words in 1970.[1] It does not accurately describe what has happened in the Arab world since the spring of 2011. The modernization of Middle Eastern polities has not rendered these countries secular; quite to the contrary, religion and politics have become ever more thoroughly intertwined. Politics permeates virtually every aspect of religion, and religion permeates almost every aspect of politics.[2]

At first the demonstrations in Tahrir Square against the Mubarak regime seemed to involve secular youth, but they were attacking the authoritarianism of the government, not its substantial support for religious institutions. In a few days the Muslim Brotherhood joined the protests, greatly increasing the size and power of the demonstrations, but that organization, too, focused on the abuses and corruption of the regime, rather than a religious agenda. Coptic Christians, salafists, and even Sufis joined the fray. But as soon as Mubarak was gone, the military and the Brotherhood emerged as the most powerful players, the one seen as a primary force for secularization, the other as the primary champion of

Islamization. With its victory in the presidential elections of June 2012, the Brotherhood appeared poised to further strengthen the relationship between state and religion.

The immixture of religion and politics has been a primary characteristic of political development in Egypt since 1800. At every moment, the state has been the driving force toward fusion. It has consistently sought to subjugate Islam to its purposes—the modernization of the country, the strengthening of state power, the sharpening of identity, the legitimation of state authority—and in this effort at subjugation the state has empowered and politicized the religious sphere. It is the neediness of the state, not the character of Islam or the contingencies of the moment, that best explains the politicization of religion and the intermixture of religion and politics in Egypt.

The aggressiveness of the state in undermining, dominating, and reforming— hence politicizing—the religious establishment in Egypt spurred reactions from within and without. Elements of the religious establishment responded to the political opportunities afforded them by the state in its need for identity, authority, and legitimacy. Even those who might have wished to erect a wall between re- ligion and politics found political struggle the only means of defense. Ultimately assaulted by Islamists seeking to subordinate the state to their agenda, the state found itself ever more deeply involved in seeking to manipulate religion to its own advantage. The result was a spiral in the politicization of religion and the sanctification of politics that contradicts the predictions of secularization theory.

Smith proposed that religion and politics had been fused in "traditional so- cieties."[3] Moreover, he hypothesized that religion and politics would undergo radical separation under the impact of external forces. Smith then suggested that interaction between separate political and religious spheres results in an equi- librium consistent with autonomous, secular political development. Neither of these hypotheses fits Egypt. Under the Ottomans (after 1517), Egypt was a tra- ditional society in that it was largely unscathed by Western influence before the French invasion of 1798. The country was marked by visible separation of the religious and the political. Muhammad Ali, who seized power after the French left, sought to attack the autonomy of the indigenous ulama in the early nineteenth century, asserting political control over religion. There was progressive expansion of the state and its intrusion into religious affairs; overlap and tension between the religious and political that tended to increase over time; and increased pen- etration of society by politicized religion and the sacralized state.

Tensions between the religious and the political did not begin in 1800, nor are they likely to end at some precise moment, but in any society there are periods when tension between religion and politics becomes more acute and periods when it subsides. One might define moments of low tension, or relative equilibrium, as moments when neither the religious nor the political seeks major modification of the relationship. At other moments, one side or the other seeks revision. In Egypt, the state assumed the revisionist role in the nineteenth century. Religion struck back effectively in the twentieth century, with the exception of the Nasirist period (1952–1970). In the twenty-first century, religion in the form of Islamist movements still seems to have the revisionist role in Egypt and the rest of the region.

One result is that Islam in Egypt no longer resembles what it was a century ago. It has transformed itself and been transformed by the actions of the state, and the Egyptian state is likewise being reshaped by the activities of the religious sphere. While religion might become utterly pliant and secondary to a triumphant secular state, as Smith predicts, or politics might become subordinate to religious direction, as the dominance of the Muslim Brotherhood suggests it could, neither outcome now seems plausible. The question to be asked is how, after two centuries of intensified rivalry and even violent conflict, the two spheres may build an enduring, collaborative arrangement out of the unstable, conflictual relationship that prevails.

Stabilizing the relationship between religion and politics in Egypt would require consensus about the place of Islam in Egyptian identity. On the one hand, the monuments left by the pharaohs remind all Egyptians that their country does not owe its existence to Islam. The presence of a Coptic Christian minority (8 to 10 percent of the population) also predates Islam. On the other hand, Egypt was the seat of the Fatimid caliphate in the tenth and eleventh centuries. The Fatimids, builders of Islamic Cairo, were the first Islamic dynasty to arise from Shii Islam. Egypt happily claims Arab precedence in Islam and Egyptian dominance among the Arabs.

Moreover, stabilization would require further agreement about the place of Islam in the country's political ideology. The Egyptian constitution of 1971, as amended in 1980, makes the sharia the primary source of legislation, a provision reaffirmed in the new constitution adopted in December 2012. What does this mean? Stabilization would require not separation of church and state—whatever that would mean in this context—but some regularization of the relationship between political decision-makers and unauthorized preachers, the Muslim Brotherhood, Sufi orders, salafis, and Coptic Christians. Finally, stabilization would require a common understanding of the appropriate role of the state in maintaining the country's moral climate. In an era of expanding literacy and seemingly infinite demand for education in Egypt, the question is what sort of education the state should provide, what sort of moral guidance it should impose on the political culture. Islam calls upon the state to "promote the good and fight evil." Is there any political system that does not try to do that? The problem is defining good and evil.

Identity

Islam has been an aspect of Egyptian identity since the Arab conquest of the seventh century, but it has never been the only binding force in the society. Because Napoleon Bonaparte regarded Islam as the key to domination of Egyptian society, he posted proclamations on doors all over Cairo proclaiming that he would save Egyptian Muslims from the predations of those false Muslims, the Turks.[4] He tried to co-opt the ulama, who provided the leadership for Egyptian resistance, such as it was. But once Muhammad Ali seized power in 1803, he did not hesitate to attack the religious establishment in his effort to solidify Egyptian military and economic strength against European threats and Ottoman rule. Islam served to distinguish Egyptians from the French, who were allies, but not from the Ottomans, who became unwelcome masters, rivals, and then enemies. In the eyes of Muhammad Ali and his successors, impressed by all things European, Islam was a drag on change and modernization. He began a campaign to nationalize *waqf* land, set aside in perpetuity for the support of religious institutions, and to reduce the autonomy of the ulama.[5] In one form or another, successive Egyptian governments continued his policies for 150 years. The 1952 Egyptian Revolution, which ended the dynasty established by Muhammad Ali, "carried to a conclusion the secularization trend begun in the nineteenth century."[6]

Egyptians constituted a society before the advent of Islam. As inhabitants of the Nile Valley, modern Egyptians live with monuments that testify to a long history together under the pharaohs. They also live with the knowledge that Alexandria was once a center of Greek learning. The Romans later conquered the country along with most of the Mediterranean region, and early Christianity both flourished and suffered there. Christian monasticism originated in Egypt. The Arabs followed the Romans as conquerors, and the country became Arabized and Islamized over several centuries. "Slave soldiers" (Mamluks) of Turkish origin won control of the country in the thirteenth century, and then the Ottoman Empire, itself a Sunni Muslim state governed by Turks, imposed itself on the Mamluks in the sixteenth century. When Napoleon entered the country in 1798, he found a tiny Ottoman administrative class governing by virtue of a Mamluk military class and a native Egyptian religious class, the ulama. Egyptians thus had reason to think of themselves in many ways—primarily as subjects of foreign rule. Even Muhammad Ali, liberator of Egypt from the Ottomans, was a foreigner, a Turkish-speaking Albanian.

In the nineteenth century, Egyptians began to think of Egypt as a nation in the modern sense.[7] The French and American revolutions had demonstrated the potency of the idea that a group of people united by language, religion, and history might act to establish and control a geographical state. The era of empires began to wane as the new concept of the nation-state gained traction. In Egypt, Muhammad Ali and his heirs, though still theoretically subject to the Ottoman Empire and governed from Istanbul, embarked on a program of autonomous economic, military, and political development that finally led them to challenge the Ottoman dynasty for control of the empire itself. In the process, they depended on French and then British support, which entangled them in another form of external dependence. Financial dependence on Europe became political dependence after Great Britain seized control of Egypt in 1882. Thus, in subsequent decades, with liberation from the Ottomans largely achieved, Egyptian nationalism focused on freedom from British imperialism.

Arabism

It was an epoch in which Arabs, principally intellectuals in the cities of Damascus, Beirut, and Cairo, were beginning to assert that they constituted a single nation.[8] Language was the foundation of that idea, as it had been the foundation in Europe, but some of these intellectuals emphasized religion as the primary glue. For example, Jamal al-Din al-Afghani, who was actually of Persian rather than Afghan origin, flitted from capital to capital propounding his notion that only a union of Muslims could be effective in opposing European power.[9] Most European

nationalists of the era saw Arabism and Islamism as mutually reinforcing principles. The Arabs were, after all, the first Muslims, and even non-Muslim Arabs
acknowledged the impact of Islam on Arab culture. Egyptians helped generate
some of these ideas without necessarily seeing a contradiction between them
and the concept of the Egyptian fatherland.[10]

The first concrete proposal for an Arab state did not include Egypt or any
other part of North Africa. Sharif Husayn, an Ottoman official entrusted with the
care of the holy places in Mecca and Medina, made contact with the British government during World War I. He proposed to mount an Arab revolt against the
Turkish-dominated Ottoman Empire, which had joined Germany and Austria in
the war against France, Britain, and Russia. In return, he asked the British to support the creation of an Arab state after the defeat of the Ottomans and even to
support the idea of an Arab caliphate for Islam. The state he proposed included
the Arabian peninsula and the modern states of Syria, Lebanon, Iraq, Israel-
Palestine, and Jordan—but not Egypt or any Arab country west of Egypt. Presumably he thought the British would object to the inclusion of Egypt in such a
state. Who knows how he thought a Christian power could create an Arab caliphate
for Islam. The whole episode testifies to the relative weakness of both Arabism
and Islamism, or rather the weakness of the groups promoting both of those ideas.

Egyptians faced the practical problem of gaining liberation from a British
occupation that, though defined as temporary in 1882, showed no signs of disappearing some twenty years later. The British converted their unofficial tenure
in the country into protectorate status during World War I and refused the demands of a delegation (*wafd*) of Egyptians, led by Saad Zaghlul, which traveled
to Paris and asked for independence at the end of the war. Instead, Britain imposed "independence" on Egypt in 1923 with a set of conditions that the newly
created Wafd party and its leader, Zaghlul, found unacceptable. The party stood
for Egyptian independence from European domination, but it affirmed Egyptian
identity in a thoroughly modern, European way. Nationalism was simply another
step in the process of economic, social, and political modernization initiated by
Muhammad Ali.

The creation of the Muslim Brotherhood after 1928 challenged the European
model and reemphasized the identification of Egypt with Islam. The founder of
the Brotherhood, Hasan al-Banna, who was a schoolteacher in Ismailia, set out
to promote an Islamic society as the basis for an Islamic state and eventually an

Islamic world. He saw the first step as one of bringing Egyptians together through education, social activities, sports, and public meetings—all to promote morality and good citizenship as defined by Islam. In religion, Egyptians could find a common identity and the organizational strength required to achieve genuine independence.[11]

However, it was the idea of Arabism that took precedence over Islamism in the 1930s once Egyptian governments and intellectuals became more attuned to developments elsewhere in the Middle East. The Wafd party became interested in Arab issues in the late 1930s, especially after the Arab general strike of 1936 began to create turmoil in Palestine. In and out of the premiership in the 1930s, the Wafd came back to power in 1942 as part of a deal that smacked of selling out to the British and the Egyptian king. The deal, which brought Egypt squarely into the war on the British side, damaged beyond repair the reputations of the Wafd and King Faruq. In an effort to recover credibility, the Wafd subsequently took the lead in sponsoring the creation of the League of Arab States. Although the Arab states joined the league as autonomous entities, the initial headquarters was in Cairo, and the first secretary general an Egyptian who had championed the project. "The new Arab League was thus an Egyptian triumph," explain Israel Gershoni and James Jankowski, "and marked a new era of Egyptian as-cendancy within inter-Arab politics."[12] Egypt elbowed its way past Iraq to become the leader of the Arab world.

The focus on Islam proposed by Afghani and reinvoked by the Muslim Brotherhood in the interwar period served the purposes of political elites seeking the liberation of Egypt and the rest of the Arab world from European domination. Gamal Abd al-Nasir welcomed the support of the Brotherhood for the 1952 rev-olution, which swept away King Faruq and the dynasty established by Muham-mad Ali. Nasir made Islam the country's official religion in 1964, even though he had dissolved the Brotherhood and imprisoned its leaders. By subjugating the religious establishment to his political purposes and maintaining the place of Islam in the public schools, he sought to show that he was not indifferent to Islam as a source of national identity. Pious or not, he behaved as the conventional wisdom said he should: keeping his wife out of sight, drinking no alcohol in public, and playing the role of an authentic Muslim uncorrupted by European decadence. But President Nasir nonetheless made Arabism, rather than Islamism, the focus of his presidency.

It was probably more accident than design that caused Nasir and Egypt to claim supranational obligations toward the Arab world. The failure of five Arab states to defeat a fledgling Israel in the war of 1948–1949 created one backdrop for the new Arabism. Another was the efforts of the United States and Great Britain to defend the Middle East against the Soviet Union by focusing on so-called northern-tier countries (Turkey, Iran, Iraq) rather than Egypt. The United States turned down Egyptian requests for arms and for funding of a new, high dam on the Nile at Aswan. In response, President Nasir nationalized the Suez Canal. The owners of the canal (the British and the French) fussed and fumed and finally conspired with Israel to invade Egypt with the aim of overthrowing Nasir, whom the British called a "new Hitler."[13] The failure of the invasion, thanks to British and French bungling and to American expressions of outrage, made Nasir into an Arab hero. Suddenly he was an icon who could lead the Arabs out of the shadow of imperialism into an age of prosperity and unity. Egypt became an Arab state, while the leaders of the Muslim Brotherhood, champions of Islamism, went to prison for allegedly trying to assassinate Nasir in 1954.

Arabism led not to unity but to conflict. In 1958, Nasir put Egypt into union with Syria, forming the United Arab Republic, which was supposed to draw in other Arab states. Jordan and Lebanon trembled as Nasir flexed his muscles, and the Iraqi monarchy fell to revolutionaries. But rather than following instructions from the Voice of the Arabs, Nasir's radio station, the other Arab states fell to quarreling with each other and with Egypt. Syria withdrew from the union, and Nasir himself stumbled into a war with Israel he could not win. The war of June 1967, in which Israel defeated three Arab states in six days, tarnished both Nasirism and Arabism. Egypt's effort to unite the Arabs under Egyptian leadership had led to military and economic disaster.[14]

Islamism

When in the fall of 1970 Nasir succumbed to a heart attack, his fellow collaborator in the 1952 coup d'état, Anwar al-Sadat, ascended to the presidency of Egypt. Instantly he freed political prisoners of the Nasirist era, including members of the Muslim Brotherhood, who promised loyalty to the regime in return for freedom. Sadat cultivated a religious image, spoke frequently at Friday mosque, and became known as "the believer president." A new constitution (1971) proclaimed the sharia one source of legislation, and amendment in 1980 made it the "principal source." Meanwhile, Sadat sought to extract Egypt from the Arab-Israeli conflict for the sake of his own country. The other Arab states expelled Egypt from the Arab League after Sadat concluded a peace treaty with Israel in 1979. Egypt's Arabism receded in favor of a rekindled loyalty to Islam and a rediscovered enthusiasm for capitalism, liberalism, and the West.

The identification of Islam with the Egyptian state has always generated two sorts of problems. The appeal to Islam as a source of identity invokes an identification much broader than Egypt on the one hand and narrower than Egypt on the other. To identify Egypt with Islam exposes the Egyptian state to criticism not just by its own citizens but by foreign groups and states claiming to represent the universal principles of Islam. Before World War II, with encouragement from the Egyptian religious establishment, King Faruq considered advancing a claim to be the new caliph, successor to the Ottoman caliph deposed by Mustafa Kemal Atatürk in 1923. Other Muslim states, including Saudi Arabia and Turkey, made it clear they would not support such a claim.[15] Internal political forces also made their objections known.

Internally, the identification between Islam and the Egyptian state tends to separate Coptic Christians, treated as *dhimmis*—a group protected as a religious minority under Islamic law—from full identification with the state. Should Islam take precedence over identification with ancient Egypt, Christian Egypt, or the Arab world in Egyptian politics? Coptic Christians tend to see these as pieces of a single puzzle, whereas Muslims see the pharaonic age as part of the jahiliyya, or age of ignorance.[16] A state that embraced all these and other dimensions of Egyptian history would be more inclusive, but its secularism would make it suspect in the eyes of Islamist groups. The Muslim Brotherhood and groups spun off from the organization have succeeded in evoking a positive response among millions of Egyptians with a plea that spiritual renewal and societal renovation depend upon a fresh commitment to Islam. But they have also alienated many Egyptians who regard their projects as suspect and divisive.[17] David Zeidan speaks of this limitation: "Islam limits what is perceived as permitted in Egyptian society and politics, and fundamentalists today are further narrowing the limits of the possible. A radical reinterpretation of the *dhimmi* concept in favor of non-Muslim equality is at present unlikely."[18]

Under the Ottoman Empire, Christians, Jews, and some other religious minorities had enjoyed protected (*dhimmi*) status as "peoples of the book," those who honor scriptures from the Abrahamic tradition. In return for acknowledgment of subordinate positions and payment of a special tax, these communities enjoyed the right to regulate many of their own affairs. They organized their own religious communities, selected their leaders, and applied religious law to matters that concerned only their community—all within the limits established by the Ottoman authorities. As Coptic Christians acquired greater access to European education in the late nineteenth and early twentieth centuries, they sought reform and began to think of themselves as a community with its own heritage and church. As Paul Sedra says, they "rediscovered a glorious past and sought to revive it."[19]

The Coptic community took on a new militancy after the Egyptian government under Sadat's presidency sought to accommodate the Islamist "awakening" triggered by the 1967 defeat. When Nazir Gayyid became patriarch of the Coptic Church in 1971, taking the title of Pope Shenouda, he broke the "millet partnership" that his predecessor had established with President Nasir and that was built on the notion of Copts accepting their role as a minority in a Muslim state. Pope Shenouda initiated educational and social programs to help middle-class Copts and propel them into mainstream posts, even at a moment of economic contraction. He ruffled feathers, as did Islamist extremists on the other side. Arrested by the government before Sadat's assassination in 1981, Shenouda pulled back toward a more traditional stance of cooperation with the regime. Such a policy pleased Coptic business elites, content to sacrifice political influence for the sake of economic interests. Shenouda consolidated his position as the unique intermediary between Christians and the government. Sedra describes the relationship between the Copts and the state: "There exists no secular leadership of the Coptic community untainted by complicity with the government—no independent voice willing and able to voice Copts' grievances."[20]

A 2001 survey reported that some 80 percent of Egyptian respondents identified themselves first as Muslims and only secondarily as Egyptians (10 percent) or Arabs (1 percent).[21] The percentage of Egyptians saying that they are best described by a religious term (Muslim, in this case) exceeds comparable numbers for Turkey (68 percent), Israel (45 percent), Iran (62 percent), and even Saudi Arabia (74 percent) (Table 2.1). Although no direct comparison with past surveys is available, the magnitude of that number seems to confirm what many have observed: that Egyptians seem to be more religious than ever before. As Gregory Starrett asserts, "more people are praying, more people are reading about Islam and listening to its preachers, more people are discovering consciously the salience of religious ideas and practices to their private and public lives, than did a generation ago."[22] More women and more men appear in the streets dressed in ways that suggest religious commitment. More women wear the hijab (head scarf) or even the niqab (long, concealing form of modest dress that usually includes a facial veil) than in the past. Religious publications have multiplied, and the market for sermons on cassette, authorized and unauthorized, is brisk.[23] Sadat welcomed and encouraged an upsurge of religious feeling, apparently believing it useful in strengthening citizen identification with the state and support for him as president, but this upsurge in religiosity appears to complicate the question of identity. In the parliamentary elections that followed the overthrow of President Mubarak, Islamist parties won two-thirds of the seats, a fact that seemed to reflect this trend toward increasing religiosity, although the Muslim Brotherhood candidate in the June 2012 runoff for the transitional presidency received barely more than 50 percent.

TABLE 2.1 "Which of the Following Best Describes You?"

Country (date of survey)	"I am Iranian [or Israeli, Turk, Egyptian, or Saudi]" (%)	"I am an Arab" (%)	"I am a Muslim [or a Jew in Israel]" (%)	Other (%)	N (100%)
ISRAEL (2001)	31.9	6.7	44.9	16.5*	1,171
IRAN (2000)	34.9	—	62.4	2.7	2,473
TURKEY (2001)	30.8	—	68.0	1.2	3,201
SAUDI ARABIA (2003)	12.1	9.5	73.6	4.9	1,502
EGYPT (2001)	9.8	1.0	79.4	9.8	3,000

Source: World Values Surveys, 1981–2004, online analysis, question G015. Wording may have varied slightly with country.
*Among Israeli respondents, the largest "other" response was "individual, no group" (12.2%). The next largest group of "other" described themselves as Muslim (3.0%).

At a popular level, common sense may soften the importance of the identity issue. Religious belief and practice do not necessarily equate with an exclusivist version of Egyptian identity. Personal religiosity does not necessarily translate into political attitudes. Nadje Al-Ali interviewed "secularist" women who, though often religious, were able to differentiate between personal observance and the political sphere. Some women explicitly saw secularism as a way of including Muslims, Christians, and Jews in a single discourse and a single society. While Islamists tend to equate secularism with atheism, many of the women Al-Ali interviewed saw secularism as a nondogmatic view of religion, an attitude perfectly consistent with being a Muslim, a Christian, or a Jew.[24]

At an intellectual level, many Egyptians have sought to broaden the concept of national identity. A group of Egyptian intellectuals whom Raymond William Baker calls New Islamists crafted a doctrine of "civilizational" Islam that was inclusive rather than exclusive. They were highly critical of the narrow-mindedness of many Islamists, especially the extremists, but also critical of the government for its unwillingness or inability to support full equality for all citizens, freedom of the press, the right of artists to be creative, and the right of women to play public roles in society. While the New Islamists insisted that every society must establish limits to freedom based on underlying values, they claimed that those rules were as much civilizational as religious. They wanted reform of Egyptian education to make possible the emergence of a society based on Islamic values. They were skeptical of the notions of authenticity and cultural specificity, dear to both Islamism and Coptic Christianity. They portrayed an Egypt open to the world, ready to adapt and create but conscious nonetheless of fundamental values anchored in a nonexclusive Islam. Some Copts joined members of the Muslim Brotherhood to form the Wasat (Center) Party in 1995, but the state's Party Formation Committee denied the Wasat status as a political party in 1996, 1998, and 2004.[25] Centrist efforts to expand Egypt's political identity thus have not had visible effect.[26] The Wasat Party did not do well in the presidential elections of 2012.

The fundamental illegitimacy of the Egyptian state before the revolution, committed to democratic principles it did not observe, enhanced regime incentives for cultivating Muslim religiosity rather than seeking a long-term equilibrium solution to the problem of identity. Identification with all religions, or with a Muslim-Christian religious establishment that reflects underlying Egyptian morality, seems more promising than the pursuit of radical separation between the political and religious identities. But such a reformulation required more strength and courage than the Mubarak government could muster. Democratization might now open the way for a solution, but full democratization requires a regime of great strength and confidence. Lacking these attributes, political elites, Islamist or not, have an interest in strengthening the state by emphasizing its Islamic identity. More secular-minded Muslims and Coptic Christians regard that interest as a threat to democratization.

The meaning of Islamic identity and the needs of the state change with every iteration of religious-political conflict. For Muhammad Ali, Islam meant dependence on the Ottomans and dependence on an entrenched, indigenous elite out of touch with what he believed were new global imperatives. As much as Muhammad Abdu sought to alter that image of Islam by reworking its substance, the early nationalist movement did not see Islam as a defining feature of Egyptian identity. In a third period, after "independence" from the British, the emergence of the Muslim Brotherhood once again transformed Islam into a primary symbol of Egyptian resistance to British imperialism and internal moral degradation. And finally, in the most recent period, which has followed the war of 1967 and the Iranian Revolution, the meaning of identity with Islam has acquired yet another nuance. Those events, together with Nasir's death, pushed the Egyptian state toward a more fulsome (though hesitant) embrace of Islamic identity as a defense against enemies of the left and the right, internal and external. The constitutional document emerging from Egypt's Constituent Assembly some two years after the revolution appears to have maintained or strengthened Egypt's identity with Islam.

Ideology

The Ottoman Empire identified with Islam from its modest beginnings on the fringes of the Byzantine Empire in about 1300. Adhering to a Sunni model inherited from the Abbasid caliphate, the Ottoman sultans empowered religiously trained judges to implement the sharia. But Ottoman rule did not depend on a political ideology any more than did the French monarchy under Louis XIV or any other premodern political system. Political ideologies, elements of philosophy combined with recipes for action, emerged from the French, American, and Russian revolutions. Only in the nineteenth century did governments come to see any advantage in committing themselves to programmatic objectives such as liberalism, constitutionalism, or nationalism. Drawn to these ideas, Egyptian intellectuals began to regard Islam as an obstacle to economic, social, and political modernization. They began to think that Islam itself needed to change to accommodate modern needs. Far from thinking that Islam should dictate political change, they thought the needs of the polity required reform of Islamic doctrine.

Not all ideologies invoke religion, and religions do not necessarily produce political ideologies, but all religions propose notions of what is good. Because government must try (or at least pretend) to put itself on the side of "the good," it cannot be indifferent to religious conceptions of authority and general welfare. Political ideologies, such as Marxism, have often assumed an almost theological character, and theology has sometimes become ideological in a political sense. Eldon Eisenach describes these similarities:

> Every effective religious establishment . . . must have some theology defining, directing, and binding it together. Every effective political order, whether relatively open and democratic or relatively hierarchic, closed and authoritarian, must have some ideology performing these same integrative and directing functions.[27]

Both theology and ideology became more important as literacy increased and politics came to require some element of popular participation. Although they need not conflict, a theology that proclaims that God's law is all-inclusive and unchanging will necessarily clash with a political ideology that says constitutions and positive law take precedence over God's law. The advocates of reform in nineteenth-century Egypt came to see organized Islam, represented by the ulama, as an obstacle to change. Some of them tackled the problem as one of theology.

The leader of Egyptian religious reformers was Muhammad Abdu, a man trained in traditional religious schools but with an exposure to European education. Abdu studied at Al-Azhar Mosque and University, which had become the central institution of Egyptian Islam in the middle of the nineteenth century, and began a teaching career before the British invasion of Egypt. After the invasion, he was exiled for supporting a revolt against the monarchy and spent six years in Lebanon and in France collaborating with intellectuals such as Jamal al-Din al-Afghani before returning to Egypt and undertaking a legal career that culminated in his appointment as the mufti of Egypt in 1899. From that high pulpit, he propounded a doctrine of return to the Islam of the ancestors (salafi), peeling away layers and layers of traditional Quranic exegesis to identify what he saw as the fundamental impulses of the religion. The Quran brought truth, and Muslims ever since have been striving to build upon that truth with all the intellectual powers at their disposal. In the modern era, scientists have carried the search for truth into new domains and brought it to new levels. In Abdu's view, the Muslim view of truth is that it is one, absolute, and complete. Scientific truths cannot possibly conflict, therefore, with revealed religious truth. A proper understanding of Islamic law must accommodate the new realities, and theology needs to adapt to modern politics.[28]

The significance of Abdu's work may lie more in this revived interest in Islamic theology than in his own conclusions. His student Rashid Rida built on Abdu's work and edited a journal called *al-Manar*, which was dedicated to rethinking the relationship between Islam and modernity. Rida came to believe that his mentor, Abdu, had given away too much ground by making Islam into a supple, reactive, adaptive agent and undermining its qualities as an unchanging moral foundation for society. He and others contributed to the rising sense that Islam could not be ignored as an essential part of Egyptian identity, but no one, not even Hasan al-Banna, founder of the Muslim Brotherhood, regarded Islam as a modern political ideology before World War II.

The use of the word *salafi* in the contemporary era causes a student of Egyptian politics to think of Abdu and Rida. They wanted to reinterpret Islamic doctrines by invoking Islamic texts and the interpretations of the earliest Muslims, the salafis. In so doing, they were seen as modernists and progressives, breaking as they did with the traditionalists of their era. The puritanical Wahhabi movement that has dominated much of the Arabian peninsula since the eighteenth century also considered itself salafist, revolting against the prevalent Sunni practices of the day. By the twentieth century, Wahhabi Islam came to be seen as antimodern, rejecting modern innovations that Abdu and Rida had welcomed. Hasan al-Banna acknowledged his debt to Abdu, Rida, and the salafi movement, which had created a discourse about Islam's relevance to the condition of Egypt, but the movement that calls itself salafi in Egypt today seems to stand against the Brotherhood for its politicization of Islam and its betrayal of the "true Islam" of the ancestors. In Saudi Arabia, *salafi* has become a term to describe some of those who dissent from state-centered Wahhabism! What salafis have in common is looking to the distant past for wisdom in approaching problems of the present, as Europeans have so frequently done in using Ancient Greek thought as a basis for moral, cultural, or political renewal.

The Muslim Brotherhood moved from salafi thought to Islamist action. Banna insisted he was first and foremost interested in creating a moral, Muslim society. From a Muslim society might follow a Muslim state, and from a set of Muslim states might follow a Muslim world. Banna set out to generate discussion of Islam among educated Egyptians, to create schools and sports teams, to engender trust and a commitment to moral behavior among his fellow citizens. "Banna was steeped in both the theological and Sufi traditions," says Richard Mitchell, "and from both he absorbed, and in his teachings demonstrated, the nonrationalist, even nonintellectual quality which has been observed to be an aspect of Muslim thought."[29] For him the problem was not the theological one identified by the salafi movement but the practical one of renewing Egyptian society through the spiritual transformation of individuals.

The transformation of Islam into a modern political ideology followed World War II, and it came not only from the renewed interest in Islam but from efforts to articulate a secularist ideology. Between the wars, liberal secularism had taken the ideological offensive against a condition of theoretical ambiguity created by a century of modernization, state aggression against the religious establishment, and the renewed interest in Islam.[30] A government employee and member of the religious establishment, Ali Abd al-Raziq, published a book in 1925 in which he advocated separation of religion and state. Islam, as a religion, had "no application to temporal governance," he claimed.[31] The ulama of Azhar reacted by getting him dismissed as a judge (*cadi*) in the religious (sharia) court system. In this same moment in Turkey, Mustafa Kemal Atatürk, having abolished the caliphate claimed by the last of the Ottoman sultans, implemented his interpretation of secularism, which was heavily influenced by the French notion of secularism (laïcité).

In the 1930s, one Egyptian intellectual, Khalid Muhammad Khalid, renewed the secularist attack on the tenuous, unstable, ill-defined position of the Egyptian state by saying that a prophet outranks a ruler. The Prophet did not want to be a ruler and did not, as a result, establish a model for government. Khalid equated religious government with tyrannical government. Religion must speak to the religious needs of the individual, not to the questions of governance and public policy. The government permitted the book's publication but not without acknowledging objections from Azhar and thus accepting state responsibility for religion. The state had "continuing need for religious legitimacy in order to neutralize its political Islamist rival, the Brotherhood, and promote its essentially secular policies."[32]

Sayyid Qutb

The Islamist response to this ideological challenge came from Sayyid Qutb, who joined the Muslim Brotherhood about the time Banna met his death in 1949, presumably at the hands of the state in retaliation for the Brotherhood's 1948 assassination of the Egyptian prime minister. Qutb has left an account of a rather idyllic childhood in Upper Egypt.[33] His prodigious intelligence propelled him to Cairo in pursuit of modern education. He became a writer and a literary critic but was then drawn to social issues and to the Brotherhood's vision of nationalism and social justice. A visit to the United States convinced him that the Western version of modernity had produced rampant materialism and moral degradation. He returned to Egypt, acceded to an important post with the Brotherhood, and then went to prison with other Brotherhood leaders in 1954, after the attempt on President Nasir's life. In prison, Qutb wrote volumes, most of them part of a commentary on the Quran, in which he articulated an Islamic political ideology.

Banna had created an organization that effectively acquired great power in Egypt and had talked about the need for an Islamic state. Qutb offered reasons why the creation of an Islamic state was imperative and explained how the first generation of Muslims had created a revolutionary model by which it could be achieved. He asserted that Muhammad had encountered the same sort of problems that confront modern Muslims: social inequities, flagrant immorality, and human beings who exercise political authority over fellow human beings. Perhaps following a line of argument already advanced by Pakistani activist Mowlana Abul ala Mawdudi, Qutb said the condition of ignorance (jahiliyya) that marked the pre-Islamic age again afflicts humankind. Modern Muslims must therefore fight the modern jahiliyya with the same methods and weapons used by the first

Muslims, who first took counsel with themselves and strove through individual jihad to perfect their faith in God, then retreated from Mecca's hostility to strengthen their community in Medina, and finally launched a violent jihad against Mecca's power structure. The new Muslim community recognized no final authority except God. Sayyid Qutb interpreted this to mean that all human claims to sovereignty, ancient or modern, are necessarily illegitimate because they defy God's sovereignty. He saw all existing governments, including Egypt's, as illegitimate and targets for revolution, even though the leadership might claim to be Muslim. The president of Egypt, Gamal Abd al-Nasir, did not mistake the message contained in Qutb's little volume called *Signposts on the Road* or *Milestones*.[34] Qutb was tried, convicted, and hanged in 1966.

Banna had called for spiritual revival, but Qutb argued that it was unrealistic to ask Muslims to lead virtuous lives in a corrupted society, where material and sexual temptation was too great. While Banna had seen society's renewal as a precondition for political change, Qutb thought that an Islamic government based on the sovereignty of God and on the laws formulated in the sharia was a prerequisite for moral behavior. Like Marx, who thought human beings could overcome alienation only when they came to have collective ownership of the means of production, Qutb posited that Muslims would finally be free only when liberated from the domination of other human beings and the pressures of a degraded social situation. The laws of God would guide Muslims toward virtue and righteousness. He thought the entire world would eventually become Muslim in the sense of "submitting to God," whether within the established Islamic tradition or beyond it.

The ideological battle between Islamists and secularists has raged ever since. Because Qutb portrayed the modern jahiliyya as thoroughly entrenched and unlikely to give up power voluntarily, he seemed to suggest the necessity of violence against a state that had, after all, used violence to oppose the Muslim Brotherhood. Qutb lauded Muhammad's use of military force against Mecca and therefore the notion of violent jihad as well as the idea of nonviolent jihad, the striving of Muslims to know and follow God's will. Unlike the several radical groups that subsequently took inspiration from his writings in Egypt—Takfir wal Hijra, Islamic Jihad, and the Islamic Group, for example—he did not explicitly urge the use of violence or condone the use of terrorism to undermine the Egyptian regime. Abdassalem al-Faraj, who collaborated in the assassination of President

Sadat in 1981, published a book invoking some of Qutb's ideas to justify the action. In addition, he argued that a medieval Muslim scholar, Ibn Taymiyya, had endorsed the legitimacy of Muslim violence against other Muslims who had abandoned the path of God.[35] Ibn Taymiyya's question was whether Muslims had the right to revolt against Mongol rulers, who were converts to Islam. The radicals built on Qutb's distinction between Muslims and "true Muslims." A true Muslim must do more than believe and wait for eternal salvation. He must act with other Muslims to make this world better. Islam supplies the goals and the methodology. Qutb created the basis for a revolutionary political ideology.

The leaders of the Muslim Brotherhood broke with this sort of radical analysis when they emerged from prison soon after Sadat succeeded Nasir in the presidency in 1970. The group retained its ambitions of making Egypt an Islamic state but committed itself to advancing its cause within the confines of Egyptian law. Radical groups nonetheless launched a series of attacks in the 1970s and managed to assassinate Sadat in 1981. A second spurt of radicalism in the 1990s, marked especially by attacks on Egyptian police and foreign tourists, constituted a severe test for the regime. At one point, radicals established full control over two impoverished suburbs of greater Cairo. The government used military force to regain control. The radicals functioned most easily in Upper Egypt, where they launched a spectacular assault at Luxor in 1997. Some fifty-eight Western tourists and four Egyptians died at the hands of the Islamic Group in an incident that outraged ordinary Egyptians and constituted a turning point in sentiment against the radicals.[36] The government prevailed. Within a year, one of the most prominent radicals was recanting the "mistakes" of the Islamic Group. The most radical version of Qutbian ideology may continue to flourish underground, but it does not figure in contemporary Egyptian debates.

The Sharia

Current Egyptian debates turn, instead, on the place of the sharia in Egyptian politics. With passage of the democratizing constitution of 1971, Sadat opened the way for ulama to join Islamists in pushing for the application of the sharia. Abd al-Halim Mahmud, who acceded to the role of shaykh of Azhar in 1973, seized upon that opportunity to challenge the regime by advancing a proposal to codify the sharia. The proposal bore fruit in 1978, when the People's Assembly created a committee that brought together ten members of the assembly with six ulama from Azhar.

The ulama as a group were united on the principle of applying Islamic law. Whether members of Sufi brotherhoods or close to the Muslim Brotherhood, the ulama were together in demanding the *tatbiq* [application] of the sharia. It was a question of returning to Islamic law, which would be applied once codification had been completed.[37]

Mahmud also associated himself and Azhar with an effort of the Academy of Islamic Research to draft a generic Islamic constitution. Under these pressures from Islamists and Azhar, the regime agreed to modify the Egyptian constitution in 1980 to make the sharia the principal source of legislation.

Faraj Ali Fuda, founder of the new Wafd party, renewed and augmented the arguments of Ali Abd al-Raziq and Khalid Muhammad Khalid, saying that the sharia is not holy (because it was fashioned by human beings) and not relevant, although positive (man-made) law in Egypt is in fact consistent with the spirit of the sharia. He agreed that Islam is a part of Egyptian identity, that something called Egyptian Islam exists, and that religion could be a part of the public sphere, but he argued that religious governments are tyrannical "because they hold to a single absolute truth, denying the possibility of multiplicity."[38] He was murdered in 1992. Such was the intensity of debate about the sharia.

The critical sentence from the constitution, "Islamic jurisprudence is the principal source of legislation," never satisfied radical Islamists, determined secularists, or even Azhar, but it served to turn debate toward a more manageable question: whether existing Egyptian law reflected the sharia. It was this debate that preoccupied much of the flourishing religious press in Egypt during the Sadat and Mubarak years, and the government responded with its own set of religious publications to argue its point of view. At its core, the debate inevitably depended on an understanding of what the sharia is and how the sharia relates to the process of legal science (fiqh). For a secular jurist and writer such as Muhammad Said al-Ashmawi, this set of principles, anchored in the Quran, must be interpreted by every generation. In his view, Egyptian law conformed to that standard.[39] Azhar, though a participant in the debate about the sharia, could not afford to challenge the legitimacy of the regime from the inside; instead it defended the state against the radical perspective that defines the political leadership as *kufr*, nonbelievers. Before 2011, even the Muslim Brotherhood could not reopen the constitutional issue without risking its precarious legal-illegal position, and the radical Islamists, through attacks on secularists such as Nobel Prize winner Naguib Mahfouz and Fuda, made it clear that they would not tolerate a reopening of the broader issues from a secular, academic perspective. After the events of 2011, the Brotherhood seemed in a position to reformulate the constitutional treatment of the sharia but was reportedly disinclined to do so, despite pressures from salafis.

The centrists, sometimes called New Islamists, argue that fiqh is a necessarily human process open to continuous revision. Any and all Muslims, whether members of the ulama or laypersons, can and must engage in the process of *ijtihad*, by which general principles are applied and interpreted. In that view, the sharia is an abstraction, a set of foundational concepts derived principally from the Quran and to a much lesser extent from the sunna or practices of the Prophet. The early legal authorities, creators of the four legal traditions within Sunni Islam, all worked from the relatively small amount of legal material in the Quran and from the sunna, known primarily through collections of hadith, reports on what the Prophet said or did in his lifetime. Although early lawyers winnowed and compiled the hadith in an effort to eliminate the fraudulent, many hadith reports are contradictory, and modern scholars tend to be skeptical about the reliability of many or all of them. Hence, a notion of sharia that depends on a fiqh anchored in hadith does not inspire confidence among the New Islamists. For many Islamists and ulama, however, the sharia, though constructed after Muhammad's death and well after the compilation of the Quran, constitutes a complete set of instructions good for all ages, a set of instructions that should guide and take precedence over all positive law. Egyptian legislation and judicial procedures, deeply influenced by European law and jurisprudence, do not measure up, in their view.

By one line of thinking, opening the doors to full democracy in Egypt and permitting all forces, including the Brotherhood, to be fairly represented may now lead to a more stable balance between the religious and secular spheres. That has been the hope of those who focus on religion as an aspect of civil society.[40] In defending itself against Islamic revolution, the Egyptian state became significantly more religious in orientation.[41] The Islamist movement succeeded in creating a more religious society and goading the state to greater religious sensibility. The movement, however, also abandoned its revolutionary dream of a utopian Islamic state—never explicitly defined by Qutb or anyone else. Islamist ideology penetrated the Egyptian state, and the state produced a reshaping of Islamist ideology. Nathan Brown, one of the most careful and thoughtful observers of Egypt's transition, wrote in the fall of 2012: "The 2012 constitution, if completed and ratified, is likely to set the term of engagement, clarify the stakes, and shape the arenas of a long political struggle over the relationship between religion and state in Egypt."[42]

Institutions

Modernization theory predicts greater and greater separation of church and state, but in Egypt the lines between religious and political institutions, never sharp, have become increasingly blurred. When Smith wrote *Religion and Political Development* in 1970, the secular-minded state seemed to have overwhelmed religious institutions in Egypt, but the challenge of radical Islamist groups in the 1970s put the Egyptian state on the defensive. Institutions such as the office of the mufti, the head of the fatwa (religious opinion) office (Dar al-Ifta), and Al-Azhar Mosque and University, pronounced lifeless in the 1960s, achieved resurrection.[43] And the Islamist movement, though deterred in its most radical inclinations, made its influence felt in every aspect of Egyptian society.[44] The Muslim Brotherhood, now more than eighty years old, became a semiofficial part of the religious establishment even though it remained an illegal organization until the revolution of 2011.

One contemporary model of development proposes that religious organizations be seen as a part of civil society and that civil society be seen as separate from the state. By opening its doors and encouraging the growth of civil society, the Egyptian state would prepare the way for participatory democracy. All voices would find their expression through political parties vying for power. Democratic decision-making would fashion the balance between religion and politics; both religious and political power would be tamed. A liberated civil society would redefine the state.

However useful in thinking about the prerequisites of democracy, the model does not sufficiently reflect the complexities of the interlocking relationship between religious and political institutions. On the one hand, no religious organization can function without the security and regulatory framework the state provides; without the state there is no civil society. On the other hand, the state cannot function without the legitimacy provided by religious leaders and organizations, some of which escape direct control. The state is the single most important actor in the religious sphere, and religious groups exercise critical influence in the political system. The religious establishment in Egypt, represented by Azhar, the Dar al-Ifta, and the Ministry of Awqaf (plural of waqf), constitutes part of the state but also remains part of the country's religious structure. The Azhari establishment includes high officials closely beholden to the state and peripheral preachers who manage to critique the government and support militant Islamist positions from within what appears to be a state-controlled sphere.[45] And the Muslim Brotherhood, whose origins were antistate and anti-ulama, became an integral part of the political system it supposedly opposed. There was and is no clear boundary between civil society and state, between religion and politics.

The state's assault on the autonomy of the religious sphere began with Muhammad Ali's confiscation of waqf land as a means of bringing the ulama, the native Egyptian elite, under his control. The assault continued throughout the nineteenth and twentieth centuries as the state elevated Azhar to a dominant position within Egyptian Islam and then seized direct control of it, established its own educational system to challenge the Azhari system, created the Dar al-Ifta as an official source of religious opinions, attacked and then eliminated sharia courts—replacing them with state courts fashioned on the European model—and regulated Sufi practices, abolishing some of the more extreme ceremonies. Gamal Abd al-Nasir completed the long process of subjugating religious institutions to state control and making Islam a simple instrument of the state.[46] State superiority over religious institutions appeared absolute but proved short-lived, even illusory.

In the 1940s and 1950s, the Muslim Brotherhood nearly reversed the power relationship, first with its challenge to the weak governments from 1942 to 1952, and then with its assault on the Nasirist regime in 1954. (Although the Brotherhood may not on either occasion have intended a full-scale assault on the regime, it certainly did nurture hopes of creating an Islamic state.) Then in the 1970s and 1980s, the radical groups that had spun off from the Brotherhood renewed the effort at violent overthrow of what they saw as a secular state. That effort failed.

Azhar and Dar al-Ifta

Neither the state under Nasir nor the radicals who fought for power emerged
entirely victorious. As a result, the waters were muddied. The Egyptian state
that was deeply involved in, albeit not in full control of, the regulation of religious
organizations battled semiautonomous religious organizations in the political
sphere. The religious and political spheres were engaged in an embrace that neither could break. Although the state retained the upper hand, the lingering threat
of radical Islam and the mass appeal of Islamic symbols and programs drove
the state to accommodate religion. And the Muslim Brotherhood, breaking with
its past and the militant offshoots, decided to seek influence within the confines
of the authoritarian state, tempering its message and compromising with state
regulation in a variety of ways, even electing members of Parliament without
being able to organize a political party. That strategy carried the group toward
direct political participation in the system after the uprising of 2011.

At the moment of the French conquest in 1798, the Egyptian ulama consti-
Two religious-political institutions reflect the tensions at the heart of the
struggle between the religious and political under the old regime: the Azhar
mosque-university system and the Dar al-Ifta, office of the mufti. Both are, in
different degrees, creations of the state and are designed to exercise state influence
over Egyptian Islam. Before the events of 2011, both offices enjoyed dubious
legitimacy in the minds of Islamist groups, but neither office could be entirely
ignored. Both were obliged in some measure to do the will of political elites,
but Islamist pressures permitted them to stiff the regime on some issues to maintain the legitimacy they needed to do the job the state wanted them to do. They
demonstrated the way in which the state had reshaped Egyptian Islam and at the
same time made itself vulnerable to pressures from the religious sphere.[47]

At the moment of the French conquest in 1798, the Egyptian ulama constituted a small, native elite headed by a council of nine or ten, of whom the shaykh
of Azhar was one.[48] Muhammad Ali and his successors sought to subordinate
the ulama by nationalizing the autonomous source of financial support, the awqaf,
and by creating a chief among the ulama, someone who could take orders. By
the beginning of the twentieth century, the state had raised the shaykh of Azhar
to such a position.[49] Azhar successfully resisted reform of its teaching establishment on more than one occasion, declining a more effective role in the modern
world in what was a losing effort to maintain autonomy. By the end of the Nasir

regime, there was no longer any illusion of autonomy. Azhar, nationalized and reformed, constituted an arm of the state and seemed to have lost all legitimacy in the eyes of Islamist groups. Hasan al-Banna and the Muslim Brothers, although they recruited some members from among Azhari students, remained largely critical of the institution for tolerating foreign rule and political domination of Islam.

Azhar, together with the Ministry of Awqaf, became and remains the principal tool for state control of religious practice in Egypt. It administers a system of religious schools that expanded from a total of 90,000 students in 1970 to about 300,000 by 1980. The university itself came to enroll about 90,000 students; its faculty, employees of the state, constitute the elite of Egyptian ulama, all of them employees of the state. In addition, through the Ministry of Awqaf, the state employs several thousand preachers who staff official mosques, most of them products of the Azhar system, around the country. Starting in the 1960s, Azhar's Academy for Islamic Research began to claim the right to censor Egyptian publications according to Islamic criteria. It largely succeeded in exercising that right. The shaykh of Azhar, named by the government, is in theory the chief spokesman for Islam in Egypt, empowered to issue fatwas affecting every Muslim in Egypt.

The state created the Dar al-Ifta in 1895 as another tool in its effort to assert its control over the religious sphere. From the beginning, the office annually issued thousands of fatwas, nonbinding judgments on the application of Islamic principles to problems and legislation. The office's prestige rose and fell according to the ability and qualifications of the mufti, who was always a political appointee selected from men educated in the religious tradition. Surprisingly, the Dar al-Ifta, even more than Azhar, has exercised increasing autonomy since the end of the Nasir regime as a result of the state's need for protection against the verbal assault of the Islamists. The Dar al-Ifta has helped transform politics into a war of fatwas, reshaping Egyptian Islam as has the state's transformation and manipulation of an old institution, Azhar. The history of these two institutions shows how the Egyptian state has transformed the institutional structure of Islam in Egypt. By its actions, the state has politicized religion. Every religious institution must in some measure play politics to protect itself within the system. Virtually every religious act has acquired political significance. Every proclamation, every sermon, every study group, every nongovernmental organization

(NGO) operated in the name of religion, resonates within a structure defined by the government. The institutions differ in degree of government regulation and influence, but only the militant Islamist groups accused of murdering policemen and tourists put themselves outside the system.

The Muslim Brotherhood

The Muslim Brotherhood grew outside the official religious establishment but within the legal framework of the Egyptian state. Its founder, Hasan al-Banna, was a layman, and the movement included few ulama in its early years. It eschewed politics but became a political force by virtue of its organizational strength. From a small society established in Ismailia, it spread to Cairo and then to much of Egypt as a network of people drawn by Banna's charisma, by the group's schools and activities, and by its message of moral rejuvenation and nationalism. Mitchell describes Banna's appeal:

> One friendly writer describes Banna as a man who knew the language of the Azhar and of the Sufis, who knew the dialects, the traditions, and the problems of the cities and towns, of the provinces, of the delta and the desert, and of Upper and Lower Egypt; he knew the psyche of the butcher and the little girl and the various types of people who inhabited the cities, including the thieves and murderers—he spoke to them all, says this observer, and "always his knowledge astounded his hearers." In this matter "he won individual after individual," binding them in an unbreakable bond to him as a representative of an idea and as a personal friend.[50]

Banna was, in short, an extraordinarily effective and talented politician with explicit, though deferred, political objectives: the liberation of Egypt and the creation of an Islamic state.[51] Although the Brotherhood did not in the early years advance candidates for office, it enjoyed a broader base of support than any of the existing parties, even the Wafd, which dominated Egyptian politics in the interwar period with a thin base of support in the landed elites. Membership in the Brotherhood may have totaled half a million or more by World War II. It loomed as a threat to "liberal Egypt," the label commonly applied to Egypt from "independence" in 1923 until the revolution of 1952.

The Brotherhood's ability to survive first the loss of its founder and then two periods of official dissolution demonstrates the organization's strength. The government dissolved the organization in 1947. (The Brotherhood responded by assassinating Prime Minister Mahmud Fahmi al-Nuqrashi in 1948, and the government then apparently ordered the killing of Banna as retribution.) Reauthorized in 1952, the Brotherhood succeeded in putting thousands of demonstrators into the streets in a matter of hours. Banned again in 1954 and its leaders imprisoned after the assassination attempt on Nasir, the Brotherhood survived underground until its liberation by President Sadat in 1970. It soon made its presence felt with its publications, its affiliated organizations, and a strategy of capturing power in the universities and professional syndicates, such as that of engineers and lawyers. Although Presidents Sadat and Hosni Mubarak sought to harass and restrain the Brotherhood out of suspicion that it kept ties to radical factions engaged in violence, they stopped short of dissolving it a third time. The Brotherhood became a part of Egypt's religious, social, and political structures.

A 1977 Egyptian law that prohibits the formation of political parties based on religion kept the Brotherhood from running candidates under its name in parliamentary elections, but it succeeded in running candidates on other tickets or as independents. Its elected members of the People's Assembly built a tight, effective parliamentary group, boasting 80 members (of 454) after the 2005 elections. Mubarak seems to have assumed that the Brotherhood, if permitted to organize and compete in a fair election, would have won a majority. The results of the first parliamentary election held after Mubarak's overthrow suggest that he may have been correct in his assumption. One secret of the Brotherhood's electoral success in 2005 was the mobilization of women to turn out the vote. Women approached women and provided security services at the polls. Security forces finding veiled women surrounding a polling place were less likely to intervene forcibly to prevent voting or stuff ballot boxes.[52] One presumes that women also helped the Brotherhood win in 2012, but it does not follow that a Brotherhood-dominated government would necessarily enlarge opportunities for women.

Between its emergence from repression in 1970 and the overthrow of the Mubarak regime in 2011, the Brotherhood was often critical of the official religious establishment (i.e., Azhar, Dar al-Ifta, and the Ministry of Awqaf), but some of the official ulama expressed sympathy for the Brotherhood and its positions. Moreover, unofficial preachers working from private mosques echoed Brotherhood positions and even sympathized with the radicals. Their sermons circulated in an underground cassette trade that the government tried to suppress. Furthermore, many NGOs with Brotherhood sponsorship received a portion of their resources from the government, and they could not function without government permission. These organizations provided a quality of service many Egyptians saw as fulfilling important needs and as lacking from any other source. Hence, the government tolerated and even supported them. In this sense the Brotherhood constituted an unofficial, semiautonomous part of the religious establishment.[53]

Plural Voices

The triangular relationship between the government, the official religious establishment, and the unofficial establishment (the Brotherhood) remained unstable because the status quo depended upon the will of the state. The government continued to campaign against unauthorized preaching, prohibit unauthorized sermons on cassette, regulate NGOs, monitor elections to syndicates where Islamists had won power, and censure publications that stepped beyond the line of "acceptable criticism." Religious groups pushed the state toward implementation of its proclaimed interest in democratization; by resisting democratization, the state weakened its hand and exposed the instability of the situation it had created. Azhar again exercised a certain autonomy, as did the Dar al-Ifta, because the regime needed the help of the official establishment in legitimating an unstable and fundamentally illegitimate system. The Muslim Brotherhood enjoyed considerable liberty to organize, speak, and publish because its support helped the regime suppress radicals and helped affirm the state's loyalty to Islamic principles. The Brotherhood enhanced its position if it won the support of Azhar; Azhar magnified its position within the state if it helped to satisfy the Brotherhood and to keep it within the domain of state control.

Despite government efforts over two centuries, the organizational structure of Islam in Egypt has become pluralistic. Government efforts to control Islam and give it a single spokesperson have failed. Even the official agencies do not speak with a single voice, and the Muslim Brotherhood, though it would aspire to follow a single line, has suffered a splintering that further complicates the picture. The New Islamists, for example, express their conviction that Islam must be the foundation of the Egyptian state, but they welcome fresh thinking about the meaning of Islamic law from any quarter. They reject narrowness of interpretation from the Brotherhood, Azhar, and Dar al-Ifta.

As Jonathan Brown explains, Sufi orders constitute yet another element of Islamic pluralism in Egypt, an element often neglected by political analysts, because Sufism seems irrelevant to politics. Major Sufi brotherhoods, such as the Shadhiliyya, the Burhamiyya, the Rifaiyya, and the Ahmadiyya, elect representatives to the Supreme Council of Sufi Orders. "This quasi-state leadership committee is responsible for managing Sufi affairs at a national level, such as the organization of the *mawlid* (celebrations of the birthdays of major Sufi saints) festivals." The council works closely with Azhar, which is thought to be favorably oriented toward Sufism. As of 2012, the rector (shaykh) of Azhar and the grand mufti of Egypt were both known to be Sufi grand masters, that is, leaders of Sufi circles. This tight relationship between the religious establishment and Sufism irks salafis and members of the Muslim Brotherhood. "Since the 2011 uprising mainstream Sufis have become firm allies of both the transitional authorities and of liberals; they identify with the state-controlled religious establishment and are driven by a consuming fear of salafis and Islamists in general."[54]

Since the revolution of 2011, religious groups calling themselves salafis have also stepped out of the shadows and into the action. What salafis have in common is a rigorous view of monotheism. They object to Sufi notions of sainthood, ancestor worship, and inspired leadership. Typically they have emphasized faith and opposed political action, yet some salafi groups decided to field candidates in the parliamentary elections, and their success led them toward representation in the Constituent Assembly. Without the political experience of the Brotherhood or its stake in existing constitutional arrangements, some salafis apparently wanted sharp revision of the 1971 constitution and its treatment of the sharia. The Islamic Group, which engaged in violence against the state in the 1990s but renounced violence in 2002, resurfaced as a salafist voice.[55]

The de facto pluralism of Islam in Egypt and the existence of a Coptic minority have not yet produced separation of religious and political institutions. The state transformed the institutional structure of Islam in Egypt and incorporated it in various degrees into the structure of the state. The revolt of the Islamists intensified the state's need for regulation and control and contributed to an unintended Islamization of the state. Transforming Islam transformed the state. Far from separated, religious and political institutions were deeply entangled even before the collapse of the old regime and the ascension of the Muslim Brotherhood.

The case of Professor Nasr Abu Zayd, who was convicted of apostasy, illustrates the deep involvement of religion in state institutions and the partial ability of state institutions to regulate and enforce Islam. Islamists brought a civil case against Abu Zayd for teaching that, like any other document, the Quran must be subjected to close textual analysis and that understanding its implications is a human process open to continual revision. Islamists supported by some ulama brought the case to the state court system, which would enforce religious law only insofar as it is embedded in the Egyptian code. The court would normally have been concerned only with the effects of apostasy. One consequence in this case is that a Muslim who abandons Islam cannot be married to a Muslim woman. The court found Abu Zayd guilty not of abandoning Islam but of teaching and writing against it and, as a result, being illegally married to his wife. In finding guilt and dissolving his marriage, the court made it clear that Islam constitutes one of the foundations of the Egyptian state. The decision, a product of religious pressure on the state, nevertheless represented a state assertion of authority over religion.[56] In what can only be termed a humane response to an inhumane decision, the government subsequently permitted Abu Zayd and his wife to leave the country for the Netherlands, where he taught at the University of Leiden until his death in 2010.

The relationship between religious and political institutions in Egypt remains unstable for at least two reasons: First, social and economic change in the form of urbanization, social mobility, improved communication, and increasing access to education continues to transform religious institutions. These changes have increased pluralism and produced conflict within the religious sphere. Some elements of the religious sphere have sought and continue to seek revision. Second, although the state has sought to further subjugate religious institutions, to undermine the power that Islamic organizations have acquired in the past three decades, it has not succeeded. Islamic organizations have seized power in a democratic setting, though it is not certain that they will be any more tolerant of religious pluralism than was the previous regime. They, too, may want to increase the power of the state over religion. To reverse the long-standing state effort to control religion would be consistent with the Brotherhood's complaints about the former regime, but it would also compromise the power of the state the Brotherhood now dominates. To acknowledge religious plurality and conflict in accord with secular democratic theory might be difficult for the Brotherhood and other Islamist groups. The revolution has not yet led to equilibrium.

Political Culture

The notion of political culture serves to help political scientists identify a society's attitudes that are more enduring than opinions of the moment. Scholars have shown that there is a certain continuity in the way the French think about their political system and that French attitudes are distinct from those of Denmark, Great Britain, the United States—and Egypt, for that matter. Weber argued that the "Protestant ethic" affected the growth of capitalism in Europe. Inglehart claims that in European political culture, there are still traces of the distinction between predominantly Catholic and predominantly Protestant countries. He argues that respondents from Muslim countries do not differ from other cultural groups in attitudes toward democracy but do distinguish themselves from other cultures on the equality of women and on homosexuality.[57] Differences in basic attitudes—the importance of religion in society, attitudes toward minorities, trust of other people—tend to endure within countries and, perhaps, within cultural areas.

Such attitudes are not, however, permanent. There is abundant evidence for long-term change in political cultures. Catholic Europe has become as dynamic economically as Protestant Europe. The authoritarian Germans have become democrats. Eastern Europeans are shedding communist values. And, as Daniel Lerner showed more than fifty years ago, Middle Eastern Muslim culture has evolved in significant ways.[58] A trilogy of novels by Naguib Mahfouz dramatizes the shifting mentalities of a single Egyptian family over thirty years.[59] It would be helpful to document the political attitudes of ordinary Egyptians in, say, 1810, 1860, 1910, and 1960, but the modern survey, dependent on computers, became available only in the 1950s. Since then the skepticism of the Egyptian government about any survey touching on politics has slowed research, but some survey data on Egypt are available to help test impressionistic accounts. While some Egyptian attitudes have clearly endured—witness the broad attachment to clitoridectomy (female circumcision), despite legislation banning the practice—others have evolved over time. Change in social conditions would certainly be the primary explanation for long-term evolution of Egyptian political culture.

The most striking change in Egyptian political culture during the past fifty years is the apparent increase in commitment to Islam. The signs are everywhere—in dress, in behavior, in publications, in speech. The Islamist movement seems to have had an impact on the piety of ordinary Egyptians, even on many who are not formally a part of the movement. How does one explain this "awakening" in a country that seemed inclined to downplay religion in the 1950s? Many scholars have attributed the Islamist success to changing social conditions.

Islam has become a form of protest for regions and groups disadvantaged in the modernization process. The message of the militant Islamic Group, an offshoot of the Muslim Brotherhood powered by Qutbian ideology, found resonance in the underdeveloped south of Egypt.[60] By at least one analysis, the attacks on tourists and policemen represented an assault on northern dominance and southern weakness. Gilles Kepel has argued that the Islamist phenomenon has, in general, depended upon an appeal to two groups: a pious bourgeoisie and a lumpen proletariat, the wreckage of modernization. Where Islamists have succeeded, they have mobilized both groups, as in Iran.[61] Urbanization has overtaxed the state's ability to minister to the needs of its citizens. Migrants fleeing the poverty of the countryside end up in slums on the periphery of Cairo—areas that lack sanitation, decent housing, schools, and transportation. The radicals captured and held two such neighborhoods in the 1990s. NGOs, many of them supported by religious organizations, have often stepped into the breach by providing services unavailable from the state.[62] The rise in literacy and the demand for public education has resulted in overcrowded schools, declining standards in education, and large numbers of educated young people unable to find jobs. To compensate, the wealthy hire tutors for their children or send them to private universities.

Education

Social dislocation does not, however, explain why individual Egyptians have been drawn toward Islam rather than socialism, Arabism, or some other form of protest. It does not explain why so many Egyptians have ceased to think of their faith as a set of rituals and practices embedded in the social fabric and have begun to read about Islam and think about what it means to their lives. Changes in Egypt's educational system over the past century probably do more to explain the growth of the Islamist movement than does social alienation. Of course, education may itself produce alienation in those who emerge with modern degrees but cannot find work. Lack of access to modern education also alienates those who have come to understand its magic properties but cannot acquire them. The two explanations are complementary.

The Islamist awakening comes in part from a transformation in the structure of Egyptian Islam that has followed from modernization. Starrett writes:

> In documenting the role of the contemporary school in teaching Islam, I hope to show how the expansion and transfer of religious socialization from private to newly created public sector institutions over the last century has led to a comprehensive revision of the way Egyptians treat Islam as a religious tradition, and consequently of Islam's role in Egyptian society.[63]

As education has reached a larger proportion of the population, it has enabled more and more Egyptians to evaluate their faith and its implications. The Nasirist state forced reform upon the Azhari educational system after 1961, and one result has been ulama better prepared to lock horns in contemporary political battles, ulama whose backgrounds more closely resemble those of Islamist leaders, many of them products of state education. The Muslim Brotherhood and all its Islamist successors are products of modern education and protagonists of it. Already in the 1930s and 1940s the Brotherhood was publishing newspapers and journals to recruit and hold members. Since the 1970s, the number of religious publications has multiplied, and the government has been obliged to compete by mounting a publishing industry of its own.

Religious and political institutions find support in political culture. They respond to the culture as they find it, but they also seek to transform it. The Brotherhood exemplifies both sides of that assertion. It arose from its ability to respond to the sentiments of Egyptians caught in a process of change they could not fully comprehend. It sought to re-create a moral society inspired by the Quran and committed to a comportment consistent with Islamic law. The Muslim

Brotherhood wanted to transform the existing political culture as a prelude to changing the state. Similarly, Gamal abd al-Nasir transformed a military coup into a popular "revolution" by virtue of his ability to reach ordinary Egyptians. His government launched land reform, formed agricultural cooperatives, and pushed medical clinics into villages. He appealed to the political culture as he found it, but he also set out to transform Egyptians into good citizens, good Arabs, and, eventually, good socialists! The Brotherhood saw that education was the key to bringing Egyptians back to Islam. Nasir understood education as the key to secularizing society. Consensus on educational policy remains vital to stabilizing the relationship between religion and politics in Egypt.

Although Jamal al-Din al-Afghani revived the idea of using Islam as the rallying cry against European imperialism in the late nineteenth century, the British never came to see Islam as an obstacle to colonial rule. Instead, as Starrett shows, they sought to finish the job begun by Muhammad Ali and his successors, undermining the traditional elite by providing an alternative source of education in the society.[64] Despite reaching only a relatively small part of the population, the elementary schools they established included instruction about religion, which the British saw as a necessary component of citizenship.[65] In so doing, the schools opened the way for a transformation of Islam in Egypt in ways that made possible the Muslim Brotherhood and the identification of Islam—a good Egyptian is a good Muslim—with the Egyptian state. But this was no longer the Islam of the traditionalist ulama but the Islam of the Egyptian public schools.[66] The old Quranic schools based on memorization of the Quran began to lose sway.

Successive Egyptian governments, first under British tutelage and then independent of British rule, have followed the British line. Islamic identity reinforces Egyptian identity as long as the Islam in question is Egyptian Islam, a product of a curriculum designed and supervised by Egyptians. A survey of Egyptian university students found that 73 percent favored teaching religion in the national curriculum. A third wanted religious instruction extended to the university level. Most respondents said the current educational system in Egypt conflicts with Egyptian national character, presumably because it is insufficiently influenced by Islamic learning and culture.[67] According to Starrett, Egyptians see public education as the principal means of transmitting Islam to the younger generation.[68]

Nasir's regime sought to move that culture toward an Arab version of socialism, but those efforts did not succeed; nor did Islamist efforts to transform

Egyptians into militant Muslims, willing to countenance violence in the name of an insurgent Islam. Both the state and the Brotherhood worked at shaping the existing belief system through education, social services, and a barrage of mediated messages, but neither was capable of transforming that culture as it wished. Instead, the competition accentuated a bifurcation of the political culture between attitudes that one might term "religious" and those that one might term "secular," and it seems unlikely that one tendency will vanquish the other. Islamists have regularly pushed for greater attention to religion at every level of Egyptian education. The Brotherhood has never ceased to champion the idea of Hasan al-Banna: that a moral revolution was the key to social and political change. It will be interesting to see whether a more democratic government dominated by the Brotherhood or other Islamists will make cultural transformation a high priority. A political culture that resists change is not necessarily immutable. The old saws about the incompatibility of democracy with Islam or Arab culture, built on notions that cultures are unchanging, seem utterly untenable. But, as Leila Ahmed observes, change occurs not because a modern culture erases the traditional, but because participants in a culture find ways to preserve and innovate at the same time.[69] Are women who join Islamist groups and embrace "traditional" subordination of women to men acting in a modern or traditional way? They are both agents of change and agents of preservation.[70]

Maintenance or Transformation?

Socialization is the key to maintaining and transforming culture. It is not surprising, then, that education has been a primary battleground between the religious and the political spheres in Egypt as elsewhere. From Muhammad Ali's initial effort to create European-style schools to the contemporary conflict over higher education in Egypt, the battle has raged. The state weakened the hold of religious elites on the education of youth, but the resulting public school curricula reinforced the place of religion in Egyptian society. Now the Azhari system has bounced back in a new form combining secular and Islamic criteria. Secularizing liberals once constituted the forces for instability; now it is the Islamists who agitate for revision and change. The relative strength of religious and political institutions has determined the outcome of the struggle over education much more clearly and directly than it has the shape of Egyptian political culture as a whole. Education does not necessarily produce an intended result, as colonial powers and independent governments alike have discovered over time.

A study conducted in the waning years of the Mubarak regime identifies both areas of clarity and others of ambiguity and even ambivalence in the teaching of religion in the schools. In textbooks used at all levels, James Toronoto and Muhammad Eissa found clarity about the unacceptability of violence: "There is no material that justifies violence or that can be construed as an incitement to commit terrorist acts. We noted a complete absence of vitriolic rhetoric directed toward either Muslims or non-Muslims."[71] The textbooks offer less clarity on matters such as religious liberty and tolerance. The texts defend religious liberty with reference to Quranic passages, but ignore issues of apostasy or contemporary restrictions on Coptic Christians in Egypt.[72] (Copts have their own religious instruction and their own texts.) The general spirit of the Muslim texts is inclusiveness: "The emphasis is almost entirely on promoting tolerance and respect among Egyptians," but there is also insistence that Islam is the superior universal religion, which may encompass the other religions of the book in the sense that Christians and Jews are Muslims because they "submit" to God. But even in the curriculum as revised for the 2002–2003 school year, there are also diatribes against the Jews, which the authors of the study note is "curiously anachronistic" in a country that has been at peace with Israel since 1979. The textbooks sound alternatively modern and old-fashioned on issues of gender, purposely broad-minded on questions of dress, but quite decisive in saying that there is no Islamic basis for female circumcision. Strangely, the texts make no effort to introduce the practices and varieties of Sufism that are prevalent in Egypt and no effort to acknowledge non-Sunni Islam. "The curriculum, from beginning to end, leaves Muslim students with the impression that Sunni Islam is the only and correct version of Islam in existence."[73] The texts urge students to distinguish true religious ideas from false religious ideas by encouraging them to listen to those who have authority, such as Azhar and the Dar al-Ifta.

Religious instruction in Egypt aims to reinforce the dominant religious and political authorities, but it may undercut all authority because it objectifies religion. Once studied in school, religion is no longer mere tradition or custom. Educated Egyptians must now think about what sort of Muslims or what sort of Christians they want to be. If they choose to follow the old ways, it will be a matter of choice, not habit. They may choose to wear the hijab or the niqab, or not. They may choose to vote for candidates of the Muslim Brotherhood, or not. Islam is thus a variable and not a constant. To know whether an Egyptian is a Muslim may be less important politically than knowing how religious he or she is and whether the person sees a relationship between faith and politics. Whether the average Egyptian actually has become more pious or whether piety itself strengthens or weakens identification with the state remains uncertain. Tessler and Nachtwey found that Egyptians who ranked high on piety did not necessarily support Islamist parties, and half of those who support Islamist parties did not report high levels of piety. They found no correlation between policy issues and religiosity measured by an index of piety.[74]

Formal education is one means of shaping and reshaping political culture. Political elites tend to imagine that law will reshape political attitudes. Religious elites rely on preaching, publications, and fatwas in an effort to heighten the public's moral perceptions and religious practices. Both groups necessarily acknowledge a set of habits and practices that resist change. To proclaim clitoridectomy illegal does not necessarily eliminate the practice. To declare certain Sufi rituals contrary to Islam or to intone against drunkenness does not necessarily change behavior. From the perspective of both religious and political elites, political culture often appears static.

Both political and religious elites must respond to popular conceptions of ethics and rightful authority. For example, the Egyptian government appealed to the public's general sense of right and wrong in its efforts to suppress radical attacks on tourists and policemen in the 1990s, and it was largely successful. The Muslim Brotherhood had success in attacking the government for its hypocrisy and corruption; where possible the regime responded by accusing the Brotherhood of corruption in its involvement with municipal administration.[75] There was no need for detailed Quranic exegesis to make these points, although both sides invoked expert opinion to support arguments that most Egyptians, Christian or Muslim, accept without thinking. In these cases, there is coincidence between the law and the common sense of morality.

Instability

Divergence between morality and the law can destabilize the relationship between religion and politics. The importation of civil and criminal codes from Europe in the nineteenth century constituted an effort of the state to reshape moral sentiments, something a thoroughly authoritarian state, willing to ride roughshod over religious objections, could attempt. The reduction in authority of the sharia courts and their ultimate abolition constituted a wholesale assault on a political culture in which justice had been seen as a function of religion more than politics. The many tales of villagers ensnared by a law they did not comprehend testify to the conflict between law and morality.

The tables turned, perhaps after 1967. Common perceptions of morality started to undermine the law and thereby threaten the state's authority. The Islamist movement emphasized the responsibility of citizens to one another and put renewed emphasis on the need for respectability in sexual relations. It was a matter not of creating a new morality, but of reemphasizing aspects of morality embraced by most Egyptians, both Muslims and Copts. The result was that court cases often became public causes, not because the law was or was not applied, but because the law seemed inadequate to express the morality of the case.[76] Public policy on matters such as clitoridectomy, AIDS, and prostitution reflect rather than challenge general conceptions of morality.[77] Individual citizens can drag other citizens into court on charges of immorality. That is what happened to Professor Abu Zayd.

In the nineteenth century, the Egyptian state thought it was changing the standards by which all citizens, including those in the religious sphere, would be judged; now it increasingly appears that the state is to be judged by a set of criteria emerging from the religious sphere. Or rather, it is the religious sphere (of which state-supported actors are a part) that is reemphasizing old standards of respectability and responsible citizenship the government can scarcely deny or ignore. By acceding to these standards, leaders ceded their power to the Islamist forces and thereby demonstrated weakness. In resisting these standards, the government appeared illegitimate and hypocritical; in fact, the old regime invoked them itself to ward off attack from radical elements. It remains to be seen whether a state dominated by Islamist forces will seek to reflect existing culture or change it.

This domain of encounter between religion and politics in Egypt is thus quite different from that of previous eras. The strength of the political culture and its evolution does not depend on the state's Islamic identity or on ideological disputes about sovereignty. Both secular and religious tendencies depend upon the prevailing political culture in Egypt. Both orientations reflect ideas about morality, authority, and participation contained in that culture and have limited means to alter that culture in the short run.[78]

Social, economic, and political conditions appear to shape political culture more than does ideological discourse. The religious and political institutions do, however, reshape political culture in the long run by influencing social, economic, and especially educational policy. Outcomes necessarily reflect the relative strength of political and religious institutions. Institutions must function within an existing set of cultural conditions but must also protect their future welfare by attempting to mold culture in a way that favors their prosperity. Christians must socialize young Christians. Muslims must train new generations of Muslims.

Conclusion

The burgeoning literature on religion and politics in Egypt shows that modernization theory, with its predictions about the secularization of politics and society, does not accurately describe what has happened there. Religion and politics have become more and more thoroughly intertwined as social, economic, and political changes have affected all four domains in which politics and religion necessarily interact: identity, authority, morality, and organization. Destabilized by Muhammad Ali in the early nineteenth century, the religious and political spheres remained locked in an increasingly intense, uncomfortable, and unstable embrace. Neither sphere could be characterized as a force of tradition or modernity. Neither sphere could realistically contemplate victory. The question is now whether a relaxation of military authoritarianism in favor of democratic dialogue can create movement toward a more stable relationship.

The pattern of instability bears the imprint of Islam. The relative lack of hierarchy in the Islamic establishment as Muhammad Ali encountered it in the early nineteenth century made it easy for him to seize waqf resources and reorganize the ulama. (Because of this lack of hierarchy, D. E. Smith calls Islam an "organic" religion as opposed to a "church" religion, such as Roman Catholicism.)[79] The egalitarianism of Islamic doctrine opened the way for lay challenge to the Islamic establishment; the plurality, even chaos, in the current configuration of Egyptian Islam stems in some measure from this fact. The character of the sharia has certainly conditioned the debate about legitimate authority.

Islam has shaped the nature of the interaction, but the dynamism and instability of the relationship come from forces of social and economic change—forces that go beyond Egypt or even the Muslim world. They also result from developments peculiar to Egypt. Would indigenous rulers, beholden to the ulama, have been as aggressive as the Albanian Turkish dynasty of Muhammad Ali in seeking to subordinate the religious establishment to their agenda of modernization? Might not the relationship have evolved quite differently in the early twentieth century without British intervention, pushing modern education and galvanizing dissent? It is commonplace to see Egyptian politics as a product of British imperialism, the failure of liberalism, and the Nasirist fling with Arabism. But these are also the forces that have transformed the religious sphere in Egypt into the vibrant, cacophonous, polycentric force it is today.

The development of an Egyptian national state required the development of an Egyptian Islam. How does religious identity square with the claim that Egypt is a state distinct from others in the Muslim world? How do Copts fit into that identity? How does the authority of the nation-state square with God's authority? Does an Egyptian government represent truth and justice as it is commonly understood, or do religious leaders speak for general perceptions of morality? How do national political institutions relate to religious institutions? The development of the nation-state created these questions and requires answers.

The state was needy, and religion responded to this neediness. Religion evolved in response to changing political opportunities, gaining influence and authority along the way. The state fought back by limiting and altering those opportunities, trying itself to exploit the pluralistic structure of Egyptian Islam, and the result was an ever greater intermixture of politics and religion. In moments of tranquility, the two spheres conducted a sharp but civilized dialogue; in moments of trauma, violence broke out on the margins.

How might one envision a move toward stability in Egypt? It is difficult to imagine an Egypt that does not eventually become liberal and democratic, whether or not the events of 2011 come to be seen as a step in that direction. It is equally difficult to imagine an Egyptian state willing to forgo the legitimacy that a link to Islam provides, whether or not the Muslim Brotherhood or other Islamists dominate politics in the near future. What sort of state will the religious sphere outside of government be willing to tolerate? Which religious doctrines and organizations will political elites, religious or not, be willing to permit? In what encounters and forums is compromise likely to emerge? The lesson of the West suggests that the answer will be forthcoming from a long progression of interactions of religious and political actors.

Chronology

1513 to 1798	Ottoman Empire governs Egypt.
1798	French under Napoleon Bonaparte conquer Egypt.
1805	Muhammad Ali establishes a dynasty that endures until 1952. Modernization begins.
1869	Suez Canal opens.
1881	British invade and establish informal control, retaining monarchy.
1914	British establish a protectorate.
1923	British grant Egypt "independence," against will of Egyptians.
1928	Hasan al-Banna founds the Muslim Brotherhood.
1936	New treaty of "independence" from Great Britain is signed.
1939–1945	Egypt is forced into war on side of Allies. British troops again occupy Egypt.
1948	Muslim Brotherhood assassinates prime minister.
1949	Government kills Hasan al-Banna.
1952	"Revolution" brings military to power. Gamal abd al-Nasir emerges as leader.
1954	Muslim Brotherhood attempts to assassinate Nasir.
1956	Nasir nationalizes Suez Canal. Britain and France fail to overturn regime. With "victory," Nasir becomes Arab hero.
1958	Egypt merges with Syria into United Arab Republic with Nasir as president.
1963	Syria withdraws from the United Arab Republic.
1966	Sayyid Qutb, radical ideologue of the Muslim Brotherhood, is executed.
1967	Egypt suffers humiliating defeat by Israel.
1970	Nasir dies. Anwar al-Sadat takes power and initiates an opening to the West, liberates political prisoners, including Muslim Brotherhood leaders.
1979	Egypt signs peace treaty with Israel that requires withdrawal from Sinai peninsula, leaves Gaza under Israeli rule.

1981	Islamist radicals assassinate President Sadat. Hosni Mubarak ascends to presidency.
1990s	Radical Islamists (the Islamic Group) create chaos by attacking policemen and tourists. Repression ensues.
2005	Mubarak wins another term in election seen as unfair. Muslim Brotherhood wins eighty-nine seats as "independents," to become primary opposition in Parliament.
2011	Demonstrations force resignation of President Mubarak. Supreme Council of the Armed Forces (SCAF) assumes power.
2012	Mohamed Morsi of the Muslim Brotherhood wins presidency in an election widely viewed as fair. SCAF accepts, appears to defer.

3

The Transformation
of Judaism in Israel

The state of Israel illustrates the inadequacy of dichotomies between secular and religious, modern and traditional. A product of Jewish nationalism, Israel is thoroughly modern in its economic, social, and political orientation, but it is not secular. Some dimensions of law bear the imprint of religious law (halakha), and religious institutions intertwine with those of the state. Yet the mixing of religion and politics in Israel reflects the decisions of an elected legislature always dominated by secular elites. Religious parties have influenced political outcomes but have failed to win control of the state. Secular elites of the left and the right have accepted the collaboration of the religious parties and concurred in funding religious institutions, in order to perpetuate secular dominance. Only small minorities at the two ends of the spectrum, secularist ideologues and some ultraorthodox groups, find the Israeli pastiche of secular and religious unacceptable. That is one reason why the political system has been stable.

The evolution of the Israeli system, from the early articulations of Zionism through independence to the transformation produced by the Six-Day War of 1967, illustrates the primacy of politics. Both Orthodoxy and Zionism emerged in nineteenth-century Europe in response to the emancipation of Jews from a ghettoized existence. The movement toward Orthodoxy, which eventually produced a political party called Agudat Israel, constituted a response to the breakdown of the communitarian organization (the *kehilla*) of Jewish life.[1] Orthodoxy sought to fight assimilation by ensuring a separate life for Jews in Europe. Zionism responded to the apparent failure of assimilative processes and called for the regeneration of the Jewish people, who had been fragmented by geography and rejected in many societies. It was a modern, secular movement driven by a political objective.

Politics, not religion, drove the Jews toward independence, and politics dictated forgoing a constitution opposed by the forces of religion. David Ben-Gurion, a socialist who led the Jewish community in Palestine to independence, shunned the separation of religion and state because he wanted to control religion.[2] Twenty years later, it was politics, not religion, that pushed Israel to victory in 1967 and to domination of the West Bank and Gaza Strip areas. The conquest, however, triggered an outburst of religious enthusiasm that fostered pressures for settlement and long-term retention of the conquered territories.

Ben-Gurion, the first prime minister of Israel (1948–1953 and 1956–1963), had no reason to feel threatened by the power of religion, nor did he probably imagine that state control would eliminate religious influence on the state. Were he alive today, he might nonetheless be astounded at the extent to which the religious organizations and authorities controlled by the state have strengthened themselves to play a part in their own control. The state of Israel, though surely not in full control of even official Jewish Orthodoxy in Israel, has reshaped the Jewish religion within and outside Israel's boundaries. The religion that shapes Israeli politics bears the distinct mark of Israeli policy. Even anti-Zionist ultraorthodox groups have been seduced into playing the democratic game and into acknowledging the supremacy of positive law over Jewish religious law, the halakha.

Israel declares itself a state that is both Jewish and democratic. Whether it can be both remains open to question. Full democracy would imply equal rights for non-Jews, mainly Palestinian Arabs, who are predominantly Muslim and who might come to be the majority. It would mean equal treatment for Reform and Conservative congregations in Israel, and under the Law of Return, acceptance of immigrants who are not Jewish by halakhic standards, which define Jews as persons whose mothers are Jewish or who have converted by Orthodox procedures. For those on the secular end of the spectrum, a "Jewish" state suggests imposition of halakhic law on those who do not wish to live by it. Such a state evokes rigorous enforcement of the Sabbath and of Jewish dietary rules (*kashrut*) and alienation of much of the American diaspora, dominated as it is by Reform, Conservative, and secular Jews. For Arabs who are citizens of Israel living within the borders established by the armistice of 1949, a Jewish state means formal citizenship but not full rights.

Judaism does not appear inherently more democratic than Islam or Christianity. (In fact, Jewish history provides only the sketchiest of suggestions about what a Jewish state might look like.[3] Israel is the first such state since classical times.) While some writers have found pluralistic tendencies in the Jewish tradition, it is God rather than human beings who dominates the Jewish version of history.[4] Many Jews who have resisted the Hellenistic and modern conception of the world as centered on human beings have joined the hurly-burly of Israel's democracy despite theology. If Israel is largely democratic today, it is despite Judaism, not because of it.

Can the Israeli mix of secularism and religion, of Jewishness and democracy, of modernity and tradition, be maintained? Is the relationship between religion and politics conducive to political stability? Boat designers think in terms of primary and secondary stability. Primary stability is how a boat responds to small waves. A boat with good secondary stability can undergo considerable rocking but nonetheless show excellent resistance to capsizing. In the case of Israel, sharp debates about identity, the role of institutions, political culture, and ideology suggest primary instability fostered in part by religious issues. The debates in the Israeli parliament, the local press, and the platforms of political parties suggest that the boat rocks continuously. Despite predictions that the ship of state will capsize, this has not happened.[5] Democratic procedures have so far garnered legitimacy and led to a continuous retouching of the balance, and secondary stability has been achieved. But to the chagrin of political scientists, the result does not conform to any external model. In practice, the Israeli polity permits both the observant and the nonobservant to go on claiming it as their own, "Jewish and democratic," without being fully satisfied that it is either one.

Identity

Religion shapes Israeli identity. This identity causes critics to charge that Israel is a racist state. The opening line of the 1948 Declaration of the Establishment of the State of Israel, which is also called the Declaration of Independence, proclaims: "Eretz Israel, the Land of Israel, was the birthplace of the Jewish People," and goes on to declare the establishment of "the Jewish State in Palestine, to be called Israel." Yet, the same document promises the non-Jewish inhabitants of the Israeli state "full and equal citizenship and due representation in its bodies and institutions—provisional or permanent." While the declaration promises that the state will be "open to the immigration of Jews from all countries of their dispersion," it guarantees the "full social and political equality of all" Israeli citizens, "without distinction of race, creed or sex." The perplexing paradoxes contained in this document frame the debates that still dominate Israeli political discourse over national identity.

Who composes this "Jewish People"? What is the relationship between the Jewish people and the Jewish religion? What constitutes the Jewish character of the state of Israel? Is it possible for the Israeli state to be Jewish in character while guaranteeing full citizenship to all of its inhabitants?

"Secular" Versions of Israeli Identity

For the first twenty years of Israeli statehood, Labor Zionism attempted to define Israeli identity by linking it to Jewish tradition without subordinating political decision-makers to traditional religious authorities and to the ritual practices and the theological worldview of Orthodox Jewry. Labor Zionism attempted to remove religious ritual and rabbinical law from the core of Jewish identity and replace it with a common nationalistic affiliation (*am Yisrael*) and with a historical connection to the Land of Israel (*Eretz Yisrael*) and the state of Israel (*Midinat Yisrael*). The construction of the state and the settlement of the land was, for the Labor Zionists, the reentry of the Jewish people into the history of nations. The attainment of a national homeland meant that the Jewish identity could be rebuilt through the worldly activities of settling the land and forging political independence.

The founders regarded the otherworldly orientation of the Orthodox (*dati*) community, with its emphasis on ritual observance and religious study, as a dysfunctional symptom of the Jewish nation's long exile from its homeland and inability to govern itself politically.[6] Rather than looking to religion, the founders sought to create a national identity based on cooperative effort to build a new Jewish civilization in the Land of Israel. "For this generation," Ben-Gurion wrote, "this land is more holy than for the tens of generations of Jews who believed in its historical and religious sanctity; for it has been sanctified by our sweat, our work, and our blood."[7] For Ben-Gurion, the labor of the settlers preempted the Torah as the basis of Jewish claims.

Far from abandoning tradition, however, the Labor Zionists tried to seize the "spirit" or basic values of the Jewish religion and present them as moral and cultural foundations of the Jewish nation. The Declaration of Independence, though it makes scant mention of religious ritual and law, credits the Jewish people with the creation of "cultural values of national and universal significance" and with giving "to the world the eternal Book of Books." This statement acknowledges the connection between Jewish nationhood and Jewish religious texts and ethics. Yet it describes the Bible not as a divine mandate but as a cultural accomplishment of the Jewish nation, and designates Jewish values not as a binding moral code but as an aspect of Jewish national character and ethos. Nahum Levin, a member of Ben-Gurion's team, went further:

> We have freed the biblical texts of their archaic quality and restored to them their concrete content: "Six days thou shalt labor—Thou shalt love thy neighbor as thyself—that which is altogether just shalt thou pursue—Proclaim liberty throughout all the land unto all her inhabitants." . . . These have become foundations of the world view which we have sought to achieve in the cooperative and communal settlements in particular, and in the Labor movement in general.[8]

Labor sought to invoke Jewish values without reference to rabbinic Judaism or belief in God. The "New Jew" would be the product of collective political and social endeavor.

This effort to define the Jewish state by land and labor failed on two counts. It did not incorporate many who were already living in the land, including the Orthodox, as well as Jews who lived beyond the state's borders and who were not part of the effort.[9] The notion of identity constructed on the basis of collective effort to build the Land of Israel excluded Diaspora Jews. Were those who declined to help build the state really Jews? Moreover, the symbols Labor Zionism used to forge a Jewish nation came from the theological, ritual, and cultural tradition referred to as the Jewish religion. Ben-Gurion acknowledged this stubborn reality: "Even for a free-thinking Jew like myself, our faith is still something that requires respect and any Jew who does not revere Judaism in one way or another is alien to Jewish history."[10]

Even the Jews who immigrated in the first years of independence fit awkwardly into the dominant notion of the New Jew. Between 1948 and 1951, the number of Jews living in Israel more than doubled.[11] Most of the immigrants who arrived during the first twenty years of Israeli statehood came from the Muslim countries of the Middle East and North Africa. They had not experienced European discrimination or suffered from the Holocaust. Religious practice defined them as Jews, whereas the concept of the New Jew depended on a Labor Zionist view of Jewish ethnicity.

In the 1960s and 1970s, as these Oriental immigrants (Mizrachim) began to make their influence felt, and especially after Israel's conquest of the Sinai, the West Bank, and the Golan Heights in 1967, the discourse of Israeli identity began to shift from what Gershon Shafir and Yoav Peled call "republican virtue"—identified with collectivism, settlement, labor, and state-building—toward a new form of reference they call "ethno-nationalism."[12] This new discourse pulled the Jewish heritage from the periphery to the center of Jewish identity but still stopped short of embracing religious Orthodoxy. Prime Minister Golda Meir expressed the shift with her call for "the deepening of Jewish education, an increased awareness and understanding of the Jewish faith and heritage"—elements, she argued, that were crucial to the "spiritual continuity of our people and the reservoir of commitment and strength for the future of Israel."[13] Ethno-nationalism credited Jewish customs and culture with preserving Jewish life in a hostile gentile world.

In this emerging perspective, the Holocaust became central to Israeli identity. Whereas the concept of the New Jew treated the Holocaust as a product of Jewish passivity attributable to the "Old Jew," ethno-nationalism extolled instances of Jewish resistance to persecution, such as the Warsaw Ghetto uprising. The subtitle of the Yad Vashem Holocaust memorial, begun in the late 1950s, reads: "Memorial Authority for the Holocaust and Bravery," and the name of the official day of Holocaust remembrance is "Memorial Day for the Holocaust and Ghetto Uprisings." Israeli identity emerged from a tradition of suffering and bravery.

This emphasis on persecution and resistance fit conveniently with Israel's ongoing conflict with its Arab neighbors. The resistance of the Israeli Defense Forces against Arab aggression echoed the rebellion of the Jewish communities of the Holocaust against gentile oppressors. The central myth of the Jewish nation, therefore, became the heroic resilience of the Jewish people and their vigilant determination to defend and maintain their culture (including religious traditions) rather than the Labor Zionist myth of a transcendent New Jew whose identity sprang from cultivation of a new Jewish civilization.

Labor Zionism and ethno-nationalism have both cloaked the state in traditional symbols of the Jewish religion for secular reasons. The Israeli flag bears the *magen* David (star or shield of David), a Jewish symbol said to date from the period of the First Temple (957–597 BCE). Israel adopted the seven-branch menorah, another ancient religious symbol, as its national symbol. Biblical verses adorn Israeli government buildings and stamps and figure frequently in speeches by Israeli politicians.[14] Furthermore, as a result of compromise in Israel's constituent assembly, the Israeli parliament (Knesset) contains the same number of representatives as did the Great Knesset, a governing body of the Second Temple period (516 BCE to 70 CE).[15] Saturday, the traditional Sabbath, is the official day of rest in Israel, and the state sponsors ceremonies on Jewish holidays.

Doubts About the Jewishness of Israel

These gestures give substance to the Declaration of Independence, which proclaims Israel a Jewish state, but they do not constitute divine sanction. From the Labor Zionist perspective, Israel is Jewish because Jews have built it. In the ethno-nationalist ethos, it is Jewish because Jews have suffered, and Israel is a refuge. For many religious Jews, these standards do not suffice. Religious authorities do not rule the state; the halakha, "defined by religious authorities and encompassing all aspects of human activity," does not preempt or even guide positive law in most domains.[16] Most Israelis reject the claim of some religious Zionists that Israel represents a step toward messianic redemption. The ultraorthodox and some secularists deny that the state has any religious significance whatsoever. Finally, in the eyes of some, the effort to define nationality independently of religion and to accord equal rights to all religious groups threatens Israel's identity as a Jewish state.

Since the first stirrings of modern Zionism, elements of the Orthodox Jewish community have regarded the "secular Zionist" movement with deep suspicion. For these rabbis and their followers, to admit that the modern state of Israel was

Jewish in character or to acknowledge any relationship between Jewish identity and Israeli nationality was considered blasphemous. The memory of many false messiahs, including Jesus, Bar Kochba, and a seventeenth-century rabbi named Shabatei Tzvi, drove the prominent rabbinical authorities of the Diaspora into a deep conservatism regarding the migration of the Jewish people to the Holy Land. In the main, these rabbis taught that only miraculous, divine intervention could transport the people to the land.

To acknowledge Israel as a Jewish state carried troubling messianic implications. Benjamin Mintz, a prominent member of an Orthodox political party, triggered scandal when he admitted to saying that the formation of the Israeli state "might" have been the first step toward redemption.[17] The leaders of the Jewish state considered themselves secular, even atheist, and the laws they adopted diverged from the mandates of the Torah. Thus, for Mintz to acknowledge the state's Jewish character signified approval of what the Orthodox rabbinical establishment considered an illegitimate form of Judaism.[18]

A group known as Neturei Karta (Defenders of the City) and its leader, Amram Bloy, expressed an extreme version of this ideological conviction. The existence of a secular state in the Promised Land so appalled Bloy that he refused to recognize the legitimacy of the Israeli state, declared his unwillingness to defend the country, and announced that Neturei Karta would accept the rule of "any nation that the United Nations would choose, or the rule and protection of all of them together."[19] For this faction of the Orthodox community, there could be absolutely no concrescence of Jewish and Israeli identities.

Elite intellectuals of the Israeli left, including a group of scholars from Jerusalem's Hebrew University, formed a group known as Brit Shalom (Covenant of Peace), which distinguished Jewish national identity from the identity of the state. This group advocated the foundation of a binational (Arab-Jewish) state in the Land of Israel and curtailment of Jewish immigration to mandatory Palestine. Martin Buber, himself an Orthodox Jew and one of the leading Jewish scholars of the twentieth century, insisted that establishing peaceful coexistence with the Arabs was the primary religious challenge of the Jewish people in modern times.[20] Members of the peace movement, including Hashomer Hatzair, a party based in utopian communities called kibbutzim, made similar arguments on behalf of binationalism.[21]

An even more extreme attempt to dissociate Jewish national identification from the Israeli state came from Uriel Halperin, publicly known as Yohanan

Ratosh, a charismatic Israeli poet and the founder of the Hebrew Youth movement in the 1940s. The Hebrew Youth, commonly referred to as the Canaanites
in the Israeli media, argued for the existence of a "Hebrew" nation that included
people living in the Land of Israel and other parts of the Middle East. "Now it
is possible," Ratosh declared before the Knesset, "for a new Hebrew nation to
arise, young and strong and mighty, the liberator of its homeland . . . hand in
hand with all its inhabitants . . . Jews, Christians, Moslems, Druze, and others."[22]
The Hebrew Youth's formulation of a Hebrew nation that enveloped Jews and
non-Jews in a Middle Eastern superstate constituted a radical secular effort to
dissociate religion from national identity in Israel.

Who Is a Jew?

Both Labor Zionists and ethno-nationalists assume that Jews are an identifiable
group. In 1950 the Knesset passed the Law of Return, which gave every Jew
the right to join the nation as an *oleh*—one who immigrates by "rising up" to
citizenship, but the law offers no conclusive specification of who qualifies as a
Jew. Quite predictably, this legislation generated long and intense debate. In
1958 the Knesset established a three-person committee to suggest a legal framework for determining who qualified for Jewish status. It proposed that "any person declaring in good faith that he is a Jew shall be registered as a Jew and no
additional proof shall be required."[23] The Orthodox member of the committee
resigned from the cabinet in protest. Leaving many issues unsettled, the Knesset
went on to adopt a definition of Jewish identity that closely resembled the halakhic rule.

Some of the unsettled issues arose in a pair of court cases. In 1969 Binyamin
Shalit, an Israeli citizen born of a Jewish mother, married a non-Jewish woman
outside the country and settled in Israel. He then challenged the Israeli government to make the identity cards of his children read: "Nationality: Jew; Religion:
None." Although Shalit admitted that his children did not qualify as members
of the Jewish religion, he argued that they should be accepted as members of
the Jewish nation. Despite much ambivalence, the Supreme Court found legal
reasons to deny Shalit's request.[24]

The 1970 case of "Brother Daniel" exposed further contradictions in Israeli
legislation. Brother Daniel was born in Yugoslavia to a Jewish mother. Named
Oswald Rufeisen, he survived the Nazi occupation of Yugoslavia in a Catholic

monastery. Later he became a Catholic monk, changing his name to Brother Daniel. He then requested that the Israeli government grant him permission to immigrate to Israel as a Jewish oleh, to become an Israeli citizen, and to live in a Catholic monastery in Jerusalem. Refused an oleh visa, he appealed to the high court, using the Talmudic argument that "a Jew, even if he has sinned, remains a Jew."[25] The Supreme Court ruled against Brother Daniel and denied him Israeli citizenship. In doing so, the court acknowledged a distinction between Jewish religious identification and Jewish national identification.

In response to political pressures and the legal crisis caused by these cases, the Knesset amended the Law of Return in 1970. The amended law declared: "For the purposes of this Law, 'Jew' means a person who was born of a Jewish mother or has become converted to Judaism and who is not a member of another religion." This change confirmed that only persons who qualify as halakhic Jews may become members of the Jewish nation but also established that some halakhic Jews, who happen to have adopted another religion, may be denied legal Jewish status. The amended law also declared:

> The rights of a Jew under this Law and the rights of an *oleh* under the Nationality Law, 5712–1952, as well as the rights of an *oleh* under any other enactment, are also vested in a child and a grandchild of a Jew, the spouse of a Jew, the spouse of a child of a Jew and the spouse of a grandchild of a Jew, except for a person who has been a Jew and has voluntarily changed his religion.

This amendment diminished the importance of Jewish national identity by permitting close relatives of Jews to attain oleh status and Israeli citizenship.

The amended law has also affected subsequent immigrant groups. As many as a fourth of those who have immigrated from the former Soviet Union under this amended Law of Return are not Jewish by halakhic standards.[26] Yet there is no sharp divergence in political and social behaviors between these people and the rest of the Jewish population. These immigrants have, in effect, joined the Jewish nation without joining the Jewish religion. To become Jewish in a religious sense, these non-Jewish immigrants would have to undergo conversion, and under the 1947 status quo agreement—a letter from Ben-Gurion to the leadership of Agudat Israel—only institutionalized Orthodox rabbis can administer conversion in the state of Israel. Orthodox leaders and politicians fought fiercely against establishing a Joint Conversion Institute, which would have given Reform and Conservative (*masorti*) rabbis a role in the conversion process.

It matters who is a Jew in Israel. The approximately 23 percent of Israel's legal citizens, roughly 1.5 million people, who are not considered Jews under Israeli law, most of them Arabs, do not enjoy full citizenship rights in the state of Israel. While the Declaration of the Establishment of the State of Israel promises non-Jews "full citizenship," the religious symbols of these "minority" populations do not appear in Israel's institutions. Although minority religions receive funding from the state, the monies come from a fund separate from the one that subsidizes Jewish (Orthodox) institutions. Furthermore, the Israel Land Authority controls 93 percent of the land within the pre-1967 boundaries of Israel and decides who is entitled to lease property for which purposes.[27] Serving the needs of Jewish immigrants has been a primary purpose of public policy since the founding of the Jewish National Fund, a quasi-governmental NGO, in 1901.

Recent developments suggest some willingness to lessen the privileges of Jewish identity. The Supreme Court decision in the Qaadan case of 2000 challenged the right of the Jewish National Fund to discriminate between Jews and non-Jews in leasing land, and amendments to the Law of Return extended rights at least as far as relatives of Jews. These changes constitute an ideal of citizenship more in line with liberal-democratic ideology. The recent activism of the Supreme Court, coupled with the Knesset's adoption of two basic laws—Human Dignity and Liberty, and Freedom of Occupation—constitutes a gradual shift toward a value system that prizes equal application of the law over Jewish collective objectives. However, both the Law of Return and the Israel land laws grant Jews preferential status as citizens of the state of Israel.

Israel's Jewish identity has proved stable in its inconsistency. On the one hand, the state cannot renounce its Jewishness without undermining its reason for being. Hard as Zionists might try, they did not succeed in defining a Jewish people without some reference to religion. Beliefs, scholarship, rabbinic leadership, common rituals and ceremonies—all these held Jewish communities together in the Diaspora. An Israel without Jewishness cuts itself off from the Diaspora and from its links with Jewish history. On the other hand, Israel cannot adopt unmitigated Orthodox definitions of Jewishness without cutting itself off from the nonorthodox Diaspora and from important elements of its own population, such as the Russian immigrants. Even a watered-down commitment to Jewishness makes it difficult if not impossible for Israel to achieve the democratic commitment contained in the Declaration of Independence. Non-Jews lack full status in the state. Arabs, who are Christians and Muslims, are third-class citizens behind the Jews of European origin (Ashkenazim), who enjoy primacy in the society, and the Mizrachim, who are still struggling for parity with the Europeans.

The conflict between Israelis and Palestinians may help stabilize the inconsistencies inherent in Israeli identity. The unexpected victory of 1967 opened the way for a new religious Zionism committed to settle the West Bank and Gaza—lands linked to Jewish history. These initiatives tipped Israeli identity toward the religious. The ratio of Israelis who put their Jewishness ahead of their identity as Israelis increased slightly and became a majority. The settlers and their supporters saw themselves as Jews doing the work of God. They attacked "mere" Israelis, who wanted to trade land for peace with the Arab states and the Palestinians. More generally this conflict reinforces Israelis' self-perceptions as a persecuted minority. Until this conflict ends, it seems unlikely Israeli society will embrace full democratic inclusion of its non-Jewish citizens.

Israel's identity remains distinctly Jewish. The Jewishness of the state results from a set of political decisions that reflect divergent and even contradictory notions of Judaism and Jewishness. The state remains too Jewish for some and insufficiently Jewish for others. The privileges accorded Jewish identity make the goal of full and equal citizenship for non-Jews unattainable. The elaborate use of religious symbols to legitimate the secular state strike some as a travesty. Yet many religious Zionists see the state as halfhearted and even hypocritical in its commitment to its sacred mission, the realization of God's promise to the Jews. Ultimately the Jewishness of Israel reflects a set of political decisions taken to realize the ambitions of Zionism. Nationalism requires an identity for a people, and no one has yet devised a definition of the Jewish people that does not refer to religion. The religious identity of the state is not a result of religious imperatives but of nationalist necessity.

Ideology

Israel's Declaration of Independence frames one of the central debates over Israeli political ideology. Ratified in 1948, it promises that the Israeli state will be "based on freedom, justice, and peace as envisaged by the prophets of Israel." While the document recognizes the visions of the Jewish prophets, it denies political authority to rabbis and makes no claim that the law of the state will reflect or abide by the traditional rabbinical laws of the Jewish religion. Instead the declaration explicitly promises that elected authorities will govern the state of Israel in accordance with a constitution written by an elected constituent assembly. How much and in what ways should the law of the Jewish state reflect the religious law of the Jewish tradition? Should the Jewish state be governed exclusively by elected politicians and bureaucrats? Or should the traditional leaders of the Jewish faith who serve as interpreters of divine law hold positions of authority?

Pre-State Discourse

The most powerful politicians of the Zionist movement had no interest in turning over government power to rabbinical leaders. The religious conceptions of these men and women reflected the socialist and democratic ideals of the modern Zionist movement. The founders framed their call for the Jewish state in terms of political necessity, as had Theodor Herzl. They saw themselves as champions of a homeless people dispossessed from its native land, not of a movement to create a religious state. David Ben-Gurion, Israel's first prime minister, assured the devout that the government would show "understanding of your religious feelings and those of others," and would be "devoted to the values of Judaism" but would not make Israel into a theocratic state or impose religious law upon the people.[28] In the constitutional debate that followed the ratification of the declaration, a member of the Knesset loyal to Ben-Gurion proclaimed: "As a socialist and an atheist, I could never endorse a program that included a religious model."[29]

Few ultraorthodox Jews of the pre-state period regarded the Zionist project as divine. While Orthodox Jews did regard the Land of Israel (Eretz Yisrael) as sacred, most did not attribute holiness to the state of Israel (Midinat Yisrael), whose architects largely considered themselves secular Jews. Consequently, few Orthodox Jews believed in a divine mandate for the creation of a halakhic state and were thus willing to accept compromise on religious matters.

In the early nineteenth century, much of the Orthodox establishment evoked a rabbinical tradition that discouraged the formation of a Jewish political entity in the land of Palestine. Although Orthodox Jews everywhere believed that the "End of Days" and the coming of the Messiah would eventually bring the dispersed Jewish communities back to their homeland, most Orthodox rabbis taught that this migration would be of a miraculous nature. The Mizrachi movement among Orthodox Jews began a cautious shift in this long-held tradition. Created in Vilna in 1902 among Orthodox delegates to the Zionist Congress, Mizrachi sought to foster cooperation between two separate responses to modernism: Orthodoxy and Zionism.[30] In 1912, Agudat Israel split with Mizrachi to engage in Jewish settlement of Palestine outside the auspices of the World Zionist Organization (WZO). Both groups regarded the secular Zionist movement with suspicion but came to cooperate with the WZO on a practical level during the 1940s, when European persecution of Jews reached catastrophic proportions.

Suspicion of Labor Zionism led a large portion of deeply Orthodox Jews in Palestine in 1948 to reject the formation of a halakhic state and to deny that the modern Israeli state was holy or theologically significant. These groups feared that an Israeli state claiming a basis in modern Judaism would undermine the Orthodox cultural establishment in Israel. They attempted to persuade the Labor Zionists to refrain from engaging in Jewish cultural activities.

In the early twentieth century, however, there emerged an alternative Orthodox discourse that invested the Jewish state with religious meaning. Rav Abraham Isaac Kook argued that the establishment of a Jewish state in the Land of Israel was an "advent of redemption" and had not only religious but also messianic implications.[31] Yet he was willing to accept that Israel would at least temporarily be a secular, nontheocratic state. While he hoped and anticipated that Jews who had rejected rabbinic authority and traditional law would repent in the final stage of messianic redemption, he welcomed the work of the Labor Zionists in taking the land and creating a space for the physical salvation of the Jewish nation. These were necessary conditions for the spiritual salvation he believed would come later. Kook helped to create a discourse that permitted the formation of a sacred but nonhalakhic Israeli state. These Orthodox discourses eased the burden of the early Zionist leaders, who feared and rejected the idea of a halakhic state. Significant portions of the Orthodox population of Palestine and important Orthodox leaders discouraged involvement in the Jewish state, lest the integrity of traditional Judaism be compromised. Other Orthodox Jews and leaders accepted the sanctity of the state of Israel without demanding that it be governed immediately by religious law or religious leaders. Consequently, no significant movement for theocratic government surfaced as the Jewish community in Palestine (the Yishuv) prepared for statehood.

The Founding

Lack of demand for theocracy did not, however, prevent fierce debate over the role of halakhic law in Israel and the allocation of governmental power to Israel's religious leaders. Those questions dominated debate in the constituent assembly, which quickly declared itself the sovereign parliament, the Knesset, and eventually prevented the adoption of a constitution. One member representing Agudat Israel argued that "only the Torah Law and tradition are sovereign in the life of Israel."[32] While the religious forces recognized that the creation of a halakhic state would be impossible, they fiercely opposed the drafting of a secular constitution, which they feared might sever the tie to the past.[33] "If the time is not yet ripe for our constitution to be based on the laws of our Torah," argued Agudat Israel, "it is better that no constitution be passed and that we not be untrue."[34] The Knesset quit trying to draft a constitution, but the ideological battles over the role of religion in government were far from over.

Israeli leaders used two strategies of tempering ideological debates and creating a degree of ideological stability. Their first strategy was to frame policy and law so that they conformed to the basic tenets of Jewish tradition even if they did not precisely reflect the halakha. Ben-Gurion used this strategy frequently, as demonstrated in one of his speeches: "Our activities and policy are guided not by economic considerations alone but by a political and social vision that we have inherited from our prophets and imbibed from the heritage of our greatest sages and the teachers of our own day."[35] Politicians such as Ben-Gurion embraced the political and social vision of Jewish religious leaders in an attempt to legitimate modern interpretations of ancient principles and traditions.

This rhetorical strategy required a clever ability to avoid discussing religious legitimacy with the Orthodox rabbinical establishment. Ben-Gurion insisted that the "Rock of Israel (*tsur* Israel)" was to be found in the "State of Israel and in the Book of Books."[36] And on at least one occasion, he referred to the modern Israeli state as the Third Kingdom, comparing it to the ancient Jewish communities of biblical times. By focusing on the Bible and on ancient Israeli civilization,

Ben-Gurion attempted to steer ideological debate away from the Talmud and the halakha. This strategy permitted him to argue for the sanctity of state policies without deferring to the authority of contemporary religious leaders, who claimed to be the rightful interpreters of religious law.

Ben-Gurion's approach amounted to more than rhetoric. Attempts to embrace the basic principles of Judaism, and to couch legislation and institutions in the language of religious tradition, influenced the character of Israeli institutions and law. A letter Ben-Gurion wrote to the ultraorthodox Agudat Israel has long served as the foundation for political debate over religious issues in Israel. In this letter, which came to be known as the status quo letter, Ben-Gurion promised that the religious character of the Jewish state would be respected and reflected in the policies and practices of the Israeli government. The first two points of the letter reflect the strategy of Israeli political leaders, described above. "Saturday shall be the national day of rest," the letter reads, and "the laws of *kashrut* will be observed in all government kitchens." These promises did not guarantee observance of halakha, but committed the state to honor Jewish tradition in some domains.

To implement the promises of the status quo letter, the government passed the Law of Working Hours and Rest in 1951, limiting the workdays of Jewish employees and effectively barring most industrial activity on the Sabbath. Framed in modern legal language, the law did not, however, apply to self-employed Jews or to government utilities and services crucial to the proper functioning of the state. While the legislation honored a principle, it did not adhere to the letter of the halakha. Neither did it interfere with the practical necessities of the state.

A similar strategy led to compromise on kashrut. While the Israeli government was not willing to pressure its citizens to maintain these dietary laws in their own homes, the government did maintain kashrut in its kitchens and other facilities. Positive law prevented state-owned companies from importing pork and any other meat not slaughtered in accordance with religious law. The state hired Orthodox inspectors to ensure that military food was prepared according to religious standards. These and other compromises served to quell ideological conflict by covering state institutions with a veneer of religion. They went far enough to secure the continued participation of Orthodox Jews in government institutions, and especially in the military, without subordinating government authority to religious leadership.

The strategy of compromise proved insufficient. Traditional religious Jews, and the rabbinical establishment of Palestine, rejected Labor Zionism's efforts at modernizing Jewish tradition to fit a nationalist agenda. While many Orthodox Jews accepted compromise over the expression of religious ideals in the state's public activities, they would make no concessions in other domains. In response, Israeli leaders used a second strategy to soften ideological debates. The status quo letter promised that religious organizations would continue to receive funds from the state to maintain their autonomous school systems and that religious courts would have exclusive authority over matters of personal status, including marriage, divorce, conversion, and burial.

Israeli citizens considered Jewish cannot engage in civil marriage within the state of Israel. Although the state recognizes civil marriages performed outside Israel, government employees appointed by religious courts of the fourteen religious denominations recognized by the Israeli government issue marriage certificates.[37] Judaism is but one of the fourteen, albeit the largest. These religious courts grant marriage licenses and perform ceremonies according to standards of religious law upheld by religious authorities in Israel. Governmentally recognized Jewish leaders supervise all conversions to Judaism and manage funerals and Jewish cemeteries.

In addition, the status quo agreement promises that "full autonomy of every education system will be guaranteed." At the state's inception, the Ministry of Education began to allocate funding among its many autonomous school systems according to the size of the populations they served. This includes explicitly Muslim, Christian, Druze, Bahai, and Jewish schools; all the preceding schools are free to teach religious curricula to their students as they see fit. By permitting autonomy, secular elites sought to dissuade religious groups from seeking influence over a broad spectrum of the state's laws and functions in return for domination of significant but limited spheres of policy. While government officials handle a broad range of state functions according to codes of civil law, religious officials administer other domains according to their own interpretations of sacred texts and tradition.

Early political leaders employed two major strategies to deal with the perplexing paradoxes of a Jewish republic. First, they attempted to connect the law and institutions of the Israeli state apparatus to a modified version of Judaism. Second, they tried to grant specific spheres of influence to religious leaders and some autonomy to religious institutions. While protests over religious legislation did occasionally erupt, the early Israeli leadership managed to maintain a balance. Many religious leaders expressed discontent from time to time but also often articulated their gratitude to Ben-Gurion and his allies for their cooperation. Menahem Parosh of Agudat Israel said: "Ben-Gurion gave us more than anyone else, because he understood that if the state did not make concessions to us we would have to leave the country, and this he did not want."[38] As long as their own spheres of authority were not challenged or disturbed, Orthodox leaders could accept that the state of Israel did not abide by halakha or recognize their authority on other matters. And although some citizens rebelled fiercely when they thought religious leaders and authority figures had overstepped boundaries, few citizens were willing to fight for the total disenfranchisement of these leaders.

Ideological Shift

While there were occasional challenges to the status quo agreement, its basic lines prevailed through the first twenty turbulent years of Israeli history. Orthodox leaders had no practical ideas about how a halakhic state might be governed.[39] Because a modern nation-state must operate utilities, ensure security, and maintain other services, the Israeli government could not observe the halakhic prescriptions of the Sabbath. Conversely, separation of religion and state did not seem possible or desirable. Most Israeli Jews, even those who consider themselves secular, wanted (and still want) the state to maintain its Jewish character for nationalistic reasons. Most Israeli Jews accepted the laws of the state of Israel as legitimate.[40]

In the 1960s and 1970s, however, ideological shifts in the Israeli political landscape eroded support for the fragile balance created by the status quo agreement. First, Israel absorbed more immigrants in comparison to its population than had any other country.[41] Many of these immigrant groups belonged to religious communities. They did not share the ideals of the secular Zionists or support the idea of modernizing the Jewish faith to fit contemporary needs. Government mistreatment of the immigrants bred discontent, and attempts to indoctrinate them through education fomented hostility toward the ruling coalition. Second, two deeply traumatic events, the Six-Day War of 1967 and the Yom Kippur War of 1973, contributed to ideological reconfiguration. Although the stunning victory in 1967 left many with a feeling of elation and national pride, it ended with the Israeli occupation of vast territories and Arab populations that posed new and difficult questions. The more costly 1973 war had a deeply traumatic effect on the Israeli people and divided previously unified coalitions. It led to diplomatic negotiation and eventual peace with Egypt, but Israeli sentiment remained deeply divided about giving up more territory to create a Palestinian state.

The wars of 1967 and 1973 sparked shifts in Israel's most Orthodox communities. Rav Kook's son, Rabbi Zvi Yehuda Kook, interpreted the two battles and the acquisition of the historically and religiously significant areas of the West Bank as indicative of messianic times.[42] Through the institution of Merkaz Harav, a highly influential religious academy established by his father, the rabbi began to articulate religious arguments for expanding the Israeli state and settling the occupied territories. While the senior Kook had argued that redemption of the land was a precursor to the spiritual redemption of the Jewish people and the world, Zvi Yehuda Kook portrayed the conquest of the land as a holy endeavor in and of itself.

A new generation of religious leaders began to utilize the vocabulary of Jewish tradition and to formulate a new ideology that justified and even commanded the forceful conquest of the Land of Israel. Rabbis such as Moshe Rom interpreted wars of conquest as "mandatory in Jewish tradition and argued against ceding any land to non-Jews as a religious sin."[43] Moshe Moskowitz, a leader of Agudat Israel, declared, "Do not doubt that the land and the people will find their mutual redemption."[44] These militant religious Zionists spread their ideas through a large network of yeshivas, academies of Jewish learning, where they found audiences of thousands of young, idealistic Jews.

The new ideology sparked settlement, and settlement solidified ideology. In 1968 Rabbi Moshe Levinger moved with a small group of pious followers to the city of Hebron. As one of four Jewish holy cities and the site of the cave of *machpelah*, thought to be the burial place of three of the Jewish patriarchs and their wives, Hebron held enormous religious significance to religious Jews. But the city was inhabited almost exclusively by Arabs, most of them Muslims who, like Jews, honor Abraham as the founder of their religion. Levinger began a settlement called Hameuchad, often considered the first religious settlement established in the occupied territories. A short time later, religious settlers in

Hebron organized the Gush Emunim (Bloc of the Faithful) around the militant religious ideology of Zvi Yehuda Kook. These settlers saw conquest of the entire biblical land of Israel as the divine right and obligation of the Israeli state; they claimed that this divine mandate transcended positive law. "We are commanded by the Torah according to the will of God," proclaimed one official Gush Emunim publication, "and therefore we cannot be subject to the standard laws of democracy."[45]

Rabbi Meir Kahane, who moved from the United States to Israel in 1971, took the new ideology of militant religious Zionism a step further by explicitly justifying the use of violence to secure the whole Land of Israel. Kahane not only hailed conquest as a noble and sacred activity, but also claimed that militant conquest was the primary, divinely inspired purpose of the Israeli state. In an essay written in 1976, Kahane declared, "The State of Israel was established not because the Jew deserved it, for the Jew is as he has been before, rejecting God, deviating from his paths and ignoring his Torah." Kahane argued rather that the divine purpose of the state was "a Jewish fist in the face of an astonished Gentile world that had not seen it for two millennia."[46] Kahane proclaimed that "when the Jew is beaten, God is profaned!" He preached that the state of Israel was God's instrument of holy war.

Kahane expanded his ideological formulation into a full-fledged apocalyptic prophecy. In 1980, after being arrested by Israeli police for his involvement in a plot to blow up the Dome of the Rock, Kahane claimed that on the basis of biblical texts, the formation of the Jewish state in 1948 was a sign of the impending messianic redemption. According to Kahane, the forty years following the establishment of the state were a grace period in which Jews could choose to repent their sins, obey God's law, and experience "a great and glorious redemption," or choose to remain in defiance of God and face a redemption brought about through "terrible sufferings and needless agonies; . . . holocaust more horrible than anything we have yet endured."[47] Predicting an impending catastrophe, Kahane advocated a "truly Jewish state, not a Hebrew-speaking gentilized one."[48] He argued, among other things, that democracy should be suspended in Israel, that Arabs should be stripped of political rights and excluded from all spheres of work, that Jewish sovereignty should be proclaimed over all of the Land of Israel "by virtue of the promise of the Almighty," that Israeli public schools should teach a fully religious curriculum, and that dietary laws, censorship laws, and dress codes should be strictly enforced in public venues according to halakha.[49]

While Kahane's religious ideology and apocalyptic predictions galvanized his inner circle, the rabbi also managed to appeal to a larger audience by couching his ideas in more secular and pragmatic language. He warned Israelis that the demographics of Israel were the real danger, playing on nationalist anxiety felt throughout Israeli Jewish society that a Jewish majority would no longer exist in Israel.[50] He appealed to poor Mizrachim by claiming that cheap Arab workers were undermining the Israeli labor market, and he utilized racist biases to garner support. After several electoral bids to gain a seat in the Knesset, Kahane's party, Kach, gained 1.2 percent of the vote in 1984, enough to win a seat in parliament, but the Knesset barred Kach from taking its prize.[51]

The ideology of the settler movement developed on the fringe of the Israeli political spectrum, but the religious parties used the movement's precepts and spirit to mobilize political coalitions and push for favorable policies. In 1977, the defection of the National Religious Party after a series of disputes over Sabbath regulations brought down a Labor government under the leadership of Yitzhak Rabin.[52] The right-wing, nationalist coalition that took power in 1977 shared many common interests with religious settlers, although it never adopted the ideological discourse of the militant settler movement. The religious parties exacted a high price for their support of the coalition in terms of increased state support of religious institutions and religious education.

The compromises and strategies derived from the status quo agreement did not work in the new political circumstances. While the Orthodox community had been primarily concerned with preserving its own privileges in the Israeli establishment, the ideology of militant religious Zionism demanded radical action. Because the radicals believed that the conquest of the land was a divine duty, they were unwilling to dismiss the actions of the Israeli state as theologically inconsequential, as had non-Zionist Orthodoxy. And believing that they were living in times of impending messianic redemption, militant religious Zionists were unwilling to agree with the elder Kook that Israel could wait to fulfill its halakhic obligations.

Ideological debate sharpened after a government of the left returned to power in 1993, interrupting a sixteen-year period in which the Likud party dominated coalitions. In an attempt to forge a peace process that would lead to a sovereign

Palestinian state in the West Bank and Gaza, Yitzhak Rabin's government encountered resistance from a religious Zionist movement that regarded the surrender of the Holy Land to gentiles as a religious sin. Rabin pushed his peace plan in largely pragmatic terms, arguing that the social, economic, and moral cost of maintaining the occupation of the territories was unnecessary and damaging to the Israeli state.[53] As Rabin saw it, a government must pursue the best interest of its citizens, but the militant religious Zionist movement saw the state as God's designated instrument for the conquest of the Land of Israel.

A young Orthodox Jewish militant named Yigal Amir assassinated Rabin in 1995. When questioned, Amir offered the following explanation for his actions: "I acted alone on God's orders and I have no regrets. . . . I know Jewish law and *din rodef* means that if you have tried everything else and nothing works, then you have to kill him."[54] Amir took it upon himself to defy positive law to impose halakhic law on the state. The leader of the opposition, Benyamin Netanyahu, proclaimed Amir a "madman," implying that the logic Amir used lay beyond the legitimate spectrum of Israeli political discourse. Amir had, however, studied in a West Bank yeshiva with rabbis who propounded such ideas. Many secular Israelis accused right-wing politicians of tacitly cultivating a hostile political environment and of failing to denounce religious extremists who called Rabin a murderer and a traitor. A fourth of Orthodox Israeli teenagers condoned the assassination.[55] Majority opinion sustained the government, however, in its use of positive law to punish the self-appointed enforcer of the halakha.

Already in the 1990s the ideological struggle had begun to transform itself into a struggle between two major institutions of the Israeli political system. Since 1977 the right has usually dominated the Knesset and welcomed religious parties into coalition governments. These coalitions have encouraged and protected settlements, taken a hard line with the Palestinians, and cultivated Israeli particularism. Israelis of Middle Eastern and North African origins (the Mizrachim), now the majority, have kept the right in power and enabled the meteoric rise of Shas, a party with ultraorthodox leadership and a generally observant following. The Knesset became the champion of a *Jewish* democracy (i.e., emphasis on Jewish), while the defense of Jewish *democracy* (i.e., emphasis on democracy) passed to the Israeli Supreme Court, which began to set itself up as the champion of religious freedom, equality, and human rights. The court challenged the power of religious authorities and proclaimed a "constitutional revolution." Compromise and agreement (not to disagree) gave way to a test of wills between the branches of government, each of them sustained by political forces.

Institutions

The history of Judaism contrasts with that of Islam in its relationship to political authority. In the first two centuries after Muhammad's death, the architects of Islamic law and doctrine worked in a context of political dominance. In contrast, Jews never enjoyed self-government after the destruction of the Second Temple (70 CE). Rabbinic Judaism produced the Talmud in exile. As long as the Abbasid caliphate survived, the exilarch of Baghdad enjoyed special authority within the Diaspora. Jews and Christians enjoyed some autonomy as peoples of the book under Muslim rule, but not since 1042 have there been Jewish institutions with any claim to centralized religious authority over world Jewry, dispersed across the globe under gentile rule.

Israel emerged from Zionism, and Zionism came from Eastern Europe, where Jewish communities survived by closing themselves off from the mainstream. In relatively small groups, they sought to follow the halakha, which had been articulated for just such circumstances. In Poland and Russia, the community (*kahal* or *kehilla*) shouldered responsibility for its own court system, for taxation, and for discipline of its members. While some Jewish bodies brought together communities to deal with central authorities, most decision making lay within the individual communities. The halakha defined Jews as persons born of Jewish mothers, prohibited intermarriage, and prescribed a rather complicated set of rituals and ceremonials that preserved the community by setting it apart from society as a whole. The community took precedence over the individual, and the community functioned in the context of overarching political authority exercised by gentiles.[56]

The European Enlightenment of the seventeenth and eighteenth centuries brought nationalism and the destruction of the kahal. After the Peace of Westphalia in 1715, sovereign states with sharp boundaries sought increasing control over their own citizens. Napoleon made Jews full citizens in France, and the lure of assimilation affected German and English Jews, as well. In Russia the czar sought to centralize authority to push reform. He abolished the kahal in 1844 and transferred its functions to municipal councils, where Jews were in the minority. As Jews came to see themselves as citizens in the new "imagined community" of the nation-state, or as governments began to treat them that way, the internal solidarity of the kahal began to break down. Judaism, like Christianity, acquired a new shape as a result of Westphalian geography.[57]

Two political forces emerged within the Jewish community to challenge these threats to the old order. Orthodoxy was the first in order of appearance. It sought to resist the breakdown of the kahal by creating a set of ideas and organizations to protect the Jewish way of life from destruction. Rabbi Moses Sofer took a negative view of secular culture and responded by founding a yeshiva in Pressburg, Hungary, which became the largest in Europe. The Volozhin yeshiva founded in Lithuania in 1803 became even more important than Pressburg as a model. "The yeshiva became the locus of a Jewish counter-culture," explains Jonathan Sacks.[58] Whereas schools in the kahal had been local in character and conservative in message, these yeshivas responded to the new universalism of Europe by rejecting it.

Then came Zionism. Moses Hess, Ahad Haam, and Theodor Herzl regarded assimilation as a failure but sought remedy not in resurrecting the kahal but in realizing Jewish peoplehood. Nationalist theory, with debts to Immanuel Kant and to romanticism, argued that peoples deserved to control their own political destiny. If the Jews are a people, then they deserve a state. Herzl argued that Jewish survival depended on it. Haam welcomed the possibility of cultural renewal. And these ideas reverberated with great success in Eastern Europe, where the herding of Jews into areas of settlement and official acts of discrimination violated the promises of the Enlightenment. Masses of Jews sought emigration.

Jewish settlement of Palestine began under Ottoman rule and continued after World War I under the mandate for Palestine awarded to Great Britain. The Ottomans had treated Christian and Jewish communities as *millets*, non-Muslims worthy of autonomy in administering some of their own affairs, especially matters of family and personal status—matters directly affected by religious law. The British carried this system into the mandate; the mandatory power treated Christians, Muslims, and Jews as separate communities, a practice Arabs regarded as unfair because it split them into two groups, Muslims and Christians. Moreover, the mandate document entitled the Jews to "an appropriate agency" to serve as a liaison with the British government. Initially the World Zionist Organization (WZO) assumed the role, even though its leadership lived outside

Palestine. Even in the first decade of the mandate, 1920–1930, the Labor settlement movement dominated the WZO and, hence, spoke for the Jewish community. A decidedly secular force thus represented the Jews, who were nonetheless defined by the mandatory power as a religious millet!

Labor Zionism dominated the Yishuv, and its leader, David Ben-Gurion, took the community to independence in 1948, but Israel's institutional structure came to reflect not so much the will of the majority as it did a power-sharing arrangement between secular and religious forces. Several authorities have called it consociationalism.[59] The majority could proceed only with the consent not just of religious Zionists but also of ultraorthodox elements whose attitude toward Zionism and the new state of Israel was anything but unambiguously positive. As Agudat Israel prepared to testify before the United Nations Committee on Palestine in 1947, its leadership met with Ben-Gurion about conditions for supporting the state. Ben-Gurion, with the help of religious Zionists, supplied the status quo letter. Even then, Agudat avoided firm commitment to the state.

The Status Quo Letter

Ben-Gurion opposed separation of church and state, because he wanted the state to control religion. He avoided insistence upon a constitution, a document that the religious parties unanimously opposed. They said the Torah provided a sufficient backbone for the republic. Yet the religious Zionists welcomed state control of religion to assert their primacy over their ultraorthodox rivals. They favored the creation of a chief rabbinate, supported by a rabbinical council. The rabbinate would supervise both Jewish religious courts, which would retain exclusive control of marriage and divorce for the Jewish community, and local Jewish religious councils, which would supervise synagogues, ritual baths, and kashrut.[60] These institutions would depend on state funding.

The status quo letter promised that ultraorthodox schools would not come under state control. Before independence, the Jewish community in Palestine had supported four streams of education: Labor Zionist, General Zionist (liberal, nonsocialist), religious Zionist, and ultraorthodox. Labor now agreed to abandon its own schools and establish a single secular track, but religious Zionists insisted upon state-run religious schools, as well. Agudat maintained its schools, and the state established schools for Arabs. State monies flowed toward all these schools, even the Agudat yeshivas. The intensity and adequacy of state supervision constituted a greater point of dispute than the fact of funding.

Today, the state controls religious institutions, and secular elites dominate the state. But the consociational nature of Israeli politics requires governments to win the cooperation and even support of the religious parties. The National Religious Party has normally supported the governing coalition and has normally dominated the Ministry of Religious Affairs, which is only one of many sources of funding for religious institutions. Ira Sharkansky writes: "A variety of Israeli government offices provide aid to Orthodox and ultra-Orthodox bodies, but there is no central recording of how much goes to which institutions. The style of Israeli political competition may have something to do with this lack of record keeping."[61] He notes that the Ministry of Construction and Housing, the Ministry of Finance, the Ministry of Education, the Ministry of Welfare, and local municipalities all help fund religious institutions. The religious parties have focused their political efforts on winning cabinet-level appointments to at least some of these ministries. Because the religious parties have traditionally cared most about issues directly related to religion, they have been willing to accommodate the secular parties on other matters.

State control, mediated by Orthodox and ultraorthodox influence over state policy, has created an Israeli Judaism utterly at odds with much of the Diaspora. By virtue of its controlling mission, the state has effectively fashioned a Judaism that is distinct from American Judaism or the Judaism imagined by Agudat Israel in the years before independence. Reform and Conservative Jewish rabbis have no standing, get relatively little state support, and cannot legally perform marriage ceremonies or convert anyone to Judaism.[62] Yet these non-Orthodox congregations dominate Judaism in the United States. Perhaps 5 percent of American Jews can be considered Orthodox, and the United States boasts more Jews than any other country in the world, including Israel.[63] Muslims, Christians, Druze, and many other religious groups enjoy considerable autonomy in managing their institutions and ceremonies in Israel, but the state defines the institutional parameters of Judaism. Even some of the new generation of students in the ultraorthodox yeshivas now acknowledge the Israeli context in which they live.

Secular critics argue that Jews lack religious freedom in Israel, which accords rights to persons of other faiths, though it denies them first-class citizenship. Jews of Conservative or Reform congregations would be freer if the state treated them as non-Jews! The harshest among Orthodox rabbis would do just that, while the more lenient see these congregations as defective and misguided, worthy of citizenship but unworthy of official religious rights and privileges. State control of religious institutions permits the logic of Orthodoxy to prevail.

From 1948 until 1967, the stability of the Israeli political system helped maintain the equilibrium of political and religious institutions sketched by the status quo letter. Mapai, the party of David Ben-Gurion, dominated the Labor settlement movement with its commitment to break with Jewish passivity, victimhood, and exclusivism through pioneering, cultural regeneration, and state building. Labor depended upon the cooperation of religious Zionists in the National Religious Party and only occasionally on the support of the ultraorthodox Agudat Israel. There were skirmishes about respect for the Sabbath, the rules of kashrut, and the Law of Return, but neither Labor Zionism nor the religious parties sought revision of the understanding Ben-Gurion had championed in place of constitutional regulation.

Threats to the Status Quo

Even before 1967, the immigration of Jews from the Middle East and North Africa, cultivated and welcomed by Labor Zionism, began to threaten the balance between religious and secular forces. Secular Israelis traveled to Iraq and Yemen, among other places, to encourage Jews to come to Israel. They trumpeted the virtues of Israel as the Holy Land to reinforce an identity distinct from Arab-Muslim culture. The immigrants who arrived from these and other Muslim countries tended to be more observant of Jewish tradition than their European predecessors. They tended to prefer religious schools for their children. Fearing that these students would strengthen National Religious Party schools, Ben-Gurion and his colleagues moved quickly to establish a single state-school system, albeit one divided into state general schools and state religious schools. To this day, students from Mizrachi families constitute an overwhelming majority of students enrolled in state religious education.

Israel's unexpected conquest of the West Bank in 1967 proved to be a key event in further destabilizing the balance between religious and political forces. While mainstream Labor leaders such as Ben-Gurion talked about trading the conquered territories for a peace agreement with the Arab states, religious Zionists exulted not just in the freedom to pray at the Western Wall of the old temple but to go live in places of biblical significance, such as the city of Hebron. Labor-dominated governments authorized settlement for reasons that are unclear. Some settlements were supposed to protect Israel's eastern frontier along the Jordan River, but the pressures for settlement came increasingly from religious voices brought together in 1973 in the Gush Emunim (Bloc of the Faithful).

Powered by a fresh version of Zionism and by an outburst of organizational talent and energy, the Gush became the primary pressure group for the Land of Israel Movement. The Six-Day War, in which Israel had seized the West Bank from Jordan, the Sinai peninsula from Egypt, and the Golan Heights from Syria, constituted an act of God and the beginning of the promised redemption of the Jews, the group said. It was providential that Jews could now live not just in Tel Aviv, a new city of no religious significance, but also in cities of ancient Judea and Samaria, the land most closely identified with the ancient Jewish king-doms. This was land God had given the Jews, and the Jews needed to settle and defend this territory. The Gush organized settlements, the most daring of them in the center of Hebron, surrounded by a hostile Arab population. With consid-erable support in the National Religious Party and in the nationalist party, Likud, the Gush pushed ahead and dared the government to stop it. Shafir and Peled write: "They grafted their own messianic religious discourse onto the old dis-course of republican virtue [propounded by the Labor settlement movement], and claimed the mantle of the moral community attending to the common good by settling the Land of Israel."[64]

The institutional balance defined by the status quo agreement tipped further toward the religious forces in the so-called earthquake election of 1977. Me-nachem Begin, Ben-Gurion's great antagonist and critic, won power in a smash-ing victory of his Likud party over the Labor Alignment. The primary reason was clear: Mizrachim now dominated the body politic, and Likud won a majority of their votes. It was, in Shafir and Peled's words, a victory of "ethnic nation-alism" over "republican virtue." The ideology of Likud, an offshoot of Vladimir Jabotinsky's Revisionist movement, did not emphasize religious claims to the Land of Israel. Revisionism had always emphasized military power as the key to building and preserving a state. For reasons of security, Likud opposed Labor's ostensible policy of trading land for peace. The party distrusted the Arabs, the United Nations, and great power guarantees. Israel under Likud would not be content to trust God for protection, but Begin himself was personally observant as well as charismatic. Religion became a more important foundation of the so-called Second Republic than it had been of the first, the era of Labor dominance.

Designated as the new prime minister, Begin pleased Mizrachi supporters by inviting the National Religious Party and ultraorthodox forces to join his coalition. They accepted. State subsidies began to flow more generously toward religious institutions, and the government began officially encouraging settlement. The Land of Israel Movement, powered by the Gush Emunim, gained strength, though it suffered temporary disillusionment when Prime Minister Begin agreed to pull back from Sinai in return for peace with Egypt. The Gush took the 1981 withdrawal of settlers from Yamit, required by the treaty with Egypt, as a sign of betrayal.

The birth of two new political parties in 1984 epitomized the shifting institutional balance between religious and secular forces. The first of these, Kach, openly proposed expelling Arabs from the West Bank. The Israeli Knesset ultimately banned Kach (see "Ideology" above). The second party called itself Shas. Its founder was Rabbi Ovadia Yosef, former chief Sephardic rabbi of Israel. He split with Agudat Israel to establish an ultraorthodox party of Middle Eastern and North African Jews. Of Iraqi origin, Yosef chafed at the lack of adequate Sephardic schools for rabbinic training. He dreamed of restoring Oriental Judaism to its past glory, identified in his mind with Muslim Spain. At first Shas split the ultraorthodox vote with Agudat Israel, but it soon achieved much wider appeal among Mizrachim, thanks in large measure to Arie Deri, of Moroccan origin, who felt he had suffered discrimination at the hands of the establishment. Deri demonstrated remarkable political talents and found himself director-general in the Ministry of the Interior after Shas joined the governing coalition. Soon he was acting minister and diverting large sums of money to religious institutions. The party, which won 3.1 percent of the vote in 1984, advanced to 4.7 percent in 1988 and 5 percent in 1992. In 1996 it leaped to 8.5 percent after a change in the electoral system created two ballots, one for parliament and one for prime minister. When Shas joined a new coalition headed by Netanyahu, it received two ministerial posts and two slots for deputy ministers; three years later, even after charges of corruption forced Deri to stand aside, the party reached 14.1 percent of the vote and claimed four ministries.

Shas reached well beyond the ultraorthodox in its appeal by targeting Mizrachi resentment against Ashkenazi dominance in society, economy, and politics. The party began to see itself as the representative of underprivileged Israelis. It established a special program to help marginal youths in the Oriental community by bringing them into Orthodoxy. At the same time, it reached out to a mystic, Rabbi Yitzhak Kaduri, who helped legitimize religious practices common among North African Jews, including belief in charms and the power of saints. "Six to seven million persons annually are reported to make pilgrimages to tombs of saints in Israel," writes Lilly Weissbrod.[65] Despite their commitment to Orthodoxy, Shas leaders have avoided criticizing such practices.

In the 2003 election, Shas suffered the loss of one-third of its seats in the Knesset. It dropped from 14.1 percent to 8.9 percent of the vote but remained the fourth-largest party in Israel. For the first time in nineteen years, Shas was excluded from the governing coalition. The shift back to a single ballot probably is the single most important explanation. Voters needed to calculate how their votes for party lists would affect the selection of the prime minister, as they had before 1996. Some voters apparently thought Shas had failed to fulfill its promises to help the underprivileged, but Yosef campaigned with a more presumptuous, religious assertion: "Those who are for God follow me."[66] A secular political force of the center-right, Shinui, identified Shas as its principal enemy. In return, Yosef called on the electorate to vote against the evil Shinui. The viciousness of the attacks and rebuttals showed that both sides feared that the balance of religious and secular forces might be jeopardized.

The electoral success of Shas—it won 9 percent of the vote and 11 seats in the January 2013 parliamentary election—and its resulting influence in the ministries have permitted the construction of an educational system that guarantees lasting influence. Weissbrod reports that Shas established 270 centers in poor Mizrachi communities and neighborhoods to provide adult religious education, supplementary religious education for school-age children, hot meals for the needy, nursery schools, and more.[67] It moved toward providing modern education as well as religious instruction for both girls and boys, and seemed prepared to move toward professional training in fields as diverse as social work and finance—all in the name of advancing the social well-being of the Mizrachi community. Whether these programs succeed in moving Mizrachim toward Orthodoxy remains to be seen, but they strengthened Shas as a political force.

Immigration and war explain much of the threat to institutional balance in Israel since 1967. The influx of Jews from the Middle East and North Africa after independence created an underclass of Israeli Jews susceptible to political mobilization. Menachem Begin and the Likud party succeeded in reaching some of this group, and then after 1984, Shas rode Mizrachi votes to power and influence. Meanwhile, the war of 1967 triggered new cries for "settlement of the Land of Israel." Religious Zionists flocked to the Occupied Territories, bolstered by convictions that they were carrying out the will of God, supported by the Gush Emunim and rabbinical proclamations. A few extremists such as Kahane jumped into the mix. The threat represented by Shas and by the Gush Emunim, on the other hand, came through the electoral system and the Knesset. Nothing could prevent the Knesset from changing things, other than a constitution that impinged on the Knesset's authority.

"Constitutional Revolution"

The Knesset usurped its authority at the birth of the state of Israel. Elected as a constituent assembly charged with preparing a constitution, it transformed itself at its very first meeting into a legislature and postponed the constitutional task. In 1950, after intense discussion of constitutional issues, including the place of religion in the state, the Knesset adopted a resolution proposed by Haim Harari. It said, in essence, that the constitution of the state would take shape one chapter at a time in the form of a set of basic laws. Hanna Lerner explains what the resolution accomplished: "The Harari Compromise . . . enabled circumvention of the ideologically controversial issues which divided the religious and the secular publics by avoiding any explicit formulation of the relationship between religion and state in Israel."[68]

The Knesset adopted a set of basic laws that defined the way Israeli government functions. These laws, which mostly confirmed established practices, elicited little controversy until 1989, when the minister of justice, Dan Meridor, proposed the Basic Law on Human and Civil Rights. The religious parties objected that such a law would undermine the status quo. That proposal failed, but pieces of it reemerged three years later in two parts: the Basic Law on Human Dignity and Liberty and the Basic Law on Freedom of Occupation. These bills won passage but only after an amendment provided that existing law would not be affected. The religious parties wanted to protect prevailing practice.[69]

Justice Aaron Barak of the Israeli Supreme Court proclaimed that passage of these two basic laws represented a "constitutional revolution." "Israel has transformed itself from a parliamentary democracy to a constitutional democracy," he said, because the Supreme Court had acquired the right to review legislation. In making these claims, he sharpened the lines of conflict: court against Knesset, secular against religious forces. By one account, Ashkenazi Jews, having lost control of the Knesset, were using the court to reassert their control over the state of Israel.[70] The "constitutional revolution" threatened to neutralize, if not reverse, the advances made by the religious parties since 1967. Secular forces on the left and the right cheered these changes. Rising electoral fortunes made Shas the principal opponent of the "revolution."

The bitterness of this confrontation suggested the possibility of instability, if Justice Barak pursued his constitutional aims. In fact, much of the ensuing controversy emerged from cases that produced modest change in the interpretation of Israeli law, nothing worthy of the term *revolutionary*. The "pork case," involving the importation of nonkosher meat, showed the potential explosiveness of the issues, but the resolution also illustrated the secondary stability available in the Israeli system. The Knesset, upon recommendation of the government, undercut the apparent victory of the court system and defused the "constitutional revolution." The case (*Mitral v. Prime Minister*, 1993) arose after the Knesset privatized the frozen-meat industry in 1992. Mitral, a meat importer, appealed a government decision that even private importers could not bring in nonkosher meat. Mitral said the decision violated the Basic Law on Freedom of Occupation, which guarantees any resident of Israel the right to practice any occupation, profession, or trade. The Supreme Court, sitting as the High Court of Justice, accepted the appeal and ruled that any further legislation of the Knesset that sought to ban nonkosher meat would contradict the clause of the basic law preventing the negation of previous legislation. But the government then won Knesset approval for an amendment to the Basic Law on Freedom of Occupation specifying that future legislation could constitutionally contradict the basic law, if the legislation included a clause exempting it from the provisions of the basic law![71]

Despite the clarity of that victory of Knesset over court, which was a victory of religious over secular forces, the antagonism did not end. On one side, the court chipped away at the authority of religious courts in matters such as the division of matrimonial property in divorce and the right of women to pray at the Western Wall. As Frances Raday writes, the Supreme Court has "established the right to equality as a fundamental right," but "the Knesset has put personal status law . . . beyond the reach of the principle of equality and the courts have not challenged this."[72] Feminists and others concerned with civil liberties find the "constitutional revolution" rather tame, but religious forces nonetheless attacked the Supreme Court and the chief justice repeatedly and viciously. Rabbi Meir Porush, a leader of Agudat Israel, proclaimed he was ready to die in the struggle against Justice Barak. In 1999 ultraorthodox (*haredi*) religious leadership forbade its own leadership, members of the Knesset, and civil servants to obey rulings of the High Court of Justice on exemption from military service, conversions to Judaism, and the inclusion of Reform and Conservative Jews in local municipal councils. More than a quarter of a million Orthodox Jews demonstrated against the Supreme Court in February 1999.[73] Proposals to create a constitutional council to replace the Supreme Court in that role reached the Knesset. Those efforts met defeat in 2002, but ultraorthodox hostility to the court and to Barak continued. Barak's successors in the position of chief justice have not bowed to the pressure or abandoned Barak's "constitutional revolution."

The smoldering institutional rivalry that marks the relationship between politics and religion in Israel probably stems from an underlying clash of ideologies. Shafir and Peled call it an encounter between ethno-nationalist discourse and liberal democracy. Barak was explicit about wanting to put Israel more squarely in line with the Universal Declaration of Human Rights and with democratic principles. He declared that "the meaning of the Jewish nature of the state is not in the religious-Halacha sense, and hence the values of the State of Israel as a Jewish state should not be identified with Jewish Law."[74] Lerner portrays the conflict as one between consociationalism and majoritarianism. The religious parties seek to maintain the consociational structure that has given them an effective veto power over Israeli political life. Those who champion equality want greater majority control in all matters and a reduction of what they perceive as religious privilege. The change of the electoral law to permit direct election of the prime minister seemed to be a step toward majoritarianism. Yet the unintended result was growth of the smaller parties, including Shas, a modern defender of the enduring consociational arrangements. Repeal of the provision for direct election of the prime minister after 2001 signaled a resurgence of consociationalism.

Political Culture

Independent Israel grew out of a nationalist movement of European origin. European Jews, products of czarist rule in Poland and Russia and some of them survivors of Nazi Germany, brought with them a set of aptitudes and attitudes that continue to mark Israeli politics. When Israel took its independence, its political culture already accepted labor unions, political parties, and proportional representation. It also knew something of dictatorship and repression. As Ben-Gurion and his colleagues began to shape a new political culture, they were not working with virgin clay or starting from that hypothetical "state of nature" so important to liberals from Thomas Hobbes to John Rawls.

At independence, Israel distanced itself from the World Zionist movement and from the movement's longtime leader, Chaim Weizmann. Ben-Gurion seized the controls as prime minister, but Weizmann's presence on the stage as the state's first president and Israel's obvious debt to the WZO evoked an issue of enormous importance. Did the Israeli state respond to the Jewish people as a whole, or was it responsible only to its citizens? What was Israel's relationship to the Diaspora? More Jews lived (and still live) outside Israel than live within. For some Jews, both within Israel and outside it, Israel suddenly replaced God as the center of Judaism. In the first euphoria of independence, leaders seemed to have expected that most Jews would return "home." Constitution making could be postponed until the great flood of immigrants had arrived. Any Jew who did not go there was not "fully" Jewish. To this day, 83 percent of Israelis believe they have an obligation to the Diaspora, and a high proportion of American Jews support Israel even if they do not intend to move there.[75] For some, Israel is so much identified with the Jewish people as a whole, that to oppose Israeli policies is tantamount to anti-Semitism.

Zionism asserted the existence of a single Jewish people, but the emergence of an independent Jewish state including only a minority of world Jewry created a political culture quite distinct from that of the Diaspora. In Israel, Jewishness can become trivialized. As a twenty-year-old Israeli woman put it, "My Jewish identity is as much a part of me as my name—but really of no greater consequence."[76] Israelis divide evenly on whether they see themselves first as Jews or first as Israelis. An American Jew is more likely "to seek personal and spiritual meaning in religion than is his Israeli counterpart."[77] For many American Jews, political activism, not religion, cements identity. American Jews help define American political culture.

For some Jews, Israel has no religious significance. Yeshayahu Leibowitz argues that the deep involvement of the state in religious affairs damages religion:

"Religion as an adjunct of a secular authority is the antithesis of true religion."[78] Israel uses religion to bolster its identity and its standing with the Diaspora, but "nationalism and patriotism as such are not religious values."[79]

In a similar vein, Joe Lockard writes: "It is not religion that makes me be ashamed of being Israeli today, but nationalism."[80] For Leibowitz and Lockard, nationalism separates Israel from the "Jewish people" and, of course, from the "Arab people" as well. The ultraorthodox accept Israel as a reality of their existence but stop short of sanctifying the state and seeing it as the center of Judaism.

The attitudes of the Diaspora constitute one element of Israeli political culture, but Israeli nationalism—propagated by Labor Zionists intent upon settling the land and building a state, and more recently by ethno-nationalists preoccupied with security issues—has emphasized the uniqueness of the setting, the problems, the people, and the relevant solutions. The land itself, including the Occupied Territories, has become central to Israeli identity. The political system reflects and responds most directly to the attitudes of its Jewish citizens. The nation-state outweighs the Diaspora as the popular context of Israeli politics.

Secular or Religious?

Highly devout segments of the Israeli body politic fear majoritarian rule from their sense that the Israeli political culture is highly secular. The conventional wisdom, propagated by academics and the media, was that a third of Israeli Jews observed most religious traditions and that of this third, roughly half voted for the religious parties. (The ultraorthodox Agudat Israel and Poalei Agudat Israel garnered less than 3 percent of the vote.) The Guttman Institute report, based on surveys taken in 1991 and 1993, provided a much more complete and complicated picture. It confirmed that a minority of Israelis are highly observant of religious traditions, but it also showed that an ample majority of Israelis observe some religious traditions. Israelis rated their own degree of religiosity this way:

Strictly observant	14 percent
Observant to a great extent	24 percent
Somewhat observant	41 percent
Totally nonobservant	21 percent[81]

Four-fifths of the population appears to be observant, and even this number may understate religious practice. The study reported that 77 percent of the respondents regard the Sabbath as important to their lives, "including 39 percent of those who consider themselves 'totally nonobservant.'"[82] Charles Liebman underscores this observation: "The report found that the Jewish religion retains an influence that many had heretofore refused to acknowledge."[83]

The Guttman report undermined the conventional wisdom about Israel's "secular" majority, but it did not convince everyone that Israelis are deeply religious. Bernard Susser asks, "Why do 50% think good deeds will be rewarded but 27% think bad deeds will be punished? Why do 50% see Torah as divine while only 14% observe commandments?"[84] Many Israelis may follow religious traditions for family or nationalistic and patriotic reasons.[85] One in six thinks public life in Israel should be more religious, and one in three thinks it should be less religious, but the rest of the Jewish population would keep the balance of religion and politics where it is.[86] "Israeli society has a strong traditional bent," write Levy, Levinsohn, and Katz, "and, as far as religious practice is concerned, . . . there is a continuum from the strictly observant to the nonobservant rather than a great divide between a religious minority and a secular majority."[87]

These numbers help explain why neither secular nor religious forces have been successful in their efforts to tip the balance of Israeli politics. Secular opposition to restrictive Sabbath policies has not produced legal change, but the state does not enforce all the rules dear to religious Jews. "Could anyone in the 1960s have predicted that movie theaters, restaurants, and pubs would operate undisturbed in downtown Jerusalem on Friday nights?" asks Friedman.[88] Orthodox rabbis continue to perform all marriages, but fewer and fewer Israelis choose to get married in Israel. Cyprus is a popular venue. Survey results do not directly confirm a great divide on religious matters, but neither do they affirm a consensus.

Political culture in Israel appears to be evolving toward postmaterialism in the manner Inglehart predicted.[89] The spirit of the early Yishuv was decidedly collectivist. The kibbutz represented the collective, socialist spirit better than does any other institution. Building the economy, the society, and the state required the subordination of the individual to group aims. Bourgeois Zionism stayed in the background until the 1960s, when economic prosperity began to produce a new emphasis on liberalism, individualism, self-realization, and secularism, at least among people of European origin. Israelis as a group may be relatively observant, but the elites are overwhelmingly secular, postmaterialist, and Western in orientation.[90]

Political attitudes slipped in the opposite direction, however, as a result of the immigration of Middle Eastern and North African Jews. These immigrants found themselves at the lower rungs of Israeli society, fighting for material gain and political influence rather than postmaterialist values. They swelled the ranks of the observant and mostly observant, categories that came to be described as *masorti* (traditional). To secular Jews from Europe, the Mizrachim appeared remarkably religious, and to Orthodox Jews from Europe, the newcomers appeared remarkably eclectic in their patterns of religious observance. The label *traditional* carried all the baggage associated with it in the "traditional-modern" distinction made by Inglehart and other modernization theorists, who argue that tradition must give way to modernity. Immigration thus produced an increase of religiosity that tended to counterbalance the decreasing religiosity of the long-established Ashkenazim. The relative stability of survey numbers disguised offsetting changes.[91]

Change threatens both sides. S. N. Eisenstadt asserts that the religious feared the rising tide of secularism in the 1950s, whereas heightened religiosity and the strength of the religious parties cause fright among secularists now.[92] The proportion of citizens who see themselves as Jews rather than Israelis has edged upward. The commitment to land as a sacred object has increased. The haredim seem to have advanced in strength relative to the Orthodox. Shinui has played on these fears to advance its political standing.

Remaking Political Culture

From the beginning, Zionism aspired to transform Jewish political culture. It sought to break with Jewish passivity and to create a new image of the Jew as adventurer, pioneer, worker, activist, and good citizen of the state. Israel was to be a visionary democratic state rather than a service state. The dominant Labor party, Mapai, operated its own school system before independence, invoking the Jewish heritage, explains Tom Segev, "mainly in historical terms, as a humanistic tradition, whose expression lay in the commandment 'Thou shall not kill.'"[93] The Labor schools saw the Sabbath as a day of rest, Passover as a festival of liberty. While perhaps not antireligious, the schools were nonetheless anti-clerical. The schools run by the secular, liberal parties taught more Jewish subjects than did those run by Labor, but tended to emphasize the Bible rather than the Talmud, the principles of Judaism as opposed to the rabbinic tradition. After independence, in 1953, these two streams of education merged into the state general schools. Julia Resnick concludes that the national image conveyed in these schools in the 1950s was one of a "nation with a right to a state," a right seen as coming from Jewish history and international recognition.[94] The socialism of the Labor schools gave way to a message of nationalism in the merged general schools, which accommodated about 70 percent of Jewish pupils at the moment of merger.[95] Mainstream schools sought to transform Jews into citizens of the new state, distinct from Jews in the Diaspora.

The haredim, whether supportive of Zionism or not, found this transformative vision unacceptable, because it threatened the ability of the religious minorities to sustain themselves. Even before independence, about one-fourth of all Jewish pupils attended religious schools. Religious Zionists resisted a single, secular school system, and the Labor movement resisted complete autonomy for the religious schools. The resulting compromise produced two streams of state education: general and religious. In addition, groups such as Agudat Israel could and did establish independent schools. Thus, the religious forces sought to protect their distinctive cultural niches from the corrosive power of the secular schools.

Already in the 1950s, the transformers began to be transformed. As immigrants poured into Israel from North Africa and the Middle East, Labor Zionists established camps and set up schools, but these immigrants preferred religious schools. Fearful they would all emerge as eventual supporters of the National Religious Party, dominant elites began to nudge the general schools toward greater consideration of religion. The governing coalition settled on new "basic principles" for education in 1955:

In primary, secondary and higher education the government will take care to deepen Jewish consciousness among Israeli young people, to root it in the Jewish people's past and historical heritage, and to strengthen its moral tie to world Jewry based on the awareness of a common destiny and the historical continuity which links all Jews from all countries.[96]

Resnick calls this image a "nation by right of religion" and says it came to be broadly implemented in the 1960s.

The objective of consciousness raising outlined in the principles was to incorporate the Diaspora and to overcome the ever more visible split between religious and nonreligious Jews, between Sephardim and Ashkenazim. The evocation of religion as a treasure chest of memories and symbols available for political purposes did not, of course, satisfy even religious Zionists, much less the non-Zionist Orthodox groups. This deflection of Labor Zionism toward religion reflected a sense that arriving waves of immigrants and a growing religious-school system might threaten secular domination. The threat warranted a tempering of the message to acknowledge more explicitly the role of religion in uniting the Jewish people. The state general schools still do not teach religion as much as they teach *about* religion.

Far from disappearing, state religious education gained in numbers but suffered in quality from the influx of immigrants. In the early 1990s, Mizrachim constituted 80 percent of the enrollment in state religious schools, compared with 57 percent in the general schools. Since the 1967 conquest of Sinai and the West Bank, those schools have acquired fresh significance in justifying retention and settlement of the whole Land of Israel. The schools teach that Israel constitutes a step toward the redemption of the Jews. They are also supposed to prepare their students for modern life and teach that it is possible to "live as a Jew" in a democratic country.[97] The claim is that about 70 percent of the students in this track emerge as observant Jews. Since roughly 20 percent of Israeli pupils attend such schools, some 14 percent of the population would maintain or acquire Orthodox habits in these schools. Another 10 percent of pupils attend non-Zionist Orthodox schools, which emphasize religion but do have some state supervision. Roughly 4 percent of all pupils attend ultraorthodox schools, which follow religious curricula. If the independent religious schools succeed in keeping all pupils within the realm of Orthodoxy, then about 30 percent of Israeli youth would be drawn along in Orthodox patterns. This suggests relative stability in patterns of belief.

Religious education acquired new resources after the right won the parliamentary elections of 1977. It also suffered at home and abroad from the actions of settlers who took the law into their own hands. In the state general schools, there emerged a new emphasis on Israel as a democracy and a champion of universal human rights, pluralism, and the rule of law, in response to the abuses of Israeli rule in the West Bank and Gaza. Religious forces saw Labor's return to power in the early 1990s as a fresh assault of Hellenism and universalism on Jewish particularism. The Oslo Accords opened the way to possible peace with the Palestinians and to ceding much of the West Bank. When Yigal Amir assassinated Prime Minister Rabin, religious education took some of the backlash. Overall, though, religious education does not appear to be gaining or losing strength.

Education has not fashioned a homogeneous political culture in Israel. A case study of ceremonies commemorating Rabin's death suggests that the two school systems differ in the way they socialize students into politics. On the one hand, the religious schools portrayed the assassination as "abrogation of a religious commandment rather than a political act." They used readings from the Torah to stress the need for tolerance, the sanctity of life, and the need to prevent civil war. The general schools, on the other hand, devoted much more time to the ceremonies, which included music, dance, and speeches. They emphasized the need for peace with the Palestinians and Arabs, and the need to work for goals by democratic means. From interviewing students, the author of this study found that those from religious schools used the term "us" to mean religious Jews, and those from the general schools used "us" as the equivalent of peace-loving democrats. She noted that the ceremonies in the state general schools, like the better-established ceremonies commemorating the Holocaust, did not pertain to Arab schools—or even to yeshivas, for that matter.[98]

The autonomous yeshivas of the ultraorthodox contrast even more sharply with the state general schools in their approach to political socialization. In such schools, boys don traditional garb and devote themselves to the study of the Torah, to the exclusion of almost everything else. They enjoy deferment from the military service imposed on all other qualified Israeli males. Some students remain in the yeshivas until age forty-two, when deferments become exemptions, remaining all the while a burden on the state and delaying any contribution to the economy. Deferments for yeshiva students, which numbered about 500 in the 1950s, now total some 30,000 a year.[99] Criticism has mounted with the numbers, but the ultraorthodox, some of whom still disdain the state, fend off critics by saying that learning is the greatest asset of the Jews and because of this, yeshiva students contribute to the defense of the nation. The lure of military deferment has increased the power of the yeshivas as a socializing force and increased the state's financial burdens. It is estimated that two-thirds of the haredim live on welfare.[100] The Netanyahu government proposed to limit the number of exemptions for the ultraorthodox and to conscript Arab citizens but then backed off from its own proposal in the summer of 2012.

Despite the intent of Labor Zionists to create a single civil religion, the Israeli school system has solidified pluralism. State general schools are too secular for religious tastes. The state religious schools are insufficiently Orthodox for some and insufficiently secular for others. The autonomous yeshivas run by ultraorthodox forces constitute an unwarranted refuge from military service, in the eyes of some, as well as an inadequate preparation for modern life. The Hesder yeshivas run by the National Religious Party produce poor scholars and poor soldiers, in the eyes of critics. Schools for Arabs remain separate but include heavy doses of Jewish history and inadequate treatment of Islam. No single set of schools can satisfy the fragmented political culture of Israel. Only a segmented school system can sustain the plurality of attitudes that has shaped the polity from the early days of Zionism.

Politics has "created" and maintained the religious diversity that divides the body politic. Secular Zionism generated religious Zionism. Religious Zionism sharpened the reactions of Orthodoxy, which was, like Zionism itself, a reaction to modernity. Independent Israel separated itself from the Diaspora at the same time that it welcomed Jews from the Diaspora, and especially from the Middle East and North Africa. Immigration produced a split in Orthodoxy and the creation of Shas. The dominance of Orthodoxy ensured by the state fostered secular reactions of the Meretz party on the left and the Shinui party on the right. All these groups, including most of the ultraorthodox, avail themselves of politics to protect their organizations and their constituents. Does this mean that the political culture is religious or that religious culture is thoroughly politicized? Both seem to be true.

Stability of Israeli political culture is a by-product of the interdependence of religious and political attitudes. The effort to instill a single understanding of democracy may not have succeeded, and many proponents of the halakha may still remain theoretically opposed, but not even they can afford to put themselves outside the democratic maelstrom. How they behave politically may be a more important lesson for their students than what the halakhic proponents teach. They may teach that politics depends on religion, but the behavior of all the groups also suggests that religion depends on politics.

Conclusion

Israel calls itself a Jewish state and thinks of itself as democratic. Insofar as it is democratic, the reason is not because Israel is Jewish. Some of the most religious elements of the society have rejected participation, and others have used their influence in democratic politics to block measures to liberalize and democratize the society. The early Israeli settlers, most of them secular in orientation, brought democratic ideas with them from Europe. Consociational political arrangements emerged not from the Talmud but from the practical need for cooperation within the Jewish community in Palestine under British mandate. The democratic procedures initiated in those years carried over directly into the independence period.

Israel is Jewish because, by a process of negotiation and democratic decision-making among its Jewish citizens, it has decided to be Jewish. Zionism began as a secular movement but found itself obliged to invoke religion, if only as a source of cultural commonality, to explain the common identity of the Jews. Labor Zionism flaunted its irreverence as it launched its program of settlement and state building, but it could not in the end ignore the political strength of Orthodox groups. The status quo letter acknowledged the power and prestige of the Orthodox. The National Religious Party demonstrated its effectiveness at the polls and earned a lock on cabinet positions, guaranteeing the enforcement of status quo policies. The heavy immigration of Middle Eastern and North African Jews after independence pushed both left and right to sustain and even enhance their secular commitments to uphold religion. In these new demographic circumstances, the right recruited voters more successfully than the left and came to power in the earthquake election of 1977. In the aftermath, coalition governments based on the right catered to the needs and desires of the religious parties, further solidifying the state's religious character. Israel has become progressively more religious by virtue of its democratic politics. The Arabs who live within the Green Line borders established in 1949 and enjoy full voting rights have been unable to exert significant influence over this process.

By becoming a Jewish state, Israel has transformed Judaism. For many Jews, Judaism acquired a center, a focus, and a structure it had not had since the destruction of the Second Temple. Many Israelis saw themselves as occupying holy ground and playing a central role; the word *aliya*, used to describe immigration, evoked religion. Those who did not immigrate suddenly found themselves less Jewish than those who did. Reform and Conservative congregations, dominant in America, found themselves at odds with the Orthodox establishment, which had for political reasons achieved preeminence in Israel. A whole new line of religious thinking, initiated by Rav Kook, argued that the formation of the state might open the door to messianic times. Political bargaining led to the creation of parallel Orthodox rabbinates, one for the Jews of Europe, the other for those of the Middle East and Africa. Judaism, previously fractured into communities all over the Diaspora, acquired elements of order and hierarchy that brought parts of the world Jewry together but divided Israelis from the Diaspora, Zionists from anti-Zionists, Orthodox from Reform and Conservative congregations, West from East. If Judaism is the sum of what Jews believe, think, and do, then it is substantially different from what it was a century ago.

While religious doctrine and practice has indubitably affected the state of Israel in at least superficial ways, political opportunities and necessities have shaped religious thinking in more profound ways. The state agreed to honor the Sabbath, to practice kashrut in its establishments, and to protect the autonomy of religious institutions, but never agreed to wholesale implementation of the halakha. It does permit Jews to live their lives according to the halakha, as long as they don't violate the positive law of the state. The disciplining of Kahane and Amir demonstrates the supremacy of state law over halakha. Moreover, it was state action, the conquest of the West Bank in 1967, that triggered change in religious ideology. Suddenly, for an activist minority of Orthodox Jews, the Zionist project of settlement became a sacred enterprise of helping God fulfill a promise to the Jews. Retention and settlement of conquered lands became a religious imperative as a result of political conditions.

Conflict over institutions similarly arose not from religious doctrine but from the outcome of particularistic political bargaining. As the religious parties gained political clout and the control of key ministries, they reinforced their educational facilities and programs through the allocation of government funds. Representative government became the tool by which religious forces protected the Sabbath, encouraged settlement, ensured the future of religious education, and secured ongoing settlement in the West Bank and Gaza. These forces exploited their electoral strength and encountered resistance only in an unelected institution, the Supreme Court under Chief Justice Barak. The court challenged the sovereignty of the Knesset in the name of an Israeli "constitution" invoked against the legislative will. The strength and autonomy of religious institutions in Israel reflect the politics of the country more than the politics reflect religious institutions.

Religion has prevented Israel from achieving a single, unified political culture. Only a unified educational system common to people of all faiths and to the secular as well as the religious could build a unified political culture. Particularistic religious groups would not, however, be able to perpetuate themselves if they were not permitted to run their own schools. (The same thing might be said of Christian sects in the United States.) It is not Judaism that prevents unification. Rather, the diversity of the political culture and the consociational spirit that emerges from that diversity provides the political guarantees of religious diversity. Democracy of the Israeli sort helps create and sustain religious fragmentation.

In these three domains—ideology, institutions, and political culture—the intermixture of religion and politics seems not to thwart democracy but to be a result of it. Israeli politics has reshaped Judaism, and as conditions change, it may do so again. Religion is a variable in this perspective and largely one that depends upon political circumstances and political interaction. Religious forces have become formidable players in Israeli politics because they have shaped and reshaped themselves to win elections, control ministries, approve budgets, and administer programs. They have seized their political opportunities and transformed themselves in the process. What they become in the future depends less on religious doctrine than on future political opportunities.

With the question of national identity, the prospects seem somewhat different. Early Zionism sought a national identity that was distinct from religious identity, but it could not define a Jewish people without reference to Judaism. Jewish leaders decided Israeli identity depended upon the invocation of religious symbols. This decision precludes full democracy in the state by denying non-Jews full citizenship. While it is theoretically possible to untangle national and religious identity, it is much more difficult to imagine separation than it is to imagine political decisions to give back the West Bank or to limit deferments to yeshiva students. Unlike many of the decisions Israel has taken about ideology, institutions, and political culture, the state's identification with Judaism is not a product of democratic politics as much as a product of world history. The identification came out of medieval anti-Semitism, Russian pogroms, Hitlerian atrocities,

British imperialism, American guilt, and much more. The identification of Israel and Judaism necessarily comes from politics, but it is not clear that a mere majority in Israel could undo what history has done.

Chronology

1896   First Zionist Congress meets.
1917   Great Britain issues Balfour Declaration.
1921   British accept mandate for Palestine.
1936   Arabs revolt and organize a general strike.
1947   Ben-Gurion writes status quo letter.
1948   Declaration of Independence establishes the state of Israel.
       Ben-Gurion becomes head of Labor-led government.
1956   Britain, France, and Israel attack Suez.
1967   Israel celebrates victory over Arabs in Six-Day War. Israel occupies
       West Bank, Sinai, Gaza.
1973   Israel suffers defeat on Yom Kippur.
1977   The Earthquake Election: Likud defeats Labor. Menachem Begin
       becomes prime minister.
1979   Israel signs peace treaty with Egypt and cedes Sinai.
1982   Israel invades Lebanon.
1987   Intifada begins. Uprising occurs in West Bank and Gaza.
1993   Israel and Palestinians sign Oslo Accords.
1994   Israel concludes peace with Jordan; Kach and Shas are founded.
1995   Prime Minister Rabin is assassinated.
1996   Netanyahu wins direct election as premier under two-ballot system.
2001   Second intifada begins. Ariel Sharon takes power as prime minister.
2002   Construction of wall between Israel and West Bank territories begins.
2003   Return to single-ballot system rewards Likud, punishes Shas.
2005   Israel withdraws from Gaza.
2006   Israel fights thirty-four-day war with Hizbullah in southern Lebanon
       and northern Israel.
2009   Benyamin Netanyahu becomes prime minister.
2013   Parliamentary elections favor the center-left.

4

The Politics of Religion
in "Secularist" Turkey

The first nation-state to emerge from the defeat and breakup of the Ottoman Empire in World War I, the Republic of Turkey decided to separate religion from
public life. It accepted the idea that modernization requires secularization of society and politics. From a Western perspective and from that of many Turks,
Turkey became proof that a Muslim country could become modern, liberal, and
democratic. From another perspective, advanced ever more insistently in the
past forty years, Turkey had betrayed its heritage, its neighbors, and itself.

Today Turkey is demonstrating that an overwhelmingly Muslim country of
the Middle East can sustain democracy. Under a government led by Islamists,
Turkey has since 2002 achieved a strong record of economic growth, reasserted
a role in regional affairs, and become a model for other countries of the region
trying to break with their authoritarian pasts. Seen in the Ottoman era as impe-
rialists, Turks now position themselves as liberators. In this new role, Turkey
wins praise from those who believe it is blazing a much-needed trail for the
Muslim world, but it also encounters skepticism from those who think Turkey
has betrayed the Western, secular tradition established nearly a century ago.

Mustafa Kemal Atatürk, the first president of republican Turkey, pursued
policies he regarded as secularist, *laik*. Many writers took the regime's self-
proclaimed secularism as a description of fact, even though Turkish secularism
never meant separation of church and state. Quite the contrary, secularism in
Turkey "refers to state control of all aspects of religious life."[1] Secularist elites
proclaimed the liberation of the country from the strictures of Islamic doctrine,

customs, and what they called superstitions inconsistent with modernity, but they never convinced most Turks to abandon their religious beliefs and practices.

The Kemalists, followers of Atatürk, who seem to have interpreted their dreams as reality, fueled the efforts of Western social scientists to propose Turkey as a model for modernizing societies. The Turkish case confirmed the theory that secularization leads to modernization. But recent scholarship suggests a definition of *laiklik*, the Turkish term for secularism, that conflicts with the one propagated by Kemalists and Western scholars of an earlier epoch. The new scholarship portrays a continuum of development in which a series of political changes has altered the balance between religion and politics in Turkey.

When Atatürk created an official Islam, he also outlawed nonofficial versions. As a product of the democratization process undertaken since World War II, however, the outlawed strands of Islam have been progressively reintegrated. The search for a new equilibrium of religion and politics reflects changing political opportunities and the responses of religious groups to these opportunities. Modern Islamic movements, reshaped by the politics of the past century, are now reshaping politics. They have helped bring neglected segments of the Turkish population into the political process. The rediscovery of Islam in Turkey has resulted from and promoted modernization and democratization.

Atatürk sought to create a Turkish nation whose identity depended on Turkishness rather than on Islam. Under the Ottoman Empire, a true citizen was both a Turk and a Muslim, although many Ottoman subjects were neither Turkish nor Muslim. In winning the war against the Greeks that set the Turks free of European ambitions, a group of military officers, including Mustafa Kemal, invoked Islam to rally the country and especially the Kurds against the foreigners. Yet, once the war was won, the new Turkish republic made the Turkish language and Turkish history the foci of national identity, making it difficult for Kurds, speaking a non-Turkish mother tongue, to feel a part of the state. In fact, the Kemalist elites cut themselves off from much of rural Turkey by virtue of their apparent hostility to religion. The emphasis on Turkishness and official Islam "helped to politicize nascent identities such as Kurdish ethnicity and Sunni/Alevi Islam."[2]

The gradual reconciliation of Islam with Turkish identity began in the 1950s but progressed more quickly with the emergence of Islamist parties in the 1970s.[3] The election of an Islamist mayor of Istanbul in 1994, and the accession of

Necmettin Erbakan to the premiership two years later, pulled the country toward reintegration of Islamic symbols with those of the republic. The old Ottoman capital, Istanbul, began to reassert itself against republican Ankara, the country's modern capital. Even the military, a bastion of Kemalist secularism, fostered the growth of religious schools, and the graduates of these schools slipped into the bureaucracy. Since 2002 the government headed by Prime Minister Recep Tayyip Erdoğan, himself a product of the Islamist movement, has reopened Turkey's connections to its Ottoman and Muslim past without negating the nationalist tradition constructed by Atatürk.

While Islam served as a foundation for Ottoman law and morality, it can scarcely be regarded as an Ottoman ideology. Ottoman rule depended upon both dynastic legitimacy and the linkage of the dynasty to Islam. Ideology is a modern concept. Most modern political ideologies have emerged from revolution, and the Turkish revolution against Ottoman rule—a revolution led by Mustafa Kemal and his band of Young Turks—produced a secularist ideology that has marked Turkey ever since. The idea of divorcing politics and religion drove changes in language, dress, social habits, and even the choice of the capital city. Atatürk sought to remake Islam into a state-supporting ideology, propagated by official preachers and public schools—an ideology dedicated to eradicating Islam from public life. To implement his secularizing ideology, Atatürk created a set of central institutions to define and direct religion. He disbanded the religious hierarchy and outlawed public meetings of unofficial religious organizations such as the Sufi brotherhoods, which were forced underground. The Republican People's Party, guardian of the revolution, won support from an educated, urban, secular elite that regarded religious practices as badges of backwardness. The institutional monopoly seemed unassailable, and yet, forgoing politics, religious leaders such as Said Nursi nurtured a modernist, nonconfrontational set of Muslim study groups and organizations. Some of these groups eventually moved toward political action through the National Outlook movement, which spawned a series of political parties. The regime banned one and then another of the parties, but always there was a successor to replace it. It became apparent that the Turkish state, despite its best efforts, had not succeeded in maintaining control of all religious institutions, although it had made religion invisible in public life.

The Kemalist state partially succeeded in remaking Turkey's political culture in an image of European enlightenment and secularism. Elites adopted European dress, manners, and entertainment and the European attitude that religion is a private matter. Yet Turkish society as a whole remains religious to roughly the same degree as the peoples of Egypt and Iran. About 80 percent of all three populations report that God is "very important" in their lives.[4] The regime found itself teaching religion in the public schools to advance the "correct" Islam, and in the 1950s it opened special schools for preachers. Immensely popular, these religious schools were soon pumping graduates not just into the mosques and teaching positions but also into business and the bureaucracy. Muslim organizations did their part with study groups and scholarships. "Islamic businesses" began to flourish, and prosperous businesses funded Islamist organizations. The political culture, never as broadly secular as the Kemalists would have wished, began to appear more and more religious in attitude even as it advanced toward liberal democracy. Any Kemalist hope of generating a monolithic, secular political culture in Turkey had disappeared by the twenty-first century.

Religion has again become an important element in Turkish identity.[5] Two Turkish scholars write: "Although Turkey has been strictly secular since 1928, Islam is becoming the semi-official religion of Turkey."[6] Pinar Tank calls contemporary Turkey a "semi-secular state."[7] The secularist ideology demanding complete separation of religion from political life has broken down, and state monopoly of religious life has failed. The political culture has come to be marked by high religiosity, strong commitment to democracy and liberalism, and marked plurality of religious and political commitments. Turkey seems to be reintegrating the religious and the political as it charges toward more democratic political arrangements.

Identity

To speak of equilibrium under the Ottoman Empire would be to suggest that religion played the same role in 1300 as it did six hundred years later. While Islam constituted an element of Ottoman identity from beginning to end, the role and significance of religion changed continuously. The founder of the eponymous state, Ösman (Turkish version of Uthman, the name of the third caliph), won fame as a warrior for the faith on the southern frontier of the Byzantine Empire. M. Hakan Yavuz writes: "Frontier societies tend to be fluid, institutionally fragmented, and multiple in their loyalties and shared understandings—laws, norms, customs, and overlapping roles."[8] Islam was one basis, but not the sole basis, of the Ottoman state. David Kushner writes:

In time the dynasty acquired the sanctity which kept it in power for centuries. An Ottoman gentleman, until well into the nineteenth century, would therefore identify himself as a Muslim and an Ottoman, never as a Turk, a term which was used either to differentiate between Turks and non-Turks, or as a derogatory reference to the ignorant peasant or nomad of Anatolia.[9]

The Ottoman state built its legal system on the sharia (*şeriat* in Turkish), but the periphery "maintained its segmentary Sufi and eclectic character."[10] The empire came to encompass multiple ethnic groups—Turks, Kurds, Arabs, Armenians, Greeks, and so forth—and multiple minority religions, including Judaism and Christianity. The Ottomans saw themselves as Muslims but also as the successors of the Roman Empire.[11]

The identification of the Ottoman state with Islam came under pressure in the nineteenth century both from within and from outside the empire. Ottoman losses to the Russians in the north and then to the French in Egypt led the sultans, starting with Selim III, to begin a process of modernization, first of military forces and then of political institutions. The suppression in 1826 of the janissary corps, which had once been the fearsome heart of the Ottoman infantry, and the issuance of the Rose Chamber Rescript in 1839 demonstrated an Ottoman effort at defensive modernization. The principles of the *tanzimat* (reorganization) first articulated in the Rose Chamber Rescript, such as equal rights for and protection of minorities, derived from European thought and practice. The nationalist idea was driving European development in the wake of the French Revolution. Now the Ottomans began to cultivate the idea of a national monarchy. With a new emphasis on Ottomanism, they sought to bring together "all peoples living in Ottoman domains, Muslim and non-Muslim, Turkish and Greek, Armenian and Jewish, Kurd and Arab."[12]

By the second half of the century a group of intellectuals calling themselves the New Ottomans began to criticize these policies. Namik Kemal, perhaps the most prominent thinker of the group, faulted the Ottomans for inattention to the sharia: "The Ottoman state is based on religious principles and if these principles are violated, the political existence of the state will be in danger."[13] Kemal saw Islam as the key to legitimacy and believed the sharia to be consistent with constitutional politics and educational reform. Any such appeal to Islamic identity tended, of course, to divide the empire's Muslim and non-Muslim subjects.

At the end of the nineteenth century, a powerful, reform-minded, autocratic sultan, Abdülhamid II, took some of Kemal's advice. Although the sultan ignored Kemal's plea for constitutionalism—in fact, in 1876, Abdülhamid had set aside the constitution accepted by his predecessor—he invoked Islam as a rallying point for the empire. He called himself caliph, a title initially adopted by the immediate successors to the Prophet Muhammad as leaders of the entire Muslim community. In doing so, he reached out to Muslims beyond the Ottoman domains as well as to Sufi orders within, even as he promoted reform. He opened new schools at the elementary and secondary levels to offer both European education and Islamic instruction under the same roof. These schools began to produce graduates who entered the bureaucracy and began to influence policy. "In other words," writes Yavuz, "in the process of transforming society, the state itself was transformed by societal forces."[14] Abdülhamid used Islamism to further reform.

In 1906 the Young Turk movement staged a revolt and won control of the empire. The insurgents appealed to Turkism rather than either Ottomanism or Islamism as the rallying point of the endangered empire. That decision exposed Armenians, Kurds, and other minorities to discrimination and even subsequent massacre. Suspected of sympathizing with Russia, the Armenians of eastern Anatolia died during World War I in what contemporary Armenians and most scholars regard as genocide. (Turkey has systematically denied wrongdoing.) The Young Turks opted to join Germany and the Austro-Hungarian Empire in that war, a choice that brought defeat and partition at the hands of the victorious allies. Russia, Britain, France, Greece, Italy—all were to have their piece of the Ottoman pie at the end of World War I.

The Europeans imposed the Treaty of Sèvres on the defeated Ottomans in 1920, but a group of Young Turk officers refused to accept foreign occupation. They challenged Greek forces for control of Anatolia and did not hesitate to use Islam in their efforts to rally non–Turkish speakers, especially the Kurds who dominated southeastern Anatolia, to the armed struggle. Mustafa Kemal, an officer in the Ottoman military and a Young Turk who had distinguished himself at the battle of Gallipoli in 1915 against British, French, and Australian forces, emerged to lead the struggle for Turkish independence.

Breaking with Islamic Identity

After the war waged for Turkish independence, religion temporarily preempted language in defining nationalism for those who had fled the new Turkey for Greece and who had left Greece for the new Turkey.[15] Only after victory was secure and an independent Turkey had emerged from the 1923 Treaty of Lausanne did Mustafa Kemal take radical measures against both the political and the religious establishments of the truncated empire. Breaking with the Ottoman dynasty proved much less difficult than distancing the new Turkey from Islam. The proclamation of the Turkish republic in 1923 ended the Ottoman experiment with a "national monarchy."[16] However, the attachment to Islam depended on more than just Abdülhamid's proclamation of the caliphate—which the new republic now abolished. The attachment also depended on the power and prestige of the ulama, a legal system the ulama helped administer and schools they ran, Sufi orders such as the Bektaşis and the Nakşibendis, and a set of symbols that tied Turkey to Islam and to the old regime. Mustafa Kemal and his supporters (subsequently referred to as the Kemalists) acted against all these dimensions of the Ottoman heritage.

The Kemalists sought to revive Turkishness as an identity for the new nation-state and to portray Ottoman Islam as a symbol of backwardness. Istanbul had been the capital of the Ottoman Empire ever since its conquest from the Byzantines in 1453, a trophy city that, as Constantinople, had been the most important city in Christendom before it became the most important city of Islam. Its mosques and palaces are among the most famous in the Muslim world. Yet the Kemalists abandoned Istanbul as their capital in favor of Ankara, a small town in Anatolia of no particular religious or political distinction, dramatizing their intent to reshape Turkish identity. The decision to abandon the Arabic script used to write Ottoman Turkish and to adopt the Western alphabet for modern Turkish further emphasized the shift. Arabic is the language of the ulama and the Quran everywhere in the Muslim world. Its alphabet also serves the Persian language, which was the literary language of Ottoman elites. By adopting the

European alphabet, Mustafa Kemal tipped Turkish identity toward Europe and favored an elite already familiar with European languages.

The Kemalists exalted in "pure" Turkishness as the badge of authenticity, evoking pre-Islamic Turkish history and customs to justify social changes such as the uncovering of women in public places.[17] Women in ball gowns and bathing suits became symbols of the new Turkey.[18] A Turkish woman introduced as the granddaughter of the last shaykh al-Islam, the chief religious official of the Ottoman Empire, won the Miss World beauty pageant in 1932.[19] Ibrahim Kaya writes: "The appearance of women who broke with the Islamic tradition was to be a major sign of a new form of social life."[20]

Mustafa Kemal Atatürk convinced much of the world that he had effectively cut Turkey free of its identity with Islam. The West applauded. Scholarship of the 1960s portrayed him as a secularizing, modernizing hero, a model for the Middle East.[21] Some Muslims described Atatürk as one of the great enemies of Islam. Both views now appear extreme. Rather than suppressing Islamic identity in Turkey, Atatürk actually cultivated it, politicizing religion and making religious reaction almost inevitable. By abolishing sharia courts and closing the meeting places of the Sufi brotherhoods, he struck blows against versions of Islam he deemed inimical to the new Turkey, even as he created the Directorate of Religious Affairs to control and propagate an Islam he thought benign. Ümit Cizre has written: "Atatürk set in motion the republican tradition of employing Islam to promote the ideas and policies of the secular state."[22] The Turkish masses outside the capital and even in the middle- and lower-class neighborhoods of Istanbul remained attached to the substance and symbols of Islam.

The failure of the Kemalists to establish a viable equilibrium of religion and politics became evident after 1950. When Atatürk's successors opened the system to competitive elections after World War II, the Republican People's Party lost its control of the country. The victors of 1950, the Democrats, made clear their sympathies with the rural areas and their sensitivity to religious belief. In the next decade, the Democrats began a long process of bringing Islam back into public life. The process continued in the 1960s under the Justice Party and further accelerated in the 1970s with the emergence of the National Outlook movement, which spawned a series of Islamist parties, including the National Order Party, the National Salvation Party, the Welfare Party, the Virtue Party, and, finally, the Felicity Party.

Bringing Back Islam

The transition from the Kemalist effort to separate Turkey from centuries of identity with Islam toward the reintegration of Islam into Turkish identity has already spanned more than half a century. Three moments stand out as turning points in the progressive modification of the Turkish identity.

The first moment came when the army, intervening in 1980 after a decade of conflict and violence, recognized the needs of ordinary Turks by making religious instruction mandatory in primary and secondary schools. The military wrote this requirement into the 1982 constitution.[23] President Kenan Evren, dressed in military uniform, delivered sermons "as if he were the Grand Mufti," writes Ersin Kalaycioğlu.[24] As representatives of Atatürk's memory and policies, the military legitimated the reintroduction of Islam into politics.

The second important moment came in the form of a remarkable leader, Turgut Özal. Once the military had returned politics to the politicians, Özal assumed power at the head of the Motherland Party. By breaking with protectionist policies and opening the country to international competition, he triggered economic expansion and political liberalization. He also spoke publicly about his religious devotion. Henry Barkey describes him as being "as comfortable with Western leaders as in a mosque."[25] Özal was the first prime minister of the Turkish republic to identify openly with Islam and, even more particularly, with Sufism, a variety of Islam disdained by early Kemalism. He was a member of a Sufi order, and "to him, rather than being a burden, [Islam] was an asset that could be utilized for the stability and prosperity of the country."[26] By recalling Ottomanism and its acceptance of plural identities, he sought to bring the Kurds, alienated by Turkish unwillingness to recognize their culture, back into the political fold: "Our state is secular. But what holds our nation together, what serves in a most powerful way in our national cohesiveness and what plays the essential role, is Islam."[27]

The sweeping victory of the Justice and Development Party in 2002 under the leadership of Recep Tayyip Erdoğan constitutes the third moment. Erdoğan came out of the National Outlook movement, which sought to identify Islam with Turkish nationalism and the future of Turkey. Elected as mayor of Istanbul in the 1990s, he scandalized Kemalists by proposing a mosque in the city's Taksim Square with a minaret among the tallest in the Middle East. Taksim is the neighborhood the Kemalists had chosen for their administrative hub to escape the Islamic architecture and influence of the old city center south of the Golden Horn. Istanbul became the capital of "an alternative, Islamist, nationalist project."[28] Erdoğan welcomed a United Nations conference on habitat in 1996 in an effort to advance a new vision of national identity. The accession of his Justice and Development Party (AKP) to power with an overwhelming parliamentary majority in 2002 demonstrated that the Turkish political system, far from purging itself of Islamic influence, had been Islamized even as it sought to democratize and liberalize as preparation for entry into a predominantly Christian Europe.

This account neglects the contribution of Necmettin Erbakan and the National Outlook movement (Milli Görüş). His party, Welfare (Refah), assumed the leadership of the Turkish government in 1996 as part of a coalition. The soft coup that brought Erbakan's resignation in 1997 reflected his inability, despite his rather mild but awkward attempts to enact the Welfare Party's agenda, to bring Kemalists and the military into his project. Yet his effort was one of enhancing and enlarging the Turkish national identity, not undercutting it in the name of an internationalist Islam. He saw himself and his movement as saving the Turkish state by restoring its Islamic identity. His party advocated a Just Order (Adil Düzen) to effect a "division of labor and equality among the Muslim brothers comprising all ethnic groups of Turkey."[29] Banned from politics after the dissolution of the Welfare Party, Erbakan must have watched with some amazement when only five years later his protégé, Erdoğan, managed an electoral victory without triggering further military intervention. Erdoğan had tweaked the Islamist message and wooed support in quarters where Erbakan could not have hoped to be successful.

Contemporary Islamism

The reemergence of Islam in Turkish identity opens the way toward reconciliation with the Ottoman past, which in turn links Turkey to Europe. The Ottomans constituted a formidable European power from the moment they outflanked the Byzantines to establish a beachhead in Europe until their defeat in World War I. The core of Istanbul stands on the European side of the Bosporus, together with a smidgen of hinterland that permits a continued geographic claim to be a part of both Europe and Asia, the bridge between the two. Ottoman elites hailed from the Balkans, and Balkan refugees swelled the population of Anatolia in the last years of the empire, as it progressively lost European provinces.[30] If the European Union (EU) were to admit Turkey to full membership, one would expect even greater dependence on Ottomanism and its tolerance for ethnic and religious minorities in the further construction of Turkish political identity.

However, the renewed identification of the Turkish state with Islam may complicate the Turkish case for entry into the EU, although Europeans have never ceased to identify Turkey with Islam and Muslims. Kemalist secularism did not change the political complexion of the country any more than laïcité stripped France of its underlying Catholicism. Ninety-nine percent of all Turks carry identity cards indicating they are Muslims. The Turks were supporters of Bosnian Muslims after the breakup of Yugoslavia, as they are naturally advocates of Turkish emigrants who reside in Germany and elsewhere in Europe. Under Islamist tutelage, the Turkish state has continued and even intensified its efforts to meet European conditions to qualify for entry into the EU. But its progress in this regard, together with Turkey's size and the power of its economy, both partly attributable to the success of the AKP government, have set off alarm bells in Europe and may end up defeating Turkey's application for membership.

The rediscovery of Islamic identity should facilitate the integration of Turkey's Kurdish minority—distinct in language from the Turkish majority but united with most Turks by religion. The National Outlook movement and the AKP have enjoyed strong support in the Kurdish areas, but the government has not been able to translate that support into a remedy for the Kurdish problem. According to one analyst, Prime Minister Erdoğan sees ethnicity as a lesser form of identity, subordinate to nationalism anchored in Islam and a broad under-standing of Turkishness. The AKP owes much of its success to support in the rural, backward, peripheral parts of Turkey, of which the southeast, where most Kurds live, is a part. In this posture, the party opposes the urban, intellectual elites who have dominated the state. The AKP shares Kurdish votes with a secular party linked to the PKK, which has long demanded regional autonomy and engaged in violence. But the AKP under Erdoğan shows no signs of di-minishing the reach or strength of the centralized Turkish state created under Kemalist rule.

The downside of heightened emphasis on Islam lies in the alienation of hard-line Kemalists, some of them heterodox Muslims known as Alevis. The Ottomans identified formally with Sunni Islam. The Islamist movement in Turkey has been Sunni in general orientation, while Alevis, who believe that Ali, the nephew and son-in-law of the Prophet, should be seen as his rightful successor, have much in common with Shii Islam. The syncretistic beliefs and practices of Alevism, however, make Alevis suspect in the eyes of many Muslims, both Sunni and Shii. Faruk Bilici argues that Alevis have, in fact, played an important role in Turkish Islam by raising questions such as "Which Islam? Which Quran? Which Sunna?"[31] Asking those questions and implying that there is more than one possible answer does not win them friends among devout Sunnis and many in the Islamist movement. Alevis constitute between 10 percent and 25 percent of the Turkish population. Some are Kurds.

A majority of Alevis have been sympathetic to the secularism of Kemalism, and some have gone beyond Kemalism to support parties of the extreme left.[32] Some highly religious Alevis feel close to Iranian Shiism and share its belief in twelve legitimate imams, starting with Ali. They want a return to the sharia. Another strain of Alevism centers on Bektaşi Sufism, its associations, and its lodges. It tends to be mystical and apolitical. Ultranationalist Alevis tend to see themselves as authentic inheritors of ancient Turkish tradition. Alevis have thus been anything but united in their political views, but the rise of the Islamist parties triggered an Alevi revival both in Germany and in Turkey. An Alevi manifesto issued in 1990 called for acceptance of the Alevi faith and culture and equal opportunities in education and politics. Many Alevis fear that Islamist efforts to reassert the centrality of Islam will lead to suppression of their own heterodox practices.

The greatest benefit of the gradual reintegration of Islam into Turkey's political identity lies, however, in the solidification of Turkish democracy that appears to have occurred with the victory of Erdoğan and his Justice and Development Party. The party captured not just support of National Outlook voters, who had brought Erbakan to office in the 1990s, but a broad swath of center-right voters who had swelled the ranks of the Democratic Party in the 1950s, the Justice Party in the 1960s, and Özal's Motherland Party in the 1980s. Erdoğan's victory was as much about class as religion, as shown by Turkish reactions when he sent his daughters to the United States for education: "He is no longer a Muslim."[33] It was said he had betrayed his class and his religion, but his actions also demonstrated that he was not a religious ideologue. His colloquial

Turkish, his inattention to dress on some occasions, and his clumsiness at ballroom dance all helped him cement his identification with the rural, nonelitist classes neglected by the Kemalist tradition. The Islamic idiom has helped him to do that.

Political identity is always a work in progress.[34] Islamism, Ottomanism, Turkism, Westernism—all became tools for the construction of a national identity, even though each of the concepts lends itself to transnational interpretation. While Turkey has reached out to the Turkish-speaking republics of Central Asia, those states have not warmed to the formation of a trans-Turkish union. Turkey has shown little enthusiasm to unite with all Muslims in a revival of the umma (the community of all believers), and none for the revival of Ottomanism. The drive to enter Europe reflects a desire to further strengthen the nation in economic and political terms rather than a wish to escape the nation-state formula and the bundle of identities it represents. Fortunately for the Turks, the EU remains a group of states with multiple identities, not a superstate with a monolithic perception of itself.

Ideology

Kemalist ideology emerged in the context of late-nineteenth-century European ideologies, spurred by a philosophical movement called logical positivism, whose proponents argued that truth must be empirically verifiable. Natural science produced hypotheses. When those hypotheses could be verified empirically, positivists took them as truth. Observations such as "God exists" cannot be verified and do not satisfy the positivist criterion for truth. Marx claimed to be a scientist whose theories explained the dynamics of history and the workings of the capitalist system. While rejecting Marx, Weber and other sociologists offered theories of modernization and change that pushed religion to the margins of society. Durkheim posited that societies create religions to satisfy social needs. The more modern the society, the less it needed religion. In positivist perspective, the secularization of European society had come to be fact, not mere theory, at the end of the nineteenth century and the beginning of the twentieth. Positivists came to see religion as superstition. In Turkey those educated in science who imbibed this notion felt estrangement from those who followed a course of religious study. The Ottomans had looked to France to help them modernize education.

The military schools in which Mustafa Kemal and other Young Turks received their educations reflected the influence of the French curriculum. At a moment when France was regarded as the quintessential modern country, the Third French Republic (1871–1940) found itself deeply at odds with the Catholic Church. Not until 1896 did the Catholic Church rally to support the republic, but the Radical Party, largely defined by its hostility to the Church, joined socialists to press for the secularization of education and the body politic. The French vision of secularism comported overt suspicion of the Church and produced a political arena where any reference to personal religious belief came to be seen as improper.

Kemalism

Mustafa Kemal established an ideological state in Turkey. "All new ideologies are in essence oppositional," writes Mansoor Moaddel.[35] The republicanism and nationalism of the French Revolution responded to the monarchy. Marxism emerged in opposition to capitalism. Secular nationalism in Turkey, fueled by positivism, used the Ottoman Empire as its foil. Mustafa Kemal set out to reshape the lives and even the consciousness of his fellow citizens by indoctrinating them with the new ideology, which was unabashedly Western.

> This state not only claimed the monopoly of the legitimate use of the physical means of violence, to use Weber's terminology, but also a monopoly of the means and content of legitimate discourse. . . . Cultural expression was at the same time political expression. Cultural opposition was also political opposition.[36]

Questions of dress were fundamental. The fez, adopted by the Ottomans in the early nineteenth century as modern headgear, was proclaimed passé. Only the European hat was suitable for a modern man. In 1926 a decree prohibited the wearing of the veil in public places. Images of Atatürk in a tuxedo, the elegant host of ballroom dancing, suggested a new standard for the elite. Not even clergy could wear traditional Muslim garb, except when they were exercising their functions.

By putting costume at the forefront of cultural concerns and by focusing on the role of women in society, Kemalists responded to the Western image of the Muslim world. The Orientalist fixation on the veiled eroticism of the East stirred

Kemalist response. The adoption of a secular civil code in 1926 replaced the sharia and opened the way for the advancement of women. It continued to treat men as heads of households and required women to obtain permission to work outside the home, but it outlawed polygamy and marriage by proxy and accorded equal rights to women in divorce, custody, and inheritance. Women received the right to vote in 1934–35.[37] While rural women remained largely beyond the scope of this "state feminism," the results were nonetheless impressive. Jenny White calls Turkey "one of the most important success stories of women's empowerment in the early twentieth century."[38]

The empowerment began with the adoption of the Swiss Civil Code in 1926, which Yeşim Arat calls "arguably the most revolutionary undertaking of the Kemalist regime in the newly founded Republic."[39] When feminists finally managed to achieve amendment of that code in 2001, removing reference to men as the head of their families and changing rules of property ownership, the debate in Turkey's parliament, the Grand National Assembly, turned primarily on the original rationale for Turkey's adoption of the Swiss code. That rationale provided a powerful statement of Kemalist ideology:

> Not to change is a necessity for religions. For this reason, that religions should remain matters of conscience is one of the principles of the civilization of the present century and of the most important elements that distinguish the new civilization from the old. Laws that derive their principles from religions . . . constitute one of the major factors and reasons impending progress. . . . As a matter of fact, the stipulations of the religious Ottoman code are doubtlessly irreconcilable with contemporary civilization. But it is also obvious that the Ottoman code and similar other religious regulations are not reconcilable with Turkish national life.[40]

Islamist parties, among them the newly organized AKP, objected to including such language in the amended version, arguing that it was demeaning of religion and Turkish traditions. But there was relatively little debate over the substantive changes in the amendment or even on the role of women in the society. The question was not whether Turkey should continue to modernize and Westernize, but whether the progress of women depends upon the elimination of religious influence from public life.[41]

The armed forces came to epitomize and defend secular values. Atatürk took power on the shoulders of the Turkish military, victorious over the Greeks in the fighting that followed World War I. His army saw itself as the vanguard of the modernization movement. The military still occupies a privileged position in the constitution. It enjoys "an autonomy that no other democratic state would accept," powerful in its control of the National Security Council and solid in its relationship to big business.[42] The officer corps enjoys superior schools and acquires a sharp sense of duty to protect the state against external threats and "dangerous" people and ideas. As Stephen Kinzer writes, "an officer who prays, shuns alcohol or is married to a woman who wears a head scarf not only is an unlikely candidate for advancement but runs the risk of being cashiered."[43] The military has been the guarantor of secularist ideology.

Secularist ideology must be distinguished from mere secularism. The Kemalists did not merely abolish the sultanate or caliphate and undermine the political authority of the ulama. They established an official version of Islam and sought to outlaw or discredit every other version. Propelled by positivist thinking, Kemalist ideology drew a line between modern and traditional, urban and rural, "white Turks" and "black Turks," the cultured and the uncultured, enlightenment and superstition, elites and masses.[44] Yavuz says that "members of Turkey's elite and foreign dignitaries marched to Chopin music, while the masses marched to Qur'anic chants."[45] Or, as Orhan Pamuk, born into a wealthy Istanbul family, recalls:

> As westernized, positivist property owners, we had the right to govern over these semiliterates, and we had an interest in preventing their getting too attached to their superstitions—not just because it suited us privately but because our country's future depended on it. If my grandmother discovered that an electrician had gone off to pray, even I could tell that her sharp comment had less to do with the small repair job he had left unfinished than with the "traditions and practices" that were impeding "our national progress." [46]

Turkey's enemy, "medieval" Islam, lurked within the country.[47]

Kemalist ideology posited a dichotomy between science and religion, modernity and tradition, but that dichotomy began to erode even as ideological Kemalism continued to dominate the political scene. One important factor was an extraordinary individual, Said Nursi, who suffered through government harassment, trials, and imprisonments to attain the status of sainthood among his followers. Bediüzzaman ("without equal in our times") Said Nursi combined popular religion with an appeal to literacy and reason that challenged the dichotomy Kemalists were making between tradition and modernity. A nationalist from start to finish, Nursi denied he was undermining the state by using religion for political purposes, but the Kemalists felt threatened by the following he generated no matter where they forced him to live.

The Nur Movement

Said Nursi crossed intellectual boundaries. Born into a Kurdish family in Bitlis near Van in eastern Anatolia, Nursi struggled to bring modern, university-level education to the Kurdish region. The son of an *alim*, a man of religion (the plural term is *ulama*), he distinguished himself as a boy by his prodigious memory and capacity for learning, but he never permitted his erudition to separate him from the Nakşibendi (Sufi) environment that nurtured his spiritual instincts or from popular religion that deviated from the practices of the formal Sufi orders. Endowed with personal magnetism and the qualities of a Sufi shaykh—sometimes he acknowledged divine inspiration and sometimes he denied it—he gathered disciples and followers in the traditional Sufi pattern but then insisted on burial in an unknown tomb, to prevent his worship after death.[48] Unlike a traditional Sufi shaykh, he created a body of writing called the *Risale-e Nur* (*Epistle of Light*), which he regarded as his legacy. He pushed his followers toward the study of text and away from the adoration of a holy man in the Sufi tradition.

Nursi fought Kemalist secularism without trying to create a counterideology. He had sought to shore up the failing Ottoman state in its final decade. He joined the army to fight against the Russians on the Eastern Front in World War I without jumping on the anti-Armenian bandwagon. He supported the republic from its beginnings in 1923 and redoubled his efforts to get a university established in Kurdistan. As Mustafa Kemal steered the country toward a radical separation of religion and state, the proposal for a university languished in the Grand National Assembly, and Nursi, "the New Said," gave up on politics and launched a spiritual renaissance. Nursi quoted himself as having told Atatürk, who had offered him a job in the public service as a preacher: "The New Said wants to work for the next world and cannot work for you, but he will not interfere with you either."[49] Bringing Islam in line with science and modernity was part of Nursi's project. Merging the lessons of formal Islam with those of popular religion was another. Nursi's idiom was Sufi even though he did not try to found a new Sufi order.

Although Nursi did not support the Kurdish Revolt of 1925, the government used that uprising as an excuse to move Nursi out of the east and into forced residence in the province of Isparta in western Anatolia. The government claimed that Nursi represented the superstition and mysticism that Mustafa Kemal identified with the Ottomans. Nursi irritated the authorities by wearing his turban in defiance of dress laws. ("The turban comes off with the head," he said in 1943.) He wrote his great work, the *Epistle of Light*, in the forbidden Arabic script. Nursi had learned Turkish as a third language after Kurdish and Arabic. His somewhat stilted prose, heavy in words of Arabic derivation, evokes the spirit of the Quran. He believed that the Ottomans had fallen on hard times not from devotion to religion but because they had neglected Islam. Modernism with its emphasis on materialism was diverting Turkish Muslims from their ethical responsibilities. Nursi nurtured a spiritual revival.

It was probably Nursi's modernism even more than his traditionalism that irritated the Kemalist authorities. Nursi had supported the Constitutionalist movement and the deposition of Sultan Abdülhamid. He favored progress and opposed despotism.[50] He argued for the integration of a modern curriculum into the advanced schools of religious learning, the *madrasas* (*medrese*). Nursi must have seemed dangerous to the government, because he pushed his followers to read texts and analyze them, to think about religious issues in a modern way, to go beyond oral transmission of scripture and clerical intermediaries to confront spiritual questions on their own. Secular culture was book culture.[51] Nursi pushed his followers toward book culture to oppose secularism, weakening the government effort to link Islam with superstition and backwardness.

Even without a printing press at his disposal, Nursi managed to reach a broad public. The government prevented publication of the *Epistle of Light*, but his disciples copied it by hand and distributed it in channels beyond government control. It is estimated that various versions of this work had been copied 600,000 times before it reached print in the new alphabet in 1956.[52] At his trials (and there were many, because the government would not give up on prosecuting him), Nursi argued that genuine secular government would make all citizens free to practice any religion they wished.[53] He professed utter loyalty to the Turkish republic and Turkish law. This modern savvy saved his neck and irritated the Kemalists.

Nursi threatened the regime by exposing the ideological, positivistic, and religious character of the Kemalist commitment to secularism. His fearlessness, willingness to endure deprivation, ability to inspire devotion in his followers, and eloquence in articulating his message made him a formidable opponent for the Kemalists. His work opened the way for challenges to Kemalist practice in the 1950s, after the Democratic Party took power. Nursi even modified his apolitical stance to endorse the Democrat program, which put religion back in public schools and led to the creation of Imam-Hatip schools to prepare preachers and teachers. But the Nur movements that were inspired by Nursi's book and that continue to animate modern Turkey have, for the most part, retained the founder's distaste for ideology and honored his fondness for education and spirituality. Fethullah Gülen, the most prominent of Nursi's disciples (who are known as Nurcus), continues to combine pragmatism, modernism, and a commitment to education with a core belief that Turkey must be true to its Islamic heritage.[54]

The Kemalist elite cut themselves off from the masses with their ideology of secularism and authoritarian approach to enforcement. Yavuz writes: "By suppressing Islam, the state ruptured the formative ties between politics and culture, and this estranged the majority of the population from the state."[55] Nursi addressed that estrangement. Şerif Mardin suggests Nursi responded to aspirations arising from the mobilization of a "new class," "the middling level of the rural and small-town population of Turkey."[56] Nursi was pulling this class toward a modern, text-based world once reserved for the elites but was doing it in a familiar, recognizable idiom. New economic opportunities and modern schools had begun to produce fresh ambitions together with frustrations at the erosion of established customs. The communications revolution had begun to bring the countryside in touch with the shocking, Westernized habits of the Turkish elites and a government bent on steamrolling particularistic customs into a smooth, monolithic culture.

The Nurcus were not alone in reaching the relatively disempowered segments of Turkish society before 1950. The Kemalists had banned the Sufi orders (*tariqat*) and bolted the doors of their meeting places, the *tekkes*, but the orders merely went underground. Hamid Algar discusses one such order: "The Naqsh-bandiya, with its sobriety and emphasis upon the sharia, could well dispense with the tekkes, and it was thus particularly well-equipped to defy the attempted abolition of the tariqats."[57] Nursi had himself come from a Nakşibendi environment. The Nakşibendi, who take their name from Baha al-Din Naqshbad from Bukhara (d. 1389), look to Maulana Khalid (b. 1776) of Kurdistan as their founder. In the modern era, the order has split into many sections following different shaykhs, some oriented toward Kurdistan and others involved in opposing Mustafa Kemal's secular state. One spin-off group, the Süleymancis, engaged themselves in creating underground Quranic schools with the explicit aim of colonizing the government's Directorate of Religious Affairs, which controlled official Islam.[58]

When Atatürk's successors opened the door to multiparty competition, the opposition parties sought votes among the "black Turks" of the hinterland, where the Nur movements and the Sufi orders had been carefully working the terrain. The ideology of the Republican People's Party did not change, and even the opposition parties—first the Democrats and then their successors in the Justice Party—did not challenge the notion of the secular state. Instead, they reached out toward popular Islam with small reforms that produced important long-term consequences. They co-opted the Nurcus and the Nakşibendi, or at least important segments of their groups, to support Imam-Hatip schools for the training of preachers and prayer leaders, to create a faculty of divinity at Ankara University, to permit the use of Arabic in the call to prayer, to authorize religious radio broadcasts, and to make religious instruction available in primary schools on a voluntary basis. The Democratic Party enacted these measures to win votes.[59]

The military coup of 1960 threatened to interrupt this movement toward the accommodation of popular Islam, but in fact the military junta, which produced a new constitution and then put government back in the care of civilians, did not reverse the trend. In fact, General Cemal Gürsel, interim president, proclaimed: "The cause of our backwardness is not our religion but those who have misrepresented our religion to us. Islam is the most sacred, most constructive, most dynamic and powerful religion in the world." For him there were, however, two Islams: "one secular and dispassionate, the other reactionary."[60] It was both a restatement and a softening of Kemalist secularism.

The military had abolished the Democratic Party and executed its leader, Adnan Menderes, but the Justice Party, which emerged to dominate in the 1960s, endorsed many of the Democratic Party's policies toward Islam. Fear of communism and the Soviet Union dominated Turkish politics in both the 1950s and the 1960s. The Justice Party saw Islam as a counterforce and a link to its allies on the right. The government brought a few Muslim technocrats into the government and cultivated the support of the tariqat and the Nurcus, but it did not launch a direct assault on the long-standing ideology of secularism.[61]

Islamist Ideology

Ideological opposition emerged first in the 1970s with the National Outlook (Milli Görüş) movement, which spawned a series of political parties over the next thirty years. The founder was a prominent Nakşibendi, Mehmet Zahid Kotku (1807–1980), who believed that much of Turkish society would support a politics based on identity and justice.[62] The name *Milli* (*millet*, a term used by the Ottomans to designate religious groups) already evokes religion as the national focus and suggests opposition to cosmopolitanism and Westernism. "National View" is an alternative translation of Milli Görüş.[63] With Just Order (Adil Düzen) as its only genuine platform, the movement suggested a return to the sharia without actually committing itself to that objective. The National Outlook movement appealed directly to the "other" Turkey, with a "reconstruction of Ottoman-Turkish norms and associations to challenge the alienating aspects of the Kemalist project of radical positivism."[64]

The state suppressed every political party created by the National Outlook movement, repeatedly enforcing a law against religious parties, the names of which hinted at religion but did not refer directly to Islam. The National Order Party, banned in 1971, became the National Salvation Front, which eventually gave way to the Welfare Party. When Welfare was outlawed, the Virtue Party surfaced, only to disappear quickly in favor of Felicity. Every name bore religious connotations. And the leadership fell primarily to one man, Necmettin Erbakan, first elected in 1969 to the Grand National Assembly. In 1974 he became a deputy prime minister when his National Salvation Party joined a coalition government. But the great success of the National Outlook movement came twenty years later, when the Welfare Party took control of twenty-nine large municipalities.

In the parliamentary elections of the following year, it won 21.4 percent of the vote and 158 of 550 seats. Erbakan stepped to the fore as prime minister of a coalition government.

The National Outlook movement did not initiate the politicization of religion in Turkey. The Ottomans had taken steps in that direction, and Mustafa Kemal had moved several steps further by attempting to force a single official version of Islam on the country. The opposition parties of the 1950s and 1960s had used Islam to enhance their appeal in the rural areas and small towns of Anatolia. But it was the National Outlook movement that imparted an ideological fervor to Islamism. It offered an alternative version of Turkish nationalism to the secular ideology (and official religion) of the Kemalist state.

The appeal of Islamist ideology suffered from the policies of Turgut Özal, the soft coup of 1997, and the acts of an extremist group, the Turkish Hizbullah.[65] First as prime minister and then as president, Özal opened Turkey to the world with his policies of economic liberalization. He resisted secularism, state control of the economy, and nationalism as homogenizing influences in favor of tolerance for minorities, whether ideological, religious, or ethnic. A devout Muslim, he worked to bridge the differences between the religious and secular communities. Yet, despite his efforts to blunt the Islamist appeal, an economic downturn in the 1990s, combined with international tensions, brought the Welfare Party to power in 1995.

The Turkish armed forces, with their eighteen directives to Prime Minister Erbakan on February 28, 1997, seemed to have struck Islamism a fatal blow. In Yavuz's words, "the goal of the military was to roll back the Muslim sectors of civil society by closing off their opportunity spaces."[66] When the Constitutional Court closed down the Welfare Party in January 1998, it said the party had violated "the principles of the secular Republic." It enforced Kemalist ideology.

A shootout at a villa on the Bosporus in January 2000 led to the discovery of a reign of terror by a Turkish organization known as Hizbullah, whose victims were thought to number at least sixty. Hundreds of arrests followed. Asli Aydıntaşbaş suggests that the state might have looked aside as Hizbullah built strength in the Kurdish areas, looking on it as a means to counter the radical Kurdistan Workers' Party, or PKK.[67] Hizbullah spread from the Kurdish zone into the squalid urban milieus of western Turkey. Aydıntaşbaş writes: "While not organically linked to the Islamists of the Virtue Party, Hizbullah certainly grew out of an atmosphere of tension between the secular state and the desires of political Islam." It was the first time that Turks had seen violence from Islamism, and the image of the Virtue Party and the National Outlook movement in general suffered as a result.[68]

The parliamentary elections of 2002, in which Recep Tayyip Erdoğan, the former Islamist mayor of Istanbul, led his AKP to overwhelming victory, may come to be regarded as the end of two ideologies: Kemalism and Islamism. Erdoğan appealed to the Islamists of the National Outlook movement, from which he came. But, unlike Erbakan, who was prime minister in 1996 and 1997, Erdoğan did not announce an Islamist agenda or even take immediate action on what Kemalists had long regarded as the headline issue, the head scarf. Pulling Islamists toward the system, he pushed them toward full support for global initiatives and entry into Europe. His policies were post-Islamist and post-Kemalist. He attempted to depoliticize religion.

Erdoğan takes his place among a set of Turkish leaders who have sought to bring Turkey back toward its Ottoman, Muslim heritage. Even the military, especially after the 1980 coup, has edged in this direction, even if the directives of 1997 represented a throwback to an earlier era.[69] By gradually separating themselves from the ideological secularism of Kemalism, these leaders have extended the reach of Turkish democracy to minorities and the rural areas, to those who have left the rural areas for the slums of the urban areas, to those who are just now feeling the effects of education and higher standards of living, to the nonelites whom Kemalists hoped to convert to "modern ways," and to all those for whom the Islamic idiom rings true and familiar.

Kemalists brought Turkey toward a liberal, democratic system, but their ferocious secularism eventually impeded further democratization. Islamism as an ideology helped undermine Kemalist ideology and brought conflict and crisis rather than reconciliation, but the return of Islam as a bridge to a plural, heterodox cultural heritage appears to be moving Turkey forward toward liberalism and inclusiveness. Nursi and the Nakşibendis initiated this change. Nurcus such as Fethullah Gülen have carried it forward. Islam as an identity draws together Kurds and Turks, Alevis and Sunnis, Sufi orders, various other practitioners of popular Islam, and so-called secular Muslims. In Turkey, the intensity of ideological conflict may be diminishing.

Institutions

Turkish secularism has never meant separation of church and state. Rather, the Turkish state sought to take complete control of every aspect of religion—prayer, language, preaching, teaching, meetings, doctrine, places of worship, personnel, calendar, finances, everything. A government agency called the Directorate of Religious Affairs was the state's primary tool. The Kemalists abolished, at least in theory, unofficial religious organizations and outlawed analysis or propaganda from any source suggesting that religion should count in public affairs. In taking these measures, they thought they were promoting modernity and condemning Ottomanism.

Democratization and liberalization opened the way for political parties. To combat the Kemalists and their Republican People's Party, the new parties needed to mobilize the minorities and the rural areas—the "other Turkey." The only organizations with strong roots in the "other" Turkey depended on religion as a bond. As industrialization and urbanization pulled people away from their familiar settings, they turned to religious associations for support, comfort, and advice. These parties and organizations found financial backing in a newly prosperous, small-town and rural bourgeoisie, partly created by the economic liberalization programs undertaken in the 1980s and partly held together by association with the Islamist movement. Their money financed newspapers, magazines, and television stations, where Islamist intellectuals talked and wrote about the relationship of religion to public life. More and more graduates of religious schools, funded by the state in deference to the pressures of these parties and movements, invaded the sanctuaries of the secular state, including the Directorate of Religious Affairs. In short, liberalization led to a relationship between organized religion and the state utterly different from that imagined by the early Kemalists.

The Ottomans looked to the mainstream Sunni tradition for legitimacy. They accorded a place of honor and responsibility to the ulama, scholars and prayer leaders who were the defenders of the sharia. Ottoman judges, the *cadis*, applied the sharia as well as the positive law (*qanun*) adopted by the Ottoman sultans. Many of the *qanun* reflected dispositions of the sharia. Not a part of the military-bureaucratic elite recruited by the *devshirme* (forced conscription) in the European provinces and converted to Islam, the ulama achieved a measure of autonomy from state control. As in other parts of the Islamic world, gifts in perpetuity for the support of religious institutions (*vaqf* in Turkish, or *waqf* in Arabic) ensured financial well-being. The ulama enjoyed close family connections with the Muslim bourgeoisie. The sultan appointed the shaykh al-Islam, chief of the religious establishment, from the corps of ulama, which tended to reproduce itself in a bourgeois milieu. Most important, the ulama derived power and influence by virtue of their specialized knowledge of Arabic and Islam.

As the Ottoman dynasty undertook modernization in the nineteenth century, it began to regard the ulama, some of whom objected to the guarantees of rights to minorities and to the moves to secularize schooling, as obstructionist. Bureaucrats began to echo the positivistic tendencies of European thought. Meanwhile, the Nakşibendi order expanded its networks all across Anatolia, perhaps as a response to the pressures for change. Islam itself appeared to be in flux. The last powerful Ottoman sultan, Abdülhamid II, renewed the dynasty's appeal to Islam, while other voices called for an Islamic constitutionalism that Abdülhamid had renounced. In short, the Ottoman state never enjoyed full control of religious organizations even at the height of its glory. Even Hamidian efforts to restore sultanic authority failed to counter the subversive effects of liberalization, which opened the way toward still greater pluralism and "multiple modernities."[70]

State Control and Beyond

The state has become much more realistic in assessing its influence on religion than it was in the early days of the republic. Ali Bardakoğlu, president of the Directorate of Religious Affairs from 2003 to 2010, acknowledged three sorts of influences over the public perception of Islam in contemporary Turkey: official agents, unofficial agents and institutions, and the mass media.[71] The directorate employs the official agents, who number 80,000. It controls 69,000 mosques and employs some 63,000 chaplains and preachers.[72] "Unofficial agents and institutions" run the gamut from local holy men through Nurcu and Sufi groups to political parties. The mass media have opened space for a new set of religiously oriented intellectuals.

Bardakoğlu insisted that the directorate did not impose a single understanding of Islam: "The Diyanet [directorate] does not support an essentialist idea of Islam." Yet he said his organization generated "authentic knowledge" and encouraged "sound knowledge and scholarship." He implied that some religious knowledge is inauthentic and unsound. The directorate does not regard religion merely as a "theoretical belief system," he said, but as a "sociological phenomenon."[73] With that statement, he acknowledged the diversity of Islam, ranging as it does from "mystical and folk Islam to a conservative and more moderate understanding of Islam." The directorate aims to foster "social peace and trust" by promoting tolerance, education, "independent" research, and "moderate" understandings of Islam. Bardakoğlu said that the Kemalist state created the directorate in an effort to create "moral religiosity."[74] The opposite would probably be "political religiosity" or perhaps "religious activism" rather than "immoral religiosity"!

The unofficial agents of Islam in Turkey fall into three categories: nonactivist and nonpolitical, activist and indirectly involved in politics, and explicitly political. The first category would include local holy men practicing varieties of folk religion loosely derived from a multiplicity of religious traditions and some of the Sufi orders. The mystical Alevism associated with Haci Bektaş Veli would be an example.[75] The second would include many offshoots of Nakşibendism, including the Nurcus, the Süleymancis, and the most prominent of the neo-Nurcu groups, the Fethullahci (followers of Fethullah Gülen), which have promoted education, economic development, and social mobilization. The third category consists of political parties, principally those associated with the National Outlook movement since 1969, together with their supporting groups.

The second category paved the way for the third. The Nakşibendi and the Nurcus supported the loosening of Kemalist secularism championed by the Democratic Party in the 1950s and the Justice Party in the 1960s, but their activities were aimed at promoting modern ideas and economic progress in the name of religious identity. Their success cannot be separated from the emergence of a new Islamist bourgeoisie capable of financing the movements and from the development of mass media—newspapers, radio, television, book publishing— by which their message was spread. The prominent Nakşibendi, Shaykh Kotku, "transformed the structure of the mosque-based community into a semi-political movement."[76] He became a spiritual adviser to Turgut Özal, the first prime minister to acknowledge his Sufi ties. Another major Nakşibendi leader, Süleyman Hilmi Tunahan (1888–1959), who took on consumer culture and secularism but also Wahhabism and Shii Islam, generated a following of some 4 million members. The Süleymancis dominated the Directorate of Religious Affairs until

1965, controlled a large number of mosques in Germany, and ran a network of dormitories for university students in Turkey.[77]

Said Nursi died in 1960 but his followers continued to meet and read aloud his *Epistle of Light*. The emphasis on text freed them from control of the official ulama and distinguished them from Sufi groups. Their meetings generated socioeconomic and even political networks. Yavuz writes: "The Nurcus are mostly university graduates who either work for small companies or own small businesses." He reports that their networks served as the means of distribution for a number of household products.[78] As time went on, they split into more than ten groups, the most prominent of them headed by Fethullah Gülen, who started his career as a state preacher in Edirne. He read Nursi and other Islamist thinkers and by the late 1960s had begun to build an organization. His basic thesis: In Seljuq and then Ottoman times, the Turks achieved an Islamic synthesis that draws not just on the Quran and the sunna but also on Sufism. In Gülen's own words, "Sufism has spread among Turks more than others."[79] Modern intellectuals must work from this synthesis, he argued. "He drew much of his support from engineers, the new Anatolian bourgeoisie, academics, and other professionals."[80] By the 1980s and until the soft coup of 1997, the Fethullahci exercised increasing influence in public life, with great emphasis on rationality, education, moderation, tolerance, and pursuit of the good life based on a religious understanding. More than Nursi, Gülen emphasized action. The movement bought a newspaper and made it into a leading daily, the fifth-largest newspaper in Turkey by 2002 and one distributed in thirteen countries with large Turkic, Muslim populations. The movement also owns a television station and radio stations.

The media explosion included many groups besides the Fethullahci. By 1994, Islamic groups owned nineteen television stations and forty-five radio stations.[81] The outpouring of books, journals, magazines, and newspapers reflected the advances in literacy achieved in Turkey and furthered the "creation of a new genre of Muslim intellectuals."[82] It represented a quantum leap in a trend initiated by Said Nursi that pulled Turks toward new forms of imagined community based on text and interpretation rather than personal, oral communication. While government agents and publications could compete in this new marketplace of ideas, they could not control the production of religious "knowledge."

The liberalization of economic policy under Turgut Özal in the 1980s favored this pluralization of Islam. As prime minister, Özal opened the Turkish economy to international competition and thus unleashed a more competitive business environment in Turkey itself. Soon these changes produced a new prosperity and a new Anatolian, Islamist middle class. Small and medium-sized businesses emerged to challenge the state-favored monopolies. Some of these new businesses made specific appeals to a religious clientele. Barber shops, bakeries, restaurants, resort hotels—even some in the luxury category, such as the Caprice on the Adriatic Coast—hung out signs that proclaimed friendliness to devout Muslims. Nilüfer Göle describes the trend: "The hotel suggests that Islamists are not immune to the seductive powers of consumption, pleasure, commodity, and property acquisition—the patterns dictated by global and local trends in the market economy. It underscores the transformative power of the market system in which leisure is 'Islamicized.'"[83]

Islamist businessmen formed an association called MÜSIAD, which built a membership of some 3,000 companies, in parallel to the older, Kemalist-dominated industrial organization called TÜSIAD, which claimed only some 400 members, most of them larger enterprises with bases in Istanbul.[84] The economic strength of the Islamist business community and the creation of a new modern, attentive middle class supported the expansion of mass media aimed at an Islamist public. Islamist businesses also became the material foundation of the openly Islamist political parties, which emerged in Turkey after 1969.

These developments diminished the capacity of official agents to keep Islamic ideas and sentiments out of political life. The collective activities of the Nakşibendis, the Nurcus, the new media, the new Islamist bourgeoisie, and the new Islamist intellectuals transformed the conditions of Turkish politics, even if many of the individuals continued to sidestep direct political involvement. The military leaders who took power in 1980 furthered the change in atmosphere by their appeals to Islam as a source of national unity. Özal's economic and social policies furthered the growth of the Islamist movement without government acceptance of Islamist ideology.

Islamist Success

The organizational success of the Islamist parties in Turkey reflected international context, the Turkish past, the Kurdish problem, internal migration, economic growth, the mass media, the veil as a symbol, and the tireless efforts of activists, many of them women. The wave of Islamist activity ignited by the Arab defeat by Israel in 1967 seems to have also affected Turkey, a non-Arab state. The Iranian Revolution of 1979 accelerated the growth of Islamism all across the region, even though Turkish Islamists, most of them Sunni, did not rally to the Iranian plea for Muslim unity under Shii leadership. In the case of Turkey, the National Outlook movement sought to reconnect the country with its Ottoman past without negating the Turkish nationalism on which Mustafa Kemal had sought to construct an independent state. As Kurds and other rural Turks moved to the suburbs of the big cities in the 1970s and 1980s, they found themselves drawn into the Islamist networks providing social integration, education, economic support, and more. Ownership of media gave the Islamists access to a large public even without access to the mosques. The head scarf, or the "turban," as it came to be called to distinguish it from the more traditional head scarf, became the symbol of the movement.

The Islamist movement brought new categories of women into political activity at the same time that it reasserted a set of traditional family values. Powered in good measure by men and women educated in religious schools, the movement drew more women into education, study groups, voluntary associations, and even local government. On the one hand, the conservative Islam that women imbibed from the male leadership of the movement discouraged them from employment outside the home.[85] On the other hand, work with other women for the benefit of the party constituted acceptable activity. Many highly educated women who were forgoing professional opportunities to rear their children in traditional ways worked long hours to advance the cause.[86] The Welfare Party mounted grassroots campaigns without precedent in Turkey and won political control of twenty-nine large cities, including Istanbul, in 1994. Then in the 1995 parliamentary elections, the party won 21.4 percent of the vote and 158 of 550 seats in the legislature. The victory, coupled with the disarray of the secular parties—none of them able to capture even a fifth of the electorate—enabled the party to enter a coalition government as senior partner.

Neither the success of the Welfare Party in the 1990s nor the 1997 soft coup that appeared to jeopardize the achievements of Islamism transformed the relationship between religion and politics. Necmettin Erbakan's government undertook ill-considered initiatives that alarmed Kemalists. He reoriented Turkish foreign policy away from Europe and toward the rest of the Muslim world.[87]

The directives handed down by the military on February 28, 1997, did seek to weaken Islamism by pulling back on state-supported religious schools, but not even powerful non-Islamists such as the center-right Motherland Party supported the changes. The courts banished the Welfare Party and banned Erbakan from politics but could not prevent successor organizations from emerging. At that point, however, the National Outlook movement split, and Recep Tayyip Erdoğan engineered a new party with a post-Islamist outlook, the Justice and Development Party (AKP), which stormed to victory in 2002.[88] The Turkish word *ak* (as in the AK Party) means "white" and "clean," suggesting freedom from corruption. The party icon is a shining lightbulb, and the slogan was "continual light."[89] In its emphasis on enlightenment, the imagery is strikingly Kemalist. It also evokes Nursi's *Epistle of Light*.

That victory, followed by assurances that the AKP planned no major overhaul of the system in the name of Islam, did not provoke further military intervention. Female AKP candidates did not wear head scarves.[90] The AKP lacked incentive to attack the Directorate of Religious Affairs or even official policies on the wearing of the turban, because many Islamists had already penetrated the directorate as well as other parts of the Turkish bureaucracy, most of them products of the religious schools. The state had already stopped strict enforcement of the rules against beards and turbans in public places, such as universities. The new government portrayed itself as the protector of all religions and all types of Islam. "Official Islam" had become more circumspect, unwilling to endorse one version of Islam, quite willing to acknowledge that official preachers were not the sole voices of Islam. Kemalist fears appeared to diminish.[91]

The election of 2002 showed that Islamists could win in the democratic marketplace of Turkey. Islamists transformed Turkish democracy by expanding political participation and became democrats by virtue of political expediency. They pulled the rural elements, the poor, the uprooted, the alienated, toward the political system, not by virtue of following instructions in the Quran or the hadith or by proposing a reversion to the past, but by proposing an alternative, progressive, inclusive future. The support and funding of a newly prosperous bourgeoisie from the hinterland made it possible. The military, which had vetoed the earlier Islamist success under Erbakan, decided to stay in the barracks rather than overrule the democratic decision-making of the Turkish public on yet another occasion. The retreat of the Turkish military from its perch as the protector of the Turkish republic and Kemalist secularism constitutes the most significant institutional change in the first decade of AKP rule. The military sought to block the accession of Foreign Minister Abdullah Gül, longtime associate of Prime Minister Erdoğan, to the presidency of the republic in 2007, but that effort failed when voters in the parliamentary elections of that year rewarded the AKP with increased representation in parliament. The National Security Council had been the primary means of military influence in the governing of the country. Officers had for years expressed their contempt for the quality and honesty of civilian politicians; politicians regularly consulted the security council to make sure their initiatives would not rattle military medals. Over a ten-year period, the Erdoğan government managed to assert civilian control with the intent of averting future coups. A primary motive, or perhaps an excuse, was the need to comply with European rules for accession to the EU. When top military leaders appeared at a Republic Day celebration in October 2012 with the president, the prime minister, and their wives—fashionably attired, heads covered with scarves in deference to Islamic tradition—the event suggested a sharp change in the institutional power structure.[92]

Political Culture

As Turkey has edged its way toward liberalism and democracy, it has also moved toward an understanding of politics that incorporates elements of both secularist and Islamist ideologies. State institutions play a leading role in shaping religion, and nonofficial religious organizations help shape the political debate. The lines between public life and religion are much less sharp than the Kemalists thought (or think) they should be. One explanation of these developments lies in Turkish political culture, which combines religiosity, modernism, nationalism, liberalism, and democracy.

Modernization theory hypothesizes that the secularization of societies depends primarily on their degree of economic and social development. Norris and Inglehart argue that "postmodern" societies are more secular than "industrial societies," which are more secular than "traditional societies." They classify Turkey as an industrial society and the United States as postmodern. Yet these two societies score equally high in religiosity. The United States ranks higher than Turkey in the degree to which respondents report religious participation

("How often do you attend services?") and somewhat lower than Turkey in people who say religion is "important" to them. The Turks are slightly more inclined toward "traditional" values than Americans, but both these countries fall outside the norms of their respective groups (postmodern for the United States and industrial for Turkey) by virtue of the religiosity and "traditionalism" of their views.[93] Even more than the Turks, the Americans are outliers, far removed in attitudes from the secular norms of Northern and Eastern Europe. Turkey and the United States resemble agrarian societies more than industrial or postindustrial groups in their relative attachment to religion.[94]

The United States appears exceptional in the context of liberal, democratic states of the postindustrial sort. Turkey appears exceptional among Muslim states struggling with Westernization and modernity. Mardin traces that exceptionalism to the Ottomans, who, of their own accord, decided to embrace change—in education, the military, even in politics—without abandoning the old. They sought to strengthen religious commitments and dynastic authority as a means of achieving modernization. They resisted seeing modernity as the negation of tradition, as the Kemalists later did.[95]

The Ottomans cultivated and maintained a second source of Turkish exceptionalism: religious heterodoxy. Although Ösman built his reputation as a warrior for the faith (*gazi*), his successors never sought to convert all their subjects to Islam. While the Ottomans came to rely on Sunni orthodoxy for dynastic legitimacy, they seem to have done so only rather late, after Safavid Persia had decided to adopt Shii Islam as the national faith. Never did they seek to suppress the rich traditions of popular Islam that marked the Muslim portions of the empire. Several authors assert that the Turkish proclivity for Sufism exceeds that of other Muslims. Some link the proclivity to ancient Turkish shamanism. The Ottomans never sought to create a monolithic religious culture.

A third strand of exceptionalism in Turkish political culture stems from its lack of colonial experience. In most of the Middle East, modernization arrived as a set of policies propounded by the agents of foreign domination. Napoleon arrived in Egypt in 1798 and imposed change. In North Africa, from Morocco to Libya, and in the Fertile Crescent—Iraq, Syria, Lebanon, Palestine—Christian powers brought "civilizing" agendas and often saw Islam as an obstacle. The colonizing powers favored Christians and other minorities, took control of mosques, created European-style schools, and wrote constitutions that reflected

European experience. In the minds of many Egyptians, liberalism served the purposes of the British. For some Egyptians and many other Muslims, modernity meant replacing traditional morality with materialism, wantonness, and corruption. Turkey, spared direct colonial intervention, avoided this identification of modernism with imperialism. Quite the contrary, the hero of the independence movement, Mustafa Kemal, unabashedly and wholeheartedly adopted Westernization as his program.

The Kemalists wanted to create a monolithic culture based on the Western model, and they failed. They launched a cultural revolution, which unquestionably changed attitudes in the urban areas, especially among the bourgeoisie. To be a true Turk was to do everything the European way! Pamuk remembers a member of the upper class with nothing better to do than have tea at the Hilton Hotel "because it's the only place in the city that feels like Europe."[96] The Kemalists created a bifurcated political culture in which only the secularized, Westernized elite of the cities represented the real Turkey, the new Turkey, the exceptional Turkey.

The Islamists who have dominated Turkish politics since 2002 have proposed an enriched version of Turkish exceptionalism by reaching back to the Ottoman tradition and by reaching out to "black" Turkey, rural Turkey, the old Turkey. They have encouraged the opening of museums and the making of films about the Ottoman Empire. What the Kemalists took as a source of shame to be hidden, the Islamists have begun to extol. Their vision is that the growth and progress the Kemalists imagined and cultivated can be achieved without sacrificing continuity with the cultural heritage. Turkey's exceptional escape from the colonial heritage makes it possible to think about entering the European Union; the Ottoman experience as a European power makes it plausible. It is not certain, though, that Islamists any more than Kemalists have come to embrace the sort of religious and ethnic heterodoxy that constitutes the third sort of exceptionalism attributable to the Ottomans. Nor is it clear that they are prepared to reconsider a less admirable aspect of Turkish exceptionalism, the treatment of Armenians during World War I.

Education

Museums, films, history books, propaganda, speeches by political leaders—all these things contribute to the shaping and reshaping of political culture in the short run. In the long run, it is probably education that matters most in forming a culture of citizenship. The Kemalists certainly thought so. They imagined that the new Roman alphabet they adopted would cut the country loose from its Islamic and Ottoman past, but the change immediately affected only the literate, perhaps 3 to 5 percent of the population. Many of those persons would have acquired literacy in Quranic schools, which lacked any modern elements in the curriculum. Some of the most prominent people would have been ulama, such as Said Nursi, whom the Kemalists were happy to exclude from public discourse. The Kemalists needed schools to propagate the new culture. Education, re-education, and consciousness raising would be vital training for citizens. The genius of Nursi, who combined his Islamic learning with European philosophy and history, lay in his understanding that education would be the key to combating Kemalist secularism.

Even the most liberal and democratic governments normally seek to shape their public school curricula to support political legitimacy. The Kemalist version of civic education promoted Turkish nationalism, the heroism of Atatürk, and the values of modernity. The government took control of all schools in 1923 and adopted the Law on the Unification of Instruction the following year. The law imposed a single curriculum, thus abandoning the dual-track (religious-modern) system of the Ottoman period. Soon-Yong Pak explains: "It meant the abolition of public religious education as well as religious education provided by various religious orders."[97] These schools offered no instruction in Islam. There was initially no provision for training mosque personnel. Only in the 1940s did the Republican People's Party, then the only legal party of the state, permit the creation of optional courses of religious instruction in elementary schools, and a few courses in secondary schools to train preachers and prayer leaders. The state also created a faculty of theology at Ankara University. The Kemalist intent was "to ensure that religious instruction remained within the secular principles of the state," but the state could not sustain official Islam without teaching Islam.[98] The alternative was to let the Nakşibendis, Süleymancis, Nurcus, and others supply religious education.

After 1950, with the Democratic Party in power, the state increased the place of religious instruction in public schools. In elementary and secondary schools, children took optional courses in religion unless their parents requested in writing that the student be exempted. The courses for preachers and prayer leaders became separate Imam-Hatip schools, which were initially established in seven cities and then extended to sixteen. By 1997 Imam-Hatip schools numbered 600 and were turning out 50,000 graduates a year.[99] By then almost a third of the graduates were female, even though women could not become imams. By the 1990s only 15 percent of the graduates of these schools were entering the religious sector; many graduates went on to universities, where their options expanded.[100] Some ended up in business, the professions, education, and the state bureaucracy, adulterating the secular climate in the state apparatus and penetrating the ranks of the Turkish elite. After the soft coup of 1997, the military insisted upon closing down the middle-school sections of these Imam-Hatip schools, greatly restricting the overall enrollment, but the state continued to maintain the Imam-Hatip high schools to limit radicalism, appease the public, and train functionaries. The state also manages about 5,000 Quranic schools with some 200,000 students.[101] The forces of Islamism continued to support these schools, despite suspicion of state control, as the best way to nurture their bases of support.

The constitution adopted under military rule in the wake of the 1980 coup provided for the mandatory teaching of "religious culture and moral education" in primary and secondary schools. Section VI, Article 24, of the constitution of 1982 (amended in 2001) specifies that the state is to supervise the control of "education and instruction in religion ethics." But it also refers to "other religious education and instruction." Presumably that phrase refers to higher education.[102] A manual of instruction to teachers produced by the Ministry of Education says schools must offer "correct" information about religion so that "others" do not "brainwash" students on religious matters. The ministry urges teachers to explain the utility of religion: "For example, in this context ablution helps keep one sufficiently clean; daily prayers discipline one into being organized; and fasting is good for one's health."[103] Teachers must uphold the secularist gospel of the Kemalists, which requires utter separation of religious and political affairs.

The courses themselves may violate that precept, however, by virtue of efforts to sanctify nonreligious values. Texts on religion used in the schools vaunt patriotism, the homeland, religious duty, the military, and social harmony. "Because 'protecting the homeland from all kinds of attacks is a sacred responsibility,' 'it is improper for a Turkish man to evade conscription or avoid joining the army using various excuses.'"[104] "The state, from the religious point of view, is an institution that Allah created for mankind's benefit."[105] Islam serves the cause of social stability. It holds diverse groups together in the interests of the nation, imparting happiness even when differentials of wealth or status may give reason for jealousy. "Thus justice does not mean the eradication of wealth differentials but 'equal' treatment of people without reference to their level of material well-being."[106] The rush of students toward the Imam-Hatip schools and the protests occasioned by the decision after 1997 to eliminate Imam-Hatip middle schools show that some Turkish parents found the official treatment of religion in the ordinary public schools inadequate.

Outcomes

As in Egypt, the efforts of the Turkish state to promote and control Islamic education may have helped elevate religiosity in the society. Results from a pair of surveys conducted among university students, the first done in 1978 on the eve of the Iranian Revolution, the second in 1991, when Turgut Özal had become president of the republic, suggest sharp changes in attitude toward religion. Table 4.1 gives the percentage of students responding positively to a series of statements. The average increase for the first five items was 24 points. The statement "Religion is a search for truth and beauty" won roughly equal support from both cohorts, but the idea of "making decisions by Qur'anic principles" actually diminished in support; heightened religiosity did not translate into support for an Islamic state that would enforce the sharia. A 1999 survey indicated that 21.2 percent of Turks wanted such a state but only 10 percent thought Islamic law should regulate marriage, divorce, and inheritance, and a mere 1.4 percent favored Quranic punishments, such as stoning for adultery.[107] Whit Mason explains these apparent differences: "When the implications of Islamic law for marriage, inheritance, or criminal penalties are made clear, support for sharia falls away to nothing."[108] There is presumably heavy overlap between the 21.2 percent of the population favoring the establishment of an Islamic state and the 21.4 percent of the electorate who voted for the Welfare Party in 1995.

Whether Turks are more or less tolerant than other Middle Eastern peoples is not clear. Nine of ten respondents to the 1999 survey "found tolerance of differences of faith and belief to be important for social peace." Four-fifths said one could be a good Muslim without fasting at Ramadan or, in the case of a woman, without covering one's head, although three-fifths said women who are

TABLE 4.1   Turkish Student Attitudes Toward Religion
(percentage agreeing with statements in two surveys)

STATEMENT	1978	1991
"God really exists"	54	81
"Day of Resurrection exists"	64	77
"There is a Heaven and a Hell"	36	75
"Qur'an is God's commandments"	47	77
"Day of Judgment exists"	59	70
"One should 'make decisions by Qur'anic principles'"	39	26
"Religion is a search for truth and beauty"	64	66

Source: Kayhan Mutlu, "Examining Religious Beliefs Among University Students in Ankara," *British Journal of Sociology* 47 (June 1996): 355.

Muslims ought to wear head scarves.[109] Responses to the 1991 survey of university students also revealed considerable tolerance. Four respondents in five agreed that minorities should be able to worship freely, but more than a third were intolerant of deviation from religious norms. The minority said (1) head scarves are necessary for women; (2) only Muslims will go to heaven; and (3) only a Muslim can be a "truly good person." A fourth of the respondents said that the "secularist" policies of the Turkish state should change, even though two-thirds favored secularism.[110] These responses portray Turkey as relatively tolerant, but in a 2007 survey, one-third of the Turkish sample, given a choice among sorts of people they would not want as neighbors, selected "people of a different religion." That is about the same proportion as in Egypt and Iran.[111] (Three percent of Americans replied to the question that way.) Turkey does not appear exceptionally tolerant by this measure.

While religiosity in Turkey remains high—83 percent of the 2007 sample said they considered themselves religious persons—Turks also show commitment to democratic ideals.[112] Mark Tessler and Ebrin Altinoğlu, analyzing data from the World Values Survey of 1997, found support for democracy higher (86.5 percent "high" or "somewhat high") than support for freedom (52.5 percent "high" or "somewhat high"). While religiosity did not help explain support for democracy among these respondents, religiosity and "traditionalism" did correlate negatively with the support for political liberty. Tessler and Altinoğlu found that social tolerance, trust in ordinary citizens, attentiveness to public affairs, and positive attitudes toward government performance helped explain why about one-third (the so-called high-high group) of the sample showed "high" support for both democracy and freedom. Traditionalist attitudes correlated negatively with "high" support.[113] Female respondents with less education, low trust in other people, and low attentiveness to government affairs tended to show low support for both democracy and freedom (25 percent of the sample fell in this "low-low" group). Religiosity did not emerge as a significant independent variable in either the high-high or the low-low groups.[114] One might well imagine that a high level of religious uniformity (more than 95 percent Muslim) would produce a high level of interpersonal trust, a quality often seen as a prerequisite for democracy. But the 2007 survey portrayed Turks as the least trusting of peoples in the area. Five percent said "most people can be trusted," compared with 40 percent of Americans. Other responses from the Middle East ranged from 11 percent for Iran to 41 percent for Iraq.[115]

The Turkish educational system initially designed by the Kemalists has produced notable successes, as demonstrated by these surveys. It has produced a highly literate society of men and women who support democracy and individual liberty. It must surely be given much of the credit for advancing women to a degree that is exceptional in the Muslim world. It has cultivated Turkish nationalism, support for the armed forces, and admiration for the founder of the republic, Mustapha Kemal Atatürk, who would surely be proud of these accomplishments.

If Atatürk were alive, he might be surprised and disappointed by other developments. He may have hoped that a public educational system would create a single Turkish Sunni political culture that would be content to separate individual belief from the political sphere. First, the minority Alevis have remained faithful to this vision, but they have not abandoned their beliefs and practices. Second, despite initial intent, the state never achieved a monopoly on education;

Said Nursi started a tradition that continues among his followers, including Fethullah Gülen, whose community has nurtured its version of religious education both inside and outside the country. Contemporary Kemalists complain that the products of Gülen's educational system have now penetrated so much of the Turkish bureaucracy that it no longer reflects secularist principles. What is more, by creating Imam-Hatip schools to train religious leaders, the state provides a religious education to many who would enter public service, with or without influence of Gülen or other Nurcus. While Erdoğan has faced resistance from the courts and other public institutions, he has also found support within the Turkish state for his Islamist orientation. Third, what is perhaps the greatest failure of the Kemalist system is that it did not convince Kurds that they were Turks and therefore full citizens of the country. Instead, the Kurds demanded the right to teach their own language and their own history, but the Kemalists were not prepared to sacrifice their notion of a monocultural Turkey. Finally, while even the Islamists have sought to advance education for women and argued vociferously for the admittance of covered women to university classrooms, the group has not promoted women within its own organizations. Sultan Tepe points out the inconsistency: "In fact, although the JDP's [AKP's] party program strongly commits itself to gender equality, according to the world economic forum Turkey's below-average gender parity index score regressed significantly between 2006 and 2010, moving the country from 103rd in 2006 to 126th in 2010 (among 134 countries)."[116]

The government of the AKP and Recep Tayyip Erdoğan, however eager to invoke the Ottomans to bolster conceptions of exceptionalism, may be no more ready than the Kemalists to accept Ottoman heterodoxy. The Alevis fear that the Islamists intend to impose a Sunni version of Islam that would impinge upon the religious freedom of all Turks. Erdoğan has not reached out to Muslim minorities. The Kurds, although supportive of Islamists over Kemalists at the voting booth, have not fulfilled the Islamist expectations and abandoned their protests. Erdoğan has softened the state's policies toward the use of the Kurdish language, but he has been unwilling to envision the autonomy, much less the independence, that the Kurdish region and Kurdish parties have sought. He sought to use the pressure of the conditions imposed by Europe to rectify injustices in southeastern Turkey without alienating the Turkish military, which is still dominated by Kemalists. There have been moments of apparent progress and moments of reversion to violence between the PKK and the state. The creation of a no-fly zone in northern Iraq that turned into an autonomous Kurdish area and still threatens to become an independent Kurdish state has complicated the issue, as has the continued imprisonment of the Kurdish leader Abdullah Öcalan, who was saved from execution by European pressure. The Erdoğan government appears almost as wedded to Turkish monoculturalism as have the governments of his predecessors. It may be that Erdoğan is more nationalist than Islamist.[117]

Liberal democracy and a healthy respect for human rights have not been fully integrated into Turkish political culture. Under increasing pressure from Europe, the Turkish government has often blamed "exceptional circumstances" for human rights abuses. It continues to deny Turkish responsibility for the Armenian massacres of the World War I era and even to deny the right of Turks to talk about that problem. Pressures from Europe make human rights a question of national pride. Foreign governments and NGOs have their interests and agendas. Pressures from the Islamists on the head-scarf issue awaken Kemalist fears of Islamist imposition of the sharia, but the Kemalist agenda to unify and democratize Turkey has itself all too often led to the employment of force against groups, such as the Kurds, believed to stand in the way of unification. Human rights issues cannot be divorced from contemporary politics in Turkey or from history. Ümit Cizre writes: "Most of all, integration of human rights into a liberal democratic order requires coming to terms with the past."[118] Turks are still in the process of doing that.

Turkish exceptionalism has nonetheless found reinforcement in the events of the Arab Spring in 2011. Turkey has shown that an overwhelmingly Muslim country can make rapid economic progress and move toward democracy without authoritarianism. An Islamist movement has played the democratic game in Turkey, achieving an important share of power and maneuvering the military toward a full acceptance of civilian control. The movement has done so while the state is aligned with NATO and the Western powers and has accepted the presence of Israel in the neighborhood, but Turkey has also asserted its independence by denying the United States access to northern Iraq in 2003 and by pushing Israel to change its policies toward Gaza. Turkey has demonstrated a new willingness to align itself with other Muslim countries without necessarily embracing dictators. It has renewed its membership in the Middle East by taking a greater interest in developments there without abandoning all hope of joining Europe.

Turkish political culture remains exceptional but it is also conflicted. Some secularists fear it is sliding toward an Islamic republic bent on enforcing a narrow-minded sharia. Tensions remain high in classrooms and beyond. Secularists have taken on the role of aggressors. The government repressed a protest demonstration of secularists on Republic Day in October 2012, when leaders were celebrating at the presidential palace. Journalists and others who have criticized policy, especially on the Kurdish issue, have either been imprisoned or pressured to refrain from criticizing the administration. The government's attitude alarms critics, who fear a lack of commitment to freedom of expression.[119] These are disconcerting signs that mar, but do not negate, the considerable economic, social, and political progress of the country. Ideological conflict may have diminished, but it has not vanished.

Conclusion

To judge by the Turkish constitution, religion is much less central to the Turkish state than it is to Egypt, Israel, or Iran. The preamble says that "as required by the principle of secularism, there shall be no interference whatsoever by sacred religious feelings in state affairs and politics." It does not mention Islam. Article Two, which is qualified as an "irrevocable provision," defines Turkey as a "democratic, secular, and social state governed by the rule of law." The article also refers to the "fundamental tenets set forth in the Preamble," thus making "the principle of secularism" an irrevocable part of the constitution. Yet the overwhelming majority of Turks are Muslims, perhaps 99 percent if one includes atheists (3 percent), who are presumably of Muslim background. In a population now put at 75 million, there are about 100,000 Christians, 23,000 Jews, and 10,000 Bahais. At about 60,000, Armenian Orthodox Catholics constitute the largest Christian group.[120] Ali Bulaç, a leading Islamist intellectual, claims that no other country in the world is so overwhelmingly Muslim.[121] He complains that the Turkish state inadequately protects both Muslim and non-Muslim rights.

The Kemalist fear of identifying state and religion came out of a particular period and a particular notion of modernity. The elites who hailed from that period and shared positivist views of modernity imposed a secular Turkish identity on the state, which survives in a formal sense but suffers steady erosion. Nothing symbolizes the erosion better than dress. The head scarf and the beard, traditional symbols of religiosity, never disappeared from rural Turkey, but the return of the head scarf and the beard to the universities and to fashionable, educated, modernist milieus suggests that the identity issue is anything but resolved.[122] The Kemalists made dress a central element in their effort to define modern Turkey. Said Nursi was attached to his turban, and young Islamists now flaunt various types of Islamic fashion to express their identities, drawing praise in some circles and derision or even prejudicial action in others.[123]

External factors also push Turkey toward a sharper identification with Islam. Europeans identify Turks as Muslims and Turkey as a Muslim state. The Bosnian crisis caused Turks to identify with fellow Muslims. As prime minister, Necmettin Erbakan overplayed his hand when he traveled to Iran and Libya to reopen dialogue with these Muslim pariah states, but he will surely be remembered, too, for trying to spring Turkey from its self-imposed isolation from its region. Other Muslims identify Turkey with the Ottoman Empire and with long-term struggles against Christian Europe. Turkey is itself a member of the Organization of Islamic Cooperation, an organization composed of fifty-seven states and originally sponsored by Iran, Saudi Arabia, and Morocco, in part to coordinate the annual hajj (pilgrimage). These forces pull Turkey inexorably toward an identity that Mustafa Kemal sought to shed.[124]

The Turkish republic under Mustafa Kemal Atatürk did not succeed in its efforts to reduce Islam to a personal religion, eliminate the identification of religion with the state, subordinate all religious institutions to state control, and reduce the religiosity of the society via public education. But the actions of the state under Atatürk and his successors provoked creative reactions among individuals and groups, who generated a new dynamic in Islam. That dynamic contributed to democratization and to a gradual modification of state policies that fed a re-Islamization of the society. The new Islam in Turkey is, however, quite different from that of the Ottoman Empire or from that of Egypt. As Turkey has transformed itself in economic, social, and political terms, it has transformed Islam as well. Modernization has brought Turkey closer to Europe by virtue of capitalist development, social mobilization, and political liberalization, but modernization has not eliminated the unique qualities of the Turkish attachment to Islam.

Despite the impact of globalization, the Turks have accentuated the distinctiveness of their approach to religious politics. Mustafa Kemal Atatürk surely deserves less of the credit than is usually attributed to him. (The Turkish constitution, prominent monuments, government Web sites—all these elements give him full credit for everything that is good about Turkey!) He did, however, initiate a process of revamping Islam to suit the needs of the nation-state. European states had already done it with Christianity. Other Muslim states of the Middle East are still following his example, even though the times no longer permit the version of secularism he espoused.

Chronology

1300–1918 Ottoman Empire.
1923 Treaty of Lausanne is signed. Mustapha Kemal Atatürk and Republican People's Party come to power. Republic of Turkey is established.
1938 Atatürk dies; Ismet Inonü accedes to power.
1950 In multiparty election, Democratic Party wins.
1960 With coup d'état, Turkey is under temporary military rule. Justice Party emerges.
1960 Said Nursi dies.
1971 Another coup d'état results in temporary military rule. National Outlook movement emerges.
1980 Another coup d'état results in temporary military rule.
1982 New constitution is written. Civilian rule returns.
1983 Motherland Party and Turgut Özal win elections. Turkey undergoes liberalization and openness to religion.
1995 Necmettin Erbakan and Welfare Party win elections. Coalition government is established.
1997 Military threatens to intervene; Erbakan's government resigns.
1999 Abdullah Öcalan, PKK leader, is arrested and tried. European Union decides to consider Turkish candidacy.
2002 Justice and Development Party (AKP) wins parliamentary election.
2007 AKP and Prime Minister Erdoğan are again victorious. Parliament elects Abdullah Gül of the AKP as president of the republic.

5

State Shiism in Iran

A casual observer might easily conclude that religion has dictated the course of political development in Iran, but careful analysis suggests, to the contrary, that politics has refashioned religion in that country. Political decisions and opportunities have recast a version of Islam (Twelver Shiism) from a passivist, minority stance into a badge of national identity, a religious establishment like no other in the Muslim world, a set of competing political ideologies, and an authoritarian effort to promote religion. Neither Islam, nor Shii Islam, nor even the Iranian variant of Shiism as a set of doctrines and beliefs constitutes a sufficient explanation for the major events of modern Iranian history, including the revolution of 1978–1979, but those events go far to explain the place of Islam in that country today. Politics and religion have become intricately entangled for political reasons.

Few are the states whose national identity depends as heavily on religion as does Iran. Israel seems similar, because its religious identity is its raison d'être, but Iran differs from Israel in that it is only one of many Muslim states, whereas Israel is the only country to identify itself as Jewish. Iran identifies with the Muslim community as a whole but nonetheless uses that identity to distinguish itself from all other states and to reinforce Iranian nationalism. In Iran, political and social revolution brought to power a clerical class that turned Islam from one of many cultural characteristics of the country into the defining element of its identity. Iran became the country of bearded men and veiled women, an "Islamic" form of government, and a rhetoric of Muslim rectitude reinforcing a version of Iranian identity.

The Iranians do not get full credit for turning Islam into political ideology. Jamal al-Din al-Afghani, Abdülhamid II, Hasan al-Banna, Mowlana Abul ala

Mawdudi, Sayyid Qutb, Mustafa Kemal Atatürk, and others played roles in that transformation. Within Iran, Ruhollah Khomeini and Ali Shariati probably did the most to convert Shiism from a set of beliefs, customs, rites, and ethical principles into a political program. Khomeini, Shariati, and a few others discovered in Shiism the resources they needed to construct ideologies of combat and governance. Like others before them, they claimed knowledge of the revolutionary intent of Muhammad, the spiritualism of Ali, the tradition of the designated imams, and the truth of the Quran. But if theirs were the only possible readings of the tradition, then the ulama of Twelver Shiism ought to have come to the same conclusions centuries sooner. As a matter of fact, the doctrines of Khomeini, Shariati, Morteza Mutahhari, Muhammad Kazem Shariat-Madari, and Abdolkarim Soroush are unimaginable except in the modern circumstances of the late twentieth century. These writers responded to the cultural cacophony of modernity, the onslaught of imperialism, and the authoritarianism of Iran's Pahlavi dynasty. The peculiarities of the Iranian situation closed the door on other ideologies and opened the way for Islamist thinking.

The clerical establishment in Iran proved to be the great secret of revolutionary success. Never before have the scholars of Islam, the ulama, taken political action themselves. It is commonplace to assert that there is no separation of church and state in Iran, but the power of the clergy in Iran resulted precisely from the relative autonomy the clerical establishment achieved and maintained under the Qajar dynasty (1796–1925) and especially under Pahlavi rule (1925–1979). The Islamic Republic brought government to the clergy and the clergy closer to government, but not even thirty years of republican rule have wiped out the distinction between government and the religious establishment, some members of which declined to endorse constitutional arrangements; refused to endorse Khomeini's successor, Ali Khamenei; and deplored the authoritarianism of the regime. By making religion a civic duty, the Islamic Republic renders suspect all professions of belief, undercuts religious rites and rituals by making them political, and undermines respect for the independence of the ulama. Clerical rule appears to have divided the religious establishment that gave birth to the revolution.

It is by no means certain that the Islamic Republic has transformed the political culture of Iran. One form of authoritarianism has followed another. Iranians bowed to the shah with an obsequiousness tinged with contempt. Scholars reported high levels of personal distrust in prerevolutionary Iran.[1] Iranians lived in fear of the secret police (Savak), berated the bureaucracy, and mocked efforts to proclaim and teach about the glories of the monarchy in Iran. The postrevolutionary regime has certainly sought to transform these and other aspects of political culture through policies, propaganda, and changes in school curricula. To judge by the way women dress, the content of the media, and the propaganda of the regime, Iran has become more moral, more honest, and more Islamic than it was under the shah, but it is no less focused on individualism and competition. Local elections still seem to turn on garbage collection, parks, recreational facilities, and taxation. The society is more bureaucratic rather than less, and perhaps no less a victim of corruption, mutual suspicion, fear, and authoritarianism than it was before the revolution.[2] Authority by emanation, once anchored in the myths of monarchy and nobility, and now reflected in the mystical superiority of the clergy, seems secure.[3] The Islamic Republic has sacralized familiar patterns of behavior more than it has transformed them.

What is it about Iran that is obstructing the constitutional promise of liberalism and democracy? The success and failure of the reform movement suggests that neither religious doctrine nor the religious class is the primary obstacle. The reformist president Muhammad Khatami was himself trained as a cleric. His supporters invoked the legacy of the Ayatollah Khomeini, founder of the Islamic Republic, in support of their advocacy of greater openness and flexibility by pointing out that Khomeini himself repeatedly invoked the "public interest" over narrow interpretations of Islamic law. Clerics of great authority, such as Ayatollah Husayn Ali Montazeri, have accepted both the principle of Islamic government and the need for democracy. The obstruction of liberalism and democracy comes from Supreme Guide Ali Khamenei and his traditionalist friends, who invoke religion to legitimate their position and who exploit a complicated and contradictory constitution to support their agenda. Their manipulation of the presidential election of 2009 and the suppression of the protest (the Green Movement) that followed the reelection of President Ahmadinejad affirm that judgment.

Identity

The revolutionary government of Iran reinvented that country's identity by creating not just a republic (as opposed to a monarchy) but an Islamic republic.

The preamble to the constitution says the Islamic Republic reflects the wishes of Iran's "Muslim people." The new government claimed that the previous regime had ignored or neglected the Muslim character of the country and propagated instead a vision of Iran as a product of the Persian language, Aryan race, ancient dynasties, and devotion to monarchy. The revolutionary government attempted a major overhaul of Iranian self-perception and of the country's image in foreign affairs.

A sharp shift in identity has often accompanied the great revolutions of modern history. The French discovered that they were not just part of a state ruled by a king but also a nation capable of determining the future of that state. The Russians discovered that they were a multiethnic empire of workers held together by a commitment to communism. Enlightenment thinking proclaimed universal rights, and Marxist ideology denigrated national identities in favor of communist internationalism. The Iranian revolutionaries called upon all Muslims to join them without distinction of race, ethnicity, or nationality. Yet all three revolutions, however much they began with a commitment to universalist principles, ended up creating or solidifying a conception of national identity.

Although Muslims constitute a majority in about forty countries and although several countries proclaim Islam as the state religion, very few have equated national identity with Islam.[4] One constraint on most Muslim states is the existence of significant non-Muslim minorities. Another is the apparent conflict generated by invoking a universal, transnational religion as the principal defining element of a nation. Proclamation of an Islamic state implies that it is coterminous with the umma, the community of believers. To identify with the umma suggests utopian expectations of unifying all Muslims in a single nation-state or, alternatively, the dissolution of the nation-state and the incorporation of its people into some larger agglomeration.

How, then, can one explain that Iran, a country with a national history that predates Islam—a country quite unlikely to seek union with Pakistan, Saudi Arabia, Morocco, or any other Muslim state—would undertake the bold and improbable action of identifying the nation with Islam?[5] One hypothesis relies on the prevalence of Twelver Shiism in Iran; Shiism has perhaps predisposed Iranians to thinking of themselves first and foremost as Muslims. Iran is not just another Muslim state; it is a unique Muslim state, where religion and state are inseparable concepts.[6] A second hypothesis attributes the recourse to Islamic identity to the "prism of colonialism" and the "mirror of modernity."[7] Because these external forces affected many Muslim countries besides Iran, it was the particular Iranian encounter with colonialism and modernity that pushed Iran to think of itself in religious terms. Finally, one might explain Iranian identity with Islam in terms of the political context of Iran under the Pahlavi dynasty. "We are Muslims" served to unite revolutionaries against a nationalist monarchy dependent on Western support. It solidified the nation by opposing the secular nationalism of the shah and the international system of nation-states. By that hypothesis, Islam has become an identity of political convenience.

The first hypothesis surfaced almost immediately after the revolution in the minds of many Sunni Muslims. As Egyptians, Saudis, and others awoke to the change of regime in Iran and heard Ayatollah Khomeini invite others to follow him into a supranational Islamic umma, their leaders were quick to observe that Iran is predominantly Shii. Muslims and non-Muslims alike made Shiism a primary explanation of the Iranian phenomenon. Many said that Shiis are more devout than Sunnis; Shiism is more violent than Sunnism; Shiism cultivates revolt and dissent while Sunnism promotes obedience and submission. Shiism requires religiously inspired leadership; Sunnism accepts a separation between religion and politics. So went the explanations of why Islamic revolution had swept Iran but no other Muslim countries. Sunni elites dismissed Iranian claims to lead the Muslim community as a whole, because the Shia remain a distinct minority (perhaps 10 to 20 percent) in the Muslim world as a whole.

There can be little doubt that Shii Islam has contributed to Iranian identity, but it is difficult to disentangle cause and effect. Neither the history nor the doctrines of Shiism as a whole constitute a sufficient explanation of its importance or development in Iran. Shiism was not born in Iran and it has never been limited to Iran. Moreover, Iran includes an important Sunni minority, and the Iranian variant of Shiism, called Imami or Twelver Shiism, includes adherents beyond the frontiers of Iran. For those reasons, the decision of the Safavid family in 1501 to make Twelver Shiism the state religion in what was then called Persia outweighs all other factors in explaining the linkage between national identity and Shiism. The Qajar and Pahlavi dynasties nurtured this connection.

Early Shiism

The Shia trace their history to the struggle for leadership of the Islamic community between Ali ibn abi Talib, cousin and son-in-law of the Prophet Muhammad, and Muawiya, governor of Syria. Muawiya, belonging to a distinguished Meccan family that opposed the Prophet early in his career, won appointment from the second caliph, Umar, to govern the new province of Syria. After Umar's death in 644, Muawiya's kinsman, Uthman ibn Affan, acceded to the leadership of the Muslim community. The assassination of Uthman in 656 by a band of Muslims disaffected from the caliphate triggered the first civil war in Islam.

The Shia later argued that Muhammad had chosen Ali as his successor and that the companions of the Prophet had wrongly overlooked Ali when they selected Abu Bakr as the first caliph. The Shia believe the injustice continued with the selection of the next two caliphs, Umar and Uthman. Ali finally won the position of leadership after the assassination of Uthman, but he refused to denounce those guilty of taking Uthman's life. Incensed by the treatment of his kinsman, Muawiya declared war on Ali. An army recruited in Syria marched into Iraq to oppose Ali and the force he had recruited in Arabia. A series of fateful events led ultimately to Ali's defeat and the transfer of authority to Muawiya and his family, the Umayyads, who came to rule the Islamic community from Damascus.

The followers of Ali, or at least some of them (whom scholars call Alids in the early centuries), remained permanently alienated from the mainstream. The Alids found symbolic support for their alienation when the second son of the heroic Ali, Husayn, marched into a battle he knew he would lose against the Umayyad caliph Yazid in the year 680. The massacre of Husayn and his little band constitutes an annual occasion of mourning and self-flagellation in the Shii community to this day. During the revolutionary days of 1978–1979, the annual passion plays commemorating the martyrdom of Husayn ibn Ali cast Shah Muhammad Reza Pahlavi in the role of the evil Yazid. The Ashura celebrations honoring Husayn fueled the fervor of the protest against the ancien régime.

While Alids played some role in bringing down the Umayyads in what is known as the Abbasid Revolution (750), they found themselves disappointed with their treatment by the new dynasty in Baghdad. But another century or more passed before there emerged a set of doctrines one might call Shii. Watt argues that Shiism emerged as a response to the development of a mainstream Muslim body of jurisprudence and theology.[8] Jonathan Berkey suggests it was the other way around. The development of Shii doctrines pushed the mainstream to generate the ideas that came to be identified with Sunnism.[9] Shiism needed a doctrine to hold it together. Sunnism needed a doctrine only once it encountered ideological challenge from the Shii minority.

The common thread of Shii doctrines is charismatic leadership. While the Shia avoid putting Ali on the same plane as the Prophet Muhammad—whom the Quran describes as the seal of the prophets, the last in a long line of human beings called upon to carry God's message—they believe Ali embodied inspired religious leadership and inherited primary responsibility for the spiritual welfare of the Muslim community. Only from him and "designated" descendants can the Muslim community look for legitimate leadership. The historic leaders are imams. For all Shia, Ali is the first designated imam; his first son, Hasan, is the second; his second son, Husayn, is the third; and the line continues from there. Some Shia look back to five such historic figures, some cling to seven, but the largest group came to believe in eleven such imams and a twelfth, who disappeared as a child but will someday reappear. These are the Twelvers, or the Imamis, who dominate in Iran.

Sunni doctrine downplays any notion of divine leadership after the death of the Prophet and emphasizes the development of a moral code, gradually built into four schools of law, that governed rulers and ruled alike. A class of scholars who codified the law and articulated theological doctrines became the primary spokesmen for Islam. The caliphs, few of them noted for their piety, found themselves ever more dependent on the ulama for the fragile legitimacy they enjoyed. Their power was bureaucratic and military, and even that power diminished as non-Arabs seized effective control of the empire, leaving the caliphs in place as figureheads.

With the disappearance of the twelfth imam and the beginning of a period called the Greater Occultation, the Twelver Shia lacked divinely inspired leadership. Many interpreters see the Greater Occultation as a rationale for passivism, which perhaps reflected the condition of the Shia as a minority in most Muslim settings. Even the tenth century, often called the Shii century because Shii families ruled in Persia, Egypt, and parts of Arabia, did not raise the Shia from minority to majority status in the Muslim world. As minorities in most areas, the Shia kept a low profile, waited for the return of the Twelfth Imam, and lied about their beliefs if challenged by the Sunni authorities. Their doctrine permitted this sort of dissimulation.

While Iran looks with pride upon this history of the early Alids and of Shiism more generally, there is no unique link between Iran and Shiism as a whole or Twelver Shiism in particular before the Safavid dynasty took control of the country in 1501. As Nikki Keddie puts it:

Before then, although there were many Iranian Shiis, the great majority of Shiis were non-Iranian and the majority of Iranians were Sunni. The Zaidi, Ismaili, and Carmathian Shiis are still found mostly outside Iran; the great majority of Shii dynasties were outside Iran, with only the Buyids as a major partial pre-1501 exception; and the great majority of Iranian dynasties have been Sunni. . . . The legendary marriage of Imam Hosain [Husayn] with a Sasanian princess, which has no historical basis, was useful in cementing the identification of Iran with Shiism, but such legends are usually available when needed.[10]

Although conversion to Islam began after the Arab overthrow of the Sasanian Empire in the seventh century, Iran became Shii as a result of the Safavid conquest. By the time the Safavids lost control of the country to Sunni Afghans in 1722, most Iranians had apparently come to identify with Shiism.[11]

Monarchy and Modernization

The Safavids (1501–1722), like the Qajars and the Pahlavis who followed them to the throne, invoked both Iranian (monarchical) and Islamic legitimacy, but the Safavids emphasized their religious legitimacy and permitted creation of a religious establishment largely subservient to their monarchical ambitions. The Safavids were Sunnis from Ardebil in Azerbaijan with strong affinity for Sufism. They found themselves drawn toward Twelver Shii teachings, apparently from contact with nomadic tribes in Anatolia. Exhibiting the energy of converts convinced of their divine empowerment, the Safavids mustered tribal followers and swept to power in Tehran. Only then did they begin to concern themselves with Shii orthodoxy, recruiting a set of theologians inside and outside of Persia to articulate a legal and religious order supportive of their rule. "More than most Islamic dynasties the Safavids worked for conversion to their branch of Islam and for ideological conformity."[12] The identity with Shiism helped the Safavids differentiate their empire from that of their principal enemies, the Ottomans in the west and the Uzbeks in the north; both these foes of the Safavids were Sunni.

In the nineteenth and twentieth centuries, Iran's encounter with imperialism served to reinforce the identity with Islam. Imperialism and modernity arrived later in Iran than in the Ottoman Empire to the west, and the impact was perhaps more devastating as a result. The decision of the Russians and the British to partition Iran into zones of influence in 1907, only about one year after the country had adopted a new, liberal constitution, represented a cynical response to Iranian weakness, and the response has lingered in the collective memory. Reza Khan seized power in 1921 as an Iranian nationalist, even though some suspected he held power only with British indulgence. Proclaiming himself king (shah), and with his eye on the reforms of Atatürk, he plunged ahead with a program of modernization and secularization in the 1920s and 1930s. With a series of measures, he continued policies initiated in the nineteenth century to secularize education. In addition, he implemented a civil code in 1928 and diminished the clerical role in administering justice. The clergy and the masses came to see Reza Shah as hostile to religious celebrations and religious institutions. In 1941, Ruhollah Khomeini wrote *The Revealing of Secrets* (*Kashf al-Asrar*), a book that expressed some of these frustrations. During World War II, when Reza resisted Allied efforts to take effective control of his country to resupply the Soviet Union, he found himself pushed into exile. His son, who replaced him, could not resist Allied efforts. The son, Muhammad Reza Shah, retained his throne in 1953 only because British and American secret services incited an uprising against the popular prime minister, Muhammad Mussadiq (Mossadegh). From that point on, the shah depended heavily on American support for his security services, his military machine, his educational establishment, and the technology for his economy.

The extended Iranian encounter with imperialism spurred secular nationalism. Mussadiq, who had opposed the Pahlavis with consistency since the 1920s, galvanized nationalist support by nationalizing oil in 1952, the act that provoked British and American intervention. A few maverick *mujtahids* (ulama specializing in the law) supported the Mussadiq government in the beginning but backed away from him as they perceived increasing leftist influence of the Tudeh Party, which was supported by Moscow, in his coalition. Tudeh support for Mussadiq also disturbed American and British policy-makers caught up in the cold war. Imperialism in Iran could never be entirely separated from modernism, and modernism came to be seen by some as a threat to Islam and to Iranian identity, by others as a promise of change. Secular nationalists such as Mussadiq thus provoked both applause and alarm among the clergy. As increasing oil revenues enabled ever more rapid change in Iran after World War II, the secularization and Westernization of Iranian lifestyles proceeded rapidly in the big cities and especially in Tehran. Muhammad Reza Shah epitomized the opulent style of the old nobility and the nouveaux riches. In 1971, evoking the memory of Cyrus the Great, he celebrated 2,500 years of monarchy in Iran by feasting on its symbol, the peacock, with a crowd of international dignitaries in the ancient Persian capital, Persepolis. Maxim's, the Paris restaurant, catered the affair. On the one hand, the king appeared to diminish and even assault the Islamic identity of his country by glorifying an authoritarian, pre-Islamic tradition. On the other hand, he cemented the linkage of progress and modernity with foreigners. It is little wonder that the Iranian writer Jalal Al-e Ahmad struck a sympathetic chord when he evoked the "Westoxication" of Iran.[13]

Before 1960, Islam seemed a remnant of the Iranian past, nurtured mainly in the superstition and backwardness of villages. From 1960 on, it started to become the Iranian future, thanks in part to Ayatollah Ruhollah Khomeini and other ulama and in part to a set of circumstances more specific than colonialism and modernity. The writings of Al-e Ahmad and Shariati played a role. So did the inability of secular nationalists to pull the shah toward genuinely liberal reform; the failure of the shah's land reform policies to produce rural prosperity; the forced pace of modernization, which began to alienate traditional sectors of the bourgeoisie; the shah's ability to ward off revolution by manipulating the "new middle class," which was dependent on his policies and largesse; and his inability to control the clergy, which maintained its standing with the public by keeping its distance from the monarchy. From a stance of separation, the clergy moved toward opposition. The defiance of Khomeini from exile in Iraq and then Paris excited the country and energized many of his fellow clerics.

The Islamization of Identity

In these circumstances the architects of revolution managed to transform Shiism into a national, revolutionary doctrine. They exploited some characteristics: "historical victimization, divine mission to restore justice, and the culture of sacrifice (martyrdom)," all illustrated in the early history of the Shia.[14] And they ignored other characteristics, such as the long subsequent period of quietism among Twelvers awaiting the return of the Hidden Imam. They also ignored the transnational character of Islam and even Imami Shiism to focus on the national struggle against monarchy. They altered the prevailing conception of Iranian identity from that of a Muslim country to that of an Islamic nation.

By renaming the country the Islamic Republic of Iran and by adopting a constitution that trumpets the state's allegiance to Islam, the founders of the new regime asserted a new national identity. In doing so, they confirmed Iran's place in the world of modern nation-states and confirmed its allegiance to constitutionalism, a thoroughly modern, secular idea. If identity depends upon constitutional confirmation, then it is conventional, not primordial. It may be true, as Ludwig Paul argues, "that Iranians cannot even think of, or 'imagine,' themselves as a political community in purely secular terms."[15] The Persian word for "nation," *mellat*, is the same as that for "people," and it connotes people of the faith. (The Ottoman millet system treated each major religious group as a community.) Yet the revolution, with its vigorous assertions about Iran's identity, sought to go beyond the natural bonds of faith that held Iranians, or various groups of them, together and to make Iran "truly Islamic." (A defining characteristic of Islamists is that they speak of "true Islam" and thereby cast aspersions on the faith of ordinary Muslims.) Iran became authentically Islamic only when it became constitutionally Islamic.

By making Islam a matter of convention rather than faith, the regime reached out to minority groups. Some linguistic minorities in Iran, such as Kurds, Arabs, Turkmen, and Baluch, are predominantly Sunni in religion. As inhabitants of outlying mountainous or desert regions, they have often been peripheral to the state, but the Islamic state, though Shii in its origins and instincts, pulls these groups into the majority. In the Islamic state, Azeri (Turkish-speaking) Shia, who constitute 20 percent of the population, are not officially seen as a minority. Seminomadic groups such as the Qashqay, Lur, and Bakhtiari, all Shii but unorthodox in their practices and beliefs, do not attract attention as minorities, either. The only genuine minorities are non-Muslim groups, and even Christians and Jews enjoy some status as "peoples of the book." However, the Bahais, who number perhaps 200,000 to 300,000, do not command even this sort of respect. Because they put themselves beyond the Muslim community, as the regime defines it, by their belief in prophets beyond Muhammad, they do not qualify as Iranians.

Language takes second place to religion as a determinant of nationality in this scheme of things. Paul puts Shii Persians and Azeri (Shii) Turks at the top of the pyramid of Iranianness. The Sunni groups fall in the middle, and the non-Muslim official minorities occupy the bottom. The tribes are marginal, and the

Bahais are outcasts. But Paul says that anyone can be an Iranian by behaving like a true Muslim and joining the fight against imperialism and Zionism.[16] A Shii is an activist, a "true Muslim," one who is not content to believe but acts on the basis of his or her beliefs. While Arabic is the language of Islam and serves as a link between Iran and the Arab world, Khamenei called Persian "the language of true . . . and revolutionary Islam."[17] It would seem to follow that the only country with a Persian-speaking majority would be the locus of the "true Islam." Paul concludes: "The commitment to the Islamic Revolution can now be understood as generating the very commitment that it was originally meant to replace: that to the nation and the home-country."[18]

"Who is a Muslim" becomes as important in an Islamic state as is "who is a Jew" in a Jewish state. In time of revolution, it is relatively easy to say that those who join the struggle are true Muslims, whether or not they are believers. The Iran-Iraq War (1980–1988) provided ample opportunity for activism and martyrdom. Once peace was restored on that front, activists could still vent their anger against the United States and Israel. The constitution calls upon citizens to vote, which could also be interpreted as activism of the sort demanded of "true Muslims." Candidates for public office, however, by the standards enforced by the Guardian Council, must be not just citizen believers but "true Muslims."[19] They must have already distinguished themselves by their commitment to the Islamic Republic. To be an activist dissident, which was in revolutionary days the quintessential way to show one's mettle as a "true Muslim," has now become dangerous in the extreme. Many of those who criticize the repressiveness of the regime risk prison or execution, even though all profess loyalty to the Islamic state. A "true Muslim" is thus one who behaves in approved, conventional ways, whatever he or she believes. For women, that means they cover their heads and wear modest dress. If actions outweigh belief, then dress becomes a critical bit of testimony. To show too much hair or wear colors that are too bright suggests a woman is not a "true Muslim." By this logic any woman inappropriately dressed constitutes proof that Iran is not an authentic Islamic state. Perhaps that helps explain why women's behavior and dress remain a matter of inordinate concern for the regime.

Shii Islam does not account for Iranian identity, but it does help explain how that identity came to be asserted. It also helps explain why Islamic identity depends more on the rule of the clerical class than on an ideological unity or purity.

Without the conversion of Shii Islam into ideology, the revolution might never have occurred in Iran, but the success of the revolution in creating institutions, and the success of the clergy in dominating those institutions, freed the Islamic Republic from all but the most elementary ideological standards. It could afford to be a dissonant state, where competing ideological notions often paralyze action and force the elites to privilege expediency over consistency.[20] What it cannot tolerate, or will not tolerate, is a revival of revolutionary ideology that would undermine the institutions established by the revolution.

Ideology

The transformation of Islam from a set of religious beliefs into a program of political action occurred late in Iran. Iran trailed Egypt in the development of an Islamist movement by forty years. By one account, Iran achieved revolution without any Islamist movement whatsoever![21] In the early 1970s, observers such as James A. Bill who predicted Iran would undergo revolution focused on the secular nationalist movement as the likely source of revolt.[22] Influenced by the failure of Mussadiq, the nationalists contrasted the authoritarianism of the shah with liberal-democratic theory. The Marxism of the Tudeh Party also enjoyed some support. Yet it was what Hamid Dabashi calls the "theology of discontent" that powered the revolution, a theology that emerged from the writings of persons such as Jalal Al-e Ahmad, Ali Shariati, Morteza Mutahhari, Sayyid Mahmud Taleqani, Allamah Sayyid Muhammad Husayn Tabatabai, Mehdi Bazargan, Abolhasan Bani-Sadr, and Ayatollah Khomeini.[23] These thinkers deserve much of the credit (or blame) for making Islam into a political ideology in Iran in the 1960s and 1970s.

Ideologies transform values and philosophies into actionable ideas. Iran was the first country to experience modern political, economic, and social revolution under the banner of Islamic ideology. Once triumphant, the revolutionaries sought to implement one version of Islamist ideology and to stamp out competing ideologies. Forough Jahanbaksh writes:

> The dominant religious discourse, based on an ideological understanding of Islam, is by its very nature militant, exclusivist and populist; it demands unquestioning obedience and conformity to its ideological elite—the

clergy. The politicization of religion has made postrevolutionary political discourse in Iran equally stifling.[24]

While the revolution represented a triumph of Islamist ideology, the statement ignores the diversity of ideologies lurking within the revolutionary discourse. Ahmad Ashraf and Ali Banuazizi put Shariati and Khomeini at opposite ends of the ideological spectrum.[25] Dabashi concurs, portraying Khomeini as a "traditionalist" whose ideas were quite distinct from "the Islamist ideology" of Shariati.[26] The politics of the Islamic Republic came to be marked not only by repression of those who challenged the fundamental concepts but also by ferocious, open debate among partisans of competing Islamist views. Where everyone claims to be an Islamist and every proposal is made in the name of Islam, some other criterion for preferring one policy choice to another must necessarily be invoked. Policy outcomes often seem to be the product of bargaining among networks, roughly linked to ideology. These networks are often labeled traditional conservatives (around Khamenei), pragmatic conservatives (such as former President Rafsanjani), reformists (Khatami), and principlists (Ahmadinejad).[27] Who is empowered to make choices is more important than the relationship of choices to the Quran or the sunna of the Prophet.

The Iranian constitution specifies a single ideology based in the sharia. While Article 3 sketches a general set of orientations, Article 4 is precise:

All civil, penal, financial, economic, administrative, cultural, military, political, and other laws and regulations must be based on Islamic criteria. This principle applies absolutely and generally to all articles of the Constitution as well as to all other laws and regulations, and the *fuqaha* of the Guardian Council are judges in this matter.[28]

Following as it does a list of "beliefs" in Article 2 and a set of "goals" in Article 3, Article 4 makes it sound as if the Islamic Republic of Iran would function within a very narrow set of limits imposed by the sharia. References to the sharia are everywhere in the document.[29] But in fact, the tradition of law in the Shii world had long ago turned away from a single, definitive, codified understanding of the sharia. In contrast with the Sunni practice, the Shii tradition came to emphasize the ongoing work of Islamic lawyers to reinterpret the Quran and the sunna of the Prophet—the primary sources of the law in both Sunnism and Shiism—in the light of contemporary circumstances.

Shiism came to emphasize the deciders as conveying legitimacy to what was decided. Since the victory of the Usulis over the Akhbaris in the eighteenth century (see below), Twelver Shiism has typically revered several *maraji-e taqlid* (maraji is the plural of marja), who are distinguished mujtahids, or living interpreters of the law seen as worthy of emulation. Even when Shia recognized a *marja-e taqlid matlaq* (that is, a single object of emulation), this authority's interpretation was not taken as valid into the next generation. Thus the traditional plurality of authorities in Twelver Islam has enabled the current regime to avoid commitment to a single textual understanding of ideology.

Ruhollah Khomeini

As early as 1941, Ruhollah Khomeini argued that Pahlavi authoritarianism violated precepts of Islamic law: "Reason can never accept that a man who is no different from others in outward or inward accomplishments, unless maybe he is inferior to them, should have his dictates considered proper and just and his government legitimate, merely because he has succeed in gathering around himself a gang to plunder the country and murder its people."[30] The government of God is the government of reason, he said: "The duty of our government . . . is to conform to his legitimate government by making the laws passed by the Majlis a kind of commentary on the divine law." Implementation of Islamic law "will lead to the establishment of the Virtuous City." At that point Khomeini, perhaps already influenced by the writings of Mawdudi, sounded Sunni in his legalism: "If just one article of the Constitution were to be implemented, that specifying that all laws contrary to the sharia are invalid, everyone in the country would join together in harmony, and the country would move forward with the speed of lightning."

Thirty years later Ayatollah Khomeini, who had become a leader among religious scholars and the primary clerical opponent of the shah, argued a different theory, one more consonant with the history of Imami Shiism. In a series of lectures, he argued that God would never have left the Shii community without leadership during the period of Greater Occultation. As the community waited for the return of the Hidden Imam, it would necessarily follow God's law and would therefore be dependent for leadership on the legal experts, the *fuqaha* (plural of *faqih*). With great care to cite precedents and relevant hadith, he constructed a case for the governance of the leading jurist of each generation, the velayat-e faqih, placeholder for the Hidden Imam.

In the earlier work, Khomeini had written: "We do not say that government must be in the hands of the faqih; rather we say that government must be run in accordance with God's law." In his later lectures, he emphasized the need for government and the need for scholars to provide leadership. The decline of the Muslims vis-à-vis the West could be explained by "our lack of a leader, a guardian, and our lack of institutions of leadership." If justice is to prevail, Khomeini wrote, it depends upon the law. Any legitimate ruler must turn to the faqih (jurist) for advice about the law: "This being the case, the true rulers are the fuqaha themselves, and rulership ought officially to be theirs." He then argued that when a jurist with a sound knowledge of law and justice "arises and establishes a government, he will possess the same authority as the Most Noble Messenger . . . in the administration of society, and it will be the duty of all people to obey him." One cannot establish justice without law, and one cannot have a society of law without government, or government without leadership. Khomeini thus pulled his Islamist campaign toward a focus on leadership, which is the essential orientation of Shiism.

For Sunni Islamists such as Hasan al-Banna and Sayyid Qutb, both of them laymen, the scholars of Islam constituted a part of the problem, not the solution. They argued that the ulama of Egypt had been loyal servants of the monarchy and of the military regime that followed. The government of Egypt had in the space of two centuries deprived the ulama of their bases of financial support and their control of mosques and vital educational institutions. Ali Shariati made roughly the same case against the ulama of Iran. He portrayed them as defenders of tradition and authoritarianism, at roughly the same moment Khomeini was calling upon his fellow clergy to rise up against the monarchy and establish the velayat-e faqih, governance of the jurist. Khomeini's success in carrying a few of his fellow scholars and much of the country with him may have had more to do with his own charisma and political skill than the persuasiveness of his argument. The case for scholarly leadership did, however, enjoy a plausibility in Iran that it could not have had in Egypt.

Ali Shariati

The thinking of Ali Shariati, a lay preacher and pamphleteer, probably did more to inspire revolt than the lectures of the Ayatollah Khomeini. The son of a cleric from Mashad, Shariati pursued modern studies in Paris but then combined his knowledge of European thought with his own study of Islam. His lectures in Tehran in the late 1960s played to ever greater crowds until the shah felt the need to close down the Irshad Hosseini institute, where he typically spoke. "Shariati made Islam into an ideology," asserts Homa Omid, but it was scarcely a simple plea to implement the sharia and it was certainly not a call for clerical rule. Shariati feared that a theocracy would turn into a despotism of the clergy, which he termed "the worst and most oppressive form of despotism possible in human society."[31] He portrayed the clergy as a reason Islam had become sclerotic. He contrasted what he called the radical, "red Shiism" of Ali and his followers with the "black Shiism" of the Safavids and their successors—conventional, conservative, passive, and antimodern. Shariati preferred red to black.

Shariati regarded the determinism of Western thought, and Marxist thought in particular, as corrosive of human will. Evoking the early egalitarianism of Islam as an antidote for Western materialism, he found a model for Islamic feminism in the example of Fatima (wife of Ali and daughter of the Prophet) and a model for universalism in the mystical coming together of those making the pilgrimage to Mecca. Shariati's thought combined modernism with nativism, mysticism with social analysis, a denunciation of the old Islam with an appeal to the "true," "red," revolutionary instincts of the religion.[32] High-ranking clerics rejected Shariati for his lack of traditional Islamic education and, doubtless, for his harsh words about the mullahs (clerics). The shah hounded him for his hostility to the regime and his ability to attract followers. In fact, the partisans of Shariati believe he died at the hands of the shah's agents in London, more than a year before the revolution gained momentum.

For one analyst, "Islamic ideology" came to an end with Shariati's death.[33] While Shariati's ideas did not die with him, his revolutionary Shiism has not had a decisive influence on the policies of the Islamic Republic of Iran. His greatest champions, the Mujahideen-e Khalq (Leftist Fighters for the Faith), encountered repression and then obliteration by the new regime. By seizing power and then claiming legitimacy by virtue of his institutional theory, Khomeini pushed aside programmatic ideology as a foundation of the regime. After the revolution, Khomeini's ideas and not Shariati's became visible in the earliest version of the constitution, but the constitution went well beyond anything sketched in Khomeini's lectures on Islamic government. It reflected both ideas of popular sovereignty and velayat-e faqih. Its complex system of checks and balances owed something to the constitution of 1906, something to the Fifth French Republic, and a great deal to the political creativity of those who wrote it. While it intoned the need to establish Islamic principles of governance, it established processes of decision rather than a set of irrevocable, ideological standards to be followed.

Velayat-e Faqih

In the Islamic Republic, legitimacy flows from those authorized by the constitution to make decisions rather than from the coincidence or lack of it between those decisions and some preestablished template of Islamic ideology. As long as Khomeini was alive, his office, his position in the religious hierarchy, and his charisma provided such authority. When President Bani Sadr got in Khomeini's way, the elected official was forced to flee. When the Guardian Council blocked proposals of the Majlis (parliament) in the name of Islam as the constitution permits, Khomeini moved to create the Expediency Council (Council for Assessing the Interests of the System), which could move the country forward in the name of "necessity."[34] When President Khatami and his successor, Mahmoud Ahmadinejad, have attempted to assert their power—that of the elected executive—the Supreme Leader who succeeded Khomeini has utilized his powers over the judiciary and the military to thwart their efforts. The power struggle goes on.

Debates about the constitution and about policy in the Islamic Republic have always depended on arguments about Islam. Islam has become the language of politics. Every candidate, every group, every office, rationalizes positions and actions in the name of Islam. The government first opposed birth control in the name of Islam. Then it changed its mind and endorsed birth control as permitted by Islam. Some legislators have championed public enterprise and expansion of the welfare state in the name of an egalitarian Islam. Others have championed privatization in the name of Islamic commitment to private property. Khomeini found it necessary to make peace with Iraq, although the war was a jihad against an enemy of Islam, Saddam Hussein. Necessity dominated ideology, as Keyvan Tabari observes: "Ultimately, the imperative of governance has forced the rulers of Islamic Iran to resort to the same foundation for laws as used by secular states: the interests of the regime. They have rationalized that this transformation is justified by a juristic principle, *maslahat* (public interest), long rejected by Shiism."[35] Policy followed from politics, not ideology.

The great debate in Iran turns on who holds the authority and by what right. By the time he took power, Khomeini had become a marja, a model for emulation, one of a handful of clerics at the top of the pyramid. He permitted others to refer to him as the imam, which suggested a mystical relationship to the Hidden Imam, although Khomeini never explicitly claimed any such relationship. The popularity he achieved in Paris before his triumphal return to Tehran in January 1979 made him a hero from the start, a father of the revolution. Thus, he enjoyed both a spiritual and a popular legitimacy even before the constitution was adopted. Popular ratification of the constitution further affirmed his legitimacy.[36]

Three competing principles of legitimacy—*marja-e taqlid*, velayat-e faqih, and popularism—coincided in support of Khomeini as Supreme Leader.[37] They do not coincide to legitimize the rule of his successor, Ali Khamenei, who was not a marja or even a distinguished cleric. Certainly not the most distinguished jurist (faqih) of his generation, Khamenei was simply a revolutionary leader who won selection to office by the Assembly of Experts, a body made up exclusively of clerics.[38] His legitimacy is thus procedural rather than religious. Because the constitution draws its legitimacy from popular ratification and the voters choose the Assembly of Experts, albeit from a list of qualified candidates, one could argue that the faqih is the servant of public opinion, but there is little sign that Khamenei enjoys a popular mandate. Overwhelming opposition to Khamenei and his candidate for the presidency, Ali Akbar Nateq-Nuri, brought Muhammad Khatami to the presidency of the republic in 1997. Yet the Supreme Leader, Khamenei, fought off the challenge. When Mahmoud Ahmadinejad ran for a second term in the presidency in 2009, he encountered stiff competition from a reformist candidate. With the polls showing the likelihood of Ahmadinejad's defeat, Khamenei apparently felt his own legitimacy on the line and permitted or authorized tampering with the electoral process to insure the president's reelection. He also sought to frustrate Ahmadinejad's initiatives on several fronts. Traditional conservatives criticized Ahmadinejad for putting nationalism ahead of Islam.

Reform

Muhammad Khatami had assumed the presidency in 1997 with promises of reform: greater political liberty, greater freedom of expression, and expanded rights for women. He argued for the rule of law and, more specifically, for the enforcement of the 1979 constitution. Moreover, he endorsed the independence of the judiciary, warned the secret services directed by the Supreme Leader against the transgression of individual rights, and even introduced a bill to increase the power of the presidency. Although Khatami alerted Iranians to the potential of the law if it were rigorously enforced, his failure to achieve greater compliance within the executive branch only contributed to the "public's cynicism and mistrust."[39] Despite two four-year terms in the presidency, he was unable to convert two overwhelming victories at the polls into significant reform of the system. By staying in office rather than resigning on principle, he tacitly acknowledged the weakness of the presidency and reinforced the authority of the Supreme Leader—an authority based on velayat-e faqih.[40]

The election of Mahmoud Ahmadinejad as president to succeed Khatami in 2005, while a rebuke to the reformists for their failure to produce concrete results, did not resolve the underlying ideological ambiguity of the Iranian regime. Himself a populist with strong appeal in the rural areas, Ahmadinejad launched a one-man crusade to develop nuclear power in Iran, or at least he called attention to a program already in development. (Even the shah had been interested in developing nuclear power; when he announced a massive program to generate nuclear power in 1972, there were already suspicions that he harbored hopes of acquiring nuclear weapons.)[41] As Ahmadinejad's campaign put Iran increasingly at odds with Europe and the United States, not to mention Arab neighbors, many in the West seemed to assume he represented the Iranian government as a whole, even though these same analysts had come to understand that Khatami, as president, did not control Iranian policy, internal or external. As Khamenei began to distance himself from Ahmadinejad's aggressiveness and as regime spokesmen downplayed a conference Ahmadinejad organized to discredit the Holocaust, it became increasingly clear that the infirmities of the presidency affected Ahmadinejad just as much as they had hindered his predecessor. Electoral outcomes and the rule of law remained subordinate to the political interests of the ruling clerics.

President Ahmadinejad and his "principlist" allies sought to tighten the enforcement of dress codes for women. His efforts illustrate the impact of not just the "Islamic ideology" but also rival notions of ideology, and even the irrelevance of ideology. The imposition of a dress code said to originate in Islamic law constitutes the most visible effect of ideology on women. A 1983 law enacting "Islamic punishments" made it an offense to appear in public without the hijab. The regime enforced the law with vigor.[42] The dress code came as a shock to educated, urbanized, middle-class and upper-middle-class women, many of whom were accustomed to dressing in Western style in public as well as in the privacy of their homes.[43] By banning the veil in 1938, Reza Shah had made Iran look more Western, as Atatürk had similarly made women the symbol of Turkish modernity. In the Islamic Republic, women again came to symbolize the transformation of Iran.

Other actions to implement the sharia were more fundamental but also more ambivalent and impermanent. The new regime banned women from certain jobs such as judgeships. Shirin Ebadi, eventual winner of the Nobel Peace Prize, lost her post as a judge after the revolution of 1979 and was denied authorization to practice law until 1992. Subsequently, she took on the defense of prominent dissidents but was eventually forced into exile. Women were at first barred from studying certain subjects, but those restrictions were removed in 1986. Divorce laws established as consistent with the sharia were amended in 1992. Contraception, banned in the early days of the revolution, became available in 1988. Sixty percent of university students are now women. Jaleh Shaditalab says that women have been responsible for some of these changes: "Educated women's demands have led to calls for a strategic change in the governance of the Islamic state."[44]

The Islamic Republic encouraged women to participate in the economy and the body politic at the same time it emphasized their duties under Islamic law and their subordination to men. As Janet Afary observes, "this is why Iranian women reacted to the policies of the Islamic Republic in such varied ways."[45] The Ayatollah Khomeini, not generally a champion of women's rights, "called for . . . millions of Iranians including women to join the Islamic *Jihad* . . . against poverty and social deprivation."[46] Women joined revolutionary demonstrations in the last days of the shah's regime, many of them wearing hijab and chador as symbols of protest. (Thousands of Tehrani women then turned out to protest in the spring of 1980, when they learned that the new regime intended to impose a dress code.)[47] Under the Islamic regime, women received the right to vote and have exercised it in great number; some have been elected to the Majlis, where they have occasionally played significant roles.[48] Women's literacy rates, which were below 20 percent in 1966, surpassed 75 percent by 2001.[49] The rate of women's employment in Iran rose more sharply in the 1990s than it had under the shah in the 1960s and 1970s. Women constituted slightly more than 25 percent of the workforce in Iran by the year 2000, compared with about 20 percent at the moment of the revolution. Female employment in other Muslim countries ranged from a low of 13 percent in the United Arab Emirates and Oman to about 35 percent in Morocco, compared with 40–46 percent in industrialized countries.[50] Roksana Bahramitash concludes: "The rise of political Islam broke the barriers to participation in public life that had previously existed for women, especially those of lower socioeconomic background."[51] In contrast, many upper-class women have felt the pinch of restriction in the Islamic Republic.

Several men who have championed women's rights have been punished by the regime. Abdollah Nuri, a cleric who first lost his position in the presidential cabinet by the action of the Majlis, was brought to trial before the Special Court for the Clergy in 1999 for a newspaper article that criticized official imposition of the hijab. He said the hijab as a form of dress should be seen as an aspect of a lifestyle and accused the regime of trying to impose a lifestyle. But the government argued that the notion that people should live as they wished contradicts the Islamic duty to promote virtue and prohibit vice. Nuri received a five-year sentence but managed to publish a book called *The Hemlock of Reform*, reiterating his views on personal freedom, before he was incarcerated. It achieved best-seller status before the 2000 elections.[52]

Another dissident voice, that of Hasan Yousefi Eshkevari, a champion of democracy and human rights, argued that the hijab is a matter of belief, not obligation. To not wear modest dress might be a sin, but it should not be a crime. In April 2000 Eshkevari attended a conference in Berlin called "Iran after the Elections, and the Dynamics of Reform in the Islamic Republic." The conference suffered interruption from groups protesting the policies of the Islamic Republic. One protester, said Eshkevari, was a "woman wearing nothing but a bikini and a head scarf as a gesture of protest against 'the oppression of women in Iran.'"[53] Eshkevari agreed to sit on a panel about women's rights, although he had not been scheduled to do so, and there he ended up making a statement. He distinguished belief or dogma from basic values of Islam, which he called ideology. He put religious rulings in a third category and then distinguished rulings about worship, which are unchanging, from rulings that must be adapted to social circumstances. He put matters of women's rights in that category, since they emerged from a different set of social circumstances, those of pre-Islamic Arabia. On his return from Germany, Eshkevari was arrested and brought before the Special Court for the Clergy on charges of apostasy, conspiracy to overthrow the Islamic Republic by spreading lies, and insulting the regime by his presence at the conference. Originally sentenced to death, he won a reduced sentence of four years for "insulting the sanctities" and one year for going to Berlin and propagandizing against the regime.[54]

Law and Ideology

The case of women's rights in Iran illustrates the strengths and weaknesses of ideology as a determinant of politics. Khomeini's position, which emphasized governance of the clergy, prevailed over other ideological positions, including that of Shariati. The new governing institutions were supposed to defend an ideology that could not be defined with precision. One solution would have been to further open debate and give the proponents of democracy an opportunity to make their case, but this solution endangered the sovereignty of the faqih and the clergy.[55] Such openness endangered the interests of the regime, which then preferred to impose its version of Islamic ideology, however partial and incoherent, and to repress other versions. It was not the persuasiveness of the faqih but the power of the office that prevailed—not the strength of the official ideology but the political strength of those it protected from democratic challenge. The sharia, prominently mentioned in the constitution as the foundation of the Islamic ideology, affects Iranian life only where and if the political institutions decide it should. Tabari says: "The controlling factor in the Iranian legal system, in fact, has been the interests of the ruling conservative clergy."[56] The political power of the clergy is what makes the Islamic Republic of Iran Islamic.

Islamic ideology has affected dimensions of the law in Iran. Legislation has been drafted to reflect "Islamic criteria," and the Guardian Council has rejected some legislation in the name of the same criteria, but much of Iranian law remains unchanged. Ann Elizabeth Mayer writes that the legal system "remains essentially French in orientation." It is based on law codes developed originally in Europe and applied to a judicial system based on the French model. "Islamic law should not be treated as the central determinant of Iran's post-revolutionary legal system," she writes.[57] The reasons are several. First, the European law codes that Iran adopted in the early twentieth century continue to govern property, business, commercial transactions, and many other dimensions of Iranian life. Second, there is the long Shii tradition of judges who offer differing interpretations of Islamic law and the resulting clash of authorities about which "Islamic criteria" are relevant in any given situation. Finally, and most important, the regime itself is unwilling to put law above the interests of the governors.

Islamic ideology affects not just the law but also the discourse of both proponents and detractors of the regime. The ideology is hegemonic in the sense that supporters, critics, and outright opponents who do not openly seek the overthrow of the regime must formulate their arguments in the language of Islam. The greatest challenge comes not from those who would reject velayat-e faqih, as do many members of the clerical establishment, but from those who accept it and interpret it differently. The late Grand Ayatollah Montazeri, himself a participant in the revolution, advanced a theory that Islam requires the faqih to bow before democratic politics.[58] Intellectuals who have supported reform (and gone to jail, in some cases) have mostly accepted that argument. Montazeri, who died in 2009, became a hero of the reform movement.

The most notable critic of the regime, one who has nonetheless escaped punishment, is Abdolkarim Soroush, a philosopher who has sought to differentiate religion from the religious knowledge of human beings, which is inevitably fallible and changing. He has argued that genuine faith is possible only if a believer is free to choose to believe or not to believe. Faith and freedom are inseparable. Farzin Vahdat further explains the argument: "Soroush identified protection of the freedom of faith and creation of social conditions conducive to such freedom as the main tasks of a democratic religious state."[59] An Islamic state cannot, therefore, seek guidance in Islamic ideology understood as an unchanging set of principles or even understood as a principle of leadership, such as velayat-e faqih. According to Soroush, the faqih, not to mention the author of the idea (Khomeini) himself, is a mere mortal interpreting the immortal and unchanging will of God from a particular vantage point amid the vicissitudes of history.

Another dissident, Mohsen Kadivar, insists on the necessity of protecting freedom in the private sphere: "The private sphere is the sole prerogative of the individual."[60] He says the sharia starts from the assumption that no issue is public and that individuals, even non-Muslims, are protected in their options and in their private activities: "The rights of the individual in his or her private sphere are guaranteed to a higher degree in an Islamic society than in a secular one." The boundary between public and private is the question. Giving absolute power to an Islamic state, and putting the Islamic state above the principle of free choice, may reflect good intent, but the state cannot succeed in imposing belief. "Deceit, duplicity, and maintaining appearances are only some of the pitfalls of imposed religiosity. . . . Islamic thought finds absolute and despotic rule alien and does not sanction interests not already delineated in Islamic terms." Both Kadivar and Soroush remained traditionalists on gender issues. Neither would shake hands with women strangers, writes Afary, "even at academic conferences and private gatherings abroad."[61]

Iran is a place where ideas have mattered. From its rich intellectual history, there reverberate echoes of Ferdowsi's *Shahnameh* from the pre-Islamic period, the great Sufi poets, the Islamic philosophers, distinguished ulama, liberal reformers, Marxists, and Islamists. The ideas of Jalal Al-e Ahmad, Ali Shariati, and Ruhollah Khomeini affected the revolutionary outcome. The regime has chosen principles of the sharia and written them into positive law, but, as Abdullahi A. Al-Naim observes, the sharia "cease[s] to be the normative system of Islam by the very act of enacting it as the law to be enforced by the state."[62] The Islamic Republic is a product of all these ideas together with many from non-Iranian and non-Islamic sources. The state is not a result of an unambiguous Islamic ideology, because no such thing exists. The "Islamic ideology," which many would see as a force in modern Iranian politics, is best understood as an outcome of state decisions. The state is not Islamic by virtue of the ideology. State ideology is Islamic by the decision of state institutions.[63] Because one segment of the clerical class dominates the state, that segment fashions the laws, decrees, sermons, and proclamations that have come to be seen as the Islamic ideology.

Institutions

Neither an Islamic identity nor an Islamic ideology suffices to explain political and religious institutions in Iran. No concept of Islamic identity adequately ac-

counts for the emergence of a strong, relatively hierarchical religious institution
in Iran, which is quite unlike the religious structure of other Muslim states, such
as Egypt or Turkey. Nor does any concept of Islamic ideology suffice to explain
the elaboration of a constitution that owes so much to Western conceptions of
political engineering. In the wake of the Iranian Revolution, many Westerners
argued that the Islamic Republic of Iran reflected an Islamic requirement for the
complete merger of religion and politics. Scholars soon pointed out, however,
that the revolution occurred because the clergy in Iran had developed an autonomy from political domination over a period of five centuries. This autonomy
permitted the clerical class to act against a monarchy that had long striven to
control religious personnel and observance. When a portion of the clerical class
took power, it broke with another substantial group of clerics who believed in
separation. The political hierarchy does not coincide with the religious hierarchy.
Tehran, the political capital, is only one hundred miles from Qom, the center of
religion, but the psychological distance between these cities remains significant.

What distinguishes Iran from other Muslim countries is the degree to which
the religious establishment enjoys (1) internal coherence and hierarchical structure
and (2) relative independence from political interference. The Qajar and Pahlavi
dynasties tried in the nineteenth and twentieth centuries to subjugate the ulama
by undercutting their bases of financial support, eliminating the religious courts,
and reducing the role of ulama in education. But the governments never gained
full control. Instead, as early as the nineteenth century, a portion of the clergy
began to utilize its ties to the commercial middle class in particular and to the
people more generally as bases for political influence. Ruhollah Khomeini built
on this long tradition of political engagement and capitalized on the construction
of a religious hierarchy that had begun under the Safavids and matured under
the Qajars. Reza Khan (Pahlavi) benefited from the support of that hierarchy
when he had himself crowned shah in 1925, but his son Muhammad Reza Shah
found himself increasingly at odds with the hierarchy after 1963. His crude, ill-
considered efforts to throttle the rising voice of the clerics merely magnified
their prestige and authority. It was the separateness of the ulama from the political
system that made them popular and credible. Similarly, their distinctiveness (in
dress and language) and organizational coherence made them a powerful force
for revolution.

The emergence of an autonomous, distinctive corps of ulama owed something
to Safavid rule and even more, perhaps, to the eventual disappearance of the

Safavids. The early Safavids were "extremists," tribal Sufis from Azerbaijan who seized power according to the pattern outlined a century earlier by Ibn Khaldun. They were religious extremists sweeping in from the marches to seize power and establish a dynasty in the name of moral purity. Their link with theological Shiism was tenuous or nonexistent, and they took control of an Iran marked by multiple religious tendencies. The Safavids cultivated a group of ulama to bolster their legitimacy in the name of Twelver orthodoxy. The Safavids appointed the imams of the primary mosques in the cities, but there also developed a category of unofficial ulama. The most distinguished became known as mujtahids, who claimed the right to engage in the process of ijtihad, that is, offering individual opinions on theology and law. Toward the end of the Safavid rule (early eighteenth century) some mujtahids seem to have been claiming the right to give the ruler advice.[64] The weakening of the monarchy made it more dependent on the ulama. The incursion of Afghan forces into Iran in the eighteenth century ended Safavid rule and drove many of the ulama into the Shii shrine cities of Iraq, where they were largely invulnerable to the blandishments of political authority in Iran.

The Qajars and the Ulama

When the Qajar dynasty established its hold on Iran after an interregnum of relative anarchy, it did so without religious pretension or claim. The Qajars were from the beginning suitors of a religious establishment led by mujtahids, most of them living beyond the political control of the regime. A struggle among the mujtahids in the late eighteenth century pitted a group known as Akhbaris, who claimed that the role of the mujtahids was limited to the application of inherited wisdom, and another group known as the Usulis, who insisted that wisdom must be reinterpreted in every generation. They said the Islamic concept of "perfect man" must necessarily reflect time and place, and they portrayed themselves as the keeper of that tradition, as the models for the emulation of ordinary believers. Their success led to increased prestige and influence for the mujtahids in particular and the clerical class in general. In the absence of the Twelfth Imam, they asserted their claim to religious leadership of the society about two centuries before Ruhollah Khomeini proposed velayat-e faqih. The emergence of Shaykh al-Ansari Murtada as the sole model for emulation (*marja-e taqlid matlaq*) in the mid-nineteenth century provided an unprecedented unity for the Twelver

Shii world as a whole. This unity did not survive beyond the life of Murtada's successor and has rarely been re-created, but his dominance further strengthened the corporate identity of the autonomous clergy. His position as a teacher in Najaf, Iraq, put him beyond the control of the Iranian monarchy. The predominant attitude of the ulama in this period was one of disdain for the Qajars and opposition to their policies.[65]

The Qajars courted the religious establishment without advancing any religious claim of their own. They appointed an official called the *sadr al-ulama* and named imams to head mosques in key cities, but they mainly provided enforcement of religious law. The mujtahids had enforcers of their own, thugs called *lutis*, who carried out sentences pronounced in religious courts, but the clerics welcomed the help of the state, particularly in dealing with heretical minorities and practices. The monarch curried favor with the mujtahids by prosecuting Sufis and suppressing a movement inspired by Sufism called Shaykhism in the early nineteenth century. The ulama saw even greater threat in a man named Sayyid Ali Muhammad, who claimed in 1843 to be the Bab, the "door" or "gateway" to the Hidden Imam. His was an explicitly anticlerical message, although some of his leading supporters came from the lower ranks of the ulama. Only one seems to have been a mujtahid. "Had the Bab been acknowledged as the Hidden Imam, the function of the ulama would have ceased to exist," asserts Hamid Algar.[66]

The ulama responded to the Bab by seeking to discredit and repress the movement. They demanded his execution, and after outbursts of unrest attributed to the Bab and his partisans, the state finally obliged in 1850. But, as is so often the case with religious figures, death did not settle the matter. Babism became Bahaism under the leadership of Abd ul-Baha, who reaffirmed the Bab's hostile attitude toward the clergy and the state.[67] Repression of the Bahais continues to this day.

Foreign influence became the principal bone of contention between the Qajar dynasty and the religious establishment. The Qajars started to modernize their country almost a half century later than the Ottomans and did so by appealing for foreign assistance, first to strengthen the military, then to reorganize the state and the economy. The ulama resisted growing foreign influence, positioning themselves as defenders of the Iranian people and their traditional way of life. They opposed the 1872 concession to the Baron Julius de Reuter, an Englishman, of rights to exploit mineral resources, build railways, and found a national bank, among other things.[68] But the shah went ahead, saying he respected the mullahs but "refused to permit their intervention in matters of state."[69]

The activist elements of the ulama achieved greater success in their fight against the tobacco concession in the 1890s and in the struggle for a constitution in the following decade. In both cases, an alliance between ulama and the merchant class, the bazaaris, was the secret of success. The families of bazaaris and ulama intermarried. As prosperous members of Iranian society who provided financial support for the mullahs, the bazaaris helped choose the mujtahids who rose to become models of emulation.[70] Bazaaris needed the educational and judicial services of the clergy, and the clergy needed the financial support of bazaaris. Both groups found themselves threatened in their livelihood by the monarchy's reliance on foreign advice and money. In opposing royal absolutism, they joined a group of modernizing intellectuals determined to promote political as well as economic and social change.

The shah's grant of a monopoly on the production, sale, and export of tobacco in Iran in 1890 served as a warm-up for the constitutional struggle that would follow more than a decade later. A cleric who preached against the agreement in Shiraz, where there was resistance, earned expulsion to Iraq. The resistance spread to Tabriz and other cities, where ulama led mass protests. In December 1891, the clerical establishment produced a fatwa declaring that the use of tobacco constituted an attack on the Hidden Imam. The effect was dramatic. Mass demonstrations in Tehran led to violence and a number of deaths, and the government, after attempting to negotiate a partial renunciation, finally backed away from the entire concession in early 1892. The alliance of ulama with bazaaris and modernizing liberals had prevailed, and the ulama emerged as "a central force, which could be allied with, manipulated, combated, but never ignored."[71]

The same alliance proved critical in the success of the constitutional revolution in Iran. The assassination of Nasir al-Din Shah in 1896 weakened the Qajar monarchy. While scarcely an exemplary ruler—he had a lifelong zest for women, young boys, and material gain—Nasir al-Din held power for forty-eight years. His successor, Mozaffar al-Din Shah, switched from one chief minister to another in the search for resources to satisfy creditors of the throne and the "needs" of his courtiers and himself. Clerical contempt for the monarchy's moral weaknesses and indifference to national sentiment only increased. In December 1905, the governor of Tehran ordered the beating of sugar merchants who refused to lower their prices. Some mullahs and bazaaris assembled to protest, but the government broke up the meeting and provoked the ulama into withdrawing from the city. Algar calls it "a symbolic demonstration of the illegitimacy of the government."[72]

The ulama came back to Tehran once the government promised to implement a House of Justice. After further pushing and shoving between government and opposition—a struggle that lasted ten months—the first representative assembly, the first Majlis, met in October 1906 to draft a constitution, which was signed by the dying Mozaffar al-Din Shah in December. Article 1 made Imami Shiism the religion of state, and Article 2 created a five-member board composed of top religious leadership to review legislation. These would seem to be important trophies for the ulama, who were presumably less committed to the freedoms that the new document guaranteed. Unfortunately, the machinations of a new shah and foreign powers, especially the 1907 agreement between Britain and Russia to divide Iran into zones of influence, eventually brought the constitutional experiment to a standstill. The alliance of ulama, bazaaris, and constitutionalists brought change but not stability to the country.

The Pahlavis

The chance for stability emerged twenty years later, after Reza Khan, who had risen within the Russian-trained Cossack Brigade, overturned the Qajar dynasty. The religious establishment, or most of it, apparently preferred a new monarchy over a republic and the possibility of further chaos.[73] Reza Khan, who took power in 1921 and the crown in 1925, understood and presumably resented his dependence on the goodwill of the ulama. Together with his admiration for Mustafa Kemal Atatürk, his resentment helps explain why he systematically sought to undermine the power of the religious establishment over the next two decades. The creation of modern schools, begun after 1850, had already eroded the power of the ulama in education. The adoption of a civil code in 1928 diminished the power of sharia courts, and a 1932 law deprived them of the revenue generated by the registering of documents. After 1936 the ulama could not serve as judges. Shahrough Akhavi sums up the impact of Reza Shah's tenure on the religious establishment:

On the whole, the Shah's legacy in the matter of clergy-state relations was that of a ruler who sought to prohibit the public enactment of passion plays, narratives or even mourning for the death of contemporary *maraji-yi taqlid*, rather than a ruler who received petitions of redress from the clergy, solicited their support in establishing order and stability, and sought their spiritual guidance, as mandated by the Constitution.[74]

The military strength of Reza Shah, who managed to subdue tribal areas and to initiate the creation of a modern infrastructure in Iran, permitted him to disregard the views of the ulama but did not enable him to domesticate the religious establishment. His reforms marginalized the ulama and deepened the divide between church and state. The adoption of a dress code in 1928 set clergy apart by permitting them to dress in a traditional manner. Everyone else was to appear in public in Western dress.[75]

Clerical influence rebounded after the allies—Britain, Russia, and the United States—pushed Reza Shah from the throne in 1941 and permitted his young son, Muhammad Reza Pahlavi, to take power. The veil came back and, in fact, mujtahids issued fatwas in 1948 forbidding women to enter the bazaars without the veil. One faction of the clergy led by the Ayatollah Kashani favored active intervention in politics and supported the rise of Muhammad Mussadiq to the prime minister's position. Mussadiq's nationalization of Iranian oil touched off an international crisis. His popularity threatened the position of the shah, who was forced to flee the country in 1953. He returned after a coup d'état engineered by Washington and London. But most of the clergy, including the young Ruhollah Khomeini, remained loyal to the leading ayatollahs, Muhammad Husayn Borujerdi and Muhammad Musavi Bihbihani, who resisted direct political involvement. While unwilling to cooperate openly with the shah, they gave him tacit support. Grand Ayatollah Borujerdi solidified the organizational integrity of the religious establishment. Respected in his later years as the sole marja-e taqlid, he held together a set of factions and dampened conflict with the regime in the name of spirituality, the seminaries in Qom, a united front, and sufficient economic resources. Borujerdi died in 1961, leaving behind a religious establishment that was more autonomous, coherent, and prosperous than the one he had inherited.

It was by no means obvious, however, that this establishment could prevail in a contest with the monarchy. By 1961 Muhammad Reza Shah had been in power for twenty years, thanks in part to foreign assistance with police, education, and industry. He was launching the ambitious White Revolution in an effort to win the hearts of the peasantry with land reform, which some of the clergy opposed.

The religious establishment appeared weak and ineffective. Akhavi puts the total number of clergy at 10,000, of whom 100 ranked as mujtahids. They staffed 20,000 mosques.[76] There were some 138 madrasas in 1968 and some 7,500 students, and the state was progressively taking control of those institutions to modernize the curriculum. The state had taken ownership of religious endowments in 1937 under Reza Shah.[77] (The autonomous clergy still enjoyed the benefits of direct contributions from believers in the form of the religious taxes.)[78] By the 1970s the state's Endowment Organization was using funds to support students in madrasas and to create the Department for Religious Propaganda to work in the rural areas. Akhavi writes: "Together with their associates in the Literacy Corps, [these fresh products of religious education] were meant to be the 'mullas of modernization.'"[79] By seizing control of religious education and bureaucratizing religious outreach, the state sought to undermine the autonomy and power of the religious establishment.

At least two factors explain the religious establishment's transformation over twenty years (1960–1980) from a position of relative obscurity and acquiescence into a force capable of taking political power. The first factor is the remarkable leadership of Ruhollah Khomeini, who turned the regime's awkward efforts at repression into an incitement of revolution. The second was the preaching of lay radicals such as Jalal Al-e Ahmad and especially Ali Shariati, whose revolutionary but anticlerical message aroused the masses in Tehran and prepared them to follow revolutionary religious leadership.

When Khomeini began systematic verbal attacks on the shah in the spring of 1963, he was already a prominent religious leader, one of three or four leading ayatollahs and objects of emulation, or maraji. Some clerics objected to the shah's land reforms. Others protested the plan to give women the right to vote, although voting itself was largely meaningless in Iran at that point. Khomeini attacked the shah for the tyrannical nature of his rule and for his dependence on the United States. A proposed law to exempt American military personnel in Iran from prosecution under Iranian law exemplified his complaints. The regime triggered protests in major cities when it arrested Khomeini in March 1963. Subsequently released, rearrested, released again, and then expelled to Turkey in 1964, Khomeini ended up installing himself in the old stronghold of Shiism, the city of Najaf in Iraq, where he could teach—and rail upon the Iranian regime with impunity. It was there he gave a series of lectures expounding his theory of velayat-e faqih.

From Quietism to Activism

By his long patience with the quietism of the Ayatollah Husayn Borujerdi, and by his denunciation of the shah from the prestigious Faiziyeh madrasa in Qom, Khomeini acted with full consciousness of the need to pull the clerical class with him toward political activism. He articulated a theory of Islamic government that depended on the rule of a mujtahid. Quite to the contrary, Ali Shariati helped found Irshad Hosseini in Tehran, an institute that lay outside the traditional religious structure and where he and others intoned against the regime for its favoritism, elitism, and tyranny. Shariati preached a revolutionary version of Islam that categorized the clerical class as defenders of the status quo, but in the long run he helped Khomeini by portraying the shah as a threat to the authentic, democratic, egalitarian nature of Islam. After Shariati's death in 1977, Khomeini and his clerical entourage carried the message forward and transformed it into an Islamic government.

The religious establishment prevailed in Iran by virtue of its success in maintaining distance from the regime. Alone among Iranian institutions, it was relatively untainted by the crassness of authoritarianism. It prevailed because of the hierarchical structure, developed over centuries, that permitted top ayatollahs to exercise financial and political control. It prevailed thanks to a structure that reached into nearly every village. Mosques seem to have escaped the surveillance of Savak, the shah's secret police and intelligence agency. Sermons on cassette shipped from Europe carried Khomeini's message to the far reaches of the country. The religious establishment prevailed by virtue of astute leadership that caught foreigners, and perhaps the shah himself (then suffering from cancer), by surprise. The United States struggled at the last minute to make contact with the clerics and failed. Ignored and disdained by academics and intelligence agencies, Khomeini and his revolutionary cohorts could not be restrained.

The arrival of Grand Ayatollah Ruhollah Khomeini in Tehran in February 1979 united religious and political power in a manner reminiscent of Safavid Iran. Khomeini had advanced himself to the pinnacle of the Shii hierarchy in Iran. The new constitution, with its consecration of the velayat-e faqih, opened the way for him to rule as "the most distinguished jurist" of his generation. The Guardian Council necessarily included members of the clerical class, and the Council of Experts entrusted with choosing the faqih included only members of the clergy. In addition, clerics repopulated the judiciary, dominated the new foundations designed to promote the purposes of the new regime, and ran for election to national and local offices. While laymen were eligible to fill offices and run for election, clerics vetted officeholders and candidates for their religious credentials. It was not enough to be a Muslim. To get past the gatekeepers, one needed to have supported the revolution. Under Khomeini, the religious establishment became the political establishment.

Separation of Institutions

Such a statement is, however, misleading. First, a number of leading clerics stood aside and refused to acknowledge the legitimacy of velayat-e faqih. The clerical class was not united behind the regime. Some believed the clerical involvement in politics would sully Islam. At the moment of Khomeini's death in 1989, all the remaining grand ayatollahs, except for Husayn Ali Montazeri, stood opposed to the idea of velayat-e faqih; Montazeri had already been shoved aside as a potential successor and put under house arrest for advocating Islamic democracy.

Second, the constitution did not specify the relationship between the faqih and the religious establishment. Khomeini was a grand ayatollah, a marja, one worthy of emulation by believers, but his successor, hastily promoted to ayatollah from a more modest status, did not try to attain marja status. Khamenei's promotion to Supreme Leader created division between the velayat-e faqih and the traditional Shii notion of the marja. The selection of Ali Khamenei to succeed Imam Khomeini affirmed the practical separation between religious and political institutions.[80]

A leading champion of Islamic government, Ayatollah Mohammad Yazdi sought in the mid-1990s to eliminate the idea of plural models and to make the Supreme Leader the sole object of emulation. The time seemed ripe, because three grand ayatollahs (maraji) had died in the space of a few years. The Qom seminary professors responded to the Yazdi proposal with a list of seven leaders who should be considered maraji, including Ayatollah Khamenei. Apparently embarrassed by being included in a group of seven, or by not being designated the sole marja, Khamenei declined to claim the role within Iran but accepted that Shiis living abroad might consider him a marja![81] Thus, the distinction between the Supreme Leader and highest religious leadership continues, showing that the government of the Islamic Republic has not been able to bring the clerical class under its thumb despite efforts that began under Khomeini. The seminaries at Qom continue to enjoy substantial control over religious education and function with relative autonomy, independent of the government.

A third reason that the religious establishment is not fully congruent with the political establishment is that clerics no longer dominate the Majlis or the presidency of the republic, and much less do they control the bureaucracy. Khomeini said the faqih inherited all the power of the Prophet, but the constitution balances that power with institutions based on popular sovereignty. At the outset of the Islamic Republic, it appeared that clerical networks exercised their power through every branch of the inordinately complicated political structure, but the networks split into factions vying for influence within the system. Moreover, their numbers were never overwhelming. Of 5,000 clerics with the rank of ayatollah in the year 2000, Wilfried Buchta estimates that 80 worked for the government. When Khamenei took office, he held the rank of *hojjatoleslam*, a title accorded to graduates of theological seminaries. Buchta puts the number of such people at 28,000 in 2000, of whom about 2,000 served in the government. He also estimates that some 4,000 clerics (out of a total of 180,000) with little or no seminary training held government positions in that year.[82]

If these numbers are roughly correct, then the size of the formally trained clerical class has increased about threefold from the early 1960s, from 10,000 to 33,000. Mosques, seminaries, and religious associations multiplied in the 1960s and 1970s in a period of relative prosperity. Ervand Abrahamian describes this increase: "By the mid-1970s, perhaps for the first time in Iranian history, the religious establishment was large enough to be able to send preachers to the most distant of Iranian villages."[83] Nikki Keddie puts the number of people in Iran holding religious posts or having some religious training at 180,000 in the early 1980s.[84] The total might be more than 210,000 today (about 0.3 percent of the population), as indicated by the Buchta figures. The clerical class constitutes a small part of the population (1 person in about 350), and only a few of the clerical class (roughly 6,000 of 210,000, or 1 in 35) hold government positions.

While clerical rule has transformed some government departments, such as the judiciary and education, others have retained much of their prerevolutionary character, largely unscathed by clerical influence. Clerics have gained power through the great foundations created after the revolution in the name of good works and charity. The *bonyads*, as these foundations are called, may control about 40 percent of the Iranian economy.[85] Examples would be the Foundation for the Dispossessed, the Martyrs' Foundation, the Imam Reza Foundation, the Fifteenth of Khordad Foundation, and the Farabi Foundation. Enjoying nonprofit status and reporting to the Supreme Leader, these foundations engage in money-making activity but also draw heavily on the state budget. Perhaps because they depend on the Supreme Leader, or perhaps because of their ostensibly charitable purposes, clerics play key roles in most if not all of the foundations.

The political influence of the *bonyads* appeared to increase in the first decade of Khamenei's rule as Supreme Leader. In the second decade it was another group, even less tied to the religious establishment, that gained influence. Since 2000, the Revolutionary Guard (Pasdaran or IRGC), seemingly in support of the Supreme Leader's efforts to maintain or augment his control over the system, has come to exercise decisive influence in both the legislative and the executive branches. About a third of the members of the Majlis have served in the IRGC. President Ahmadinejad served there and has brought many former IRGC members into his cabinet. Taking advantage of measures to privatize the economy, the IRGC has enmeshed itself in enterprises that may now constitute 25 percent or more of the economy.[86] The Revolutionary Guard controls the Basij (5 million members, perhaps 1 million effectives), the volunteer morals police, which quelled the protest of the Green Movement following the 2009 election. Some analysts speak of Iran coming under military rule: "One of the most important implications of this development is the consolidation of a military state that can be described as a theocracy only in name."[87]

Despite the lack of a clear separation of religion and politics in Iran, the two realms cannot be described as one force. Some religious institutions, such as the seminaries, continue to function with relative autonomy. The religious hierarchy centered in Qom is distinct from the political hierarchy, which is headed by the Supreme Leader in Tehran, who is not and never was a primary religious leader. The fear he evokes inside and outside the government depends not upon his ability to allocate religious rewards but upon his control of the armed forces, police, and intelligence agencies in addition to the powers of appointment and dismissal that reside with his office. The presidency, the Expediency Council, and the Majlis, not to mention most of the government ministries, are not religious institutions. If political institutions were identical to the religious institution, there would be no need for a constitution and the complicated system of elections it creates. The constitution, the religious establishment, and Iranian tradition prevent complete fusion of religion and politics. Nevertheless, the current constitution, as interpreted by the Supreme Leader, Ali Khamenei, prevents separation. Such is one definition of "dissonant politics."[88]

Political Culture

The hope of any revolutionary regime is to transform the political culture in its image. Lenin and Stalin hoped to create a society of communists. Mustafa Kemal Atatürk hoped to make Turkey a nation of secular Muslims. The Iranian revolutionaries succeeded by appealing to the Muslim loyalties of men and women who flocked to the revolutionary standard, but the leadership also hoped to transform its countrymen into "true Muslims," those who would abandon the miniskirt, give up wine and beer, rededicate themselves to their families, and, when necessary, stand ready to sacrifice their lives for the country. The revolutionaries hoped to displace the celebration of pre-Islamic Iran characteristic of the old regime with a fresh commitment to Islam and to Iran as the leader of the Muslim world. As with every revolutionary regime, education became the key to achieving such objectives. Propaganda may sway some of the older generation, but the new, purified generation comes from the schools. Unless a revolutionary regime can transform the political culture to fit its ideals, it will eventually be forced to continue with postrevolutionary repression or relinquish its vision of utopia.

The struggle over political culture in Iran has focused on religion for a century. Reza Shah and his son Muhammad Reza Shah drew from Atatürk's vision of modernity, which called for secularization of the political culture. They worked at the level of symbols (dress codes), law (civil and criminal codes), and especially education. By creating modern elementary and secondary schools run by the state, they undercut the role of the clergy and helped propagate a message of nationalism and modernization. The schools taught religion as a tool for achieving these objectives.[89] The creation of a law school in 1936 and then modern universities after World War II offered an alternative to the madrasas run by the ulama, and even the madrasas became subject to government regulation. The Pahlavis sought to reduce the impact of the religious establishment on the law and its enforcement, on education, and on the mores of the country.

To some extent they succeeded. They succeeded among the upper classes in the great cities of Iran, especially Tehran, where Western fashion, automobiles, industry, commerce, and education wrought enormous changes. As Iran became richer from its oil production, the shah spent freely on military hardware, oil technology, and big business. New wealth and opportunities abounded for elites, but there also emerged resentment against the incursion of foreign ways. Western cinema, Western experts, Iranian students returning from abroad, American television shows broadcast in Iran—all affected the culture in Tehran. The modernizing, secularizing vision of the Pahlavis rallied an urban elite against the ulama and religion. In a survey of some 167 members of the Iranian elite in the late 1960s, Marvin Zonis found that two-thirds of his respondents

> felt that the ulama were performing a negative service for Iran—a rather conclusive demonstration of the fundamental bifurcation between the religious and political elite and a rationalization for the political campaign being waged against them. Inasmuch as the old regime was unsuccessful in mobilizing the religious elite for regime policies, the regime's response was overwhelmingly negative, both to the ulama themselves and to religion per se (although this latter point is not one that would be conceded by the regime).[90]

The Advent of Islamism

For the nonelites, the tide was beginning to shift toward religion about the time Zonis conducted his survey. With the leadership of the Ayatollah Khomeini, the ulama began to reciprocate the elites' disdain. Al-e Ahmad was writing about Westoxication. Shariati began to preach about revolutionary Islam as the proper recourse for Iran. At about the same time, other Muslim states began to experience religious revival. The Israeli victory over the Arabs in 1967 triggered new interest in Islam. While the changing tide in Iran does suggest that the shah failed in his broadest efforts to combat religion, it would be difficult to establish that Iran was naturally more disposed toward Islamism than other countries, much less to show that the religious revival in the Muslim world began in Iran. As frustration with the promises of modernizing ideologies such as socialism and liberalism mounted, religion became the language of political dissent in Iran as elsewhere in the region.

In an effort to legitimize the illegitimate, the shah sought to link his throne to Persian monarchs of the pre-Islamic era. When he celebrated the 2,500th anniversary of the Peacock throne at Persepolis in 1971, he linked himself to tales of the past reported in the great epic poem by Ferdowsi, the *Shahnameh*. Writing in the Islamic era, Ferdowsi recounts bloody tales of ancient warfare in which kings and heroes act first and reflect later. When they reflect, they often invoke concepts of right and wrong and the support of God (in the singular), but they also confront jinns (devils) and demons, monsters, and magic. Women figures are mostly bearers of children, but at least one woman dons armor and takes the battlefield to avenge a family wrong. Wine flows freely at banquets that go on for days. Regarded as one of the first and most important examples of Persian literature, the *Shahnameh* neither exalts religion in the pre-Islamic period nor banishes it from consideration. Belief in a single God seems to characterize this ancient society.

The simple existence of Persian literature demonstrates that for Iran, the coming of Islam did not mean, as it did elsewhere in the Middle East and North Africa, the victory of Arabic. Names changed, as Richard Bulliet observes in charting the slow conversion of Iranians from Zoroastrianism to Islam, but the predominant language of everyday discourse did not.[91] Moreover, the Persian penchant for mystical poets such as Rumi and Hafiz further distinguishes Iranian Islam from that of places such as Saudi Arabia, where Sufism has long been suspect. The passion plays honoring the death of the Imam Husayn draw upon a love of theater, poetry, and mysticism. On the one hand, the late shah sought to neglect elements of the Iranian heritage he considered inimical to modernization and his legitimacy. The ulama, on the other hand, tried to filter the heritage of Iran's non-Islamic and "heretical" elements (such as the Bab) in order to ensure their own dominance in religious affairs.

The Pahlavis, father and son, promoted Iranian nationalism and tried but failed to reduce the role of religion in Iranian society. The Islamic Republic has sought to enhance the place of religion by (1) establishing norms of dress and behavior; (2) establishing religious criteria for holding political office; (3) revising school curricula and devising new educational programs; (4) restricting the flow of information in the name of protecting morality; and (5) encouraging religious groups, religious celebrations, and religious language. The long-term result of these measures is still uncertain.

The regime has been successful in changing the way women dress in public, or at least the way bourgeois women dress. (Nonurban and lower-class women have been less affected, because many had always covered their heads.) Urban women have necessarily complied, but they have complied in different ways and to different degrees. Some show a bit of hair, wear some makeup, or don scarves of bright colors. Any small distinction in a sea of gray and black calls attention to the bearer and the body. Covering the body is a way of calling attention to it. In short, women still show personality and make themselves attractive. The question is whether changing dress has affected the woman's role in the family and society. Although the employment of women outside the home dropped after the revolution, it now appears to be rising again. And although girls suffered discouragement in the educational process and were prohibited from studying abroad without escort, these restrictions now appear to have been lifted. A society long steeped in misogyny is still misogynistic but nonetheless changing in directions predicted by modernization theory.

By demanding that candidates for public office hold religious credentials, the regime has sought to reduce the possibility that municipal councilors, members of the Majlis, and the president of the republic would act in ways injurious to religious rules. In fact, the criterion is loyalty to the regime. A similar requirement prevailed under the shah. Only authorized political parties were permitted to contest elections, and only authorized candidates were permitted to run. The old Majlis had little authority, and the new Majlis has rather limited authority as well. Imposing religious criteria diminishes the democratic legitimacy of the assembly, as did the vetting process of the ancien régime. Because all legislation of the Majlis is subject to review by the Guardian Council, which looks for incompatibilities with Islamic law, there is no need to have members of the Majlis who meet religious criteria. What seems to be a process to promote religion turns out to be an inherited suspicion of democratic procedure.

Educational Reform

Education is the major tool of any government for reshaping or maintaining political culture. The Islamic Republic has taken a number of measures designed to reorient the schools toward moral purpose, to energize the teaching corps as models for behavior, to reinforce the teaching of religion, to mobilize support for the Muslim world, and to rally opinion against the West and Israel. Iran continues to permit non-Muslim religious groups to provide their own religious instruction and examinations. Non-Muslim students are exempt from examination on the

Quran.[92] The texts call upon non-Muslim believers to join Muslims in opposing infidels (including Bahais). While high school students learn that the leadership of the Muslim community passed to a line of twelve imams, as the Imami Shia believe, the high school texts refrain from criticizing Sunnis, who do not believe that the imams were inspired leaders designated by God and Muhammad.[93]

The purpose of religious education in the schools is to train pious Muslims and encourage them to become champions of revolutionary Islam. The classroom is a place for the teaching of moral values, proper dress, modesty, and chastity. One of the first actions of the new regime was to separate the sexes in all schools.[94] Instructions for teachers remind them that they are models for their pupils and must therefore conduct themselves in righteous fashion. Texts appropriate to each level come from the Religion Team of the Office of Planning and Compilation of School Textbooks, part of the Ministry of Education. In 1980 the government created a separate division of the ministry, the Bureau of Fostering Affairs, which aims specifically to propagate the regime's ideology and to create followers of the faqih. In 1999 the ministry began creating centers for teaching boys and girls the Quran and Arabic in segregated settings from age five. Some 600 such centers enrolled 800,000 students by 2000–2001.[95]

The textbooks reflect an aggressive tone on behalf of Islam. In the Pahlavi era, the schools emphasized modernization and Iranian nationalism as the primary objectives. Now the textbooks advocate jihad in defense of the homeland, defined not as Iran but the Dar al-Islam, the house of Islam. They mention not just the martyrdom of the Imam Husayn, but also the deaths of others on behalf of Islam, which the texts portray as threatened. Golnar Mehran says the texts show that the regime feels insecure: "Framing the threat in terms of Islam and Shiite Muslims as oppressed victims versus ambiguous others directs feelings of patriotism toward the Islamic state and its clerical rulers."[96] The school texts treat Iran as a homogeneous country with a single, unambiguous pattern of historical development. They ignore Iranian history before Islam. They treat the great personalities of Iranian history only in their relationship with Islam and neglect, even if they largely refrain from attacking, the existence of linguistic and religious minorities. By these textbook accounts, Iran is and always has been Shii and Persian. Its fate is identical with that of the Muslim world as a whole. This notion conflicts, of course, with the reality of international relations, where Iran has often been at odds with other Muslim countries.

Efforts to politicize the teaching of Islam in the primary and secondary schools carry forward into the university, where entrance now requires not just the requisite diplomas but a religious-political screening process, says Mehran: "This means that admission to university is contingent upon evidence of praying and fasting, proper veiling for female students, and loyalty to the Islamic Republic, in particular the religious jurisprudent [faqih]."[97] The authorities closed the universities for four years in the 1980s in an effort to cleanse them of classes, faculty, and students potentially critical of the regime. Reconstructed, the universities have nonetheless generated expressions of dissent and support for reform—expressions that have rocked the regime.

The Islamic Republic has made great strides in carrying education to remote villages. Illiterate parents want education for their children, and literacy rates have risen impressively, especially for girls and women. The demand for university education exceeds capacity, and the needs of the economy and society— the oil industry, the nuclear industry, modern communications—require an emphasis on education. One result is the increase in self-reflection that Fariba Adelkhah observes in Iranian culture. She notes the outpouring of manuals on food, marital relations, physical education, and raising children. Both sexes flock to the gym for exercise and self-improvement. The birthrate has fallen. Consumers make complicated decisions befitting a modern economy. There is a passion for competitions of all sorts, including Quran contests, and the country is mad about sports.[98] A film portrays women skydiving from the mountains north of Tehran—their Islamic garb intact from launch to landing.[99] Iran's qualification for the World Cup finals in soccer galvanized the nation. Women demanded and achieved access to soccer games.

Studies have long regarded heightened individualism and self-consciousness as a characteristic of modernity, as the term is defined in the West. Individualism and self-reflection rise with levels of education as they do with exposure to the media. While the regime in Iran has often censored newspapers or intimidated their owners and sought to control the spread of satellite dishes, it fights a losing battle over access to sources of information. Adelkhah refers to great public debates about soap operas. The regime takes advantage of Ramadan to broadcast programs designed to heighten religiosity and loyalty to the regime, but adherence to Ramadan fasting appears to have diminished, and those who follow it often offer as a reason its benefits to mind, body, and social interaction—not religious tradition. Even official programming on television turns a religious celebration into a variety show. Ramadan has become a time for great consumption, gifts, travel, and sporting competition.[100]

Deeply suspicious of cinema in general, the regime has nonetheless permitted a revival of the Iranian film industry. The government understood the propaganda potential as well as the risks. The makers of the documentary *Divorce Iranian Style* struggled for months to get the requisite permissions to film a family court.[101] Told they should find a more positive subject, they replied that what would be more positive in the eyes of the government would be seen more negatively abroad. On the one hand, the film shows the obstacles women face in making a case for divorce. On the other hand, it shows women of great will and determination who outmaneuver their husbands in the courtroom, and a judge more open to their arguments than one might expect.

Religiosity

The Islamic Republic has poured religious propaganda into the schools and tried to use the media to promote political Islam. It has also made religion more convenient than it was forty years ago. The Quran is available in every size and shape. Every family can own not just one copy of the book, as was once the case, with the book needing protection from harm, but many copies. Cemeteries have been computerized and rationalized so that a family in need of a funeral service can choose from among options online with specified prices. The Web site of the Iranian embassy in Canada offers believers a choice of maraji the believers can consult for advice on a wide range of issues. The Internet offers access to the sermons of great preachers and to religious information. The regime has institutionalized, bureaucratized, and rationalized religion, and it has enormously enhanced the incentives for conforming to religious norms and supporting political Islam.[102]

To what extent have Iranians become more devoted to the spiritual life? Survey data collected in 2005 suggest that Iranians are about as religious as Muslims in Turkey, and less religious than Muslims in Egypt and Saudi Arabia. For example, when respondents in these countries were asked about the importance of God in their lives, on a scale of one to ten, 88 percent of Iranians responded with a nine or a ten ("very important," see Table 5.1). The figure was 98 percent for Egypt and 96 percent for Saudi Arabia. In Iran, Turkey, Saudi Arabia, and Egypt, the percentage of respondents saying they believe in God ranged from 97 percent in Turkey to a high of 100 percent in Egypt and Saudi Arabia (Table 5.2). In Iran, 2,504 of 2,532 respondents, or 99 percent, said they believed in God. Iranians appear about as religious as Egyptians and perhaps more religious than Turks, as measured by another survey item. Asked how often they attend religious services, 45 percent replied that they do so once a month or more. Thirty-nine percent of Turks and 45 percent of Egyptians chose those responses. Iranians were more likely than Turks or Egyptians to say they attend services only on special holy days, but few Iranians (4 percent) responded that they "practically never" attend services, while 35 percent of Turks, 25 percent of Egyptians, and 15 percent of Saudis chose that response.

The efforts of the Islamic Republic to propagate religion have not catapulted Iran into a special category of super religiosity, but these efforts have seemingly made religiosity "a primary cleavage in Iranian politics."[103] On a graph plotting religious participation against the propensity for religious beliefs, Pippa Norris and Ronald Inglehart locate Iran close to Egypt, Turkey, and Jordan—and not far from the United States, Chile, and Canada![104] On the Norris-Inglehart scale of traditional to secular-rational values (a scale heavily influenced by religious values and behavior), Iran appears slightly more secular than Egypt, Pakistan, Uganda, and Zimbabwe, and at about the same level as the Philippines, Indonesia, and Brazil.[105] But a survey conducted in Tehran in 2008 and a secondary analysis of the World Values Survey done in 2005 indicate a high correlation between religiosity and support for the regime. The less religious respondents tended to be more critical of the regime and more supportive of democracy.[106] The Iranian government has pushed its citizens to see themselves first as Muslims and only later as Iranians. In contrast, the old regime pushed national over ethnic or religious identity. On a World Values Survey question about how a respondent would best describe himself or herself, 62 percent of Iranians chose "above everything else, I am a Muslim," almost twice as many (35 percent) as those who chose "above everything else, I am an Iranian" (Table 5.3). But in Turkey, which is reputedly a more secular country, where Kemalism has been preaching Turkism for almost a century, the percentages were 68 percent for "I am a Muslim" and 31 percent for "I am a Turk." In Egypt, they were 79 and 10 percent, respectively. Israelis were more balanced: 45 percent chose "Jew," and

TABLE 5.1 "How Important Is God in Your Life?"
(1= not important at all; 10= very important)

	IRAN (2005)	ISRAEL (2001)	TURKEY (2007)	SAUDI ARABIA (2003)	EGYPT (2008)	U.S. (2006)
Less important 1–8 (%)	12.1	39.1	15.0	4.1	1.6	3.9
Very important 9–10 (%)	87.9*	58.5	85.0	95.9	98.4†	96.1
N (100%)	2655	1170	1339	1491	3000	2609

Source: World Values Surveys, 1981–2004, 2005–2008 online analysis. Question FO63.
*This number was 90.3 percent in the 2000 survey.
†This number was 91.0 percent in the 2000 survey.

TABLE 5.2 Three Questions About Religion

Country (date of survey)	"Do you believe in God?" (%)	"Are you a religious person?"	"How often do you attend religious services?"		
			Once a month or more (%)*	Only on special holy days (%)	Never, practically never (%)
EGYPT (2001)	100	98.4	44.7	24.9	25.1
IRAN (2000)	98.9	82.3	44.8	40.1	3.9
SAUDI ARABIA (2003)	99.9	70.4	44.1	17.4	15.4
TURKEY (2001)	97.4	78.8	38.9	15.7	34.8
U.S. (1999)	95.6	82.5	60.3	10.5	14.8

Source: World Values Surveys, 1981–2004, 2005–2008, online analysis, questions F050, F034, and F028.
* Combines responses of "more than once a week," "once a week," and "once a month."

32 percent said "Israeli." Once again the Iranian results appear unexceptional for a Muslim country.[107]

Other studies of the Islamic Republic reach roughly the same conclusion. Religion has always been an important element of the political culture in Iran, but it is scarcely the only factor shaping the culture or even the most important one. In 1986, M. Reza Behnam emphasized Iran's long-standing love-hate relationship with outsiders.[108] As early as the nineteenth century, Iran began to resent the outside influence that it also courted and cultivated. Behnam noted the Iranians' high degree of distrust of others (a distrust found among the elites and described by Zonis in 1971).[109] Family is a refuge from such distrust and from the class distinctions that further undermine social solidarity. One can, in the end, depend only upon family ties. This message, already conveyed in the *Shahnameh*, is not likely to disappear.

In a study done in the 1990s, Adelkhah looked at the continual adaptation of an old idea, the *javanmard*, or "man of integrity." The javanmard demonstrates four characteristics: (1) a generous, giving nature; (2) a set of contacts that show he has "back" [influence]; (3) practical skills and abilities that bring success; and (4) unifying acts that come to constitute the self. But she says that the javanmard is also a person who manages to overcome the self. In many respects

TABLE 5.3   "Which of the Following Best Describes You?"

Country (date of survey)	"I am Iranian [or Israeli, Turk, Egyptian, or Saudi]" (%)	"I am an Arab" (%)	"I am a Muslim [or a Jew in Israel]" (%)	Other (%)	N (100%)
ISRAEL (2001)	31.9	6.7	44.9	16.5*	1,171
IRAN (2000)	34.9	—	62.4	2.7	2,473
TURKEY (2001)	30.8	—	68.0	1.2	3,201
SAUDI ARABIA (2003)	12.1	9.5	73.6	4.9	1,502
EGYPT (2001)	9.8	1.0	79.4	9.8	3,000

Source: World Values Surveys, 1981–2004, online analysis, question G015. Wording may have varied slightly with country.

*Among Israeli respondents, the largest "other" response was "individual, no group" (12.2%). The next largest group of "other" described themselves as Muslim (3.0%).

Khomeini embodied the ideal, but that ideal then runs up against the need for solidarity and institutions.[110] James Bill observes that leadership in Iran has long depended on "emanation" for its success.[111] Khomeini's legitimacy emanated from the Hidden Imam and incarnated, perhaps, the Iranian ideal of the javanmard. But both these ideals conflict with the primary trends of the Islamic Republic: institutionalization and bureaucratization. Can Khomeini be reinvented without challenge to the institutions he helped create?

Adelkhah concluded that the social and economic forces propelling modernity—forces that include technological innovation, urbanization, global communications, and increasing literacy—continue to reshape mentalities in the Islamic Republic. Change compounds choice and causes the individual to develop capacities and rationales for choice. The regime claims that religion governs social policy, and Adelkhah thinks it does to some extent. Islam is "part of Iran," she observed, "certainly a central part, but not necessarily more important from the social point of view than, say, the reality of cities, the search for knowledge, the economic crisis, the upward thrust of youth, the regional environment and family obligations."[112]

Iran's political culture, long marked by contradictions such as obedience to political authority and contempt for it, continues to evolve in ways that seem to reflect the forces commonly identified with modernity. While religious rhetoric and practice have become more prominent, the changes may be more superficial than profound. The wants and desires of Iranians do not seem to differ significantly from their neighbors. Asked to choose between four priorities, 69 percent list a stable economy as their first or second choice, a slightly higher percentage than in Turkey, Egypt, and Israel. In Inglehart's terms, they are overwhelmingly "materialist" rather than "post-materialist," as one would expect from Iran's GNP per capita. They tend to support democracy but divide on whether the current regime is somewhat democratic or not at all democratic. Educated young Iranians appear more critical of the government than their elders and their less educated peers, and they are also the most favorable toward democracy.[113] One anthropologist describes a sexual and social revolution unfurling among some of the most educated youth of Tehran. She suggests that youth revolt, marked by pushing the limits on standards of dress and mixing of the sexes, has caused the regime to ease up on enforcement and thus accommodate change in mores.[114] There is, in other words, little evidence that the aspirations of the average Iranian differ significantly from those of people elsewhere. Modernization does not require secularization. It only requires accommodating modernization within traditional ideas and adapting religious practice to fit its exigencies. Iran appears to be engaged in accommodation and adaptation.

Conclusion

Religion varies with political circumstances, sometimes influencing those circumstances and sometimes changing as a result of them. The downfall of the Sasanian Empire at the hands of the Arabs brought Islam to Iran and resulted in the eventual demise of Zoroastrianism. The Safavid dynasty converted the country to Shiism and created a religious establishment that began to assert its political influence under the Qajars in the nineteenth century. The Pahlavis sought to push the establishment aside and to reinvent a national identity tied to the pre-Islamic past, but the overthrow of the Pahlavis brought Islamic revolution, which reworked the nation's identity, its political ideology, its religious institutions, and, to some extent, its political culture. The political success of the religious establishment made possible a dream of religious transformation. Politics have been more the cause than the effect of religious change.

From a long-term perspective, every aspect of the relationship between religion and politics has fluctuated. No single analytical scheme can account for a particular state of the relationship. Iran's identity with Islam, which the regime regards as total, has varied in intensity over the centuries and millennia. Persian literature ties the country to a geographical and cultural entity that predates Islam. The whims of fortune carried the country toward Shiism, then toward secular nationalism, and finally back to identification with universal Islam. Religion has sometimes been dominant in the ideological predisposition of a regime, as with the Safavids, and receded into the background at moments such as the early twentieth century, when European law codes and political ideas carried the day. While political institutions have generally prevailed over religious institutions, the religious institution has exercised greater influence in moments of political weakness—in the Qajar period, during the constitutional revolution, and in the 1970s as the Pahlavi dynasty began to come unraveled. Greater organization and greater hierarchy within the religious establishment enabled the clergy to create a revolution, which then altered the balance of power between politics and religion. The victory of the clergy led to a fresh assertion of political domination over religion. Yet the government has not been successful in translating that domination into a general transformation of the way people think about political authority and political actors.[115] The election of President Khatami in 1997 caught the regime by surprise, as did the election of President Ahmadinejad in 2005.

The key question about Iran is not how religion will transform the country. It is, rather, what the political system will do to religion. Will the system continue to insist that Islam requires rule by a Supreme Leader, the faqih, who is above the law, or will those clerics who hold power ultimately decide, with the late Grand Ayatollah Ali Montazeri, that even the Supreme Leader must be subject to the law and the constitution? President Khatami took Montazeri's position but failed in his efforts to uphold it. Future success of the reformist position would transform the Iranian system without eliminating religion from the public sphere. It would confirm the loss of sacredness in the political system, which began with the adoption of a constitution and accelerated with the death of Khomeini. It would perhaps save religion from the secularization it currently undergoes as a tool of government. Will the clerical elite who are now governing have the wisdom to liberate religion from its servitude to politics? To free it of the responsibility it bears for everything, from the price of gasoline to foreign policy?

The government has transformed the relationship between religion and politics in Iran by claiming a monopoly on truth. Those who oppose the regime from within the Islamic tradition find this claim to be the root of the problem. Such a monopoly contradicts the tradition of plural maraji, a choice among mujtahids as objects of emulation. Even though the current faqih does not claim to be a marja, much less the only marja, he cannot effectively be challenged from either inside or outside the political structure. While Imami Shiism has known periods in which there was a single marja-e taqlid, those have been exceptional periods. The regime need not be secular, but if it is to evolve toward democracy, it must become tolerant of diverse opinions, lifestyles, and religions. Such tolerance could certainly be achieved within an Islamic republic and even under a slightly modified version of the current constitution, but current elites may not permit change of that sort. Persistent rigidity would create a precondition for further revolution.

Chronology

637	Arabs conquer Iran. Conversion to Islam begins.
1501	Safavids take power, convert country to Shiism.
1722	Safavids fall. Afghan dynasty conquers much of Iran.
1780	Qajar dynasty begins.
1906	Protest leads to constitutional revolution.
1907	Russia and Great Britain establish zones of influence in Iran.
1921	Reza Khan seizes power in a coup d'état.
1925	Assembly deposes Qajars, declares Rza Khan shah. Pahlavi dynasty begins.
1941	Allies depose Reza Shah Pahlavi; Muhammad Reza succeeds his father.
1951	Muhammad Mussadiq (Mossadegh) becomes prime minister, nationalizes oil.
1953	Coup against Mussadiq is fomented by United Kingdom and United States. Shah returns from exile.
1963	Shah launches White Revolution, a land reform designed to benefit peasants.
1971	Shah celebrates 2,500 years of Peacock throne, at Persepolis.
1978–1979	Iran undergoes revolution. Ayatollah Khomeini accedes to power. The Islamic Republic is born.
1979	New constitution is approved. Khomeini is designated as Great Leader. Hostage crisis with United States begins.
1980–1988	Iraq and Iran wage war on each other.
1989	Imam Khomeini dies. Ali Khamenei is chosen as Supreme Leader to replace Khomeini.
1997	Muhammad Khatami, a reform-minded candidate, is elected president.
2001	Khatami is reelected.
2005	Mahmoud Ahmadinejad is elected president.
2009	Ahmadinejad is reelected; contestation of the result is followed by repression.

6

State Sunnism in Saudi Arabia

No country identifies itself more closely with Islam than Saudi Arabia. Its territory includes the city where Muhammad grew up and the city where he and his companions created an Islamic state. The king vaunts his role as "Custodian of the Two Holy Sanctuaries," the mosques of Mecca and Medina.[1] The rite of pilgrimage to Mecca draws some 10 million persons every year. The country proclaims that its constitution is the sharia, and it implements social policies—segregation of women and men in public places, restrictions on the activities of women, banning of alcoholic beverages—in the name of Islam. It has supported Islamic movements in a number of countries, including Afghanistan, where Islamist guerrillas fought the Soviets. Fifteen of the nineteen men who hijacked airplanes to attack the United States on September 11, 2001, were citizens of Saudi Arabia. Since then the Saudi government has struggled to dissociate itself from the band of international jihadis whose ideas it had once encouraged, but in the minds of Americans, the Saudi identification with Islam could scarcely be stronger.

Does Islam therefore explain Saudi Arabia? Do Saudis demonstrate a level of personal religiosity that surpasses Muslims elsewhere? Does equating Islamic law with a constitution prove a lack of separation of religion and politics in Saudi Arabia? Does Islam explain social policies that one American feminist scholar has called the "codification of absurdity"?[2] Is it reasonable to think of Saudi Arabia as the Islamic state it wishes to be?

To answer any of these questions in the affirmative would be a mistake. In a state without democratic institutions, public attitudes do not determine politics or policy. A basic law proclaims that the sharia is the country's constitution, but the monarchy authored and proclaimed the basic law. It is the king's will that the country follow a version of the sharia, not the sharia that authorizes kingship. If Muslims everywhere followed the practices of Saudi Arabia, one could attribute the practices to Islam, but the Saudi understanding of Islamic rites and traditions reflects a peculiar set of doctrines that developed in the central region of the country in the eighteenth century. Beyond that region, Muslims discovered these practices only as the Saudi monarchy, supported by Wahhabi ulama, conquered surrounding communities. Since the eighteenth century, three incarnations of a state based in central Arabia have built their identity on the rule of one family, the Saud family. The very name of the country suggests an important truth: Saudi Arabia is the possession of a family, not the vanguard of a religion. The monarchy has used Islam for its purposes, cultivating support and courting dangers of which it is well aware.

The case of Saudi Arabia further confirms the general argument of this study. While Islam is important to the history of that country, only politics and history can explain the peculiar version of Islam implemented there.[3] If Islam were a primary explanation, then Saudi Arabia should look more like Egypt, Turkey, and Iran. But although it is similar in its institutions and political culture, Saudi Arabia is radically different in identity and ideology. Saudi Arabia is like these other Muslim states in that all four governments seek to control religion, and like those other states, the Saudis have found themselves coming up short, unable to monopolize the interpretation of religion. Islam has become a vehicle of opposition as well as a tool of governance in all four of these states. Politics has transformed Islam in Saudi Arabia even as Islam has shaped politics.

Identity

Explaining national identity in Saudi Arabia is not simple. It is an Arab state by language and ethnicity, but it does not represent all Arabs, and the idea that the Arabs are a single people, deserving of a single-state (Arab nationalism) has never enjoyed favor with the Saudi monarchy. Saudi Arabia is a Muslim state, but it cannot claim to represent Muslims beyond its borders, and identification with a peculiar version of Islam puts the state at odds with religious minorities at home, many Muslims abroad, and non-Muslims everywhere. The Saudi state does not control all of the Arabian peninsula, which includes Kuwait, Bahrain,

Qatar, the United Arab Emirates, Oman, and Yemen. Citizens are thus not merely Arabs or Arabians. Rather they are Saudi Arabians, or Saudis for short, but only a small minority, perhaps 5,000 citizens, are actually members of the Saud family. One young man, stopped at a checkpoint and asked if he were Saudi, said no: "Am I a member of the Al-Saud family? No. Then I am not a Saudi." The policeman told him he could go to jail for saying something like that but then waved him through.[4]

In responding to Arab nationalism, the Saudis have often observed, with reason, that nationalism is a European idea. The French revolted against their monarchy in the name of the French nation, and the Americans, also throwing off monarchy, launched a new concept of citizenship. Some monarchies such as England managed to accommodate this new concept, but the Austro-Hungarian Empire and the Ottoman Empire found themselves struggling to defeat its impact on subject peoples, including the Arabs, that claimed the right to rule themselves as independent "nations." Some monarchies in the Middle East—Morocco and Jordan are two examples—have survived the transition to national identity, but others, such as those in Iran, Iraq, and Yemen, have collapsed. Nationalism implies citizen participation in governance, something that the Saud family and the ruling families of other states in the peninsula have resisted. "It may be impossible to find nationalism in this country," writes Fouad Ibrahim, reflecting the sentiments of many Shia in the Eastern Province.[5]

Origins of the State

The origin of the Saudi state was territorial, not national or even tribal. The first Saudi state (1745–1811), a product of an alliance between Muhammad ibn Saud ibn Muhammad ibn Muqrin and a reform-minded preacher named Muhammad ibn Abd al-Wahhab, started in Diriyah, a town located just northwest of the contemporary city of Riyadh.[6] The state expanded by conquest until it controlled most of the Arabian peninsula, only to collapse under military invasion by the Ottoman ruler of Egypt, Muhammad Ali, and his sons in the early nineteenth century. The capital of the emirate, Diriyah, disappeared in the onslaught, but a second state arose in the same area, the Najd region (1843–1865). That state controlled much of the peninsula but disintegrated after only two decades as a result of dissension within the ruling family. A rival family, the Rashidis, working from a tribal base in the Shammar region of the north, challenged the Saud/Wahhabi state and was eventually victorious.

Abd al-Aziz ibn Abd al-Rahman al-Saud (known as Abd al-Aziz or as Ibn Saud) launched the third Saudi state by retaking Riyadh (1902) and proceeding with British support to take back the whole of Najd and some surrounding emirates, each with traditions of autonomy and different conceptions of identity. The towns of the Najd region, marked by both settled and nomadic populations, were the foundation of Saudi military strength, but starting in 1912, Ibn Saud enlisted the help of Wahhabi ulama in creating new communities of bedouins with the aim of making them into "good Muslims," taxpayers, and soldiers. Ibn Saud managed to settle something like 150,000 bedouins in sixty such camps or communities.[7] Collectively known as the Ikhwan (or Brothers), the bedouins in these camps became fierce warriors for the faith and a vital element in the conquest of the surrounding regions. By corralling the bedouins and deploying them, the Sauds ensured Saudi control of the Najd region, pushed back the Ottomans, and took control of the areas surrounding Najd. Not even Ottoman and, eventually, British protection for the Hijaz region on the western coast of Arabia—a region governed by a family claiming descent from the Prophet—could fend off the attacking Najdi armies. The third Saudi state thus emerged victorious in war and conquest. Far from responding to demands for national identity, the state imposed the rule of a single family and a single, puritanical version of Islam.

British interests constrained the expansion of the Saudi state. During World War I, the British corresponded with the Sharif Husayn, an Ottoman official charged with governing the holy places in Mecca and Medina. Husayn's family, descended from the Hashemite clan of the Prophet Muhammad, had governed the Hijaz region for centuries under Ottoman rule. The British promised to support the creation of an "Arab state" if Husayn joined the campaign against his Ottoman superiors, which he did. But the Arab state he was promised turned out to be control of two territories. The British let one of Husayn's sons, Abdullah, become the ruler of an area called Transjordan, which later became the Kingdom of Jordan. Another son, Faysal, sought to lead an independent Syria but ended up, thanks to the British, as king of a new state called Iraq. Meanwhile the British were also subsidizing Ibn Saud, emir of the Najd region. When Ibn Saud and his Wahhabi forces, including the Ikhwan, attacked Husayn and his third son, Ali, in 1926, the British had already chosen to stand aside. The British stopped funding Husayn by 1924, when he refused to approve the terms of the British mandate for Palestine, but they funded Ibn Saud, ensuring the defeat of Husayn.[8] Although they permitted the Saudi conquest of the Hijaz region, the British made it clear they would not tolerate an assault on Transjordan or Iraq, much less an attack on the shaykhdoms of the Persian Gulf. The British had committed themselves to protect these shaykhdoms, such as Kuwait, Bahrain, and Oman.

Saudi Arabia was not the Arab state that the British had promised Sharif Husayn but it was an Arab state that bumped up against other Arab states, all of them constrained in some way or another by the British. Most other parts of the Arab world remained under European influence or control in the period between World Wars I and II: France ruled Morocco, Algeria, and Tunisia, as well as Syria and Lebanon, under a mandate from the League of Nations. Italy controlled Libya. Egypt enjoyed hypothetical independence but still fell within the British sphere of influence. There was no possibility of a single Arab state. Ibn Saud found himself nearly surrounded by separate, Arab-dominated political entities, two of them headed by the Hashemites, a rival family of more impressive religious credentials.

Nationalism

When the idea of Arab unity reemerged in the 1950s, the Saudis were anything but supportive. A coup d'état led by Gamal abd al-Nasir overturned the British-supported monarchy in Egypt in 1952 and opened the door to a new form of politics in the Arab world. After nationalizing the Suez Canal in 1956 and then weathering attack from Britain, France, and Israel, President Nasir negotiated with supporters in Syria to launch the United Arab Republic, which was supposed to attract and incorporate other Arab states. The Saudis declined to join, because they suspected that Arab nationalism meant Egyptian domination of the area and the generous redistribution of Saudi oil wealth, which had begun to mount in the 1950s and 1960s. When revolutionary, republican forces attacked the Yemeni monarchy, the Egyptian military intervened on behalf of the republicans, and the Saudis went to the aid of the traditional ruler, the imam. As the leftist champions of Arab nationalism, the Nasirists and Baathists, lined up with the

Soviet Union, the Saudis continued to identify themselves with some Arab causes (e.g., the liberation of Jerusalem from Israeli control) but also with non-Arabs such as Iran (then still a monarchy) and the United States.

Nationalism in general threatens Saudi Arabia because it implies citizen control of a country. It favors republicanism or at least a move toward a constitutional monarchy. Arab nationalism in particular constitutes a threat because it suggests the need to replace all the individual regimes of the Arab world with a single government. Saudi Arabia, with only a third the population of Egypt, would be just one of several regional divisions within the Arab state. It is difficult to imagine that Saudi Arabia would relaunch a military campaign and unify the Arab world by conquest, resuming the process stopped by British imperial interests in the 1920s. Much of the Arab world has already rejected monarchy, and even the other monarchies would surely resist Saudi domination. A state that could not defend itself against the Iraqi threat in 1990 and 1991, swallowing its pride and accepting the intervention of the United States, is not likely to embark on fresh conquest, and the international order is less tolerant of conquest than it was when Ibn Saud consolidated his power in Arabia in the 1920s.

These considerations help explain why Saudi Arabia has depended so heavily on Islam as a pillar of its identity. As the birthplace of Islam, it has a natural advantage. Its population is overwhelmingly Muslim. All Muslims pray toward Mecca and aspire to undertake the pilgrimage. Islam has helped the Saud family enhance its appeal without identifying itself with a particular tribe. Moreover, Islamic nationalism does not threaten Saudi sovereignty. Reviving the umma, the community of all believers, has been a cry of reformers since the nineteenth century, but no one has realistically imagined a single state bringing together Muslims from Indonesia to Morocco. That dream makes the idea of achieving Arab unity seem practical by comparison. Upon assuming power in revolutionary Iran, Ayatollah Khomeini spoke as if he imagined that Muslims everywhere would join his cause, but the revolution in Iran turned out to be as nation-specific as revolutions elsewhere. By sending Iranians to disrupt the pilgrimage in the early 1980s, Iran generated hostility in Saudi Arabia rather than support for a united Muslim world dominated by Shiite Iran and its ayatollah.

The Saudis depend on Islam for identity, but even that idea generates a set of formidable problems. Perhaps any state that embraces religion as a foundation of its identity nurtures hypocrisy; by its commitment to a rigorously moral society, the Saudi version of Islam is vulnerable to this charge. Intensely pursued, Islamic identity can complicate international relations with non-Muslims states, jeopardize the status of non-Muslims within the state, and even alienate the country's Muslim minorities, who see the regime as Sunni and Wahhabi rather than merely Muslim. Identity with Islam has caused the Saudis to support Muslims abroad with words, money, and volunteers to engage in jihad. Some of these jihadis have then come home to wage war against the Saudi state. In response, the Saudi government then had to convince its population that it was only doing its Islamic duty in arresting, trying, and executing Muslims who had strayed from the true path by attacking the regime—in the name of Islam!

Defending the monarchy in religious terms is itself a challenge. The Saud family, unlike Jordanian and Moroccan royalty, does not claim lineage from the Prophet. The Sunni tradition, which dominates the Muslim world, does not adhere to the idea of religiously inspired leadership descended from the family of the Prophet, as do the Shia. While the king is entitled to call himself an imam, this word does not have the same ring as it does with Shii, who believe that five, or seven, or twelve imams were the rightful successors to the Prophet. Sunnis do not believe that Muhammad designated his successor, Abu Bakr, and Abu Bakr did not attempt to inaugurate kingship.

Wahhabism

The Sauds base their claim to rule on noble status and, since the eighteenth century, on the endorsement of the Wahhabi ulama. The royal family's identification with Islam comes not from within the family but from outside it; the monarchy must act and govern in ways the ulama see as consistent within Islam. Mainstream Islamic history contains innumerable examples of kingship, and the predominant attitude of Sunni ulama has been one of urging obedience to political authorities, even those whose personal piety or whose policies are not above reproach. But as some Sunni radicals have argued, kingship could be considered contradictory to Islamic principles. Radicals emphasize the revolutionary egalitarianism of Islam and the resulting irrelevance of considerations such as race, language, tribe, or family. Nobility nonetheless underpins monarchy; it also accounts for governance at all levels of pre- and postconquest Arabia, both settled and nomadic. The royal family has governed by subjugating tribes and settled communities, imprisoning their most illustrious elements, and then depending on the vanquished nobles to help administer the state.

Saudi Islam differs from Islam as practiced elsewhere because the Saud family chose to collaborate with a somewhat obscure religious reformer, Ibn Abd al-Wahhab, who was convinced that Muslims had lost their way and become polytheists, despite the efforts of the Prophet Muhammad, his companions, and all intervening generations. Ibn Abd al-Wahhab wanted to bring Muslims back to strict monotheism, the concept of a single, undivided God worthy of undistracted human attention. For him, the Shia had gone astray in their devotion to Ali and his descendants. In the view of Ibn Abd al-Wahhab, Sufis—mystics who seek knowledge of God through recitation of his name, music, dance, or rituals devised by saintly men and women—had left the path of Islam, as had ordinary Sunni Muslims who carried amulets to ward off evil spirits, worshiped at the tombs of their pious ancestors in Mecca and Medina, listened to music, drank alcoholic beverages, or dressed inappropriately. Such persons could not be regarded as Muslims.

From the beginning, then, by teaming with Shaykh Ibn Abd al-Wahhab, the Saud family launched itself on a campaign of inclusion and exclusion. Those who would accept Wahhabi puritanism would be included; everyone else would be excluded. Not surprisingly, the residents of the Hijaz region, a more cosmopolitan region than Najd, a region long accustomed to hosting the pilgrimage, resisted Wahhabi assaults on their practices, whether of dubious sorts (prostitution) or of a more respectable type (celebrating the birthday of the Prophet). For example, in the conquest of the Holy Cities, the Wahhabis ripped the domes off historic tombs.[9] Not surprisingly, either, the Twelver Shia of the Eastern Province, and particularly the town of Qatif, had difficulty accepting Saudi/Wahhabi rule.[10] The Ismaili Shia of the city of Najran in the far south of Saudi Arabia have also suffered marginalization.

And what is the status of non-Muslims in such a country? Saudi policy has been one of quarantine: keeping foreigners away from the local population to prevent pollution of social mores. Foreigners have often been quite content with quarantine, which permitted them to violate Saudi law (think alcohol, women without veils, etc.) in a tolerated context. The overwhelming need for foreign labor has, however, made the quarantine solution less and less viable. Foreigners, whether Muslim or non-Muslim, must live by Saudi rules but do not enjoy the respect and rights accorded full citizens. The Saudi adherence to a rather narrow view of Islam has served to divide as well as unify the country.

Challenges

The Saudi relationship to the violent jihadi movement represents the most serious drawback to its strong identification with Islam. It is difficult for an Islamic state to disentangle itself from those who would destroy the monarchy in the name of Islam. A first crisis occurred when the Ikhwan defied the orders of Ibn Saud to cease and desist their attacks on neighboring territories in 1927. The king mustered his non-Ikhwani, non-bedouin troops to defeat the warriors who had played a significant role in the Saudi conquests. Defense of the monarchy took precedence over Islam. A second crisis occurred in 1979, when radicals led by Juhayman al-Utaibi seized the Great Mosque in Mecca at the end of a decade in which Saudi Arabia was encouraging the growth of Islamic movements, such as the Muslim Brotherhood in Egypt, at home and abroad. With French help and the support of ulama, the rebels were routed, tried, and executed. Violent attacks on the monarchy in 1995 and again in 2003 constituted still other crises of this sort. Many of the jihadis involved in these incidents had fought against the Soviet occupation of Afghanistan with the full support of the Saudi and American governments. In each instance, the Saudi regime had to distinguish between justified and illegitimate jihad. And in both the 1995 and 2003 attacks, the radicals accused the monarchy of abandoning its identity with religion for Machiavellian reasons.[11]

A state with less profound and public identification with religion than Saudi Arabia would not find itself as conflicted and subjected to as many charges of hypocrisy. The regime's dependence on religious legitimacy gives license to the views of Wahhabi ulama, who believe women should remain at home out of public view or, if in school or employed, at least segregated from men. Female employment outside the home is low; women constitute 5 to 10 percent of the workforce, even though schools and universities are turning out female graduates in large numbers.[12] Clearly some businesswomen and other professionals do work directly with men, but that activity, like so much else in Saudi Arabia, must be hidden out of respect for religious rules.[13] Women are still prohibited from driving cars, not because the Quran or the hadith mentions this specific activity, but because female mobility might create situations conducive to sin. The cost of building segregated facilities and sacrificing the potential contributions of an educated female labor force in Saudi Arabia is incalculable and staggering.

If identification with Islam brings these risks and threats, one may wonder why the regime relies on it so heavily for legitimacy. The answer is, apparently, weakness. The royal family has only the legitimacy that its "nobility" and religious tradition can provide. Arab nationalism threatens Saudi autonomy. Socialism is utterly repugnant to a thoroughly capitalistic, even rapacious, culture. And the government's performance in producing wealth and well-being in a place long mired in poverty, surely a major reason the regime has survived, is always vulnerable to the world market for oil. When prices slump, as they did in the 1980s, the Saudis find themselves looking at the need to increase taxes and reduce welfare programs. Dependence on religion does not suffer the vicissitudes of the market.

Regime dependence on Islamic legitimacy has varied with time and with the neediness of the monarchy. When Ibn Saud was building camps for bedouins and turning these nomadic people into soldiers for the faith, his state needed that military strength. From his death in 1954 and until 1964, two of his sons, Saud and Faysal, struggled to win and hold full command of the polity. When Faysal eventually emerged victorious, he reinforced the relationship between state and religion to shore up his legitimacy. After the occupation of the mosque in Mecca and the Iranian Revolution of 1979, the Saudis again augmented their commitments to the ulama and to religious education. Similarly, the regime responded to Islamist protests and jihadi attacks in the 1990s by seeking to co-opt leading Islamists to undercut the case of the radicals. In moments of relative weakness, the regime has sought to sharpen its identification with religion, even though its religious commitments have contributed to the very weakness it seeks to remedy.

The primary focus of Saudi identity is the royal family. The 1999 centennial celebration of the conquest of Riyadh by Abd al-Aziz (Ibn Saud) emphasized this point.[14] Portrayed as a superhero marked by daring, courage, ferocity, sexual potency, generosity, and wisdom, he has become a cult figure to match Mustafa Kemal Atatürk in Turkey.[15] Unlike Atatürk, though, the sons and other family of Ibn Saud still control the important levers of command in Saudi Arabia. Theoretically subject to a law they have promulgated, they seem to be above it. A prince who murdered a British consul, though convicted of the crime, apparently sidestepped the sentence of life imprisonment.[16] All other elements of Saudi identity are secondary to family. When Islamism, Arab nationalism, or liberal ideologies have loomed as a threat to the monarchy, they have been defeated. The young man stopped at a checkpoint may not feel like a member of the "Saudi" family, but there is currently no other way he could identify his nationality.

Ideology

Some writers consider Saudi Arabia a kind of theocracy, even though Islam is not its principal source of identity and religious leaders do not directly rule the country. Consider, for example, Joseph Nevo's assertion: "Saudi Arabia is the most theocratic state in the contemporary Sunni Muslim world."[17] The argument for theocracy necessarily rests with the Saudi insistence that Islamic law constitutes the country's constitution and serves as the basis for all legislation. Legislation, public policy, state decisions, the structure of the government itself—all supposedly reflect precepts gleaned from the Quran and the hadith. These precepts imply that an unambiguous political ideology shapes the structure and outcomes of political life in Saudi Arabia. The Saud family, with the help of the ulama, merely implements that ideology.

With this claim, the Saudi monarchy bolsters the legitimacy of its actions. Authorities agree that the pact struck in 1744–1745 between Ibn Saud and Ibn Abd al-Wahhab, the reformist theologian, triggered the expansion of the first Saudi state, which was based in Diriyah. The third Saudi state still insists—with the support of its salaried ulama—that it embraces the unvarnished, unimpeachable truth first articulated by Ibn Abd al-Wahhab. The Saudis use their schools, television networks, religious establishment, and diplomacy to propagate this political ideology.

There are nonetheless difficulties with this claim and reasons to be cautious in applying the term *theocracy* to Saudi Arabia on ideological grounds. Ibn Abd al-Wahhab believed Muslims had lost their way by the eighteenth century, falling back into the worship of idols (*shirk*) as in the period before Muhammad, a period known as the *jahiliyya*. Most Muslims, then and now, have rejected this view of history. Ibn Abd al-Wahhab never articulated a political theory of Islam that goes beyond urging followers to obey a secular ruler, whatever the virtues and policies of that ruler; neither have his successors or disciples among the official ulama. The Saudi claim that Wahhabi doctrine represents true Islam has encountered challenge from those who say that official Saudi ideology does not correctly reflect even the ideas of Ibn Abd al-Wahhab. In the last century, there have emerged a series of movements and groups seeking reform and even overthrow of the monarchy in the name of this same Wahhabi ideology that the regime calls its own. The regime has been obliged to use force in suppressing some of these movements, but voices of dissent within the Wahhabi community survive, undermining the Saudi claim to represent religious truth.

Modernism?

Ibn Abd al-Wahhab rebelled against the Islam of his day in the Najd region of Arabia, criticizing Muslims themselves more than nonbelievers and supporting jihad to promote the "true Islam" he espoused. Like modern Islamist reformers, he called upon Muslims to return to the rigorous monotheism of the pious ancestors (*salafis*) and abandon the many practices he thought diverted their attention away from God and toward persons, images, objects, and rituals. Shia encountered his disdain for their reverence for Ali and his descendants. Ibn Abd al-Wahhab also denounced Sufis for their mystical chants, music, dance, and sanctification of ancestors. He trumpeted the truth of *tawhid*, the oneness of God, and deplored *shirk*. True Muslims, in his view, were those who followed him in preaching and teaching this message to the unenlightened majority.

Ibn Abd al-Wahhab seems to have wanted a renewal of mainstream Sunni Islam, not the creation of a separate sect. An alim trained within the Sunni tradition, he espoused one of the four primary schools of legal interpretation, that of Ibn Hanbal, and he further endorsed the views of a medieval theologian named Ibn Taymiyya. Although Ibn Taymiyya argued that Muslims could kill other Muslims who had betrayed the faith or were only superficial Muslims, he was highly traditional in proclaiming that Muslims should obey even a corrupt secular ruler to avoid chaos and anarchy. In both respects, Ibn Abd al-Wahhab adhered to Ibn Taymiyya's arguments, which served the alim's purposes and those of the emir of Diriyah, Ibn Saud.

Did Ibn Abd al-Wahhab see his theological position as a state-building ideology? Did he conceive the principle of tawhid, or unity, as implying political unification as well as unity of God?[18] These would seem to be a contemporary Islamist extrapolations from his thought. Ibn Abd al-Wahhab was not reacting to the phenomenon of modernity and to the influence of Europeans, as would Muslim reformers of the nineteenth and twentieth centuries.[19] In fact, however, his ideas proved helpful to Muhammad Ibn Saud in expanding the reach of the emirate from its base in the town of Diriyah to other settled groups, where tribal loyalties were weak, and then to bedouins of the Najd region, where tribe was a critical element of identity, and finally to regions beyond the Najd, where beliefs and customs differed still more. Islam became the glue of the first Saudi kingdom.

The glue proved insufficient to solidify the second Saudi kingdom, which was marked by conflicts within the royal family and by challenges from the Rashidi family in the north, but Wahhabism reemerged in the revival of the Saudi polity in the twentieth century. By then, however, the context had changed. Nationalism had swept Europe; Marxism and liberalism were mobilizing revolutions and counterrevolutions. Political ideology was gaining in importance as European political systems began to democratize; even kingdoms and empires were invoking nationalist and liberal ideologies in an effort to motivate their armies and hold disparate peoples together. The Ottoman Empire had begun a belated campaign to rally its subjects under the banner of Islam. Jamal al-Din al-Afghani was calling for a revival of the umma, the community of all believers, to resist Western penetration of the Muslim world. In this context, the religious ideas of Ibn Abd al-Wahhab became a state-building tool, which Abd al-Aziz (Ibn Saud) put to use when he pressed bedouins into camps and made them warriors for the faith in the 1920s. Fifteen years after the establishment of the first Ikhwan camp, the emir faced a revolt of these warriors, and in suppressing that revolt, he made it clear that Wahhabi ideology would guide Saudi policy only when that ideology did not conflict with the interests of the state and the ruling family.

In the fifty years after the suppression of the Ikhwan, the Saudi state managed to avoid any serious challenge to its interpretation of Islam, but contradictions between Wahhabi principles and the interests of the state became more and more visible. First came the arrival of foreigners to explore for oil, followed by the discovery, production, and a flow of wealth unprecedented in Arabia. The community of foreigners expanded; the royal family and the favored few indulged in conspicuous consumption; and innovation followed innovation, all with the blessing of the official ulama, themselves rewarded with government salaries and comfortable circumstances. In addition, the foreign relations of the kingdom became increasingly complicated. Already, the need to cultivate British support had driven Ibn Saud to oppose the Ikhwan. Then the dependence on the United States for the development of the oil industry and the marketing of its product created new obligations to the Christian world. At one moment, the Saudis found themselves supporting Gamal abd al-Nasir when he nationalized the Suez Canal. A decade later, in the 1960s, they were fighting Nasir's forces in the Yemen, for fear he would take over the entire peninsula. Israel's crushing defeat of three Arab countries in the Six-Day War of 1967 embarrassed the Saudi regime and pushed it back toward the Arab camp. In 1973, Saudi Arabia supported an Egyptian effort to win back territory in Sinai and then participated in an oil embargo to punish the United States and other Western powers for their support of Israel. Profiting from the subsequent jump in oil prices, the Saudis then reversed course again to mollify the United States and to cultivate their market for oil. Religious ideology cannot explain these zigs and zags in policy.

Islamism

The Saudis encouraged and benefited from the renewed interest in Islam that marked the Middle East and North Africa after the war between Israel and three Arab states in 1967. Arab nationalism had failed as a recipe for united action; only Syria had joined Egypt, and the countries had remained united under Nasir's leadership for only five years. Socialism had failed as a formula for prosperity in Egypt; even Nasir had been obliged to back away from state enterprise after 1967. Although Syria and Iraq were still dedicated to Arabism and socialism, the future seemed to lie with capitalism and Islamism, both dear to the Saudis. The Muslim Brotherhood, liberated by President Sadat in Egypt when he succeeded Nasir in 1970, found support from the Saudis, who were recruiting Egyptians, many of them members of the Brotherhood, as teachers in the new primary and secondary schools they were building with oil moneys.

The Islamism that Egyptians brought to Saudi Arabia, though ostensibly consistent with Wahhabism in its insistence on religion as the answer to political and social problems, brought with it new baggage: heavy engagement with the Palestinian issue; a penchant for radical, revolutionary action; and a lack of commitment to monarchy. When Islamic revolution swept away the Iranian monarchy in 1978–1979, the new Islamism gained even greater traction. This is the context in which Juhayman al-Utaibi and hundreds of armed followers occupied the Grand Mosque in Mecca in 1979. They denounced the Saudi monarchy for corruption and for promoting Westernization, and they called for expelling non-Muslims from the peninsula, clamping down on the rights of women, and abolishing television, among other things. The objective was apparently the creation of a theocracy under the leadership of al-Utaibi's brother-in-law, Mohammad Abdullah al-Qahtani, whom they regarded as the *mahdi*, the one sent to redeem the Muslim community before the coming apocalypse. Their endorsement of a mahdi put the revolutionaries outside orthodox Wahhabism, but their demands could be defended in classic Wahhabi terms. More difficult was their position in a sanctuary where violence had been forbidden even before Muhammad's time. With the rebels taking hostages and fending off the police and military with their weapons, the state took care to get authorization of the Council of Senior Ulama to use force. The battle lasted two weeks and produced hundreds of deaths and casualties. It was the greatest challenge to the ideological foundation of the Saudi state since the uprising of the Ikhwan in 1927.

The Sahwa

Another challenge came from an Islamist movement that traces its origins to the 1960s and 1970s. It gained prominence in the 1980s and then, triggered by the Saudi appeal for help to liberate Kuwait, burst into the open in the 1990s. Members of the Muslim Brotherhood who fled Egypt for Saudi Arabia brought the ideas of the Brotherhood's founder, Hasan al-Banna, who thought Islam was the key to liberating Egypt from political and cultural domination. What was new to Saudi Arabia was the idea that ordinary Muslims, without the participation of ulama, might meet, discuss, organize, and plan to implement a society based on Islam. The more radical ideas of Sayyid Qutb, who called the legitimacy of all existing Muslim governments into question, also found their way to Saudi Arabia. Sayyid's brother, Mohammed, himself a refugee and a leader of the movement in Saudi Arabia, helped adapt and soften these ideas to avoid direct challenge with the Saudi monarchy. (In *Milestones*, Sayyid Qutb had proclaimed all existing Muslim regimes corrupt and illegitimate.)[20] By the 1970s, the Islamist awakening (the Sahwa) had taken root in Arabia; groups met secretly, listened to lectures, held Quran memorization contests, sponsored sporting events, and engaged in other social activities of the sort that had built the Muslim Brotherhood into a political force in Egypt. They also quarreled among themselves about ideology.

The Sahwa as a movement garnered support from the regime, especially in the form of employment in education at all levels. Adherents to Sahwi ideas came to occupy important positions in the new institutions of higher education, including three religious universities. The Sahwi circles, or *jamaa*, commanded resources to help promising students with scholarships and housing. The jamaa cultivated support from senior ulama even though the Sahwa came from outside the establishment circle and was implicitly critical of the establishment. Gradually, Sahwi preachers and scholars won respect and began to think of themselves as ulama, albeit ulama-in-waiting for the recognition and authority accorded the official religious establishment. Their willingness to distance themselves from Juhayman al-Utaibi and the mahdi, who had come out of Islamist circles, further enhanced the standing of the Sahwa shaykhs and intellectuals.

The Sahwis met resistance from some who called themselves Ahl al-Hadith (people attached to the Sunna of the Prophet) and who were convinced that the Sahwis were neglecting the primary duty of religion, which is to tend to religious practice and behavior. Other sources of disfavor came from radicals determined to wage jihad in Afghanistan to oppose the Soviet occupation in the 1980s. The Sahwis refused to endorse the position that jihad was an obligation on every Muslim, equivalent to the five pillars of the faith. In this position, they effectively supported the state's own policy, which offered subsidies to those who undertook jihad but which did not send conscripts. Some 10,000 Saudis are nonetheless thought to have fought in Afghanistan. The Sahwis resisted the appeals of Abdullah Azzam and Osama Bin Laden, who were building an international jihadi organization.

The Sahwa turned out crowds for its sermons and lectures. It found space in the cultural supplements of newspapers for its commentaries, and it sold cassettes in large numbers. The regime, known for suppressing any whimper of liberal opposition and censoring publications and airwaves, permitted this loosening of the rules for what appeared to be religious discussion. The competition of ideas and interchange produced a climate of excitement quite unprecedented in a country known for media that trumpeted the predictable propaganda of the regime. In effect, Wahhabism, the ideological foundation of the regime, was under examination and discussion.

Crisis

A crisis arose in August 1990, when Saddam Hussein seized Kuwait. King Fahd hesitated before accepting the American offer of assistance. Eventually convinced by Washington of the need for foreign troops to protect the country, Riyadh asked the Council of Senior Ulama, headed by Shaykh Ibn Baz, to issue an opinion (fatwa) supporting the recourse to foreign forces. Trapped between a rock and a hard place, the official ulama responded with a rather tepid endorsement, a response that served the interests of the monarchy but cost king and ulama dearly in the eyes of the Sahwa movement. The decision to accept American help demonstrated yet again that the monarchy put its own survival ahead of ideological consistency. The decision also helped bring together Sahwa ulama, a few official ulama who had been excluded from the highest positions and who had not been active in the Sahwi movement, and a number of intellectuals with Sahwi sympathies, who represented somewhat different points of view but agreed that the Saudi government was imperfect and in need of reform.[21]

United by feelings of exclusion from power and opposition to the use of foreign troops more than by a coherent ideology, these groups decided to petition for reform. The first effort, hammered out in the fall of 1990, put forward twelve demands that were submitted discreetly to the monarchy in January 1991, before Kuwait had been liberated and only shortly after a group of professional Saudi women were arrested for driving automobiles in defiance of the law. That act added fuel to the complaints of the Sahwis, who saw foreign intrigue or even regime support for this demonstration. In May a very similar document with a longer list of signatures, including those of two leading ulama, went to the king before being released to the public and the media. The document called for the application of the sharia to all legislation, which meant that some of the kingdom's laws were suspect. It was scarcely a call for democracy, although it did call for the creation of a consultative, "shura" council, which was seen as a step toward Islamic democracy. It also called for equality of rights and duties and for protection of the rights of "the individual and of society . . . in accord with the norms of the sharia."[22] The thrust of the demands was that the Saudi government did not measure up to its Islamic pretensions. In June 1991, the Council of Senior Ulama responded with a fatwa that avoided comment on the substance but condemned the public airing of the petition.

The monarchy sought to deflect criticism by issuing a Basic Law in March 1992, conceived in the wake of the Juhayman revolt and Iranian Revolution but not promulgated for a decade.[23] The Basic Law, which could be interpreted as a constitution, proclaimed the sharia as the foundation of the country and Sunni Islam as its religion. Two other decrees created a consultative council and a set of provincial councils, but the regime's lack of commitment to elections disappointed liberals, and the lack of concrete responses to religious concerns, such as abrogation of rules contrary to the sharia, left the Sahwis dissatisfied, too. Tim Niblock describes the problems with the new declarations:

> The new laws, in fact, constituted a missed opportunity to change the basis of the political system. What was needed was progress towards a political system where the radically different political trends in the country could be openly debated, where those holding particular political views could both mobilize support for them and be forced to defend them in the public arena and where provincial and national bodies would reflect the balance of opinion resulting from such a contest.[24]

The assembly and provincial councils, though not representative, did promise a broadening of input.

The Sahwa struck again in the fall of 1992 with a forty-five-page "memorandum of advice" to the leader of the senior ulama, Shaykh Ibn Baz, elaborating on the twelve demands. The memorandum called explicitly for granting greater autonomy to religious scholars, teachers, and preachers; giving ulama (by implication, the Sahwi ulama) greater power to monitor legislation; reducing the impact of foreign ideas through tougher censorship; and ending alliance with foreign, infidel regimes. Of 110 names on this petition, almost half were Sahwi ulama, about a third appeared to be Sahwi intellectuals, and a few were supporters among non-Sahwi ulama.[25] The memorandum suggested the formation of an army of 500,000 to protect the country, fight against Israel, and protect non-Saudi Muslims. This time the Council of Senior Ulama rejected the memorandum outright as illegitimate. The council said that it came from "teachers and a few individuals who lay claim to religious science," that it "sows the seeds of dissension and hatred," and that it "denigrates the state by completely ignoring its qualities, which indicates the bad intentions of its authors or their ignorance of reality."[26] This strong tone provoked equally strong rebuttals from some of the signers.

Repression

From then on, the movement lost steam. In May 1993, a group of intellectuals that did not include the leadership of the Sahwa launched the Committee for the Defense of Legitimate Rights, hoping to link reform with the international human rights movement. In the end, the group ended up talking about the defense of "legitimate rights," that is, those consistent with the sharia, rather than universal human rights. Almost immediately the government banned the group, which moved its activities abroad. London became the primary center of Saudi opposition. Within the country, Sahwis began to lose their jobs or their right to preach or teach. Some, including Salman al-Awda and Safar al-Hawali, went to jail. A terrorist attack in Riyadh on November 13, 1995, killed five Americans and two Indians and shocked the regime. Attributed to Islamist radicals, the attack undermined whatever credit the Sahwa movement still enjoyed. Stéphane Lacroix explains: "With that act, jihadis and rejectionists [those who had opposed the Islamists] violently hijacked the Sahwi protest and diverted its meaning for their benefit."[27] By 1995, the golden age of Sahwa activism had come to an end.[28]

As a movement, the Sahwa of the 1990s failed to propose a coherent alternative to official ideology. Instead, it sought reform within the frameworks of Wahhabism and monarchy. Once suppressed, it split into several factions. Some of the leaders (al-Awda and al-Hawali, for example), liberated from prison in 1999, achieved reconciliation with the regime and became apologists. The jihadis, such as Osama Bin Laden and others with experience in Afghanistan, began to speak of war against the regime. The Saudis had deprived Bin Laden of his citizenship in 1994, but his organization, built with the experience acquired in the struggle over Afghanistan, managed to establish itself in Saudi Arabia and carry out acts of terror there against both Americans and Saudi citizens in 2003. Still other Sahwis joined an Islamo-liberal camp, advocating reform but within the religious perspective.[29] None of these offshoots of the Sahwa has sought to confront Wahhabism, and only the most radical jihadis have called directly for overthrow of the monarchy.

The regime's slow but firm reaction to the Sahwa demonstrated its need to maintain its domination of ideology. It continued to censor publications, filter the Internet (mostly for pornography), prohibit the importation of some published materials, reduce reliance on foreign teachers, and emphasize religious studies at every level of education. All these policies aim at the control of ideas. Many factors nonetheless conspire to frustrate these measures. Increasing literacy is perhaps primary, reaching 90 percent for males, 81 percent for females.[30] Most Saudis can thus read the Quran, hadith, and the writings of Ibn al-Wahhab for themselves and can absorb alternative interpretations. The overproduction of religious scholars, most of them products of Saudi universities rather than of schools in Cairo or Damascus, is another factor that contributes to the openness of ideas in Saudi Arabia. There may be limits on what scholars can say and study, but the limits (beyond support of monarchy) are not precise. The porosity of national borders to modern means of communication—telephone, fax, Internet, satellite television—is still another reason why ideological uniformity is no longer possible. It is common to observe that the jihadi movement, which denounces globalization, has benefited from the globalization of communications, but so have more moderate interpreters of the Wahhabi tradition.[31]

The Sharia

Wahhabism has always focused heavily on ritual and belief. Legislation that affects consumption, dress, religious observance, behavior in public places, the rights of foreigners, art, music, and other aspects of ritual or belief must conform to the sharia. This is the domain of the ulama, who dominate the judicial system. They are the sole interpreters of the sharia. On matters such as the organization of the military, the supervision of the oil industry, the construction of housing and highways, and the preparation and enforcement of budgets, the government can and does act by "regulation" rather than legislation and avoids consulting the ulama. The regime preserves its ideological commitments without exposing important policies to critique in the light of the sharia, but this dualism of religious law and regulation is precisely the practice to which the Sahwis were objecting. They said all policies should be judged by the standards of Islam, including its commitment to the equality of all believers. In that respect, they went beyond the concerns of traditional Wahhabism and challenged the dualism of the legal tradition in Saudi Arabia called *siyasa shariyya*, governance of the sharia.

The monarchy also seeks to challenge the dualism of *siyasa shariyya*. It has proposed the codification of the sharia to make it accessible to those without religious education and comprehensible to foreigners doing business in the country. Codification would make the sharia less dependent on individual judges looking at individual cases, in the light of the vast and complicated legal literature in the Hanbali/Wahhabi tradition. Through codification, with the participation of a broad spectrum of ulama, including Sahwis, there would presumably be sharp debate about, and perhaps modification of, rules governing social behavior. The ulama and the Ministry of Justice, dominated by ulama, have consistently resisted this idea. To move that agenda forward, the monarchy has adopted "regulations" to achieve reform of the Ministry of Justice, one of the prime sources of resistance to codification. Codification would effectively make Saudi Arabia look more like other Muslim states, where the sharia has become integrated into a modern legal system.[32]

When Muhammad ibn Abd al-Wahhab struck a pact with Muhammad Ibn Saud in 1744–1745, there was a shaykh with one set of ideas and one political leader, the emir of Najd. There is still one political authority, now called the king, but those who claim to speak for religion are now many, only some of them descendants of the shaykh and only some of them official members of the establishment. The religious establishment may lose its fight against codification, but it seems unlikely that the state will be able to formulate a single, coherent ideology that will satisfy all its residents. Wahhabism is now plural, and the country includes many non-Wahhabis and even non-Muslims. While no other Muslim state appears to value the sharia as much as Saudi Arabia does, the sharia does not explain monarchy, oil wealth, population growth, urbanization, crime rates, foreign policy, or other vital aspects of life in Saudi Arabia. Rather, the struggle for power and influence in Saudi Arabia is redefining the sharia.

Institutions

Initially the relationship between religion and politics in the Saudi empire depended on personal relations between two men, the shaykh and the emir. In the twentieth century, that relationship became increasingly institutionalized in a pattern that resembles that of other Muslim countries. An institutionalized state, directed by the royal family, needs the support of an institutionalized clergy, still led by the descendants of the shaykh, and the clergy depends heavily on the power and wealth of the state. The emir dominated the partnership from the beginning, and the state plays the dominant role in the modern era as it does in Egypt, Turkey, and Iran. Saudi Arabia is not a theocracy if theocracy implies rule by religious authorities. However much Wahhabism has molded life in Saudi Arabia, it has done so only because the political authorities have permitted, encouraged, or forced this to happen.

Two families have created the institutions that dominate modern Saudi Arabia, working from concepts previously embedded in the culture. Bedouin tribes and settled communities of farmers and craftsmen lived in conflict and interdependence in the central region of the Arabian peninsula when the shaykh and the emir struck their bargain. Among the bedouins, the camel herders enjoyed greater prestige than those who herded sheep, and both these groups saw themselves as more courageous, virtuous, and noble than the farmers settled near oases, much less the craftsmen and traders of the villages. The bedouins identified with clans and clans with tribes; the tribal shaykhs enjoyed some power over their followers, but the egalitarian ferocity of the bedouin mentality mitigated shaykhly power. Raiding was a way of life. By contrast, the settled communities depended on "noble" families for leadership and protection.[33]

Muhammad ibn Saud came from such a family. He and his successors extended their domain by conquering other towns and subjugating their noble families, often taking hostages back to Diriyah (or to Riyadh after the destruction of Diriyah by the Egyptians and Ottomans in 1818). The Sauds used marriage with daughters of conquered leaders to further cement loyalty. The armies mustered from the settled populations of the Najd region, combined with the notion of nobility, constituted the secular foundations of the Saud family's success.

Shaykh Muhammad ibn Abd al-Wahhab found his strength in the prestige long accorded scholars (ulama) in the Islamic tradition. Exiled from Uyaina in northern Arabia for his ideas, he found a receptive audience in Diriyah and began a partnership with Ibn Saud. Not averse to bearing arms himself, Ibn Abd al-Wahhab's principal role was, however, to send preachers and judges into newly conquered territories to spread the Wahhabi message. A vital part of that message was the need for absolute obedience to the emir. The shaykh used marriage with as many as twenty women to produce many offspring, some of whom followed him in the scholarly tradition.[34] His descendants have found their way to secular institutions of the modern state, but no one in the Saud family has apparently become an alim. Religious and political elites have been linked but remain separate.

When Ibn Saud, creator of the third Saudi state, decided to force bedouins to settle in camps, the descendants of Ibn Abd al-Wahhab sent in religious figures called *mutawwaun* led by a few ulama and qadis (judges) to bring "true Islam" to the bedouins. The mutawwaun were effectively officers of the emerging state, tax collectors as well as propagandists. (The label *mutawwaun* persists to this day for those in Saudi Arabia who show outward signs of religiosity; it is also the common name for the morals police, the Agency for the Promotion of Virtue and the Prevention of Vice.)[35] The Saudi conquest of regions beyond the Najd, such as Asir in the south, Hasa in the east, and finally the Hijaz in the west, similarly entailed the extension of Wahhabi religious institutions.

Eventually, the Saud family and the Shaykh families asserted their control over the Hijaz region. Like the other regions outside the Najd, and perhaps more distinctly than the others, the Hijaz region never fully accepted the domination of a Najdi family and Wahhabi institutions centered in Riyadh. Jidda, the second largest city in the kingdom and the gateway for many pilgrims coming to Mecca, still sees itself as more modern, cosmopolitan, diverse, and tolerant than Riyadh. Participating in the Saudi conquest of the Hijaz region in 1925, the bedouins, or Ikhwan, encountered unfamiliar inventions such as telephones, radios, and automobiles, all dubious innovations in Wahhabi terms. Under Ottoman auspices, the Hijaz region had acquired a bureaucracy, a regular army, and secondary schools, all largely unknown in the Najd. Like Hijazis, Shia in the Eastern Province were also reluctant to acknowledge the supremacy of the Sunni Wahhabi establishment.

Royal Family

The royal family itself constitutes an institution, well known in some respects and mysterious in others, and it has gradually come to share its power with administrative institutions. The founder, Ibn Saud, used the traditional majlis, open daily to any citizen with a request or complaint, as one instrument of his rule. With the title of *imam*, he also participated in a majlis devoted to reading the Quran, where he could demonstrate his interest in religion. Apparently he also cultivated an informal circle of advisers, who met in the evening. St. John Philby, an Englishman who was part of the group for a time, reported that the king determined the topics for discussion in the group. No one else dared raise an issue. In the 1930s and 1940s the king created two ministries, Finance and Foreign Affairs, and others emerged between 1951 and 1953: Interior (police), Health, Communication, Agriculture and Water, and Education. The king created a council of ministers just before he died in 1953, but it met for the first time under his son and successor, Saud ibn Abd al-Aziz al-Saud.[36]

Ibn Saud shaped the future of the family by preparing his sons, not his brothers, for succession. Islam officially permitted men to take four wives, but Ibn Saud managed to marry as many as twenty women, divorcing some as he married others, and he fathered other children with concubines, who were declared free after bearing male children. As one historian writes, "Ibn Saud stretched the practice [of polygamy] to its limits."[37] He married not for reasons of alliance but rather to ensure the subjugation of his enemies. The royal family absorbed women from the outside but did not export women to ennoble other lines.[38] In contemporary Saudi Arabia, tribal and family origins matter significantly in determining one's place in the social hierarchy. The royal family is at the top and foreigners sit at the bottom, but sharp differences mark even the middle ranks. Alexei Vassiliev writes about these power relationships in the 1990s: "The interests and solidarity of a kinship group took priority over the interests of an individual or those outside the group. . . . Shaikhs and members of the tribal nobility continued to enjoy great authority and few people rose to the top echelons without suitable family connections."[39] Social divisions shaped patterns of marriage within each region and, especially, between regions of the country. The sharpest division was gender. The state trained 10,000 civil servants in the 1960s, none of them women.[40]

The sons of Ibn Saud—there were forty-three of them—still dominate the politics of the royal family. Son Saud, who ruled from 1954 until 1964, exceeded the father in his sexual potency by fathering fifty-three sons and fifty-four daughters.[41] Following the pattern of his father, Saud advanced his own sons in the emerging administrative structure and positioned them for succession, but the family curtailed those efforts when it pushed him off the throne in favor of his half-brother, Faysal. Some one hundred princes and some sixty-five ulama participated in the decision to dethrone Saud in 1964.[42] As Joseph Kechichian observes, "at the highest levels, the internal politics of Saudi Arabia are essentially the internal politics of the family."[43]

Because Saudi law prohibits publishing news about the royal family, the pattern of its interactions remains something of a mystery. The royals are thought to number at least 5,000, all supported by some measure of state favor. While nonroyals have sometimes occupied positions of great power, the most important ministries (Defense, Interior, Foreign Affairs, etc.) and regional governorships have normally been in royal hands. Except for the long struggle between Saud and Faysal after the death of Ibn Saud, family rivalries have been muted and obscured from public view, but the question of succession remains unresolved.[44] At the next moment of decision, when there may not be another son of Ibn Saud to step in, one may learn more about how the family functions as an institution (hierarchy, rules, and procedures) and whether it is sufficiently strong to maintain its control of the polity, which is itself increasingly institutionalized. The monarchy has fostered the growth of bureaucracy in its efforts to manage an increasingly large, complicated, sophisticated, and wealthy society. In doing so it has augmented its reach but also made itself dispensable. The kingdom is no longer a personal affair as it was under the founder, Ibn Saud.

Religious Establishment

To trace the growth of religious institutions is not much easier than providing an understanding of the royal family. St. John Philby suggested that there were about twenty ulama in the kingdom in the 1920s. He must not have been counting the mutawwaun dispatched to teach, preach, and collect taxes. In confronting the crisis generated by the insubordination of the Ikhwan in 1927, Ibn Saud held a conference with leading ulama in 1927 and again in 1928. The ulama ultimately sanctioned the use of arms against the Ikhwan, whom they deemed overly zealous in proclaiming jihad without the permission of the emir. Some of the lower-ranking ulama apparently supported the Ikhwan.[45] Madawi Al-Rasheed reports that the king met weekly with ulama in the 1930s: "This was a regular event whose purpose was to inform members of the ulama of major events and to seek their advice regarding innovations in the kingdom."[46] The gap between king and ulama widened as the country authorized oil exploration and the modernization of infrastructure.

The men of religion set themselves apart as a group in terms of origin (old Najdi families), by dress, and by residential neighborhood. A visitor to Riyadh in the 1920s would note the existence of a neighborhood different from others by virtue of its religious atmosphere. Behavior that might be tolerated in other parts of town would not be sanctioned there, just as certain behavior is not tolerated in ultraorthodox neighborhoods of Jerusalem. The grand mufti of the 1950s and 1960s, Muhammad ibn Ibrahim Al al-Shaykh, lived in that same neighborhood, which also hosted a "scientific institute" devoted to religious instruction. The regime built a religious university, the University of Imam Muhammad ibn Saud, in the neighborhood in 1974.[47]

When King Saud succeeded his father in 1954, his first purpose was "to encourage religion and the sharia."[48] But in the ensuing struggle between Faysal and Saud, many ulama lined up in support of Faysal and against a third prince, Talal, who was proposing a shift toward constitutional monarchy. Thus Faysal, whose mother was a descendant of Shaykh Ibn Abd al-Wahhab, came to power with good religious credentials and backing, but he soon confronted a sticky problem: the introduction of television in the kingdom. The ulama acquiesced only after assurances that a massive amount of programming would be dedicated to religion. The issue was images of places and people that offended Wahhabi sensibilities about polytheism. Televised images won acceptance even though certain sorts of photography were banned.

The descendants of the shaykh—the Al al-Shaykh, not those (sayyids) claiming family ties to the Prophet Muhammad—continued to dominate the ulama, who remained firmly in control of the morals police, originally created as the League for the Encouragement of Virtue and the Denunciation of Sin in 1926. By the 1950s a few offices emerged atop a hierarchy of the ulama: the Office of Grand Mufti (one who issues fatwas), the Committee of Public Morality in Riyadh, the chief judges (qadis) in Mecca and Dilam, and two judges of the sharia court in Riyadh. Under Faysal, the Office of Grand Mufti gave way to a Council of Senior Ulama after 1970. A member of the Shaykh family headed the new Ministry of Justice, which was created in 1971. He remained in that position for thirty years, defending the ulama's domination of the judiciary.

The career of one alim shows both the power of the religious authorities and their weakness vis-à-vis the royal family. As Americans began oil production in the eastern region of Saudi Arabia in 1938, ulama protested the presence of foreigners and the launching of petroleum production—a clear instance of "innovation," which is something Wahhabis say must be avoided. Abd al-Aziz ibn Baz, a judge in the town of Kharj, sixty miles south of Riyadh, lodged his complaint. When Ibn Baz was called to court to answer for his protest, the king informed him of the need for foreign experts to deal with oil, metals, and water. The alim went to jail as a threat to public order; when he was liberated, he went back to Kharj with much enhanced prominence. Eventually he rose in the ranks of the ulama to become the most influential member of the Council of Senior Ulama, which was called upon to approve the use of violence against the occupiers of the Great Mosque in Mecca in 1979 and to support the use of American troops to liberate Kuwait in 1990–1991. In both instances, he led the council in endorsing the king's actions, despite apparent contradiction with the Wahhabi doctrine he had championed in 1938. Since the death of Ibn Baz in 1999, no single personality has emerged to represent the ulama in the way he did.

Renewal

Some members of the Sahwa followed a path similar to that of Ibn Baz. As described earlier, two of its most prominent advocates, Salman al-Awda and Safar al-Hawali, led protests against the regime in the early 1990s and served time in jail. The two Sahwis then emerged to help mediate the regime's conflict with radicals in 2003–2004. By June 2004, the regime had hunted down most of a list of twenty-six persons thought to be responsible for violent attacks on American and Saudi installations. Al-Awda and al-Hawali supported the monarchy's repression of the jihadis, many of them linked to Al-Qaida in the Arabian peninsula.[49] These two Sahwa ulama, protesters in the 1990s, have become part of the establishment. Al-Awda has become a media star and may be in line to become the mufti.

The creation of religious universities may have bolstered the position of the ulama in one sense and weakened it in another. On the one hand, the influence of the ulama helps explain the creation of three religious universities in the kingdom and the great emphasis placed on religion in primary and secondary schools. On the other hand, the spread of religious education has broadened the category of religious scholars and generated competition for those entrusted with official responsibilities. The universities supplied the leadership of the Sahwa; al-Awda, with a Ph.D. from the University of Imam Muhammad Ibn Saud and teaching experience in Burayda, and al-Hawali, a student of theology and then professor at Umm al-Qura University in Mecca, are only two examples among many. Religion has become the language of both consent and dissent. As elsewhere in the Muslim world, the official ulama no longer enjoy a monopoly on interpretation of the Quran and the hadith; they can no longer define Wahhabi doctrine without provoking contradiction. And they can no longer object to royal regulations they deem contrary to the sharia with an expectation that the king will ignore their position, as Kings Saud and Faysal did during the 1950s and 1960s in their efforts to modernize. It might be harder now for the ulama to oppose outright a government decision, because they know their decision will have consequences; it might also be more difficult for the government to ignore religious opinion, knowing that the opinions of religious leaders will be broadly disseminated.

The religious "field" has remained somewhat autonomous in Saudi Arabia. Frank Vogel emphasizes the ability of the ulama to resist the monarchy on many matters over the years, including the introduction of television, the education of women, reform of the pilgrimage, and the codification of the sharia.[50] Granting, recognizing, or conceding autonomy to the religious establishment elevates the significance of its endorsement and gives the king an option of neutrality on controversial religious questions, but ultimately, the religious sphere, like every other field of endeavor in Saudi Arabia, depends on the power and will of the monarchy. In 1993, perhaps because the official ulama had not exhibited enough backbone against the demands of the Sahwi ulama and intellectuals, the government created a Ministry of Religious Affairs, Dawa, Waqf, and Guidance. By putting a loyal administrator in charge of the ministry, the government reasserted its domination of religion. At the same time, the king awarded the title of mufti to Shaykh Ibn Baz, perhaps as compensation for the authority the shaykh had lost to the new ministry, which took control of preaching, mosques, and religious propaganda inside and outside the country.[51] The title had not been awarded to anyone since Muhammad ibn Ibrahim Al al-Shaykh had left the office of mufti in 1969.

The organization of religion in the country depends on the will of the monarchy. A recent study develops an index of government involvement in religion (GIR) and applies it to every country in the world. On that index, Saudi Arabia ranks highest of all countries in the Middle East and North Africa and well ahead of the other countries of the peninsula, all of them predominantly Muslim.[52]

Political Culture

Few states in world history have been as determined as Saudi Arabia to expand their territorial base (in Saudi Arabia's case, the Najd region) and make the culture of that area (Wahhabism) the basis for a single virtuous society. The early Umayyad caliphate (661–750) tried to discourage conversion as it expanded across North Africa and into Spain, thus avoiding the sharing of its resources with fresh converts to Islam. The Ottoman Empire (1300–1918) seemed largely content to govern a plural society. The "true Ottomans" were Turkish Muslims, who constituted a minority in the empire. Perhaps the best analogy with the Saudi efforts would be the Soviet Union or Communist China, both eager to impose a uniform ideology.

Through its alliance with the Wahhabi ulama and with the help of the fierce and zealous Ikhwan, the modern Saudi state sought to fashion a society based on "true Islam"—a society promoting virtue and punishing sin according to a fixed standard defined by the Quran and the hadith. The state used various organizations and tools for the creation and preservation of a virtuous society. These included the Ikhwan, the mutawwaun, the ulama, the educational system, and the modern media. Other key factors were the state's censorship of competing ideas and its insulation from the corrosive effects of tourism. Additionally, the state confined non-Muslims—those who were needed for the development of the country—to enclaves where their influence would be minimized. The monarchy used violent conquest, punitive measures, confiscation of goods, the taking of hostages, exemplary executions, and humiliation of offending groups and individuals in its efforts to create a homogeneous society. As national wealth increased with the price of oil and the level of Saudi production, the distribution of benefits became increasingly important as incentives for obedience and conformity.

The Saudis' failure to create a perfectly homogeneous, virtuous society is not surprising, considering the history of other such efforts. The Saudis have not persuaded the Shia of the Eastern Province to abandon their beliefs and join the dominant Sunni culture. Nor has the state won over all Hijazis to support the Spartan recommendations of the ulama based in Riyadh, although King Abdullah has reached out to both of these communities. The 1979 uprising against the regime came from the Hijazi region, and the Sahwa had a strong following there, too. A majority of the Saudi hijackers on 9/11 came from the Asir, an impoverished, recalcitrant region in the south. Enthusiasm for the Saudi project to create a homogeneous, virtuous society clearly differs from region to region as well as from tribe to tribe and class to class.

Religiosity

Despite its commitment to Islam, the regime has not succeeded in rendering Saudi subjects significantly more religious than compatriots in other Muslim countries. In self-described religiosity, mosque attendance, and to some extent identity, Saudis are less religious than Egyptians or Jordanians. They are more like Iranians than like their Arab counterparts. This is astonishing, given that the kingdom is officially a religious state, the Islamic way of life is rigorously enforced by the religious police, school curricula are heavily loaded with religious education, and Wahhabi thought has maintained a strong grip on religious institutions.[53]

Fifteen percent of the Saudi respondents to a 2003 survey reported that they "never, practically never" attend religious services—a number roughly similar to the percentage of U.S. respondents with the same answer. By that measure, Saudis seem a bit more religious than Egyptians and Turks but less religious than Iranians, of whom only 5 percent said they practically never attend religious services. Almost 90 percent of Saudi respondents "agreed" or "strongly agreed" with the statement "Society should implement only the laws of the sharia."[54] Perhaps the surprise lies with the other 10 percent who took a position at odds with the official Saudi position.[55] Another survey put Saudi citizens slightly above the Arab norm on a question about what is "essential." Sixty-one percent of Saudi respondents said they "could not live without" their spiritual life, compared with 60 percent of Egyptians and an average of 52 percent for the Arab League as a whole.[56] By one estimate, 20 percent of Saudis openly demonstrate religiosity by their appearance or conduct. The term used to describe them is *mutawwaun*, the word also used for the morals police, which involves a much smaller fraction of the population. The length of beards, the length of gowns, and the ropes on headgear all have meaning for those intent on conveying religious conviction or standing.

Crime rates in Saudi Arabia, though perhaps still lower than in surrounding states, seem to be rising. A study done in the 1980s reported rates that were one-ninth to one-twelfth those of surrounding states.[57] For sexual offenses, the rates might be one-fourth as high as in neighboring countries. The study notes that homosexuality, which is defined as a crime, was largely ignored or at least went unreported. In Saudi Arabia, gays may be freer in public than unmarried straight couples, who risk confrontation with the morals police. A series of crimes reported in Jidda in 2002 created some alarm and touched off a debate on the social causes of crime.[58]

Wahhabism has stood firmly against mysticism, whether mysticism is associated with Sufi orders, local personalities deemed saintly, or sorcerers claiming they can identify and destroy sources of evil. A book denouncing sorcery and magic, written by Shaykh Wahid Abd al-Salam Bali, achieved best-seller status in Saudi Arabia in the 1990s.[59] By 1998, it had reached a tenth edition. Bali lists eight ways sorcerers get in touch with evil spirits called jinn. He also explains how one can distinguish a sorcerer from a genuine faith healer. Bali condemns the use of all amulets—objects carried or worn to ward off evil spirits—and says that sorcerers must be killed, because their methods are illegitimate. But obviously he thinks there are jinn to be fought:

> It is *shirk* [heresy] when one seeks the help of spirits, even in the almost metaphorical sense just described. It is acceptable, on the other hand, to get in touch with jinn in exorcisms, when they are forced to make themselves known and are persuaded (often by threats) to relinquish their victim.[60]

One can wonder whether Ibn Abd al-Wahhab would have found this book acceptable or whether he would have taken it as proof that two centuries after his death, polytheism is still a threat.

Social Change

Public attitudes in Saudi Arabia do not match the ideal of a virtuous society, for two reasons. First, such perfection is not attainable anywhere. Second, Saudi Arabia has been undergoing disruptive degrees of demographic, economic, and social change. Estimates put the population of the country at 5 or 6 million in the 1960s. The current number may be about 25 million, and one projection puts it at 45 million by 2025.[61] That rate of growth places burdens on social institutions as does the changing composition of the population. In the 1980s roughly a third of the population may have been nomadic, but that proportion is dropping rapidly, as is the social standing of bedouins, who were once the badge of Saudi authenticity. Riyadh has gone from a city of a few hundred thousand to one of perhaps 5 million, and Jidda, Mecca, and Medina have grown to more than a million inhabitants each. Urbanization has facilitated the growth of communication and education, but has also generated social problems uncommon fifty years ago. The arrival of foreign workers, who now number 8 million or more, further complicates the social system. Most of them come from Asia, but a million hail from Egypt.[62] Only a few foreigners of Arab descent have become naturalized Saudis.[63]

It is the oil industry that has provoked, enabled, and funded the sort of social change implied by such figures. When Ibn Saud and his troops conquered the Hijaz region in 1925, they acquired a major new source of revenue to supplement the spoils of war and the imposition of religious taxes. The annual pilgrimage remained the kingdom's primary source of income for the next thirty years. The exploration for oil began in 1933, and production began five years later, but only in the 1950s, in the last years of rule by Ibn Saud and the first years of rule by Saud and then Faysal, did the wealth begin to fill the family coffers, which were then indistinct from those of the state. When the price of oil shot upward after the October War of 1973, partly as a result of an embargo supported by the Saudis, the resources of the Saudi state rose to unprecedented levels. But prices dipped in the mid-1980s and produced belt tightening and a frustration born of high expectations.[64] The budget of the Saudi state at the end of the 1980s was barely more than a third of what it had been in 1981.[65] By the 1990s the state's income was again on the rise. As a result of its immense resources, Saudi Arabia has undertaken projects on a scale unimaginable in other parts of the world, building cities from scratch, universities with parallel facilities for men and women, highways across the desert, and satellite television networks reaching across the region.

While the state has taken the lead in economic development, it has also sought to foster private enterprise. What is commonly called crony capitalism has produced enormous disparities in wealth and income. Members of the royal family, benefiting from grants of land or tight relationships with political authorities, are at the top of the scale, while foreigners employed as manual laborers languish at the bottom. The economy has grown without much participation from the female half of the population. Only one working-age Saudi woman in twenty holds a job outside the home.[66] Religious rules specify that women cannot work in jobs where they encounter men to whom they are not closely related. Some women physicians do work with men who are not relatives, as do some businesswomen, but these are the exceptions, even though only 39 percent of Saudi women agree, according to one survey, that home is where women belong.[67] A new graduate school on the west coast north of Jidda, the King Abdullah University of Science and Technology, which opened in 2009, permits the mingling of men and women. Women attend classes with faces uncovered. The state has announced plans to create still more opportunities for women "as long as the jobs do not conflict with the Islamic teachings and traditions of the society or lead to the mingling of men with women."

Logic suggests that these extraordinary demographic, social, and economic changes must have produced an evolution of attitudes toward religion and its relationship to politics, but the state has put severe limits on survey research that would test this hypothesis. One survey done in 2009 and 2010 reported that Saudis were less likely than citizens of other countries of the peninsula, and much less likely than Egyptians, to welcome neighbors of another faith.[68] The authors of the poll, conducted at the Gallup Center, attributed the difference to the greater isolation of Saudi Arabia, compared with the peripheral states, which have a longer record of interaction with the world beyond. The Wahhabi notion that people of other faiths must be excluded from the community might also be an explanation. This is the only measure for which the Saudi responses in the survey look significantly different from those of other nations. In the World Values Survey conducted in 2003, younger age groups appeared somewhat less religious than their elders, an observation that foreign observers and religious conservatives tend to confirm. It is unclear, however, whether this phenomenon reflects a life-cycle effect—namely, whether these youth will become more religious as they age—or whether the responses suggest a secularization of attitudes or a social trend.[69] Only time-series data would help answer this question and others.

Saudi respondents to the 2003 values survey seemed remarkably in favor of democracy by some measures, though cautious about the idea in one respect. Two-thirds of Saudi respondents "agreed" or "strongly agreed" that democracy "may have problems but is better than other political systems." That proportion falls below other countries, including Iran (69 percent) and Egypt (98 percent), but on two other questions, Saudi respondents seemed to view democracy favorably. They were as reluctant as others to criticize democracies as indecisive or as unable to maintain public order. Their responses on these questions tend to support the Inglehart contention that Muslim countries do not differ significantly from the West in attitudes toward democracy; Saudis differ rather in attitudes toward women and homosexuality. One study suggests that attitudes toward democracy do vary inversely with religiosity in Saudi Arabia, at least among men, but age and education do not seem to matter. Among women, higher religiosity seems to correlate with more-egalitarian attitudes.[70] Saudi women hold more-egalitarian attitudes than do Saudi men. What the Saudi respondents who viewed democracy favorably think about the autocratic regime in their own country is not a question the surveys have dared (or have been permitted to) ask.

Education

Everywhere, the maintenance or modification of a political culture depends primarily on education. In the 1950s, the Saudis started to build a modern educational system. On the one hand, they understood that the construction of a modern bureaucracy and a modern economy would require an educated citizenry and that an educational system would require the preparation of Saudi teachers. The alternative would have been permanent dependence on outsiders. On the other hand, the regime needed reinforcement of cultural norms that sustained its rule. For this reason, the new educational system, from primary schools on up, needed to generate loyalty to the monarchy and support for Wahhabi ideology. The regime decided to educate girls and open the doors of higher education to young women even as it continued to treat women as beings who should not be seen in public. It claimed to want literate human beings capable of thinking creatively and autonomously but who nonetheless accept cultural practices deeply ingrained in the society. A Saudi publication of 1991, "Education in Arabia," described the purpose of education in that country as "acquainting the individual with his God and religion and adjusting his conduct in accordance with the teaching of religion, in fulfillment of the needs of society, and in achievement of the nation's objectives."[71]

The preceding statement sums up the contradictions in the educational project. The Saudis have put a heavy emphasis on religious instruction from the beginning—perhaps a third of the curriculum in primary schools and a fourth at the secondary level. This emphasis might not best serve the "needs of society" or "the nation's objectives," terms that suggest social and economic development.

Two fortuitous circumstances furthered the educational project. The more important of these circumstances was a treasury capable of building and equipping schools at every level. Some of the earliest demands for trained workers came from the oil industry, but those demands mushroomed with the growth of the Saudi bureaucracy and economy. Oil resources enabled the Saudis to build schools. One recent study counts 24,000 pre-university schools together with several other secondary institutions. That is more schools than there were pupils at all levels in 1950.[72] There are now twenty-four public and twenty-six private universities and colleges.[73] A whopping fourth of the Saudi budget goes to education, and public schools are free to citizens.

The second fortuitous circumstance was related to the staffing of the schools and turned out to be critical to politics. Most of the members of the Muslim Brotherhood who fled Nasir's Egypt for the safety of Saudi Arabia were well educated and literate and spoke Arabic. They found places for themselves in the embryonic educational system the Saudis were putting together. The Egyptians were able to teach modern subjects—including science and engineering—which traditional Saudi ulama could not.

The members of the Muslim Brotherhood thus gradually took over the primary and secondary educational systems, if not quite with the monarchy's blessing, then without its objection. Although they gave the impression of following ibn Abd al-Wahhab's interpretations, in fact they used the classrooms to propagate their own ideology.[74]

The members created an Islamist movement complete with informal organizations that flew below the radar of the Saudi authorities. The traditional ulama presumably felt comfortable knowing that those with proclaimed loyalty to religion were playing such a large role in an enterprise about which they were otherwise skeptical.

Critics today reproach the Saudi educational system for training too many specialists in religion and too few other specialists to match the needs of the job market. The duplication of facilities for girls and boys, and women and men, increases costs astronomically. Foreigners still constitute about a fourth of the overall teaching force. Teachers complain about their lack of autonomy in designing programs, but they also lack the sort of training that would enable them to exercise such autonomy.[75] Saudi schools are said to cultivate an intolerance toward non-Muslims and even toward non-Wahhabi Muslims, such as Shia and Sufis. Al-Rasheed writes:

Islamic history in Saudi schools is taught with a strong sense of mystification. The history is constructed as inevitable. It unfolds the story of a civilization marked by achievement and success, only to be undermined by the acts and ideas of those who abandoned the true spirit of Islam.[76]

At that point in the Saudi narrative, Ibn Abd al-Wahhab and the Saud family enter the scene to save the Islamic world. Saudi schoolbooks portray Saudi Arabia as a vital part of the Islamic world, but without any special links to the rest of the Arab world. Nomadism continues to figure significantly in the national story as a foundation of Saudi uniqueness.[77]

The particular orientations of the Saudi educational system may condition the political culture in ways conducive to the maintenance of the monarchy and its Islamic legitimacy. Nevertheless, these orientations cannot negate the change in political culture that comes with rapid increase in literacy and the enormous expansion of an educated elite. The growth of the media reflects and magnifies that change. While the regime tries to control satellite television, censor local publications, block some foreign books and periodicals from entry, and filter the Internet—the regime tries to maintain its *cordon sanitaire* around the country, as one author puts it—none of these measures, individually or collectively, can prevent the newly educated generations of Saudis from thinking, reflecting, speaking, writing, and acting.[78] Like other Muslim countries, Saudi Arabia finds itself embroiled in political discussions conducted primarily in the language of religion. An Islamist movement has generated both support for and protest against a regime that considers itself Islamic. The regime has found itself supporting elements of that movement even while it suppresses the other, more violent strands. Education fosters change, whatever the educator's intent.

The Saudi case shows, as do other cases, the extent to which political culture is not a constant but a variable. The religious attitudes that help shape a political culture are necessarily variables, too. While the regime has sought to preserve traditional attitudes in the form of a Wahhabi creed, it has been unable to deflect the impact of forces such as the Arab nationalism of Gamal abd al-Nasir, the arrival of members of the Muslim Brotherhood in Saudi Arabia, the growth of Islamist movements in the rest of the region, the Iranian Revolution, the ferocity of the anti-Soviet campaign in Afghanistan, the invasion of Kuwait by Saddam Hussein, and the U.S. occupation of Iraq. These events have shaped public attitudes in Saudi Arabia, and these attitudes have conditioned reactions of the monarchy. To credit the political culture alone with changing regime responses would be to suggest the presence of an effective democracy, which is counter-factual, but to suggest that the political culture only reflects regime manipulation is to neglect the impact of both external factors and the social forces unleashed by the spread of education. As shown by colonial experience elsewhere in the Middle East and Africa, education always produces unintended consequences. It produced nationalism even where colonial powers were trying to suppress it. Only time will tell whether it will undermine the monarchy that has so diligently promoted it.

Conclusion

The Saudi state sees itself as a representative of Islam in the international arena. Whether Islam explains the shape and behavior of the Saudi state to an extent that sets it apart from other Muslim majority states is quite a different issue. The name of the state is that of a family, the Sauds, with no special religious creden-tials. The predominant ideology of the state, Wahhabism, has never concerned itself with political theory except insofar as it calls for obedience to royal au-thority, which has proclaimed that the sharia is the state's constitution. The Wah-habi ideology, now supported and contested by a variety of Islamist movements, claims to represent "true Islam," but has no means of demonstrating the claim to non-Wahhabi Muslims, who cannot, of course, do any better in buttressing their own claims. The Saudis represent one highly contested version of Islamic law and practice.

Saudi institutions separate religious from political officials and guarantee the subordination of the former to the latter. By making preachers and scholars employees of the state, and by putting mosques and religious foundations under the management of the state, the Saudis have created institutions similar to those of other Muslim countries. By seeking to codify the sharia, Saudi Arabia seems headed along a path other countries have taken. The political culture, changing rapidly as a result of a prodigious extension of educational opportunities, gives religion a central place, but Saudis do not appear more religious than other Mus-lims. The rise of an Islamist movement has created a flowering of religious thought and a growth of social organization that draws Saudi Arabia closer to a pattern established in neighboring Muslim states, such as Egypt, Jordan, Yemen, and Syria. Joseph Nevo says: "Indeed, it is Islam that has undergone modifications and adjustments, not the state. . . . The state does not tolerate an autonomous religious domain that may compete with it for the loyalty of the citizens."[79]

The changes in political culture produced by the Islamist movement mean that religion is more central than ever to politics, but it is not now and never has been the decisive element in Saudi Arabia. The support for political reform among some elements of the Islamist movement may accelerate change, but nothing suggests that the most important question facing Saudi Arabia, the succession to the throne, will reflect religious thinking. Nothing suggests that the royal family will ask the country as a whole to share its decision about who will become king when Abdullah steps down. Will candidates be judged in part by their attitudes toward religion? Is this the moment when Saudi Arabia will move further toward representative institutions? Islam is not likely to provide the answers to these questions.

Chronology

1744–1745   Muhammad ibn Abd al-Wahhab and Muhammad ibn Saud conclude an alliance.
1745–1811   First Saudi state is established and is centered in Diriyah.
1818   Diriyah falls to Egyptians; Emir Abdullah is exiled and beheaded.
1822–1891   Second Saudi state exists in at least a formal sense.
1843–1865   Second Saudi state enjoys effective control of central Arabia from Riyadh.
1887   Royal family flees to Kuwait.
1902   Abd al-Aziz ibn Abd al-Rahman al-Saud (commonly known as Ibn Saud) takes Riyadh, begins construction of third Saudi state.
1913   King creates first *hijra* (camp) for bedouins, basis of what became known as the Ikhwan.
1925   Riyadh conquers the Hijaz region (including the holy places).
1927–1929   The Ikhwan revolts but Ibn Saud succeeds in repressing rebellion.
1932   A united Kingdom of Saudi Arabia is established.
1938   Oil production begins.
1953   Abd al-Aziz (Ibn Saud) dies. Son Saud ascends to the throne.
1964   Faysal ibn Abd al-Aziz officially pushes aside Saud after long rivalry. Faysal is endorsed by family and ulama as the new king.
1975   Disaffected relative assassinates Faysal. Khalid ibn Abd al-Aziz rises to throne.

1979	Juhayman and associates temporarily occupy Great Mosque in Mecca.
1983	Khalid dies. Fahd ibn Abd al-Aziz, who had been ruling Khalid, who was ill, becomes king.
1990	Saddam Hussein occupies Kuwait, triggers U.S.-Saudi intervention.
1990–1993	Sahwa (Awakening) movement demands reform.
1992	King issues Basic Law, forms Shura Council, and initiates provincial reform.
1995	Terrorists attack American facility in Riyadh.
2001	Fifteen Saudis participate in Al-Qaida attack on the United States.
2003–2004	Jihadis attack Saudi Arabia. Repression follows.
2005	King Fahd dies; Abdullah ibn Abd al-Aziz ascends to throne.
2009	King Abdullah University of Science and Technology, which permits mixing of men and women, opens north of Jidda.
2011	Half of seats in municipal councils filled by election. King announces women will vote in similar elections in 2015.
2013	King grants women 30 of 150 seats in advisory council.

7

Reconciling Religion and Politics

The debate about religion and politics degenerates all too frequently into exaggeration. A person living in Colorado Springs could easily imagine that religious organizations such as the New Life Church and Focus on the Family are exerting inordinate influence on local schools, state government, and even national politics. Someone from Southern California could easily imagine that secular humanism sweeps away religious traditions, including school observance of religious holidays. The campaign for the recognition of gay marriage evokes fear and objection among many of the devout. The American Civil Liberties Union plays the role of the devil in that context, as the religious right does in the other. The culture wars rage on in America without victor or vanquished.

Exaggeration also marks the discussion of religion and politics at the level of comparative politics. Some Europeans look at America with astonishment. How can a prosperous nation with a high level of literacy and education continue to have such high rates of church attendance and such large percentages of the population who believe in God? Americans view Europeans with some worry about a loss of not just religion but also moral purpose. Europeans join Americans in their deep concern about the growing strength of Islam in the West and of radical Islam in many parts of the world. They link Islam with traditionalism, the oppression of women, authoritarianism, and even terror. Meanwhile, some Islamists, both moderate and radical, see the secular humanism embedded in Western social, economic, and political theories as inimical to their own ways of life. They see threats to the survival of Islam in what they willingly call a clash of civilizations.

These observations share an exaggeration about the importance of religion (or absence of religion) in political life. Social scientific studies of the 1950s and 1960s argued that religion diminishes in importance as countries become wealthier and better educated. Those studies downplayed the importance of religious leaders and political leaders with claims to religious legitimacy. Religion loomed as an obstacle to development. Then, after 1967, came religious revival in the Muslim world, and social scientists responded with a veritable deluge of studies of Islam and Islamism. The Iranian Revolution of 1979 triggered the flood and reopened an old question: Is Islam compatible with social and economic development? In the 1980s, Professor Edward Said started a debate about Orientalism. The debate pitted skeptics such as Bernard Lewis, who doubted the capacity of Islam to evolve with the times, against optimists such as Said, who blamed Western scholars for having created distorted accounts of Islamic doctrine and experience (accounts that even Muslims themselves had come to accept). The debate about Orientalism has helped temper the deterministic modernism of social science in the 1950s and 1960s, which downplayed the importance of religion, and the reactive overemphasis on Islam in the 1980s and beyond.[1]

What distinguishes this book from others produced in recent years is its effort to establish a plane of comparison that goes beyond a single religion, Islam, and to go beyond an assumption that religion determines politics. A survey of events in Europe and North America shows that religion has played a part in shaping political life on both continents, especially at certain moments. In the great span of history, however, politics is a more important determinant of the religious configuration of a country than religion is a determinant of politics. Political necessities have driven religion to accommodate identity with the nation-state, the supremacy of positive law, and the political regulation of religious institutions in the West. Politics has required the recognition of religious pluralism and mutual toleration. Christianity, however influential, cannot account for the overall shape and course of political development in the West. Modern Christian thought and organization reflect political realities.

The investigation of five case studies in the Middle East confirms a similar pattern. Islam alone cannot explain diverse patterns of political development in four Muslim nation-states, and Judaism as a religion does not account for the state of Israel. If Islam is merely the Quran and a set of core ideas divorced from those who propound and believe them, and from the cultural settings in which people live, then one can speak of it as an abstraction.[2] If religion is not merely an abstraction, then it cannot be treated as a single, undifferentiated phenomenon.

If it were an abstraction, and if it were a determinant of specific political outcomes, such as a certain form of government, then it would create the same result everywhere. If Islam means not just a book and ideas, but people, what they think, how they are organized, and what they do, then one must study them in a physical space—a space now divided into nation-states. Describing Islam requires descending to the nation-state or even the substate level. If Judaism were just scriptures, beliefs, laws, rituals, and principles interpreted and implemented by an undifferentiated set of human beings, it should have produced the same result in Europe and the United States as it has in Palestine. In every case examined here, politics comes to explain more about religion as religion is practiced than religion can explain about politics in a particular nation-state.

Politics is the determining factor. If religious forces gain control of a state, as in Iran, they do so by political means. It is the state that determines how religion— its representatives, its organizations, its believers, and its doctrines—will be treated. The state may find itself desperately in need of the legitimacy that religious support can provide. It may discover that propagating a certain version of religion serves the state's purposes. A government may need to suppress dissident religious groups, either to please the religious majority or to prevent religious dissent from becoming political dissent. A state may have an ideological interest, as did the Soviets, in suppressing religion altogether. Perhaps more than anything, the state has an interest in a stable relationship with the dominant religious groups and their representatives. This interest in stability and legitimacy gives religious groups leverage. They may be able to bargain over national identity, the nature of the law, the regulation of organizations, and civic and religious education. Their political influence, or lack of it, will affect outcomes.

There exists a balance between religion and politics not when the two domains are equal in weight—what would that mean?—but rather when neither the state nor religious groups want radical change in the relationship. Of course, neither side may ever be happy with the balance that is struck. The culture wars in the United States constitute evidence for that point. Many Americans apparently vote in solidarity with a religious denomination or from personal religious conviction.[3] Groups resort to referenda, legislatures, Congress, the presidency, and the courts to seek modification of the ground rules governing religion and politics. Secular-minded groups push back in all those venues. The American system permits continual adjustment of policy without risk of a major shift in structure.

One may speak of an approximate balance or a settlement that is achieved in a particular context at a specific moment of history.[4]

Balance

Egypt in the nineteenth century serves as an example of imbalance where the state was the revisionist party. Starting with the reign of Muhammad Ali, the Egyptian state sought consistently to reduce the power and authority of the ulama by diminishing their financial resources and bringing them under state supervision. By contrast, Egypt since World War II exemplifies the opposite sort of imbalance. The Muslim Brotherhood assembled a political force with a capacity for armed action that challenged the monarchy and contributed to its demise in 1952. The new strongman, Gamal Abd al-Nasir, felt threatened by the Brotherhood, and he outlawed the organization. Free again after 1970, tolerated by the regime but lacking legal status, the Brotherhood spun off groups dedicated to the forcible overthrow of the Egyptian government. One of those groups assassinated President Anwar al-Sadat in 1981 for what the assassin argued was the betrayal of Islam. The Brotherhood itself remained in opposition and advocated a new moral order for the country. The official ulama, employees of the state, sought to negotiate a middle ground in an effort to isolate radicals from moderate Muslims and to show the average Muslim that the state respected religion. The relationship between religion and politics remained unsettled before the events of the Arab Spring, which suggested the possibility of realignment.

The relationship remains unsettled in Israel, too, but there the temporary looks much more permanent than in Egypt. Without a formal constitution, the country has forged ahead on the basis of informal arrangements. The status quo letter provided assurances to the ultraorthodox to bring them toward support of the state. In response to the influence of Orthodox and ultraorthodox groups in the Knesset, the state has provided progressively greater benefits to these groups. Leftist, secular groups have resisted and called for a radical reduction of religious influence, but they are playing politics within the system. The assassination of Yitzhak Rabin by an ultraorthodox yeshiva student from the West Bank, who declared that Rabin had violated religious law, shook the system momentarily but only solidified existing conventions in the long run. Secular law takes precedence over halakha. The state remains stable in its mix of religious and secular.

Turkey seems to be moving toward ever greater stability in the relationship between religion and politics. The long-term stability of that relationship under the Ottoman Empire came under pressure in the nineteenth century. Sultan Abdülhamid II played the Islamic card to shore up his empire. When those efforts failed and a new, scaled-down state called Turkey emerged in the 1920s, the leader committed himself to a complete reworking of the relationship. Atatürk sought monopolistic control of religion but failed in the long run to achieve it. Sufi orders, though prohibited from public meetings, lurked underground. Said Nursi cultivated a new religious sensibility. By relying on force to sustain its efforts at monopoly (which it termed *laiklik*, or secularism), the state opted for apparent over genuine stability. As the Turkish government moved toward multiparty competition after World War II, the parties that challenged the Republican People's Party, the party of Atatürk, sought to reintegrate the forces of religion. Then, after 1970, an Islamist movement arose to pursue that objective with greater intensity. Turkish democracy finally empowered Recep Tayyip Erdoğan, a product of the Islamist movement. The government of Erdoğan may be fashioning a sustainable equilibrium between religion and politics—an equilibrium that both Islamists and the Turkish military are willing to accept—but the evidence is not yet in. Fearing a sharp break with the Kemalist tradition, secularists threaten to rock the boat.

Iran has veered from one sort of imbalance to another. Like Atatürk, Reza Shah tried the strong-armed approach to reducing the role of religion. His son, Muhammad Reza Shah, took greater care to cultivate religious authorities until the early 1960s. Then, rather than seeking accommodation of the strident complaints of Ayatollah Khomeini, who was concerned about Westernization and foreign privilege in the country, the shah reverted to the repressive tactics of his father. He exiled Khomeini, who settled in Iraq to study, teach, and preach. Khomeini ultimately convinced many of his fellow clerics that revising the relationship between religion and politics required revolution. He fashioned the forces of religion into a revisionist party.

Since the Iranian Revolution, the tables have turned. The government led by clerics now seeks stability and, like the Pahlavi monarchs, has resorted to force to maintain it. Leading clerics who object to the new arrangements have been silenced by trial in special courts or, in the case of Ayatollah Ali Montazeri, once in line to become Khomeini's successor, placed under house arrest and kept there until he died. Challenge to the notion of Islamic government would be unthinkable, but even those who pushed for reform within the Islamic model—for example, the supporters of President Khatami and those who protested the reelection of President Ahmadinejad in 2009—have been harassed, imprisoned, or even executed. Since the regime insists on cloaking its actions in religious language, every protest necessarily affects the relationship between religion and politics. While there is apparent stability in the relationship, appearances backed by repression often prove deceiving in the long run.

The long-term relationship between the Saudi monarchy and the Wahhabi religious establishment looks as solid and stable as ever, but the stability depends not only upon force—the regime has been quick to repress radical dissent—but upon the considerable wealth of the Saudi state. The Saudis co-opted, deflected, and repressed an Islamist movement that originated in the 1960s and 1970s and that threatened in the 1990s to force recalibration of the relationship between religion and politics. When American troops arrived to retake Kuwait in 1990–1991, the regime weathered the instability that resulted. Later it weathered the storm generated by 9/11 and the terrorism that followed. The most serious challenges to Saudi rule have all come from groups and individuals invoking religion against a state that depends in large part on its religious identity for legitimacy. The lack of democratic institutions makes it difficult to know whether contemporary stability reflects genuine balance or merely the strength of the state.

Seeking Stability

Instability in the relationship between religion and politics—defined as a situation in which either religious forces or the governing powers seek revision of the relationship—makes liberal democracy difficult to achieve. Hobbes understood the dangers of religious discontent and proposed radical separation as a solution. But his remedy of strict state control of religion under a "mortal god," subject only to review by the immortal God, did not hold up in the West.[5] He thought only an absolute sovereign could dominate religious passions and enforce an enduring settlement, but Locke, Rousseau, and Kant did not follow his proposed solution. The liberal state that owes so much to their ideas came to depend on moral principles anchored in a universalistic religion that did not require scriptural verification. The great separation of religion and politics envisioned by Hobbes never occurred, although it remained the ideal of French secularism and, by extension, Turkish laiklik. Judeo-Christian secularism of the sort practiced in England and especially in the United States sought instead to reconcile religious and secular values within institutions designed to prevent religious strife.[6] Religion became a bulwark of the state. Once in place, liberal democracies in Europe and the United States provided the mechanisms for "partisan mutual adjustment" in such a way that stability in the relationship between religion and politics could be maintained.[7]

Liberal democracy provides a set of formulas for stability. Nonliberal monarchies in many parts of the world have sought to settle the religious issue in other ways. Some European monarchs claimed divine right to rule and depended on the church for support of their claims. In the modern Middle East, several kings claim family ties to the clan of the Prophet and ally themselves closely with the ulama. Jordan and Morocco have achieved considerable stability on the basis of relationships that bear some resemblance to the Saudi model. What Samuel Huntington defined as the "king's dilemma"—to promote modernity would be to undermine the notion of monarchy, but not to modernize would be to provoke revolt—has proved less daunting than he thought in 1968, perhaps because monarchs have often used religion effectively.[8]

Ibn Khaldun, the astute observer of history and politics who wrote from North Africa a century before Machiavelli, believed that there could be no permanent reconciliation of religion and politics. His cyclical theory of government presupposed periodic renewal by virtue of a process in which governments, established by military conquest and boldness, settle into a comfortable, debilitating lifestyle, lose their will to fight, neglect the dictates of their religion, and expose themselves to conquest by ferocious bedouins driven by puritanical religious fervor. His model served to explain some Islamic history, and the history of North Africa in particular, but the Ottoman Empire, which was in its infancy when he wrote, far outlasted the five generations allotted it by the Khaldun model. The Ottomans achieved much greater stability than he imagined possible. The relationship they established between political and religious establishments, between bureaucrats and the corps of ulama, constitutes one secret of Ottoman success.

What causes stable formulas to erode? Ibn Khaldun blamed human nature. Regimes that establish themselves on piety fall prey to the soft life of city-based power. Contemporary modernization theorists argue that social and economic modernization affects both politics and religion. People are pulled from their villages toward increasing opportunities in the cities. They educate their children, who seek jobs in the modern economy and participate in modern organizations. Eventually, they come to want to participate in political decisions. As Huntington observed, an increase in political participation via unions, associations, political parties, demonstrations, protest movements, and so on, will likely produce political instability, unless there is institutional growth and adaptation to these new phenomena.[9]

Social Change

Modernization theorists argue that this same set of changes produces a more secular society. Ronald Inglehart identifies a syndrome of traits that he calls "traditional" attitudes, many of them grounded in religion. Modernity, he says, means moving away from these attitudes and away from a number of religious beliefs. The United States has not, however, moved in the predicted direction of secularism on this scale, even though it has clearly become a postindustrial society and scores high on Inglehart's postmaterialist scale (with its emphasis on freedom and self-expression over materialism). Inglehart dismisses the United States as an anomaly. Western European countries best exemplify his model by virtue of their ultramodernity (i.e., high degree of secularism) and postmaterialism.[10]

What Inglehart's surveys do not consider is how religion can change without ceasing to be religion. Several studies have linked Islamist movements in Muslim countries to increasing literacy rates and the spread of higher education. Contrary to modernization theory, more education seems to be producing more religious commitment rather than less. Literate believers suddenly have direct access to the Quran and Quranic exegeses that have previously been inaccessible. Women's study groups abound. Religious publications have multiplied with the size of the literate audience. Sermons recorded on electronic media give even the illiterate access to interpretations they would likely never have heard a generation ago. Religion has become a matter of choice, not just habit. Dale Eickelman and James Piscatori refer to the "objectification" of religion.[11] A believer who comes to reflect on his or her own beliefs, to see religion as an object among other objects, and who chooses one version of that object over another is quite a different person from one who performs religious rituals in deference to the practices of ancestors.

The religious attitudes of a society can thus undergo change with the opportunities offered by modernizing societies. (To call this "secularization of religion" does not serve any useful purpose.) This change in religious consciousness can result in instability in the relationship between religion and politics. Egypt, Turkey, and Saudi Arabia all bear witness to the impact of the Islamist phenomenon, the emergence of groups demanding revision of the place of religion in politics. These groups have been more successful in Turkey and Egypt than in Saudi Arabia.

In Iran the relationship between religion and politics eroded from both sides. On the one hand, rapid economic and social modernization fueled by oil wealth created new political demands that the monarchy found itself hard-pressed to satisfy. On the other hand, education created a growing elite that was receptive to the messages conveyed by Jalal Al-e Ahmad, Ali Shariati, and other dissident intellectuals who came to argue that Islam meant revolution. The Ayatollah Khomeini found a receptive audience for his Islamist appeal, first among his fellow ulama and then in a broader public. Changes in the political and social environment thus affected both the political and the religious spheres. The tenuous relationship achieved under the shah and maintained by repression became unstable.

Exogenous Factors

Social change within a society necessarily affects the relationship between religion and politics, but instability may also result from exogenous political factors such as imperialism, nationalism, and socialism. Imperialism propelled subject peoples toward religion in a search for reasons why the lands of Islam were unable to defend themselves. The success of socialism in the Soviet Union during the first fifty years of its existence probably encouraged the forces of secularism, but it was nationalism, itself a product of imperialism and a reaction to it, that required major readjustment of the older relationship between religion and politics.

Nationalism arrived in Egypt as a reaction against the Ottoman Empire and against European intervention. In Turkey, nationalism arose as a revolt against the empire and against foreign domination. Iranian nationalism grew as a movement opposed to British and Russian imperialism and subsequently as a parliamentary majority supporting Mussadiq in his move to nationalize Iranian oil. In the Jewish community, nationalism ultimately created a Jewish state where there had been none before. In each case, nationalism created change in the relationship between religion and politics. Religion served to unite the nation against outsiders. Saudi Arabia is a peculiar case because the monarchy cemented its relationship to Wahhabi Islam to build its own empire in the Arabian peninsula with a bit of help from the British. Neither opposition to imperialism nor the creation of a national concept were the factors there that they were elsewhere.

Zionism represents the most dramatic example of the impact of nationalism. In the Diaspora, Jews related to a variety of states in which they lived in one of two ways: assimilated into a state dominated by non-Jews or unassimilated as a ghettoized community with great internal coherence and organization but third- or fourth-class status in the society at large. With assimilation, religion was irrelevant. With ghettoization, religion constituted a glue for the community, a reason for holding oneself apart and a manual for doing so. An assimilated Jew, Theodor Herzl, took the Dreyfus Affair in France as evidence that even Jewish citizens would never achieve genuine equality there. He revived the idea of a Jewish state, and while few of his fellow assimilated Jews responded to the appeal, the ghettoized communities of Eastern Europe responded with enthusiasm. The possibility of a state began to transform the relationship between Jews and the states of Europe, especially in the East; then came Hitler in Germany, whose persecution of Jews solidified efforts in Palestine to create an entirely new state whose identity depended in part on religion. There was no precedent for establishing a relationship between religion and politics in this new entity.

All the states included in this book have experienced instabilities in the relationship between religion and politics as a result of both the indigenous forces of modernization and exogenous factors, including nationalism. Building or rebuilding stability necessarily entails revising the relationship between religion and politics in one or more of the four arenas where religion impinges on political life. If powerful religious organizations oppose political arrangements, political instability is a likely result. If an authoritarian government imposes its vision of religion on its citizens via proclamations, laws, institutions, and education, it generates hostility and potential instability. Establishing or reestablishing stability means achieving some sort of consensus on identity, ideology, institutions, and political culture.

Identity

Hypothesis 1: A state built upon religious identity and reflecting major elements of national history may be able to construct institutions seen as indigenous in origin and capable of generating among its subjects and citizens a loyalty that other governments do not enjoy.

This first hypothesis is the claim of authenticity. The monarchies all claim to represent it. Some have not survived (Iran, Libya, Iraq, and Yemen, for instance) but others have done well. The World Values Survey has turned up strong evidence of a relationship between religiosity and nationalism, but the jury is still out on whether a state can generate greater religiosity and thereby enhance loyalty to the nation by using religion. Iran has tried to promote religiosity, without much apparent effect, if one is to believe the surveys. Egyptian, Turkish, and Israeli leaders have not cultivated religiosity as much as they have sought to exploit it for national purposes. Patriotism runs high in all these countries, but higher in Egypt and Iran than elsewhere.

Two of the five countries included in this study—Iran and Egypt—have long histories as states. These societies are older than those of Europe, but they followed European states toward nationhood in the nineteenth and twentieth centuries. Because Arab Muslims conquered Egypt and Iran in the seventh century, Islam is an important element of national identity in those countries. Roughly 60 percent of Iranians and 80 percent of Egyptians think of themselves first and foremost as Muslims (see Table 5.3).[12] Ninety percent of Iranians and 80 percent of Egyptians declare themselves "very proud" of their nationality. The comparable figures for Turkey and Israel are significantly lower: 54 percent and 65 percent. These differences seem to distinguish old states from new ones, Saudis fall in between at 75 percent, as do Americans at 72 percent.[13]

The two venerable societies, Egypt and Iran, encountered nationalism in different ways than did Turkey and Israel. For Egyptians, nationalism meant liberation from the French occupation launched by Napoleon Bonaparte and then from Ottoman rule. Later, after the occupation of Egypt by the British in 1881, nationalism came to mean genuine independence from imperialism—something not fully accomplished until 1952. Similarly, nationalism in Iran took the form of protest against the monarchy and its efforts to modernize the country by leasing its resources to Europeans. After World War II, Muhammad Mussadiq as prime minister led the forces of nationalism and challenged the shah and the West by nationalizing Iranian oil. The shah himself invoked Iranian nationalism but came under attack for his dependence on the United States. Nationalism in these two countries thus assumed anti-imperial and anti-Western forms, even though the idea of nationalism itself is of European origin.

In both countries, Islam emerged in stages as the principal source of alternative identity, even though other possibilities were available. In Egypt, ulama provided indigenous leadership when the French invaded. Muhammad Ali and his successors, themselves foreigners, tried to manipulate and control religion for their purposes as they sought to modernize the country. Meanwhile, the monarchy permitted foreigners to explore and even take home precious artifacts from the ruins of ancient Egypt. The linkage of the pharaohs with the monarchy, foreigners, and absolutism pushed nationalists toward two other sources of identity. One was Arabism, pursued with special vigor by the regime of Gamal Abd al-Nasir from 1952 to 1970, but Arabism led to quarrels with other Arab states and a disastrous war with Israel. The most successful effort to reformulate Egyptian identity in religious terms came with the creation of the Muslim Brotherhood in the 1920s. Its founder, Hasan al-Banna, saw himself as a nationalist opposed first to the British and then to the monarchy, which remained caught in British snares. The Brotherhood urged Egyptians to see themselves as Muslims and to become "good Muslims" by supporting Brotherhood activities—cultural, social, political, or even military. President Anwar al-Sadat sought to tip the country away from its Arab identity and toward Islam, but his assassins called him "pharaoh." Religion emerged as the badge of Egyptian authenticity for the Sadat and Hosni Mubarak regimes as well as for the Islamist opposition.

In Iran the story was similar. The ulama began to align themselves with the nationalist movement, first in the successful protest against the tobacco concession in 1891 and then in the constitutional revolution of 1906–1909. The ulama supported the creation of a new dynasty under Reza Khan, who crowned himself shah, in the belief that he represented the best chance for order and stability for an Iran free of foreign domination. A part of the clergy initially supported the nationalist government of Mussadiq, and a leading member of the ulama, the Ayatollah Khomeini, led protests in the 1960s against concessions to foreigners, particularly the grant of immunity from Iranian courts accorded to American military personnel in 1963. Shah Muhammad Reza Pahlavi, son of Reza Shah, sought to bolster his legitimacy with references to ancient Persia. Such claims pushed the protest movement against the shah toward an alternative form of Iranian identity, the Islamic identity solidified by the Safavid dynasty's conversion of the country to Shii Islam after 1500. In both Egypt and Iran, Islamist movements extricated Islam from its reputation of antimodernism and fashioned it into a recipe to rescue the "authentic" nation from foreign influence. In both cases, pre-Islamic identities suffered by association with previous regimes eager to assert their autonomy from the Islamic world and their solidarity with the West, but today nothing precludes an eventual revival and further reworking of national identities, if ever the issues of foreign influence recede in prominence.

The "new" societies of Turkey and Israel faced the problem of creating states and then national identities. Neither felt as much threat from foreign influence as did Egypt and Iran (Table 7.1). The Young Turks fought off foreign domination to establish a new Turkey, but they saw their own past as a greater threat to legitimacy than foreign ideas. Mustafa Kemal Atatürk identified Islam with the Ottoman Empire and with antimodernism. He suppressed many religious organizations and subjected an official Islam to government supervision. Islam was to serve the interests of the secular state, which identified itself with Turkism, even though the country included only a fraction of the world's Turkish-speaking population and even though non-Turks constituted a substantial part of the new nation. The Kemalists pushed Turkey toward the French model of laïcité. Although circumstances have changed in Turkey since World War II and Islam has reemerged as a factor in politics, the country seems increasingly capable of reintegrating Islam and even Ottoman history into its identity without giving up its commitment to modernism and to membership in the European Union. President Erdoğan has sought to recognize popular identification with Islam without downgrading the achievements of Atatürk or joining the anti-Western chorus.

Israel also emerged from a piece of the Ottoman Empire via a British mandate and, like Turkey, sought to dissociate itself from that element of its past. For its creation, it depended on foreign, imperial forces, and although it eventually fought against British occupation, it turned to the West for further assistance once independence had been achieved. The agreement to accept reparations from Germany in exchange for friendly diplomatic relations illustrates the decision. The early settlers were predominantly secular Jews, who saw the Zionist movement as creating a refuge for Jews, a pioneering effort to establish a new community in a strange land, an experiment in social justice, and an opportunity to build a state. Identity flowed from those who committed themselves to that effort, who saw themselves as secular Jews. The Zionist Labor settlement movement, responsible for establishing democratic procedures for governing the incipient state, found itself obliged to accommodate religion for two reasons: Zionism as an idea does not make sense without some reference to historic Judaism, and the emerging state could not do without the cooperation and support of all Jews, whether they were secular, Orthodox, or ultraorthodox. Politics dictated inclusion of religion in the state's identity.

Israel resembles Iran in the centrality of religion to its official identity. Israel is a Jewish state, and Iran is an Islamic republic. To become something different,

TABLE 7.1   Elements of Diversity

	Experience with Imperialism	Primary Religious Group	Principal Religious Minority	Language	Principal Minority Language
EGYPT	Occupation	Sunni Muslim (90%)	Christian (8–10%)	Arabic (99%)	—
IRAN	Zones of influence	Shii Muslim (88%)	Sunni (8%)	Persian (51%)	Turkish (25%)
ISRAEL	Mandate	Jewish (76%)	Muslim (16%)	Hebrew (65%?)	Arabic (20%)
SAUDI ARABIA	External influence	Sunni Muslim (85%)	Shii (15%)	Arabic (90%)	Asian languages
TURKEY	Defeat	Sunni Muslim (85%)	Alevi (15%)	Turkish (85%)	Kurdish (15%)

Note: This table reflects the author's estimates based on a variety of sources. Many of these statistics have political significance. Minorities inevitably claim larger numbers than what governments report. Governments tend to exaggerate the ethnic and religious dominance of the majority. In Saudi Arabia, noncitizens make up roughly 30 percent of the population. Most of these noncitizens seem to be Muslim but not Arab. The Saudi numbers may thus be even less reliable than others, but these numbers should be taken as indicative, not definitive.

each country would have to rename itself. If Israel were to revert to the notion of a binational state, it would presumably become Israel-Palestine or a state of some other name. If Iran were to move toward an identity more inclusive of Iran's full history, it would presumably drop "Islamic" from its moniker. Both countries could diminish the role of religion in their identities, but this would be more difficult for Israel than for Iran. Without Zionism, Israel would not have come into being, and Zionism is not conceivable without Judaism, although it is not a necessary consequence of Judaism. The concept of Iran as a state does not depend on Islam, whatever the current regime may think or proclaim.

In that sense, Israel may be more dependent on religion for its political identity than even Iran, not to mention Egypt or Turkey, even though a much smaller portion of Israelis see themselves first as Jews (45 percent) than do Egyptians, Turks, or Iranians see themselves as Muslims (62–80 percent). A plurality of Israelis see themselves first and foremost as Israelis, citizens of a state. An additional 12 percent see themselves simply as individuals, and about 20 percent identify themselves as Arabs, Muslims, Christians, or Druze.[14] Religion is thus central to Israeli identity not because its citizens are necessarily devout Jews but because the state itself owes much to religion for its coming into being. For a number of Israelis, religion has become an organizing tool for gaining political influence and protecting interests such as settlement in the West Bank, the definition of citizenship, the educational system, or the organization of religious institutions. It has been a factor in political opposition to the government, but more frequently, the religious parties have participated in parliamentary majorities. Relations with the West also reinforce religious identity, not by virtue of "authenticity" as in Egypt and Iran, but because many in the West support Israel by virtue of its religious identity. Israel has transformed Judaism; many Jews worldwide—perhaps most of them—now take Israel to be a central institution of the faith. According to an astute observer of Israeli society, this heightened emphasis on Jewishness and ethnicity has a downside. It may be causing a decrease in "Israeliness"—the state-centeredness that drove the founding generation.[15]

Israel and modern Turkey congealed as states with elites who admired the West and took democratic ideas seriously. The timing of national independence or autonomy gave these two states greater freedom to create national identities than either Egypt or Iran enjoyed. Both Israel and Turkey enjoyed some discretion about who would be citizens. Many Christians, including Turkish speakers, fled the new Turkey for Greece in the 1920s. The Israeli government pursued a purposeful policy of reducing the Arab population of its new state from 1947 to 1949. Through force and fear, Israel drove out Arabs and refused to permit their return.[16] Israel then depended upon voluntary immigration to increase the Jewish population and used war as a tool for refashioning its borders. Both states emerged as more coherent nations as a result of these adjustments, although neither managed to satisfactorily integrate the remaining minorities: the Kurds in Turkey and the Arabs in Israel.

Egypt and Iran bore the burdens of the past in the form of positive and negative associations with alternative visions of the nation. They sought to create nations in states that had long been together but largely by reason of geography or force. These states inherited multiple understandings of themselves, none of which has ever been entirely satisfactory to everyone. Much as they may try, Egypt and Iran can never expunge the past. For now, they have both tilted toward a greater identity with Islam, but history continues to offer other options. Since the military coup of 1952 brought Gamal abd al-Nasir to power, the push of the desert has been stronger than the pull of the Mediterranean in Egypt, but the pattern could be reversed. Iran could conceivably reverse course and revive its celebration of pre-Islamic glories.[17]

Most of the authoritarian republics of the Middle East have needed to identify with Islam for political reasons but have not been able to placate Islamist opposition. Egypt under Sadat and Mubarak, Syria under the Assads, Tunisia under Bourguiba and Ben Ali, Libya under Qadhdhafi, and Algeria under military rule—all ostensibly secular republics—found themselves facing Islamist dissent. The Syrian government sent the army into Hama in 1982 to suppress Sunni Islamists; the Tunisians chased the principal Islamist leader out of the country and kept him in exile and his followers in jail until the revolution of 2011. The Algerian government fought a civil war for at least eight years against Islamist militants. Muammar al-Qadhdhafi, who seized power in Libya in 1969, proclaimed his regime Islamic and populist, but it was neither. Nasir—not Sayyid Qutb or Ayatollah Khomeini—was Qadhdhafi's hero. A distinguished and influential Shii cleric from Lebanon, Musa al-Sadr, disappeared on a visit to Libya in the 1970s, presumably a victim of Qadhdhafi's regime.[18] Although civil war has ended in Algeria, it remains to be seen whether the country has achieved a stable understanding of the place of religion in national identity. Now Mubarak, Ben Ali, and Qadhdhafi are gone, and Syria has degenerated into civil war. In the construction of new political arrangements, the relationship between religion and politics will necessarily be primary. Algeria claims to have reached a modus vivendi with Islamist parties, but it may prove to be a settlement based on repression rather than consent.

The monarchies of the Arab world have, unlike the republics, been remarkably stable, with two exceptions. Revolution ended a monarchy in Yemen in 1962, and Qadhdhafi's coup ended the short-lived monarchy in Libya, a monarchy created by the United Nations Trusteeship Council in 1952. Otherwise, kings and shaykhs have done much better than Huntington predicted they would.[19] The kings of both Morocco and Jordan claim descent from the family of the Prophet. Morocco joined Saudi Arabia and Iran as creators of the Organization of the Islamic Conference, now called the Organization of Islamic Cooperation. The Saudi monarchy leans heavily on its geographic centrality to the history of Islam and its role in hosting the pilgrimage. While all these monarchies have undergone some Islamist challenge, they have been able to defend themselves successfully. Identification of the state with Islam may help explain the political stability, but the formula does not come from Islam or even from Islamic history. These modernizing dynasties have nurtured their versions of religious identity for reasons of political survival.

None of these states is as venerable as Iran or Egypt. All except Saudi Arabia experienced direct imperial intervention. In Morocco, the monarchy survived colonial control and emerged as a symbol of modern nationalism. In another state, Jordan, the monarchy owes its control of the country to British indulgence. Starting in the eighteenth century and finishing in the twentieth, the Saudis managed to fight their way to power over an area largely beyond the interests of Europe and the control of the Ottoman Empire, although they benefited from British help. In short, though these monarchies attribute their success to Islam, chance and politics have played a large role. Each monarchy has fashioned an Islam to suit its particular circumstances.

Hypothesis 2: Religious identities, when not congruent with a state's boundaries, may prevent the formation of strong polities capable of ensuring peace and liberty for its citizens.

In none of these five states is there congruence between religious and political boundaries (see Table 7.1). Does such congruence exist anywhere in the world? Israel has made a virtue of its relationship to the larger world of Judaism. Iran has thus far been less successful in identifying itself with Islam as a whole. Egypt and Turkey have not sought to do so. While this hypothesis appears to contradict the first, it nonetheless appears somewhat true. In four of the five cases presented in the book, the state's embrace of an official religion weakens the polity in some measure. The explicit linkage with Sunnism as articulated by Wahhabi ulama makes it difficult for the Saudi regime to win wholehearted support of the Shii minority in the eastern region. The Saudi hold on the Hijaz region has always been somewhat tenuous as a result of Wahhabi exclusivism. In Egypt, the Coptic minority is not about to secede from the republic, but the constitutional endorsement of Islam and the restrictions imposed on Copts make it difficult for them to be full contributors. In Israel, where all religions are tolerated, non-Jewish citizens do not feel undiluted loyalty to a Jewish state and do not receive all the rights and privileges enjoyed by Jews. Furthermore, the linkage of the state with Orthodox Judaism complicates the relationship for Jews who do not consider themselves religiously observant or who practice Reform or Conservative Judaism. In Iran, the Bahais have been virtually excluded from the body politic, but they are not a significant political force. The regime tries hard to demonstrate that its identity with Shiism does not marginalize its Sunni minority, which is much more significant. The renewed Turkish identity with Islam may actually help integrate the Kurdish minority, but no great breakthrough occurred in the first ten years of Islamist rule. The ideological Sunnism of the Islamist movement has not, quite to the contrary, done anything to reinforce Alevi confidence in the regime. In short, religion has been helpful to the consolidation of power and the development of legitimacy in all these states, but it brings complications and human rights issues in every case.

Ideology

Ideological stability in the relationship between religion and politics requires general consensus about the place of religious values and ideas in the political system. Such a consensus can be achieved through either process or substance. Consensus on a decision-making process satisfactory to religious groups might mean protection, citizenship, and a measure of influence. Consensus might be substantive in the sense that the state might recognize religious holidays, follow a religious calendar, and require religious observance in public institutions without necessarily permitting religious access to the decision-making process. The stability achieved in Western Europe and the United States reflects both sorts of consensus, with process being the more fundamental. Religious groups have access to the system, reap concrete benefits, and forgo ideological opposition to liberal democracy.

All five states included in this book have struggled with ideological stability. In the four Muslim countries, the state assumed an aggressive, secular stance coupled with state control of religion. Mustafa Kemal Atatürk pointed Turkey in that direction, Reza Shah Pahlavi followed his lead in Iran, and President Nasir earned a secularist reputation by suppressing the Muslim Brotherhood, nationalizing Azhar University, venting hostility toward the conservative monarchies, and endorsing socialism. In the pre-state period, the dominant political force in Israel, Labor Zionism, also waxed ideological against religion but came to see the need to accommodate Orthodox Judaism.

All these states faced ideological opposition from religious groups. The Muslim Brotherhood, born as an expression of nationalism, became increasingly radical after the death of Hasan al-Banna and Sayyid Qutb's rise to prominence within the movement. Groups with origins in the Brotherhood advocated revolution in the name of Islam in the 1970s. It was then that the National Outlook movement emerged in Turkey, turning its version of Islam into a political platform. Iranian intellectuals began to develop an Islamic critique of their regime at about the same time. In Israel, the victory of 1967 (which sparked despair and Islamic revival in neighboring countries) gave rise to a new ideology of settlement championed by the Gush Emunim, the Bloc of the Faithful. The Gush championed a Judaism that proclaimed Israeli achievements a step toward the millennium and incorporation of the holy places in the West Bank and Jerusalem as a religious duty. The assassin of Yitzhak Rabin pursued the basic premise of this thinking: Israel reflects God's will and must bow to religious revelation.

Hypothesis 3: The progressive exclusion of religion from the body politic would undermine the state's legitimacy. The most fundamental principles of liberal-democratic government cannot be reduced to empirical propositions.

It is impossible to show empirically that people are equal. That proposition, like others, requires a leap of faith or a normative judgment. Religion can help nurture faith in democracy.

None of the five states discussed in this book provides good data to test this proposition. None has sought "progressive exclusion of religion from the body politic." The successor states of Eastern Europe constitute better examples for exploring that idea. Surveys suggest that Marxism did render these states more secular in attitude than other countries at their level of development.

Marxist and anti-Marxist theorists of modernity viewed religion as an obstacle to progress. A state that seeks to control all religious institutions and observances can scarcely be called secular, but it will surely be regarded as secular by the religious groups it suppresses. Proponents took secularism to be an integral component of modernity. State control of religion was supposed to transform an obstacle into a tool, because religious doctrine and practice could be reshaped to suit political needs. Separation of church and state would have exposed the state to possible resistance from religious leaders invoking God's name against modernization policies.

Ideological secularism, whether driven by the state as in Turkey or by modernizers as in Egypt or Iran, contributed to the growth of religious movements in all five countries. Secularism was destined to fail, for two reasons: its fundamental inconsistencies and its need for compulsion. Modernization meant education, literacy, communication, global awareness, individuality, and choice, all of which powered religious resurgence and undermined state-controlled religion. The inconsistencies became increasingly obvious and the compulsion increasingly repulsive. Ideological religious movements took up the complaint but doomed themselves to eventual failure because they, like the secularists, failed to command a consensus in the society. They, too, appeared inconsistent in their attitudes toward modernity and religious freedom. Among some who resented forcible secularization, the ideological religious movements evoked hope, and among others, the movements evoked fear that their triumph would result in the forcible imposition of religious practices.

Resolution of the ideological dilemma cannot come from either the complete separation of church and state or their complete integration. The states that show the greatest progress toward resolution are Israel and Turkey, where relatively democratic political processes have helped to transform abstract ideologies into candidates and issues. The Gush Emunim has succeeded in winning state approval for some settlements and de facto acceptance of others. It enjoys wide support in several political parties, but its ideology has not become the official ideology of the state. Recep Tayyip Erdoğan led his Justice and Development Party to electoral victory in Turkey because he abandoned the ideological Islamism characteristic of the early incarnations of the National Outlook movement. He has sought to blunt the ideological secularism of the Kemalists without violating the Kemalist rule that religion ought not to dictate government policy. Secularist ideologues compete successfully for votes in both the Israeli and the Turkish systems, but they no longer dominate. Religious ideologues win offices and benefits but must give up antisystem ideology to do so. By playing the game, they acknowledge the superiority of political logic over religious doctrine.

Hypothesis 4: Some religions, such as Roman Catholicism and Islam, are undemocratic in tendency. Others (varieties of Protestantism) seem to be linked to the growth of democratic institutions. Hence, some types of religion must give way or engage in reform if political development is to occur.

This set of case studies provides no means of testing this hypothesis, because it does not include any Catholic or Protestant states. The differences in the nature of Islam among the four Muslim states studied here, however, make one instinctively skeptical of characterizing Islam as either democratic or undemocratic. The question of religious law and its impact on secular law arises in Israel and Turkey. Many Turks voice their support of the sharia, but few seem to want to see it implemented; they seem to take the sharia as a concept that deserves to be honored, not as a list of commands. A prime minister of Islamist conviction is hesitant to evoke the sharia in Turkey. Only some of the ultraorthodox in Israel might put the halakha above the law of the state, even though most Jews would acknowledge the importance of religious law. Secular courts struggle with the question of religious law in Israel. Debate in these countries thus turns not so much on whether religious law should be implemented but whether secular law should acknowledge the relevance of religious law in specific contexts. Debate over the requirements for citizenship remains critical in Israel. Women's dress codes still concern Turks.

The ideological pressure for the implementation of the religious law has been greater in Iran, Saudi Arabia, and Egypt than in Turkey and Israel. The reason in Egypt may be that the Muslim Brotherhood, chief element of the political opposition and advocate of greater implementation of the sharia, did not achieve a full stake in the government and was not forced to take responsibility for its positions under Sadat and Mubarak. The Brotherhood could afford to rail on the government for "violations" of the sharia, the official ulama for sanctioning such "violations," and the secular courts for failing to invoke it, without having to look at practical solutions to modern problems. It took a position that the sharia is known, complete, unchanging, and clear, a position that is dubious. Under Presidents Sadat and Mubarak, the government paid homage to the sharia to shore up the state's otherwise shaky legitimacy. Both government and opposition used ideology for their purposes. With the overthrow of Mubarak in 2011 and the access of Mohammed Morsi to the presidency in 2012, government and opposition have switched places. Logic suggests that the Brotherhood may moderate its demands for further implementation of the sharia, and the secular opposition may turn more shrill in its criticism.

In Iran the control that clerics and their Islamist supporters have over the government renders the situation different from what it was in Egypt before 2011, when Islamists were in the opposition. Because a specific institution, the Guardian Council, is entrusted with ensuring the compliance of all legislation with Islamic law, the sharia remains a subject of continual discussion in Iran. Charged with resolving practical problems, the president and the Majlis must invoke religious arguments to advance their legislation. They invoke the "interest of the community" to justify apparent deviations from the sharia or reversals of policies already proclaimed to be consistent with holy law. The Expediency Council speaks to the needs of practical action. An authoritarian regime founded upon Islamic legitimacy must continuously demonstrate its faithfulness to the sharia. It must defend itself not only from secularists—few dare to speak freely—but also from critics working within the Islamic tradition, who must be treated with more care.

The authoritarian regime in Egypt, with its origins in a military coup, feared Islamist violence. It could not afford to denounce the sharia and push moderate Muslims into the arms of the Muslim Brotherhood or extremism. Hence, it honored the sharia and courted the official ulama with its rhetoric, if not its acts. If the Muslim Brotherhood succeeds in holding on to power in the new Egypt, the group may, like the regime in Iran, face greater challenges from religious hardliners than from secularists. Of course, if Egypt moves definitively into the democratic camp, the government would necessarily abandon the repressive tools that sustained state ideology under Mubarak and that continue to sustain this ideology in Iran. Procedural legitimacy stemming from free and fair elections would presumably diminish the importance of ideology.

In Saudi Arabia, where the sharia is said to be the constitution of the country, Wahhabi ideology appears to thwart any possibility of democratic decision-making. The sharia is said to be complete, perfect; it is not subject to change or any need for interpretation. In fact, the monarchy has promulgated the rules and regulations required for the development of a modern economy and state without hindrance from the guardians of the sharia—and without democratic consultation. As elsewhere, the sharia is as flexible in Saudi Arabia as the state-employed ulama are willing to make it. The monarchy, not Islam, thwarts the development of democratic institutions.

Ideology remains more important in authoritarian regimes such as Saudi Arabia than in parliamentary systems, such as those of Turkey and Israel. Both the Islamic Republic in its first thirty years and Egypt before 2011 had constitutions with important elements of democracy. Both states invoked the rule of law and the importance of elections, but political considerations determined the application of the law in these countries, and neither country met commonly accepted standards of free, fair, competitive elections that mattered. Iran and Egypt depended in some measure on ideological legitimacy. The very notion of velayat-e faqih comes from Khomeini's interpretation of Shii Islam. Mubarak's regime in Egypt resisted the Brotherhood's calls for further implementation of the sharia, but the state also engaged in ideological propaganda to demonstrate its loyalty to Islam. The regime found itself dependent on its dependents, the ulama, to defend its policies against the Brotherhood. It needed to make concessions to maintain its pretentions as an Islamic state. If Egypt effectively veers away from authoritarianism in the wake of 2011, one would expect it to rely less on ideology and more on process as a source of legitimacy, even if Islamist forces dominate. Since the contested reelection of President Ahmadinejad in 2009 and his apparent loss of power and prestige within the government, ideology seems to have triumphed over process in Iran.

The dependence on Islamic ideology, albeit of different sorts, renders the relationship between religion and politics less stable in Egypt, Iran, and Saudi Arabia than in Turkey and Israel. The Brotherhood's critique of the Mubarak regime in Egypt was probably not decisive in the overthrow of the regime, but the uprising exposed the sharp differences in Egyptian opinion about the proper relationship of religion to politics. In Iran, Abdolkarim Soroush and other leading intellectuals argue that the Iranian regime misinterprets the sharia, which they say requires respect for freedom of religion, universal human rights, and democratic process. Their ideas surfaced in the reform movement under President Khatami and the Green Movement in the wake of the 2009 election, which revealed sharp conflict about the nature of the sharia and its place in modern legislation. The ideological conflict simmers in Iran, because the political process does not require compromise of opposing views. Saudi Arabia appeared to reaffirm control of Wahhabism after the Sahwi uprising of the 1990s, but the authoritarianism of the regime makes it difficult to assess the extent of ideological dissent. Exclusion and repression prolong potential instability.

Institutions

Hypothesis 5: Religious organizations engaged in projects promoting the common welfare—education, medical care, child care, and the like—can help generate a set of nongovernmental institutions that train citizens and open the way to a stronger, more inclusive state. They can contribute to the construction of civil society. Politicization of religion produces a pluralization of religious groups that may eventually contribute to pluralism in the political arena.

Some have argued that religious organizations such as the Muslim Brotherhood in Egypt constitute a part of civil society and that the growth of civil society can move a regime toward democracy. This book suggests the contrary sequence: Once a regime decides to democratize, it will permit more freedom for autonomous religious organizations. This was the sequence in Turkey and Israel. Secular leadership, dedicated to creating democratic polities, saw that it needed the support of a religious public and needed to accord that public a legitimate place in the body politic. Democratic principles pushed these countries to permit freedom of association, the right to form political parties, and the right to personal belief. Predominantly secular political organizations opened the way for greater religious influence in the system, without directly attacking the existence of an official religious establishment. The European dynamic was similar. Countries such as the United Kingdom maintained an established religion but gradually permitted equal access to other groups, even Catholics and atheists.

In none of the five countries does the government-managed religious establishment have a monopoly on religious organization. In Egypt new mosques appear and function without government knowledge or control. Dissident preachers manage to propagate their sermons. Sufi groups continue to meet within and without the establishment, and Coptic Christians maintain their own hierarchy of religious authority. The Muslim Brotherhood, itself tightly organized, engages in semipolitical, semireligious activities. In Turkey the variety of religious activity is even greater, and the Directorate of Religious Affairs is more open in acknowledging plurality. In Israel, even the hierarchy of the official establishment splits between Ashkenazim and Sephardim, each community with its own chief rabbi. But the ultraorthodox go their own way, Conservative and Reform congregations struggle for recognition, and the state recognizes fourteen non-Jewish groups. The Saudi government has sought to protect its monopoly of religion through the hiring and firing of preachers, domination of the airwaves, censorship of publications, harassment, and imprisonment, but satellite television, the Internet, and globalization have made maintaining the monopoly difficult. Not even in Iran can one speak of "monopoly" in describing state Shiism, even though control there may be tighter than in the other four states.

It is difficult to imagine an end to government endorsement of an established religion in these countries in any near future. Neither the American notion of separation nor the more radical French idea of laïcité seems relevant in these situations or even necessary for democratization. A progressive lessening of the monopolistic qualities of the religious establishments is both more realistic as an objective and more likely as a consequence of moves toward democratization. An organizational pluralism in the religious sphere is not so much a prerequisite but a natural outcome of the process by which all citizens acquire a larger stake and influence in government. The democratization of Turkey after 1950 eventually brought an end to Kemalist efforts to monopolize religious life. As democratic processes in Israel brought more and more Middle Eastern immigrants into citizenship, the religious establishment split to accommodate them. The victory of Likud in the "earthquake" election of 1977 opened the system to greater religious influence from groups such as the Gush Emunim and Shas, themselves outside the Ashkenazi establishment. Democratization in both countries led to a broadening of the range of elites exercising state control over religion, and the broadening led to a greater willingness to recognize religious pluralism.

The limiting factors in this process of moving toward institutional pluralism may be identity and ideology. To accord non-Jewish institutions fully equal status would be to compromise the Jewish identity of the state of Israel. To permit state Shiism to be one religion among many in Iran would call into question the identity of the Islamic Republic. Ideology poses a further constraint on democratization insofar as religious officials insist upon a single, unerring interpretation of religious law. Some theoretical acceptance of religious pluralism must follow from the sort of democratic development sketched above, if the emerging configuration of plural institutions is to acquire legitimacy. Such an evolution of ideas may already be occurring within official religious establishments as the sociology of religion changes before their eyes. Witness the testimony of one alim at Azhar in Egypt several years ago: "We are not the only people who speak for Islam in this country!" Witness also the statement of the Turkish director of religious affairs: "Secularism does not call for the interpretation of religion by the state. Rather it provides freedom to individuals and to public institutions in the interpretation of religion and in the production and transmission of religious knowledge."[20] If there is movement in the domain of ideology, then identity may loom as the greatest obstacle to genuine religious pluralism. A change of identity in Israel, Saudi Arabia, and Iran is difficult to conceive without revolution.

Hypothesis 6: Organized religion, where it takes hierarchical form, may obstruct political development by resisting state efforts to develop state authority and to provide directly for the general welfare of citizens. Only a state in which religion and politics are thoroughly separated can provide political development.

The Iranian example shows that religious hierarchy can also promote revolution. By treating the religious establishment as an obstacle, the late shah provoked confrontation and lost. Mostly, though, states have attempted to create religious hierarchy to enforce their own version of religion in the country. All five states in this study have sought to create or subjugate religious hierarchies. In doing so they may strengthen state authority, but they also undermine the religious legitimacy of the hierarchies they create. They open the way for challenge from lay leaders.

Iran, Egypt, and the Ottoman Empire, ancestor to the modern states of both Egypt and Turkey, contradicted the classic image of traditional societies when they encountered the challenge of Europe. Religious institutions, distinct from political institutions, enjoyed differing degrees of autonomy. In Egypt, where before 1798 the Ottomans ruled but depended on Mamluk militias for military control, the Egyptians retained control of religion. The ulama constituted a local elite, dependent on the Mamluk and Ottoman elites, but autonomous by virtue of function and powerful by virtue of their intimate connection to the Egyptian people. In Iran, at the outset of the nineteenth century, the ulama enjoyed greater autonomy than they had under Safavid rule, because the Qajars made no religious claims and were intrinsically weak. Similarly, regime weakness in the Ottoman Empire was both cause and effect of the debility of sultans by 1800. As sovereigns in all three of these places saw the need to defend themselves against foreign intervention by modernizing their societies, they sought to recuperate their authority by reducing the autonomy of frontier regions, far-flung provinces, military units (such as the janissaries) and militias, bureaucrats, and ulama. For these monarchies, modernization meant greater fusion of religion and politics, not separation. Separation meant autonomy, which translated into regime weakness.

The dynamic did not change with the fall of these monarchies. Campaigns to make religion and religious officials the servants of the state gained momentum in the nineteenth and twentieth centuries. Atatürk finished what the Ottoman sultans had begun. Nasir in Egypt finished the project begun by Muhammad Ali in 1800. Reza Shah won the support of the ulama in Iran and then proceeded to undermine their authority in more systematic fashion than the Qajars had ever dreamed possible. Ironically, the revolt of the clergy against the secularism of the Pahlavis has led to a regime in which religion and politics are more closely fused than ever before, although it is by no means certain that the clerics who dominate the state can effectively control the religious institutions, especially the Qom madrasas that educate the clerical elite. In Saudi Arabia, where the monarchy escaped Ottoman domination, European incursion, and Arab nationalism, not to mention revolution during the Arab Spring, the state has consistently depended on a tight relationship with the religious establishment.

The development of the state of Israel confirms this same pattern: fusion of religion and politics, not separation, as predicted by the classic modernization model. At the invention of modern Zionism, Orthodox Judaism stood opposed. The Jewish community long resident in Palestine looked askance at the new endeavors. The founders tended to look at formal religion and religious leadership with some skepticism, but Ben-Gurion wanted to harness religion to the state. The status quo letter reflected his efforts to win religious support and tie the hands of religious leaders at the same time. Organized religion became utterly dependent on the Israeli state as a result of the accommodation it accepted. The political power of the religious parties, vastly augmented by the arrival of Jews from the Arab world, enriched the terms of accommodation; by participating in coalitions, the religious parties achieved access to government jobs, concessions on citizenship policy, and guarantees for religious education.

Complete separation of church and state is an unattainable ideal, because religious organizations, even if autonomous, must function within rules established by the state. To be sure, while a state ban on all but official religious groups—a ban of the sort implemented by Atatürk—cannot abolish belief or even practice, it can make collective celebration of religious rites virtually impossible. Official hostility, such as that practiced in the Soviet Union, results in an eventual reduction in religious belief among the population. Nevertheless, Sufism did not die in Turkey, and religion did not vanish in the Soviet Union. A perfect merger of church and state, which Machiavelli thought the early Romans had achieved, is not possible, either, because the purposes of the two domains are quite different. The early caliphs of Islam discovered this difference themselves. In early Islamic societies, Quran reciters and their successors, the ulama, assumed a role quite distinct from the political and military duties of the caliph.

The five countries discussed in this book all have official religious establishments. All tolerate nonofficial religions, but nowhere are members of nonofficial religions regarded as full citizens. Can one imagine a non-Muslim as prime minister of Turkey, Egypt, Saudi Arabia, or Iran? A non-Jew as prime minister of Israel? Iran draws the line at permitting Bahais to enjoy even the rights accorded Christians and Jews. All these countries sponsor official religious establishments and have somewhat limited tolerance for the minorities within. For example, Conservative and Reform congregations operate under handicap in Israel. The Shii elite in Iran accept Sunnis as full Muslims, but conduct official ceremonies as if the country were entirely Shii. Similarly, in Turkey the Alevi minority regards the Islamist movement now controlling the government with suspicion, and the Directorate of Religious Affairs does not supervise Alevi ceremonies.

In a worldwide study of government involvement in religion (GIR), all five countries earn high numbers. Saudi Arabia tops the list of countries in this region of the world, with the highest GIR, but Iran and Egypt do not lag too far behind (Table 7.2). As one might expect, the Turkish and the Israeli GIR is somewhat more modest but nonetheless highly significant. Western democracies earn scores of zero (the United States) to 33 (Finland and Greece).[21] The study shows that

TABLE 7.2   Government Involvement in Religion (GIR)

	(1) Official GIR	(2) Official Restrictions	(3) Restrictions on Minority Religion	(4) Regulation of Majority Religion	(5) Religious Legislation	GIR Index
ISRAEL	Official religion	Practical limitations	3	2	25	36.84
TURKEY	Civil religion	Some illegal	9	5	13	47.21
EGYPT	Official religion	Some illegal	9	5	22	62.9
IRAN	Official religion	Some illegal	11	2	23	66.59
SAUDI ARABIA	Official religion	All other illegal	14	6	27	77.56

Source: Jonathan Fox, *A World Survey of Religion and the State* (New York: Cambridge University Press, 2008), 219–223.

Note: Jonathan Fox defines GIR as the opposite of SRAS, or separation of religion and state. The index depends on a set of criteria in each of five categories for each state. Variable 1, official GIR, has a value of 0 (hostility) to 8 (official religion). Variable 2 ranges from 0 (no significant restrictions on any religion) to 4 (all or all other religions illegal). There are fifteen criteria for restrictions on minority religion; ten criteria for regulation of minority religion; and thirty-three criteria for religious legislation. Each country was coded 0 or 1 on each of these criteria. A country's score could vary from 0 to 15, 0 to 10, and 0 to 33 on the three categories, respectively. The five variables, rescaled to vary from 0 to 20, carry equal weight in the index, which can thus vary from 0 to 100.

"Muslim countries consistently have the highest levels of GIR. The highest scoring countries on the GIR variables are mostly Muslim countries."[22] GIR does not measure the degree to which a country's politics may involve religious issues and invoke religious language, or whether governments offer tax advantages to religious institutions. The relationship between *government* and religion is only a part, but an important part, of the relationship between *politics* and religion. The United States would earn a much higher score if there existed a measure of religious involvement in politics.

This immixture of government in the organization and function of religion always creates problems for democracy. Citizens cannot all be equal if members of some religious organizations receive favored treatment over others. There cannot be equality before the law if some religious groups are outlawed for religious reasons, as are the Bahais in Iran, or if there is effectively no place for atheists. These weaknesses exist in all five countries, four predominantly Muslim, one Jewish. They exist in the two countries that proclaim their religious character in their name, Israel and Iran, and they exist in two countries that think of themselves as more secular, Turkey and Egypt. The two countries with more democratic institutions, Turkey and Israel, struggle with this problem almost as much as the more authoritarian states do.

The strength of these states depends in some measure on religion. All five have sought to control religious institutions as they engage in state building. Turkey and Israel have nonetheless moved rather decisively toward liberal democracy, and Egypt seems headed in that direction. Somewhat greater separation of politics and religion would be helpful in promoting democracy in all cases, but it is unrealistic to expect that the regimes will relinquish control of religion without coming under democratic pressure. Democracy probably has to come first.

Political Culture

Hypothesis 7: "Rational" types of religion may trigger individual initiative, encourage the spread of education, and spur economic growth. Economic prosperity will in turn make available resources vital to the construction of a modern nation-state, and an increasingly educated, rational political culture will support liberalization and democratization.

This book offers some support for this hypothesis. The Nur movement and its successors started Turkey down this road. The Alevis have played a rationalizing role there, too, as have some Sufi brotherhoods, though to argue that mystics can be rationalists may seem contradictory. A new Islamist economy has emerged to support publications, associations, tourist facilities, shops, and even political parties. The Muslim Brotherhood has been a modernizing force in Egypt. The post-Islamist movement in Iran has created a body of political and social theory that supports liberalization and democratization but has not yet won decisive political support. (Working within the parameters of Islam, this movement is post-Islamist in the sense of responding to the ideas and institutions of the Islamic Republic.) In Saudi Arabia, the Sahwi movement emerged from the expansion of the country's educational system to demand reforms of the establishment. In all these cases, Islamist movements nudged political cultures in both modernist and neotraditionalist directions.

The conventional wisdom is that Islam has not undergone the equivalent of a Protestant Reformation, which is what hypothesis 7 seems to require. But there may be some analogies to the advent of Protestantism, in what Islamists have brought to political culture. They have pushed for fresh interpretation of scriptures, encouraged the spread of education and literacy, empowered laypersons as well as ulama as interpreters and activists, welcomed and utilized the new means of electronic communication to build their movements and energize their cultures, and, perhaps most important, demanded that Muslims demonstrate their commitments to the faith by deed as well as belief. (Protestants quickly exploited the invention of the printing press to print Bibles. Calvinists saw public accomplishment as evidence of salvation.) Because Islamists continue to emphasize a return to customs long ago abandoned or neglected, such as modest dress for women and beards for men, they have often been seen as antimodern and irrational (e.g., the Saudi opposition to women driving automobiles). But even the most radical Islamists, such as Sayyid Qutb, are decidedly modernists and therefore "rationalists" in the idiom of modernization theory. Not all of them are necessarily liberals or democrats, however. The prediction about liberalization and democratization is the most problematic part of the hypothesis.

This book has looked at four predominantly Muslim countries, in which people show high levels of religiosity, and a Jewish state, in which the percentage of highly religious citizens is small but influential. It is no surprise that the Israelis appear unique. Rather, it is the similarities that elicit surprise, because Israel has distanced itself from the others in socioeconomic development. Inglehart's differentiation of states—preindustrial, industrial, postindustrial—causes us to expect that Israel will be different, but he does not prepare us for the differences in political culture among Muslim states or the many similarities between Muslim states and Israel.

The underlying problem in all these countries is the creation or preservation of a political culture that is congruent with the identity of the state, the predominant political ideology, and the structure of political institutions. In Israel, for example, the political culture must support a state that identifies itself as Jewish, even though non-Jews constitute a significant portion of the body politic. The political culture must sustain a prevailing ethic of liberal democracy, even though some Jewish religious groups think identity questions and legislation in certain other areas ought not to be subject to democratic debate and decisions and that the halakha should take precedence. The political culture must sustain a single unified state without destroying the religious pluralism that is a reality, and education is the state's principal tool for accomplishing these objectives. The solution is support for four educational systems, which probably produce at least four different understandings of the relationship between religion and politics and thus stabilize the diversity of perspective on religion that has characterized the state since independence. To unify education would jeopardize this stability.

Turkey seems headed for a similar sort of solution. After a long period in which state schools inculcated the Kemalist vision of secularism, the need to train imams led to the creation of a separate, government-controlled system of religious education. As Turkey became more democratic after 1950, the new political parties moved to strengthen religious education, and the products of religious education eventually made their way into government ministries to enhance and protect these changes. As has happened in other nations, a rise in literacy, fostered considerably by groups such as the Alevis and the Nurcus as well as Islamists, has contributed to a new understanding of religion and religious behavior as a matter of choice rather than habit. Education reinforces the democratic proclivities of the body politic, and those proclivities make it impossible to turn the schools back toward the narrow, secular, ideological education promoted by the Kemalists. Such politics also make it unlikely that Islamists can turn the public schools into a tool for eradicating Kemalism. The Erdoğan government disavows any such intent.

Important issues remain to be resolved. The place of Kurdish culture in the Turkish educational system is one such issue. Scholarly treatment of the Armenian massacres of 1894–1895 and during World War I is another. The relationship of independent Turkey to its Ottoman past is a third, and the place of Mustafa Kemal Atatürk in Turkish history will surely be a part of the debate about the history curriculum. The effectiveness of any national government depends on a supportive political culture. Every government wishes to enhance unity and patriotism, but as the Turks discovered, trying to achieve that end by propaganda and an educational system hostile to religion produced the opposite result.

The battle for control of education goes on in both Saudi Arabia and Iran, albeit in authoritarian settings. Democracies depend on compromise as a means of living with inconsistency and contradiction, but contradictions in Saudi Arabia and Iran are more difficult to resolve. In a highly fragmented political culture on both ethnic and religious grounds, the Iranian regime has pushed hard on a Persian Shii version of the state, with greater emphasis on religion than on language. Thus, Azerbaijani Turks, who are predominantly Shii, are not considered a minority, but all non-Shii groups feel some threat from the regime's efforts at producing a single, homogeneous political culture. Moreover, the regime's focus on creating a single Islamic state for all Muslims everywhere conflicts with Iranian nationalism. Efforts to create loyalty to the Supreme Leader, the faqih, conflict with the accepted notion that Iranians are free to select the grand ayatollah (marja), who will be their model for emulation, and with the broad acceptance of democratic principles. These contradictions have produced dissidence in the political culture, which the regime has sought to combat with repression. The contradictions in Saudi Arabia concern the Shii minority in the Eastern Province, persistent Sufi practices in the Hijaz region, and the role of women in the country as a whole. Current educational policies are preparing women for active roles outside the home, while the predominant cultural norms continue to segregate, insulate, and subordinate women to men. Dissident religious voices castigate the regime for its tentative steps toward liberalism, while others deplore the slow pace of change. As elsewhere in the Middle East, women continue to be a focal point of cultural conflict.

Egyptian culture contains serious contradictions, too. Egypt provides separate schools to maintain Muslim and Christian cultures, even though it identifies itself as a Muslim state. The modern educational system of Egypt, begun under British rules, was supposed to train good Muslim citizens, but in fact it has also trained Islamist opponents, radical Muslims, and Coptic activists. The ancien régime claimed to be secular but made concessions on all sides without apparent logic—not even the logic of democracy, where a majority carries the day. Secularists, Islamists, Copts, everyone outside the ruling party, felt insecure. Since the fall of Mubarak and the victories of the Muslim Brotherhood, secularists and Copts fear there will be a new push for homogeneity and consistency; partisans of the Brotherhood hope that they will be able (in the words of hypothesis 7) to "trigger individual initiative, encourage the spread of education, and spur economic growth," and lead a more prosperous Egypt toward "liberalization and democratization."

Hypothesis 8: A culture steeped in religion—committed to myth, magic, and faith in God rather than faith in human effort—will be unable to produce subjects, much less citizens, of a modern state. Such a culture must be secularized—that is, rationalized—if genuine political development is to occur.

Mustafa Kemal Atatürk would have subscribed to this hypothesis, but the statement is much too categorical. No state is fully secular. Many states combine liberal democracy or at least "genuine political development" (e.g., Israel and Turkey) with high commitment to religion. Stability in the political culture of these countries does not require secularism or even the disestablishment of religion. Forced secularization in Turkey did not produce a uniform, secular political culture, and it seems unlikely that the attempt to create uniform religiosity in Iran will create stability there, despite the efforts of the regime. Stability comes when government recognizes that it has no interest in promoting or damaging particular religious groups, and religious groups themselves feel secure in their relationship to the government. They feel confident in their ability to prosper and perpetuate their unique communities. Almost everywhere, this means that the religious groups have some control over the education of their own progeny, with necessary deference to state norms. Secularists must accept religious expression in the public sphere, and religious adherents must accept both secularists and other religious strains as legitimate and worthy of respect. In the

Middle East, the countries of Israel, Turkey, and Lebanon have been leaders in this regard. The Saudi monarchy, with its attachment to the puritanical Wahhabi version of Islam and its intolerance for non-Muslims and even non-Wahhabi practices in school curricula, has lagged in this domain. King Abdullah has recognized this challenge, as demonstrated by his outreach to the Eastern Province and western provinces of the country.

Any sort of stability evolves with domestic and international circumstances. A sharp increase in prosperity, as experienced by Iran in the 1970s and by other Persian Gulf states since 1990, necessarily occasions readjustments. Economic stagnation and unemployment, characteristic of Egypt in the 1990s and in Iran more recently as a result of international sanctions, produce readjustments of another sort. The wave of international opposition to U.S. policies in Palestine and Iraq has shaken political tranquility in a number of states. Some governments found the war on terrorism an excuse to further repress Islamist opposition. Tunisia would be an example. Others have found it harder to ally themselves with the United States on matters of local, regional, and international interest, for fear of provoking Islamist opposition. Saudi Arabia would be an example. One great advantage of the democratic process is that it permits continual readjustment of policy and institutions. A measure of permanent flexibility ensures stability. Authoritarian regimes such as Iran and Saudi Arabia fear even the slightest tremor of primary instability, for lack of secondary stability in the system.

Conclusion

Hypothesis 9: Politics shapes religion much more than religion shapes politics. Religion should thus be understood as a dependent variable, not a causative factor for political development.

All five case studies support this hypothesis. One cannot understand the shape of religion in any of these countries without understanding the political context in which religion has evolved. What can one predict from the nature of Judaism about the political contours of Israel? What can one derive from Islamic texts about Turkey, Egypt, Saudi Arabia, and Iran? If Islam as a set of religious beliefs were a principal determinant of politics in these countries, how could they be so different? Even if one studied the development of Twelver Shiism in Iran after 1500 and through 1960, one would still not be able to predict revolution and foresee the creation of the current political system of Iran. Political actions and reactions caused Shii Islam to become what it is today in Iran. Israel recreated contemporary Judaism, within its borders and beyond. Mustafa Kemal Atatürk is arguably the principal architect of modern Islam in Turkey, ironic as that may seem.

These cases all demonstrate the importance of religion in political life. The identity claims, the ideological foundations, the institutions, and the political culture—all reflect religious texts, doctrines, history, and practices. Religious organizations exert influence on political life in all these countries, but they do so within limits established by the state. When religious organizations attain genuine political power, they offer the best testimony to the primacy of politics. Religious leadership can only defend itself, its organization, its resources, and its principles by political activity. Of course, religious organizations can choose to shun politics, but they have that luxury only if state policies do not threaten their existence and well-being. When Turkey banned religious brotherhoods, it politicized them. Secret meetings became political acts of defiance.

The question then is not whether religion will suddenly and miraculously become democratic in the Middle East. The important question is, will democratizing states compel religious groups to accept and participate in democratic politics? Will the states themselves abandon the hope of monopolizing religious organization and observance, accepting plurality, even if they maintain an established religion? Will they compel all religious groups to accept plurality in return for the right to a realm of autonomy, including some control over religious education?

These questions presume the existence of a strong state bolstered by the allegiance of key religious groups. A state that wins allegiance by opening the political process to greater inclusiveness will in the long run be stronger than a state that imposes an exclusive religion and compels allegiance. Every state needs religious support, but religious groups need the state to survive and prosper. They have strong, long-term incentives to cooperate in the process of liberalization and democratization. Western experience supports this observation, and the five case studies presented here do not offer contrary evidence. One should not exaggerate the impact of religion in the Middle East or elsewhere. The evolution of religion depends on politics more heavily than political development depends on religion.

Notes

Chapter 1

1. See Plato's "Crito," in Thomas G. West and Grace Starry West, trans., *Four Texts on Socrates: Plato's Euthyphro, Apology, and Crito, and Aristophanes' Clouds/Plato and Aristophanes* (Ithaca, NY: Cornell University Press, 1998).

2. Sayyid Qutb, *Milestones*, rev. trans. (Indianapolis: American Trust Publications, 1990), chapter 3. See also William E. Shepard, "Sayyid Qutb's Doctrine of Jāhiliyya," *International Journal of Middle East Studies* 35, no. 4 (November 2003): 521–545.

3. "The Accession Speech of Abu Bakr (632)," in Bernard Lewis, ed. and trans., *Islam from the Prophet Muhammad to the Capture of Constantinople*, vol. 1, *Politics and War* (New York: Harper, 1974), 6.

4. N. J. Demerath III, "Religious Capital and Capital Religions: Cross-Cultural and Non-Legal Factors in the Separation of Church and State," *Daedalus* 120, no. 3 (Summer 1991): 22.

5. Jean-Paul Willaime, "Unification européenne et religions," in Jean Baudoin and Philippe Portier, eds., *La laïcité, une valeur d'aujourd'hui? Contestations et négociations du modèle français* (Paris: Presses universitaires de France, 2001), 134.

6. Robert Audi, *Religious Commitment and Secular Reason* (Cambridge, UK: Cambridge University Press, 2000), 3.

7. Marcel Gauchet, *The Disenchantment of the World: A Political History of Religion*, trans. Oscar Burge (Princeton, NJ: Princeton University Press, 1997), chapter 1.

8. Ibid., 13.

9. Ibid., 14.

10. Marcel Gauchet, *La démocratie contre elle-même* (Paris: Gallimard, 2002), 35.

11. Benedict Anderson, *Imagined Communities: Reflections on the Origin and Spread of Nationalism*, rev. ed. (London: Verso, 1991).

12. In several Arab states (Algeria, Syria, Egypt, Iraq, Morocco, Sudan, and Yemen), adult literacy remained at or below 60 percent in 1997. Clement M. Henry and Robert Springborg, *Globalization and the Politics of Development in the Middle East* (Cambridge, UK: Cambridge University Press, 2001), 3.

13. Partha Chatterjee, *Nationalist Thought and the Colonial World* (London: Zed, 1986), suggests that nationalism has been appropriated for a variety of purposes by post-colonial movements and states.

14. See, for example, Charles Hirschkind, "The Ethics of Listening: Cassette-Sermon Audition in Contemporary Egypt," *American Ethnologist* 28, no. 3 (August 2001): 623–649.

15. Jeffrey K. Hadden, "Desacralizing Secularization Theory," in Jeffrey K. Hadden and Anson Shupe, eds., *Secularization and Fundamentalism Reconsidered: Religion and the Political Order*, vol. 3 (New York: Paragon House, 1986), 22.

16. Thomas Ertman, *Birth of the Leviathan: Building States and Regimes in Medieval and Early Modern Europe* (Cambridge, UK: Cambridge University Press, 1997).

17. See, for example, David Martin, *A General Theory of Secularization* (Oxford, UK: Blackwell, 1978), on Protestantism and Catholicism and democratic development, and D. E. Smith, *Religion and Political Development* (Boston: Little, Brown, 1970), chapter 8, on Christianity and Islam and obstacles to modernization.

18. Samuel P. Huntington, *Political Order in Changing Societies* (New Haven, CT: Yale University Press, 1967), chapter 2.

19. Ernest L. Fortin, *Human Rights, Virtue and the Common Good: Untimely Meditations on Religion and Politics*, ed. J. Brian Benested (Lanham, MD: Rowman & Littlefield, 1996), 11–15.

20. Arend Lijphart, *Democracy in Plural Societies* (New Haven, CT: Yale University Press, 1977).

21. Avishai Margalit, "Sectarianism," *Dissent* 55, no. 1 (Winter 2008): 37–46.

22. William Gibson, *The Church of England, 1688–1832: Unity and Accord* (London: Routledge, 2001), 5.

23. St. Augustine demonstrated the flexibility of Christianity: "If we want to learn how the decomposition and recomposition of Christian sociolatry was related to political crisis, the place to start is the monumental *City of God*, which is still Christianity's most influential treatment of piety and politics." Peter Iver Kaufman, *Redeeming Politics* (Princeton, NJ: Princeton University Press, 1990), 130.

24. François Burgat, *Face to Face with Political Islam* (London: I. B. Tauris, 2003), trans. from the French, *Islamisme en face* (Paris: Editions La Découverte, 1996), 124.

25. Owen Chadwick, *The Secularization of the European Mind in the Nineteenth Century* (Cambridge, UK: Cambridge University Press, 1975), 26.

26. David Nicholls, *God and Government in an 'Age of Reason'* (London: Routledge, 1995), 119.

27. Ibid., 105.

28. Marcel Gauchet, *La religion dans la démocratie* (Paris: Gallimard, 1998), 155–159.

29. Fortin, *Human Rights*, 2.

30. David Nicholls, *Deity and Domination: Images of God and the State in the Nineteenth and Twentieth Centuries* (London: Routledge, 1989).

31. Ibid., 240.

32. Smith, *Religion and Political Development*, chapter 6.

33. Ronald Inglehart, *Modernization and Postmodernization: Cultural, Economic, and Political Change in 43 Societies* (Princeton, NJ: Princeton University Press, 1997), 93.

34. René Rémond, "Les mutations contemporaines de la laïcité française," in Jean Baudoin and Philippe Portier, eds., *La laïcité, une valeur d'aujourd'hui? Contestations et négociations du modèle français* (Paris: Presses universitaires de France, 2001), 347–350. Other articles in the same collection affirm that point.

35. Maurice Barbier, *La Laïcité* (Paris: Editions L'Harmattan, 1995), 173ff. The recent outpouring of literature on laïcité includes Abderrahim Lamchichi, *Islam et musulmans de France* (Paris: L'Harmattan, 1999); Saheif Bencheikh, *Marianne et le prophète: l'Islam dans la France laïque* (Paris: Bernard Grasset, 1998); Greg Bedouelle and Jean-Paul Costa, *Les laïcités à la française* (Paris: Presses universitaires de France, 1998); Bruno Etienne, *La France et l'islam* (Paris: Hachette, 1989); Guy Coq, *Laïcité et République: Le lien nécessaire* (Paris: Editions du Félin, 1995); Jocelyne Cesari, *Musulmans et républicains; les jeunes, l'islam, et la France* (Paris: Editions Complexe, 1998); and Jean Baudouin and Philippe Portier, eds., *La laïcité, une valeur d'aujourd'hui? Contestations et négociations du modèle français* (Paris: Presses universitaires de France, 2001).

36. Johannes C. Wolfart, *Religion, Government and Political Culture in Early Modern Germany: Lindau, 1520–1628* (New York: Palgrave, 2002), 172.

37. Gibson, *The Church of England*, 176.

38. Frederick C. Harris, "Something Within: Religion as a Mobilizer of African-American Political Activism," *Journal of Politics* 56, no. 1 (February 1994): 42–68.

39. Emile Durkheim, "The Elementary Forms of Religious Life," in W. S. F. Pickering, ed., *Durkheim on Religion* (Atlanta: Scholars Press, 1994).

40. Augustus Richard Norton, ed., *Civil Society in the Middle East*, 2 vols. (Leiden, Netherlands: Brill, 1995–1996). Not all chapters in the two volumes take that point of view.

41. See, for example, Sana Abed-Kotob, "The Accommodationists Speak: Goals and Strategies of the Muslim Brotherhood of Egypt," *International Journal of Middle East Studies* 27 (1995): 321–339.

42. Denis J. Sullivan and Sana Abed-Kotob, *Islam in Contemporary Egypt: Civil Society vs. the State* (Boulder, CO: Lynne Rienner, 1999), 135.

43. Robert W. Hefner, *Civil Islam: Muslims and Democratization in Indonesia* (Princeton, NJ: Princeton University Press, 2000), 218.

44. Dale F. Eickelman and James Piscatori, *Muslim Politics* (Princeton, NJ: Princeton University Press, 1996).

45. Ibid, 159.

46. Smith, *Religion and Political Development*, 7, defines the organic model as one where religious and political functions are fused. For further discussion, see 266–267.

47. Daniel Crecelius, "The Ulama and the State in Modern Egypt" (PhD dissertation, Princeton University, May 1967), 112 ff.

48. Peter Berger, *The Sacred Canopy: Elements of a Sociological Theory of Religion* (Garden City, NY: Doubleday, 1967), 90.

49. Pippa Norris and Ronald Inglehart, *Sacred and Secular: Religion and Politics Worldwide* (Cambridge, UK: Cambridge University Press, 2004).

50. Olivier Roy, *La Sainte Ignorance: Le Temps de la Religion Sans Culture* (Paris: Seuil, 2008), argues that all religions come out of specific cultural settings. Those with universal aspirations must necessarily adapt to alien cultures or, alternatively, engage in radical challenge to those cultures. The effort of universal religions to divorce themselves from culture helps explain the turmoil of the modern era.

51. Gregory Starrett, *Putting Islam to Work: Education, Politics and Religious Transformation in Egypt* (Berkeley: University of California Press, 1998), chapter 2; and Véronique Dimier, "La laïcité: un produit d'exportation? Le cas du rapport Combes

(1892) sur l'enseignement primaire indigène en Algérie," in Jean Baudouin and Philippe Portier, eds., *La laïcité, une valeur d'aujourd'hui? Contestations et négociations du modèle français* (Paris: Presses universitaires de France, 2001), 76.

52. René Rémond, "Les mutations," 347–350.

53. Max Weber, *The Protestant Ethic and the Spirit of Capitalism*, trans. Talcott Parsons (London: Routledge, 1992).

54. Inglehart, *Modernization and Postmodernization*, 231.

55. Corwin Smidt, "Religion and Civic Engagement: A Comparative Analysis," *Annals of the American Academy of Political and Social Science* (September 1999): 176–192.

56. Steven B. Smith, *Spinoza, Liberalism, and the Question of Jewish Identity* (New Haven, CT: Yale University Press, 1997), 17.

57. Gauchet, *The Disenchantment of the World*, 3.

58. Smith, *Religion and Political Development*, 114.

59. Berger, *The Sacred Canopy*, 107.

60. Gauchet, *La religion dans la démocratie*, 159, and elsewhere in the book.

61. Fortin, *Human Rights*, 11.

62. Berger, *Sacred Canopy*, 26.

63. Gauchet, *The Disenchantment of the World*, 13.

64. Ibid., 14.

65. Robert Wuthnow, *Communities of Discourse: Ideology and Social Structure in the Enlightenment, and European Socialism* (Cambridge, MA: Harvard University Press, 1989), part 1.

66. The reference is to Ertman, *Birth of the Leviathan*.

67. Leonard Binder, "The Crisis of Political Development," in Leonard Binder et al., *Crises and Sequences in Political Development* (Princeton, NJ: Princeton University Press, 1971), 16. On page 17, Binder writes, "The study of political development requires a theory of how the patterns of political life change from one set of regularities to another set of regularities."

68. Hefner, *Civil Islam*, 17, makes this point about Indonesia, but it applies to many other Muslim states.

69. Jenny White, *Islamist Mobilization in Turkey: A Study in Vernacular Politics* (Seattle: University of Washington Press, 2002).

70. Gabriel A. Almond and Sidney Verba, eds., *The Civic Culture Revisited* (Newbury Park, CA: Sage Publications, 1989).

71. White, *Islamist Mobilization in Turkey*, makes that point effectively.

72. Jeff Spinner-Halev, *Surviving Diversity: Religion and Democratic Citizenship* (Baltimore: Johns Hopkins University Press, 2000), 60, argues that culture is an "enabling constraint: it enables us to have choices just as it restricts the choices we have."

Chapter 2

1. D. E. Smith, *Religion and Political Development* (Boston: Little Brown, 1970), 2.

2. Ronald Inglehart, ever a partisan of the notion of secularization, nonetheless charts sharp variations in the degree of secularization within societies at all levels of income and all degrees of commitment to what he calls postmaterial values. See his *Modernization and Postmodernization: Cultural, Economic, and Political Change in 43 Societies* (Princeton, NJ: Princeton University Press, 1997), 93.

3. See the diagram in Smith, *Religion and Political Development*, 14.

4. See the extraordinary account provided by Abd al-Rahman al-Jabarti, *Napoleon in Egypt: Al-Jabartī's Chronicle of the First Seven Months of the French Occupation, 1798,* trans. Shmuel Moreh (Princeton, NJ: M. Wiener, 1993).

5. Daniel Crecelius, "The Ulama and the State in Modern Egypt" (PhD dissertation, Princeton University, 1967), chapter 1.

6. Ibid., 362.

7. See Benedict Anderson, *Imagined Communities* (New York: Verso, 2006), for an account of how that nationalist idea seized Europe and then other parts of the world.

8. George Antonius, *The Arab Awakening: The Story of the Arab National Movement* (New York: G. P. Putnam's Sons, 1946).

9. Nikki Keddie, *An Islamic Response to Imperialism: Political and Religious Writings of Sayyid Jamal al-Din "al-Afghani"* (Berkeley: University of California Press, 1983).

10. Sylvia Haim, ed., *Arab Nationalism: An Anthology* (Berkeley: University of California Press, 1964).

11. Richard P. Mitchell, *The Society of Muslim Brothers* (New York: Oxford University Press, 1993), originally published in 1969, remains the standard history of the organization. Saeed Haawwa, *The Muslim Brotherhood*, trans. Abdul Karim Shaikh (Kuwait: Al Faisal Islamic Press, 1985), contains extensive material from the speeches of Hasan al-Banna. The book provides an uncritical account of Banna's approach and thinking. In many passages, it is difficult to know whether Haawwa or Banna is the author of the thoughts.

12. Israel Gershoni and James P. Jankowski, *Redefining the Egyptian Nation, 1930–1945* (Cambridge, UK: Cambridge University Press, 1995), 210.

13. Robert R. Bowie, *Suez, 1956* (New York: Oxford University Press, 1974).

14. Michael N. Barnett, *Dialogues in Arab Politics* (New York: Columbia University Press, 1998), and Malcolm Kerr, *The Arab Cold War* (London: Oxford University Press, 1967).

15. Gershoni and Jankowski, *Redefining the Egyptian Nation*, 163.

16. David Zeidan, "The Copts: Equal, Protected or Persecuted? The Impact of Islamization on Muslim-Christian Relations in Modern Egypt," *Islam and Christian-Muslim Relations* 10, no. 1 (March 1999): 56.

17. "Secularist" women interviewed by Nadje Al-Ali often defined a secular society as one in which Copts and Muslims were equally free to practice their religions, not as a society (or a state) hostile toward religion. Nadje Al-Ali, *Secularism, Gender and the State in the Middle East* (Cambridge, UK: Cambridge University Press, 2000).

18. Zeidan, "The Copts," 64.

19. Paul Sedra, "Class Cleavages and Ethnic Conflict: Coptic Christian Communities in Modern Egypt," *Islam and Christian-Muslim Relations* 10, no. 2 (July 1999): 224.

20. Ibid., 239.

21. World Values Survey 9062000, Question G015, "Which of the following best describes you?"

22. Gregory Starrett, *Putting Islam to Work: Education, Politics and Religious Transformation in Egypt* (Berkeley: University of California Press, 1998), 91. See also Asef Bayat, *Making Islam Democratic: Social Movements and the Post-Islamist Turn* (Stanford, CA: Stanford University Press, 2007), 147–154.

23. Charles Hirshkind, "The Ethics of Listening: Cassette-Sermon Audition in Contemporary Egypt," *American Ethnologist* 28, no. 3 (August 2001): 623–649.

24. Al-Ali, *Secularism, Gender.*

25. Emad El-Din Shahin, "Political Islam in Egypt" (CEPS Working Document 266, Center for European Policy Studies, Brussels, May 2007), 3.

26. Bayat, *Making Islam Democratic*, 250, note 201.

27. Eldon J. Eisenach, *The Next Religious Establishment* (Lanham, MD: Rowman & Littlefield, 2000), 51.

28. On the salafiyya movement, see Malcolm Kerr, *Islamic Reform: The Political and Legal Theories of Muhammad Abduh and Rashid Rida* (Berkeley: University of California Press, 1966). See also Elie Kedourie, *Afghani and Abduh: An Essay on Religious Unbelief and Political Activism in Islam* (New York: Humanities Press, 1966).

29. Mitchell, *The Society of Muslim Brothers*, 326–327.

30. Meir Hatina, "On the Margins of Consensus: The Call to Separate Religion and State in Modern Egypt," *Middle Eastern Studies* 36, no. 1 (January 2000): 36.

31. Ibid., 39.

32. Ibid., 50.

33. Sayyid Qutb, *A Child from the Village*, ed. and trans. John Calvert and William Shepard (Syracuse, NY: Syracuse University Press, 2004).

34. Sayyid Qutb, *Milestones*, rev. trans. (Indianapolis: American Trust Publications, 1990).

35. Muhammad Abd al-Salam Faraj, *The Neglected Duty: The Creed of Sadat's Assassins and the Creed of the Islamic Resurgence in the Middle East*, ed. and trans. Johannes J. G. Jansen (New York: Macmillan, 1986).

36. Bayat, *Making Islam Democratic*, 141–142.

37. Malika Zeghal, *Gardiens de l'Islam: Les oulémas d'Al Azhar dans l'Egypte contemporaine* (Paris: Fondation nationale des sciences politiques, 1996), 156.

38. Hatina, "On the Margins of Consensus," 57.

39. William E. Shepard, "Muhammad Sa'id al-'Ashmawi and the Application of the Shari'a in Egypt," *International Journal of Middle East Studies* 28, no. 1 (February 1996): 43ff.

40. Denis J. Sullivan and Sana Abed-Kotob, *Islam in Contemporary Egypt: Civil Society vs. the State* (Boulder, CO: Lynne Rienner, 1999).

41. For Bayat, *Making Islam Democratic*, the state's action follows from the success of the Islamist movement in Egypt, which has nonetheless failed to produce revolution. Iran achieved revolution without an Islamist movement, in his view.

42. See these publications by Nathan J. Brown: "Egypt's Ambiguous Transition," September 12, 2012, Carnegie Endowment for International Peace, Washington, DC, http://carnegieendowment.org/2012/09/06/egypt-s-ambiguous-transition/drsi; "Egypt's Constitutional Racers Stagger Toward the Final Lap," *Foreign Policy*, October 1, 2012; and "Egypt's Constitution: Islamists Prepare for a Long Political Battle," October 23, 2012, Carnegie Endowment for International Peace, Washington, DC.

43. Jakob Skovgaard-Petersen, *Defining Islam for the Egyptian State: Muftis and Fatwas of the Dār al-Iftā* (Leiden, Netherlands: Brill, 1997). See also Zeghal, *Gardiens de l'Islam,* and Malika Zeghal, "'The Re-centering' of Religious Knowledge and Discourse: The Case of al-Azhar in Twentieth-Century Egypt," in Robert W. Hefner and Mohammad Qasim Zaman, eds., *Schooling Islam: The Culture and Politics of Modern Muslim Education* (Princeton, NJ: Princeton University Press, 2007).

44. See Sullivan and Abed-Kotob, *Islam in Contemporary Egypt*, for a general survey.

45. Zeghal, *Gardiens de l'Islam,* especially chapters 6 and 7, treats Azhar as a highly complicated institution that functions within and outside the political sphere, an institution

exercising some influence from within partly because it also exercises influence from the outside.

46. Crecelius, "The Ulama and the State in Modern Egypt," 362.

47. See the magnificent studies by Jakob Skovgaard-Petersen (*Defining Islam for the Egyptian State*), and Malika Zeghal (*Gardiens de l'Islam* and "'The Re-centering' of Religious Knowledge").

48. Crecelius, "The Ulama and the State in Modern Egypt," chapter 1.

49. Ibid., chapter 3.

50. Mitchell, *The Society of Muslim Brothers,* 298.

51. Sayed Khatab, "Al-Hudaybi's Influence on the Development of Islamist Movements in Egypt," *The Muslim World* 91, no. 3–4 (Fall 2001): 453.

52. Lisa Blaydes and Safinaz El Tarouty, "Women's Electoral Participation in Egypt: The Implications of Gender for Voter Recruitment and Mobilization," *Middle East Journal* 63, no. 3 (Summer 2009): 372ff.

53. Sullivan and Abed-Kotob, *Islam in Contemporary Egypt,* 59.

54. This paragraph reflects Jonathan Brown's "Salafis and Sufis in Egypt," Carnegie Endowment for International Peace, Washington, DC, December 2011.

55. Ibid.

56. Maurits S. Berger, "Apostasy and Public Policy in Contemporary Egypt: An Evaluation of Recent Cases from Egypt's Highest Courts," *Human Rights Quarterly* 25, no. 3 (August 2003): 740. See also Baber Johansen, "Apostasy as Objective and Depersonalized Fact: Two Recent Egyptian Court Judgments," *Social Research* 70, no. 3 (Fall 2003): 687–710.

57. Pippa Norris and Ronald Inglehart, *Sacred and Secular: Religion and Politics Worldwide* (Cambridge, UK: Cambridge University Press, 2004), chapter 6.

58. Daniel Lerner, *The Passing of Traditional Society: Modernizing the Middle East* (New York: Free Press of Glencoe, 1958).

59. See the trilogy by Naguib Mahfouz: *Palace Walk,* trans. William Maynard Hutchins and Olive E. Kenny (New York: Doubleday, 1991); *Palace of Desire,* trans. Hutchins and Kenny (New York: Doubleday, 1991); and *Sugar Street,* trans. Hutchins and Botros Samaan (New York: Anchor, 1993).

60. Mamoun Fandy, "Egypt's Islamic Group: Regional Revenge?" *Middle East Journal* 48, no. 4 (Autumn 1994): 611–625.

61. Gilles Kepel, *Jihad: Expansion et déclin de l'islamisme* (Paris: Gallimard, 2000).

62. Sullivan and Abed-Kotob, *Islam in Contemporary Egypt,* 25–35.

63. Starrett, *Putting Islam to Work,* 6.

64. Ibid., chapter 2.

65. Ibid. says that 31 percent of elementary-school time was devoted to the Quran in 1903, 11 percent to religion, and 29 percent to Arabic.

66. See ibid., 129–135, for discussion of the teaching of Islam in elementary schools.

67. Bradley J. Cook, "Islam and Egyptian Higher Education: Student Attitudes," *Comparative Education Review* 45, no. 3 (August 2001): 379–409.

68. "It eclipses all other institutions, programs, and facilities, including the mosque, the home, radio and television broadcasting, and print in the importance attributed to it as a publicly directing Islamizing force." Starrett, *Putting Islam to Work,* 115.

69. Leila Ahmed, *Women and Gender in Islam* (New Haven, CT: Yale University Press, 1992), 244.

70. Saba Mahmood, "Feminist Theory, Embodiment, and the Docile Agent: Some Reflections on the Egyptian Islamic Revival," *Cultural Anthropology* 16, no. 2 (May 2001): 202–236.

71. James A. Toronoto and Muhammad S. Eissa, "Egypt: Promoting Tolerance, Defending Against Islamism," in Eleanor Abdella Doumato and Gregory Starrett, eds., *Teaching Islam: Textbooks and Religion in the Middle East* (Boulder, CO: Lynne Rienner, 2007), 46.

72. Ibid, 34.

73. Ibid, 44.

74. Mark Tessler and Jodi Nachtwey, "Religion and International Conflict: An Individual-Level Analysis," in Mark Tessler, ed., *Area Studies and Social Science: Strategies for Understanding Middle East Politics* (Bloomington: Indiana University Press, 1999), 106, 113.

75. Sarah Ben Néfissa, "Citoyenneté et participation en Egypte: l'Action vertueuse selon la Gami'iyya Shari'iyya," *Monde Arabe Maghreb Machrek* 167 (January–March 2000): 14.

76. Baudouin Dupret, "Justice égyptienne, moralité publique et pouvoir politique," *Monde Arabe Maghreb Machrek* 167 (January–March 2000): 31.

77. Jean-Noël Ferrié and Saâida Radi, "Consensus national et identité morale: le sida comme analyseur de la société égyptienne," *Monde Arabe Maghreb Machrek* (January–March 2000): 36.

78. This is the general perspective of ibid.; Ben Néfissa, "Citoyenneté et participation en Egypte"; and Ferrié and Radi, "Consensus national et identité morale."

79. Smith, *Religion and Political Development*, 250.

Chapter 3

1. Jonathan Sacks, *One People? Tradition, Modernity, and Jewish Unity* (London: Littman Library of Jewish Civilisation, 1993), 27–31.

2. Tom Segev, *1949: The First Israelis*, trans. Arlen Neal Weinstein (New York: Free Press, 1986), 261.

3. Aviezer Ravitzky, "Is a Halakhic State Possible? The Paradox of Jewish Theocracy," *Israel Affairs* 11, no. 1 (January 2005): 137–164.

4. For example, Ira Sharkansky, *Rituals of Conflict: Religion, Politics, and Public Policy in Israel* (Boulder, CO: Lynne Rienner, 1996), 152.

5. Norman L. Zucker, *The Coming Crisis in Israel: Private Faith and Public Policy* (Cambridge, MA: MIT Press, 1973).

6. Charles S. Liebman and Eliezer Don-Yehiya, *Religion and Politics in Israel* (Bloomington: Indiana University Press, 1984), 51.

7. Ibid., 50.

8. Segev, *1949*, 208.

9. Ibid., 222.

10. Ibid.

11. Asher Arian, *The Second Republic: Politics in Israel* (Chatham, NJ: Chatham House, 1998), 27.

12. The Jews of Middle Eastern and North African origin are often called Sephardic as well as Oriental. Mizrachim has become the common term. For shift in Israeli identity,

see Gershon Shafir and Yoav Peled, *Being Israeli: The Dynamics of Multiple Citizenship* (Cambridge, UK: Cambridge University Press, 2002).

13. Virginia Dominguez, *People as Subject, People as Object: Selfhood and People-hood in Contemporary Israel* (Madison: University of Wisconsin Press, 1989), 57.

14. Liebman and Don-Yehiya, *Religion and Politics*, 15.

15. Segev, *1949*, x.

16. Gidon Sapir, "Can an Orthodox Jew Participate in the Public Life of the State of Israel?" *Shofar: An Interdisciplinary Journal of Jewish Studies* 20, no. 2 (Winter 2002): 85.

17. Ibid., 238.

18. Rael Jean Isaac, *Israel Divided: Ideological Politics in the Jewish State* (Baltimore: Johns Hopkins University Press, 1976), 27.

19. Segev, *1949*, 239.

20. Isaac, *Israel Divided*, 78.

21. Ibid., 78.

22. Segev, *1949*, 291.

23. Shafir and Peled, *Being Israeli*, 145, quoting Zucker, *The Coming Crisis*, 173.

24. Dominguez, *People as Subject*, 172.

25. Ibid., 172.

26. Shafir and Peled, *Being Israeli*, 318.

27. Elia Werczberger and Eliyahu Borukhov, "The Israel Land Authority: Relic or Necessity?" *Land Use Policy* 16, no. 2 (April 1999): 129–138.

28. Segev, *1949*, 258.

29. Ibid., 262.

30. Mizrachi is an abbreviation of "Mercaz Ruchani" or "spiritual center." See Bernard Avishai, *The Tragedy of Zionism: Revolution and Democracy in the Land of Israel* (New York: Farrar, Straus and Giroux, 1985), 95, for an account of its formation.

31. Shafir and Peled, *Being Israeli*, 138.

32. Segev, *1949*, 262.

33. Hanna Lerner, "Democracy, Constitutionalism, and Identity: The Anomaly of the Israeli Case," *Constellations* 11, no. 2 (June 2004): 239.

34. Ibid., citing Ralph Benyamin Neuberger, *The Constitution Debate in Israel* (Tel Aviv: Open University in Israel, 1997), 40.

35. Segev, *1949*, x.

36. Isaac, *Israel Divided*, 43.

37. Martin Edelman, "A Portion of Animosity: The Politics of the Disestablishment of Religion in Israel," *Israel Studies* 5, no. 1 (Spring 2000): 206. A 2007 law permits civil marriage for persons not considered Jews by Orthodox standards.

38. Menahem Parosh, quoted in Segev, *1949*, 261.

39. Aviezer Ravitzky, "Is a Halachic State Possible?"

40. Arian, *The Second Republic,* chapter 10.

41. Ibid., 3.

42. Yehudah Mirsky, "Inner Life of Religious Zionism," *New Leader* 78, no. 9 (December 4, 1995): 10–14.

43. Isaac, *Israel Divided*, 61.

44. Ibid., 62.

45. [Ralph] Benyamin Neuberger, *Religion and Democracy in Israel,* trans. Deborah Lemmer (Jerusalem: Floersheimer Institute for Policy Studies, 1997), 30.

46. Ehud Sprinzak, "Violence and Catastrophe in the Theology of Rabbi Meir Kahane: the Ideologization of Mimetic Desire," in *Terrorism and Political Violence* 3, no. 3 (Autumn 1991): 50.

47. Ibid., 54.

48. Raphael Cohen-Almagor, "Vigilant Jewish Fundamentalism: From the JDL to Kach (or 'Shalom Jews, Shalom Dogs')," *Terrorism and Political Violence* 4, no. 1 (Spring 1992): 54.

49. Ibid., 59.

50. Sprinzak, "Violence and Catastrophe," 58.

51. Cohen-Almagor, "Vigilant Jewish Fundamentalism," 51–52.

52. Efraim Ben Zadok, "State-Religion Relations in Israel: The Subtle Issue Underlying the Rabin Assassination," in Efraim Karsh, ed., *Israeli Politics and Society Since 1948: Problems of Collective Identity* (London: Frank Cass, 2002), 139.

53. Mirsky, "Inner Life of Religious Zionism."

54. Ben Zadok, "State-Religion Relations in Israel," 141.

55. Lisa Beyer, "The Religious Wars," *Time,* May 11, 1998, 32.

56. Alan Dowty, *The Jewish State: A Century Later* (Berkeley: University of California Press, 1998), chapter 2.

57. Lari Nyroos, "Religeopolitics: Dissident Geopolitics and the 'Fundamentalism' of Hamas and Kach," *Geopolitics* 6, no. 3 (Winter 2001): 135–157.

58. Sacks, *One People?* 61.

59. See, for example, Lerner, "Democracy, Constitutionalism, and Identity."

60. Edelman, "A Portion of Animosity," 207.

61. Ira Sharkansky, "Assessing Israel," *Shofar: An Interdisciplinary Journal of Jewish Studies* 18, no. 2 (Winter 2000): 5.

62. The state moved toward somewhat greater support in 2012.

63. Liebman and Don-Yehiya, *Religion and Politics,* 9.

64. Shafir and Peled, *Being Israeli,* 168.

65. Lilly Weissbrod, "Shas: An Ethnic Religious Party," *Israel Affairs* 9, no. 4 (Summer 2003): 96.

66. Etta Bick, "A Party in Decline: Shas in Israel's 2003 Elections," *Israel Affairs* 10, no. 4 (Summer 2004): 118.

67. Weissbrod, "Shas," 85.

68. Lerner, "Democracy, Constitutionalism, and Identity," 239.

69. Ibid., 244.

70. Ran Hirschl, "Constitutional Courts vs. Religious Fundamentalism: Three Middle Eastern Tales," *Texas Law Review* 82, no. 7 (June 2004): 1819–1870.

71. Lerner, "Democracy, Constitutionalism, and Identity," 247.

72. Frances Raday, "Women's Rights: Dichotomy Between Religion and Secularism in Israel," *Israel Affairs* 11, no. 1 (January 2005): 94.

73. Lerner, "Democracy, Constitutionalism, and Identity," 249.

74. Ibid.

75. Liebman and Don-Yehiya, *Religion and Politics,* 4.

76. Ibid., 7.

77. Ibid., 10.

78. Yeshayahu Leibowitz, *Judaism, Human Values, and the Jewish State*, ed. Eliezer Goldman (Cambridge, MA: Harvard University Press, 1992), 176.

79. Ibid., 227.

80. Joe Lockard, "Israeli Utopianism Today: Interview with Adi Ophir," *Tikkun* 19, no. 6 (November–December 2004): 21.

81. Shlomit Levy, Hanna Levinsohn, and Elihu Katz, "Believers, Observances and Social Interaction Among Israeli Jews," in Charles S. Liebman and Elihu Katz, eds., *The Jewishness of Israelis: Responses to the Guttman Report* (Albany: State University of New York Press, 1997), 3.

82. Ibid., 7.

83. Charles S. Liebman, "Academics and Other Intellectuals," in Liebman and Katz, eds., *The Jewishness of Israelis*, 69.

84. Bernard (Baruch) Susser, "Comments on the Guttman Report," in Liebman and Katz, eds., *The Jewishness of Israelis*, 170.

85. Gerald J. Blidstein, "The Guttman Report: The End of Commitment?" in Liebman and Katz, eds., *The Jewishness of Israelis*, 128; and Susser, "Comments on the Guttman Report," 169.

86. Levy, Levinsohn, and Katz, "Believers, Observances and Social Interaction," 21.

87. Ibid., 31.

88. Menachem Friedman, "Comments on the Guttman Report," in Liebman and Katz, eds., *The Jewishness of Israelis*, 142.

89. Ronald Inglehart, *Modernization and Postmodernization: Cultural, Economic, and Political Change in 43 Societies* (Princeton, NJ: Princeton University Press, 1997).

90. Charles S. Liebman, "Cultural Conflict in Israeli Society," in Liebman and Katz, eds., *The Jewishness of Israelis*, 111.

91. Elihu Katz, "Behavioral and Phenomenological Jewishness," in Liebman and Katz, eds., *The Jewishness of Israelis*, 74.

92. Quoted in Liebman, "Academics and Other Intellectuals," Liebman and Katz, eds., *The Jewishness of Israelis*, 67.

93. Segev, *1949*, 202.

94. Julia Resnick, "Particularistic vs. Universalistic Content in the Israeli Educational System," *Curriculum Inquiry* 29, no. 4 (Winter 1999): 491.

95. Mordechai Bar-Lev, "Politicization and Depoliticization of Jewish Religious Education in Israel," *Religious Education* 86, no. 4 (Fall 1991): 609.

96. Resnick, "Particularistic vs. Universalistic Content," 492.

97. Zehavit Gross, "State-Religious Education in Israel: Between Religion and Modernity," *Prospects* 33, no. 2 (June 2003): 158.

98. Jo-Ann Harrison, "School Ceremonies for Yitzhak Rabin: Social Construction of Civil Religion in Israeli Schools," *Israel Studies* 6, no. 3 (Fall 2001): 113–134.

99. Martin Edelman, "A Portion of Animosity: The Politics of the Disestablishment of Religion in Israel," *Israel Studies* 5, no. 1 (Spring 2000): 215, put the number at 28,277, or 8 percent of all eligible draftees, in 1997.

100. The National Religious Party has founded some Hesder Yeshivot, a military-educational institution where students alternate between their studies and military service.

Chapter 4

1. Whit Mason, "The Future of Political Islam in Turkey," *World Policy Journal* 17, no. 2 (Summer 2000): 58.

2. M. Hakan Yavuz, *Islamic Political Identity in Turkey* (New York: Oxford University Press, 2003), 52.

3. Christopher Houston, "Civilizing Islam, Islamist Civilizing? Turkey's Islamist Movement and the Problem of Ethnic Difference," *Thesis Eleven* 58 (August 1999): 87, writes that "Islamist best denotes those movements, groups and individuals who reject republican law and desire to substitute Islamic Law (seriat) for it, or live under its aegis." He also notes: "The meaning of Islamist then is self-referentially constructed against the state's official Islamic position, and is not a description of a person's religiosity."

4. World Values Survey, 2000–2001, Question F063, "How important is God in your life?" from 1 "not important" to 10 "very important." Analysis online.

5. There is an outpouring of literature on the topic. Yavuz, *Islamic Political Identity in Turkey*, is the most substantial. Here is a sample of other recent works that focus on identity: David Kushner, "Self-Perception and Identity in Contemporary Turkey," *Journal of Contemporary History* 32, no. 2 (April 1997): 219–233; Dov Waxman, "Islam and Turkish National Identity: A Reappraisal," *Turkish Yearbook of International Relations* 30 (2000): 1–22; Hasan Kosebalaban, "The Impact of Globalization on Islamic Political Identity: The Case of Turkey," *World Affairs* 168, no. 1 (Summer 2005): 27–37; Ihsan D. Daği, "Transformation of Islamic Political Identity in Turkey: Rethinking the West and Westernization," *Turkish Studies* 6, no. 1 (March 2005): 21–37; Feroz Ahmad, *Turkey: The Quest for Identity* (Oxford, UK: Oneworld Publications, 2003).

6. Arif Payaslyoğlu and Ahmet Içduygu, "Awareness of and Support for Human Rights Among Turkish University Students," *Human Rights Quarterly* 21, no. 2 (May 1999): 524.

7. Pinar Tank, "Political Islam in Turkey: A State of Controlled Secularity," *Turkish Studies* 6, no. 1 (March 2005): 5.

8. Yavuz, *Islamic Political Identity*, 39.

9. Kushner, "Self-Perception and Identity," 219.

10. Yavuz, *Islamic Political Identity*, 39.

11. F. Asli Ergul, "The Ottoman Identity: Turkish, Muslim or Rum?" *Middle Eastern Studies* 48, no. 4 (July 2012): 629–645.

12. Selim Deringil, "The Invention of Tradition as Public Image in the late Ottoman Empire, 1808 to 1908," *Comparative Studies in Society and History* 35, no. 1 (January 1993): 5. Deringil calls the empire a good example of what Benedict Anderson, *Imagined Communities* (New York: Verso, 2006), calls "official nationalism."

13. Joseph G. Rahme, "Namik Kemal's Constitutional Ottomanism and Non-Muslims," *Islam and Christian-Muslim Relations* 10, no. 1 (March 1999): 32.

14. Yavuz, *Islamic Political Identity*, 45.

15. Brian Silverstein, "Islam and Modernity in Turkey: Power, Tradition and Historicity in the European Provinces of the Muslim World," *Anthropological Quarterly* 76, no. 3 (Summer 2003): 510.

16. For a fascinating discussion of Ottoman efforts to create a more coherent political entity, see Deringil, "The Invention of Tradition," 5ff.

17. Nilüfer Göle, *The Forbidden Modern: Civilization and Veiling* (Ann Arbor: University of Michigan Press, 1996), 45, quotes Ziya Gökalp (1876–1924) as saying, "The most significant characteristic of the early Turks is feminism."

18. See Alev Çinar, *Modernity, Islam, and Secularism in Turkey: Bodies, Places, and Time* (Minneapolis: University of Minnesota Press, 2005), 64, for an illustration.

19. Ibid., 73. Islamists later saw this as a moment of humiliation.

20. Ibrahim Kaya, "Modernity and Veiled Women," *European Journal of Social Theory* 3, no. 2 (May 2000): 201.

21. See, for example, Bernard Lewis, *The Emergence of Modern Turkey* (London: Oxford University Press, 1961), and Robert E. Ward and Dankwart Rustow, eds., *Political Modernization in Japan and Turkey* (Princeton, NJ: Princeton University Press, 1964).

22. Ümit Cizre Sakallioğlu, "Parameters and Strategies of Islam-State Interaction in Republican Turkey," *International Journal of Middle East Studies* 28, no. 2 (May 1996): 236.

23. Republic of Turkey, Constitution, Section VI, Article 24.

24. Ersin Kalaycioğlu, "The Mystery of the Türban: Participation or Revolt," *Turkish Studies* 6, no. 2 (June 2005): 234.

25. Henry J. Barkey, "The Struggles of a 'Strong' State," *Journal of International Affairs* 54, no. 1 (Fall 2000): 99.

26. Berdal Aral, "Dispensing with Tradition? Turkish Politics and International Society During the Özal Decade, 1983–93," *Middle Eastern Studies* 37, no. 1 (January 2001): 84.

27. Quoted in Waxman, "Islam and Turkish National Identity," 17.

28. Çinar, *Modernity, Islam, and Secularism*, 127.

29. Burhanettin Duran, "Approaching the Kurdish Question via *Adil duzen*: An Islamist Formula of the Welfare Party for Ethnic Coexistence," *Journal of Muslim Minority Affairs* 18, no. 1 (April 1998): 115.

30. Silverstein, "Islam and Modernity," 503.

31. Faruk Bilici, "The Function of Alevi Bektashi Theology in Modern Turkey," in Tord Olsson, Elizabeth Ozdalga, and Catharina Randvere, eds., *Alevi Identity* (Istanbul: Swedish Research Institute in Istanbul, 1998), 62.

32. The classification is that of Tahire Erman and Emrah Göker, "Alevi Politics in Contemporary Turkey," *Middle Eastern Studies* 36, no. 4 (October 2000): 105–110. Bilici, "The Function of Alevi Bektashi Theology," uses the same categories.

33. Haldun Gülalp, "Whatever Happened to Secularization? The Multiple Islams of Turkey," *South Atlantic Quarterly* 102, no. 2–3 (Spring–Summer 2003): 394.

34. See, for example, Christopher Houston, "Profane Intuitions: Kurdish Diaspora in the Turkish City," *Australian Journal of Anthropology* 12, no. 1 (April 2001): 15–31.

35. Mansoor Moaddel, *Islamic Modernism, Nationalism, and Fundamentalism: Episode and Discourse* (Chicago: University of Chicago Press, 2005), 15.

36. Ibid., 342. In that context, he was writing about the "rise of the ideological state" in Algeria, Egypt, Iran, and Syria, but the observation applies equally to Turkey.

37. This discussion owes much to Ayşe Kadioğlu, "Women's Subordination in Turkey: Is Islam Really the Villain?" *Middle East Journal* 48, no. 4 (Autumn 1994): 645–660.

38. Jenny White, "State Feminism, Modernization and the Turkish Republican Woman," *NWSA Journal* 15, no. 3 (Fall 2003): 158.

39. Yeşim Arat, "Women's Rights and Islam in Turkish Politics: The Civil Code Amendment," *Middle East Journal* 64, no. 2 (Spring 2010): 237.

40. Ibid.

41. Ibid., 251.

42. Eric Rouleau, "Ce pouvoir si pesant des militaires turcs," *Le monde diplomatique*, September 2000, 8.

43. Stephen Kinzer, *Crescent and Star: Turkey Between Two Worlds* (New York: Farrar, Straus and Giroux, 2001), 168–169.

44. M. Hakan Yavuz, "Cleansing Islam from the Public Sphere," *Journal of International Affairs* 54, no. 1 (Fall 2000): 21–42.

45. Ibid., 27.

46. Orhan Pamuk, *Istanbul: Memories and the City,* trans. Maureen Freely (New York: Random House, 2006), 182.

47. Haldun Gülalp, "Enlightenment by Fiat: Secularization and Democracy in Turkey," *Middle Eastern Studies* 41, no. 3 (May 2005): 362, says Kemalism replaced religion as absolute truth. It became a "quasi-religion" (357).

48. Şerif Mardin, *Religion and Social Change in Modern Turkey: The Case of Bediüzzaman Said Nursi* (Albany: State University of New York Press, 1989), chapter 5.

49. Şükran Vahide, *Islam in Modern Turkey: An Intellectual Biography of Bediuzzaman Said Nursi* (Albany: State University of New York Press, 2005): 172.

50. Mardin, *Religion and Social Change*, 86.

51. Şerif Mardin, "The Just and the Unjust," *Daedalus* 120, no. 3 (Summer 1991): 125.

52. Vahide, *Islam in Modern Turkey*, 204.

53. Ibid., 220.

54. Bekim Agai, "Islam and Education in Secular Turkey: State Policies and the Emergence of the Fethullah Gülen Group," in Robert W. Hefner and Mohammad Qasim Zaman, eds., *Schooling Islam: The Culture and Politics of Modern Muslim Education* (Princeton, NJ: Princeton University Press, 2007), 149–171. For an example of Gülen's thought, see Fethullah Gülen, *Advocate of Dialogue* (Fairfax, VA: The Fountain, 2000).

55. Yavuz, *Islamic Political Identity*, 267.

56. Mardin, *Religion and Social Change*, 222.

57. Hamid Algar, "A Brief History of the Naqshbandi Order," in Marco Gaborieau, Alexandre Popovic, and Thierry Zarcone, eds., *Naqshbandis: cheminements et situation actuelle d'un ordre mystique musulman . . . : actes de la table ronde de Sèvres . . . 24 mai . . . 1985* (Istanbul: Isis Yayımcılık Ltd, 1990), 34.

58. Altan Gökalp, "Les fruits de l'arbre plutôt que ses racines: Le suleymanisme," in Gaborieau, Popovic, and Zarcone, *Naqshbandis*, 429.

59. Cizre Sakallioğlu, "Parameters and Strategies," 237.

60. Ibid., 239.

61. Ibid., 240.

62. Yavuz, *Islamic Political Identity*, 207.

63. Dağı, "Transformation," 21.

64. Yavuz, *Islamic Political Identity*, 212.

65. Rainer Herman, "Political Islam in Secular Turkey," *Islam and Christian-Muslim Relations* 14, no. 3 (July 2003): 274.

66. Yavuz, *Islamic Political Identity*, 244.

67. Asli Aydintaşbaş, "Murder on the Bosporus," *Middle East Quarterly* 7, no. 2 (June 2000): 18.

68. Ibid., 21.

69. For a list of those directives, see Yavuz, *Islamic Political Identity*, 275–276.

70. Şerif Mardin, "Turkish Islamic Exceptionalism Yesterday and Today: Continuity, Rupture and Reconstruction in Operational Codes," *Turkish Studies* 6, no. 2 (June 2005): 147.

71. Ali Bardakoğlu, "'Moderate Perception of Islam' and the Turkish Model of the Diyanet: The President's Statement," *Journal of Muslim Minority Affairs* 24, no. 2 (October 2004): 367–374.

72. Yavuz, *Islamic Political Identity*, 48.

73. Bardakoğlu, "'Moderate Perception,'" 370.

74. This paragraph reflects the views expressed in ibid.

75. Erman and Göker, "Alevi Politics," 106.

76. Yavuz, *Islamic Political Identity*, 141.

77. Ibid., 146–147.

78. Ibid., 167.

79. Fethullah Gülen, *Advocate of Dialogue*, 56.

80. Yavuz, *Islamic Political Identity*, 184.

81. Ibid., 104.

82. Ibid., 103.

83. Nilüfer Göle, "Snapshots of Islamic Modernities," *Daedalus* 129, no. 1 (Winter 2000): 111.

84. Ziya Öniş, "The Political Economy of Islamic Resurgence," *Third World Quarterly* 18, no. 4 (December 1997): 743–766, page 14 in EBSCO online version.

85. See Yeşim Arat, *Rethinking Islam and Liberal Democracy: Islamist Women in Turkish Politics* (Albany: State University of New York Press, 2005), on the work of "ladies' commissions."

86. Jenny B. White tells this story in *Islamist Mobilization in Turkey: A Study in Vernacular Politics* (Seattle: University of Washington Press, 2002).

87. Ziya Öniş, "Political Islam at the Crossroads: From Hegemony to Co-existence," *Contemporary Politics* 7, no. 4 (2001): 285.

88. The term is from Dağı, "Transformation," 31.

89. R. Quinn Mecham, "From the Ashes of Virtue, a Promise of Light: The Transformation of Political Islam in Turkey," *Third World Quarterly* 25, no. 2 (March 2004): 348, 351.

90. Ibid., 353.

91. For excellent analysis of the results of the 2002 election, see Ömer Çaha, "Turkish Election of November 2002 and the Role of 'Moderate' Political Islam," *Alternatives* 2, no. 1 (Fall 2003): 95–116, and Ümit Cizre and Menderes Çinar, "Turkey 2002: Kemalism, Islamism and Politics in the Light of the February 28 Process," *South Atlantic Quarterly* 102, no. 2–3 (Summer 2003): 309–332.

92. Tim Arango, "In Turkey, a Break from the Past Plays Out in the Streets," *New York Times*, October 30, 2012, A4.

93. Pippa Norris and Ronald Inglehart, *Sacred and Secular: Religion and Politics Worldwide* (Cambridge, UK: Cambridge University Press, 2004), 239.

94. Ibid., 226.

95. Şerif Mardin, "Turkish Islamic Exceptionalism."

96. Pamuk, *Istanbul*, 192.

97. Soon-Yong Pak, "Cultural Politics and Vocational Religious Education: The Case of Turkey," *Comparative Education* 40, no. 3 (August 2004): 326.

98. Jeremy Salt, "Nationalism and the Rise of Muslim Sentiment in Turkey," *Middle Eastern Studies* 31, no. 1 (January 1995): 14.

99. Pak, "Cultural Politics," 334.

100. Payaslyoğlu and Içduygu, "Awareness," report that 23 percent of students writing university entrance exams in 1997 were from the religious schools.

101. Sencer Ayata, "Patronage, Party and State: The Politicization of Islam in Turkey," *Middle East Journal* 50, no. 1 (Winter 1996): 47.

102. Section VI, Article 24, of the constitution as amended in 2001: "Education and instruction in religion and ethics shall be conducted under state supervision and control. Instruction in religious culture and moral education shall be compulsory in the curricula of primary and secondary schools. Other religious education and instruction shall be subject to the individual's own desire, and in the case of minors, to the request of their legal representatives."

103. Özlem Altan, "Sanctifying the Nation: Teaching Religion in Secular Turkey," *ISIM Newsletter*, June 12, 2003, 52, analyzes religious studies texts for the fourth through eighth grades.

104. Ibid., 53, quoting from religious texts by Ömer Yilmaz, Hasan Sarisoy, and Vehbi Vakkasoğlu.

105. Ibid., quoting from Samuel Kaplan, "Education and the Politics of National Culture in a Turkish Community" (PhD dissertation, University of Chicago, 1996).

106. Altan, "Sanctifying the Nation," 53.

107. Binnaz Toprak, "Islam and Democracy in Turkey," *Turkish Studies* 6, no. 2 (June 2005): 170.

108. Mason, "The Future," 60. He bases that conclusion on a study of religion done by the Turkish Foundation for Economic and Social Studies in Istanbul.

109. Toprak, "Islam and Democracy," 176.

110. Kayhan Mutlu, "Examining Religious Beliefs Among University Students in Ankara," *British Journal of Sociology* 47, no. 2 (June 1996): 356.

111. World Values Survey, 2005–2008, online analysis.

112. Ibid. About the same proportion of Iranians (84 percent) defined themselves as "religious persons" in that survey. Turks were similar to Iranians, too, in the proportion who said that God was "very important" in their lives: 76 versus 80 percent. But more Turks (33 percent) than Iranians (24 percent) said they "practically never" attended religious services.

113. Note that the "traditional" versus "secular" scale constructed from questions posed in the World Values Survey taps attitudes closely related to religion.

114. Mark Tessler and Ebrin Altinoğlu, "Political Culture in Turkey: Connections Among Attitudes Toward Democracy, the Military and Islam," *Democratization* 11, no. 1 (February 2004): 21–50.

115. World Values Survey, 2005–2008, online analysis.

116. Sultan Tepe, "Moderation of Religious Parties: Electoral Constraints, Ideological Commitments, and the Democratic Capacities of Religious Parties in Israel and Turkey," *Political Science Quarterly* 65, no. 3 (September 2012): 480.

117. For a careful evaluation of these matters, see M. Hakan Yavuz, *Secularism and Muslim Democracy in Turkey* (Cambridge, UK: Cambridge University Press, 2009), chapter 6. See also Seda Demiralp, "The Odd Tango of the Islamic Right and Kurdish Left in Turkey: A Peripheral Alliance to Redesign the Centre?" *Middle Eastern Studies* 48, no. 2 (March 2012): 287–302; Bo Ærenlund Sørensen, "The Ankara Consensus: Islamists, Kemalists, and Why Turkey's Nationalism Remains Overlooked," *Middle Eastern Studies*, 48, no. 4 (June 2012), 613–627.

118. Ümit Cizre Sakallioğlu, "The Truth and Fiction About (Turkey's) Human Rights Politics," *Human Rights Review*, October–December 2001, 75. This whole paragraph owes much to Cizre's analysis.

119. Marc Pierini, with Markus Mayr, "Press Freedom in Turkey," Carnegie Endowment for International Peace, Washington, DC, January 2013.

120. U. S. Department of State, "International Religious Freedom Report," 2011.

121. Ali Bulaç, "The Logical Basis for Religious Violence," *Zaman*, October 4, 2006.

122. Haldun Gülalp, "Whatever Happened?" 385.

123. Bulaç, "The Logical Basis," reports that landlords sometimes refuse to rent to tenants dressed in Islamic garb.

124. Jean-Paul Sartre, *Anti-Semite and Jew* (New York: Schocken Books, 1948), argues that identity stems from how one is viewed by others.

Chapter 5

1. Marvin Zonis, *The Political Elite of Iran* (Princeton, NJ: Princeton University Press, 1971).

2. Fariba Adelkhah, *Being Modern in Iran*, trans. Jonathan Derrick (New York: Columbia University Press, 2000).

3. James A. Bill, "The Cultural Underpinnings of Politics: Iran and the United States," *Mediterranean Quarterly* 17, no. 1 (Winter 2006): 22–33.

4. An additional half dozen countries are approximately 50 percent Muslim in population.

5. At 200,000 to 300,000, Bahais constitute the largest non-Muslim minority in Iran. Ludwig Paul, "'Iranian Nation' and Iranian-Islamic Revolutionary Ideology," *Die Welt des Islams* 39, no. 2 (1999): 200.

6. Ibid., 205ff.

7. The terms are those of Hamid Dabashi, "The End of Islamic Ideology," *Social Research* 67, no. 2 (Summer 2000): 502.

8. W. Montgomery Watt, "The Significance of the Early States of Imami Shi'ism," in Nikki R. Keddie, ed., *Religion and Politics in Iran: Shi'ism from Quietism to Revolution* (New Haven, CT: Yale University Press, 1983), 21–46.

9. Jonathan Berkey, *The Formation of Islam: Religion and Society in the Near East, 600–1800* (Cambridge, UK: Cambridge University Press, 2004).

10. Nikki R. Keddie, *Modern Iran: Roots and Results of Revolution* (New Haven, CT: Yale University Press, 2003), 8–9.

11. Ibid., 11.

12. Ibid.

13. Jalal Al-i Ahmad, *Occidentosis: A Plague from the West*, trans. R. Campbell and ed. Hamid Algar (Berkeley, CA: Mizan Press, 1984).

14. Mahmoud Alinejad, "Coming to Terms with Modernity: Iranian Intellectuals and the Emerging Public Sphere," *Islam and Christian-Muslim Relations* 13, no. 1 (2002): 32.

15. Paul, "'Iranian Nation,'" 195.

16. Ibid., 205.

17. Ibid., 211.

18. Ibid., 217.

19. A. William Samii, "Iran's Guardians Council as an Obstacle to Democracy," *Middle East Journal* 55, no. 4 (Autumn 2001): 650.

20. Daniel Brumberg, "Dissonant Politics in Iran and Indonesia," *Political Science Quarterly* 116, no. 1 (2001): 381–411.

21. Asef Bayat, *Making Islam Democratic: Social Movements and the Post-Islamist Turn* (Stanford, CA: Stanford University Press, 2007).

22. James A. Bill, *The Politics of Iran: Groups, Classes and Modernization* (Columbus, OH: Merrill, 1972).

23. Hamid Dabashi, *The Theology of Discontent: The Ideological Foundations of the Islamic Revolution in Iran* (New York: New York University Press, 1993).

24. Forough Jahanbaksh, "Religious and Political Discourse in Iran: Moving Toward Post-Fundamentalism," *Brown Journal of World Affairs* 9, no. 2 (Winter–Spring 2003): 245.

25. Ahmad Ashraf and Ali Banuazizi, "Iran's Tortuous Path Toward 'Islamic Liberalism,'" *International Journal of Politics, Culture and Society* 15, no. 2 (Winter 2001): 238.

26. Dabashi, "End of Islamic Ideology," 475–518.

27. David E. Thaler et al., *Mullahs, Guards, and Bonyads: An Exploration of Iranian Leadership Dynamics* (Santa Monica, CA: Rand Corporation, 2010), 41.

28. See English-language version of Parliament of Islamic Republic of Iran Web site, http://en.parliran.ir/index.aspx.

29. Asghar Schirazi, *The Constitution of Iran: Politics and the State in the Islamic Republic*, trans. John O'Kane (London: I. B. Tauris, 1997), chapter 1.

30. All the Khomeini quotations in this paragraph and the next two are from Ruhollah Khomeini, *Islam and Revolution: Writings and Declarations of Imam Khomeini*, trans. Hamid Algar (Berkeley, CA: Mizan Press, 1981), 169, 170, 171, 54, 62.

31. Homa Omid, "Theocracy or Democracy? The Critics of 'Westoxification' and the Politics of Fundamentalism in Iran," *Third World Quarterly* 13, no. 4 (December 1992): 681n32.

32. See, for example, these books by Ali Shariati: *Marxism and Other Western Fallacies: An Islamic Critique* (Berkeley, CA: Mizan Press, 1980); *On the Sociology of Islam: Lectures* (Berkeley, CA: Mizan Press, 1979); and *Red Shi'ism* (Houston: Free Islamic Literatures, 1980).

33. Dabashi, "The End of Islamic Ideology," 481.

34. Keyvan Tabari, "The Rule of Law and the Politics of Reform in Post-Revolutionary Iran," *International Sociology* 18, no. 1 (March 2003): 101.

35. Ibid., 106. See also Schirazi, *Constitution of Iran*, 233.

36. The best account is that of Daniel Brumberg, *Reinventing Khomeini: The Struggle for Reform in Iran* (Chicago: University of Chicago Press, 2001).

37. Saïd Amir Arjomand, "The Rise and Fall of President Khatami and the Reform Movement in Iran," *Constellations* 12, no. 4 (December 2005): 505. See Ervand Abrahamian, *Khomeinism: Essays on the Islamic Republic* (Berkeley: University of California Press, 1993), chapter 1, for a treatment of Khomeini as a populist.

38. Ashraf and Banuazizi, "Iran's Tortuous Path," 246.

39. Tabari, "The Rule of Law," 106.

40. Arjomand, "Rise and Fall," 503, reproaches Khatami for not taking a firm stand and provoking a constitutional crisis.

41. Ray Takeyh, *Guardians of the Revolution: Iran and the World in the Age of the Ayatollahs* (New York: Oxford University Press, 2009), 242.

42. Ziba Mir-Hosseini, "The Conservative-Reformist Conflict over Women's Rights in Iran," *International Journal of Politics, Culture and Society* 16, no. 1 (Fall 2002): 42.

43. Azar Nafisi's *Reading Lolita in Tehran: A Memoir in Books* (New York: Random House, 2003), conveys that point of view.

44. Jaleh Shaditalab, "Islamization and Gender in Iran: Is the Glass Half Full or Half Empty?" *Signs* 32, no. 1 (Autumn 2006): 19.

45. Janet Afary, *Sexual Politics in Modern Iran* (New York: Cambridge University Press, 2009), 267.

46. Roksana Bahramitash, "Islamic Fundamentalism and Women's Economic Role: The Case of Iran," *International Journal of Politics, Culture and Society* 16, no. 4 (Summer 2003): 560.

47. Afary, *Sexual Politics*, 273.

48. Azadeh Kian, "Women and Politics in Post-Islamist Iran: The Gender Conscious Drive to Change," *British Journal of Middle Eastern Studies* 24, no. 1 (May 1997): 75–96. See also Haleh Afshar, "Women and Politics in Iran," *European Journal of Development Research* 12, no. 1 (June 2000): 188–205.

49. Afary, *Sexual Politics*, 304.

50. Bahramitash, "Islamic Fundamentalism," 552. What women do in the villages of Iran (or other Muslim countries) probably does not get included in such figures. Neither does the number of women who do volunteer work, as in the campaign to eradicate illiteracy.

51. Ibid., 565.

52. Mir-Hosseini, "The Conservative-Reformist Conflict," 45–46.

53. Hasan Yusefi Eshkevari, *Islam and Democracy in Iran: Eshkevari and the Quest for Reform*, Ziba Mir-Hosseini and Richard Tapper, eds. (London: I. B. Taurus, 2006), 149.

54. Ibid., 173.

55. By one account, the election of President Khatami in 1997 constituted a direct threat to the "ideological foundations of the Islamic Republic." Ali Gheissari and Vali Nasr, "The Conservative Consolidation in Iran," *Survival* 47, no. 2 (Summer 2005): 177.

56. Tabari, "The Rule of Law," 106.

57. Ann Elizabeth Mayer, "The Islamic Law as a Cure for Political Law: The Withering of an Islamist Illusion," *Mediterranean Politics* 7, no. 3 (Autumn 2002): 139.

58. Geneive Abdo, "Re-Thinking the Islamic Republic: A 'Conversation' with Ayatollah Hossein 'Ali Montazeri," *Middle East Journal* 55, no. 1 (Winter 2001): 9–24.

59. Farzin Vahdat, *God and Juggernaut: Iran's Intellectual Encounter with Modernity* (Syracuse, NY: Syracuse University Press, 2002), 208.

60. All quotations by Kadivar in this paragraph are from Mohsen Kadivar, "An Introduction to the Public and Private Debate in Islam," *Social Research* 70, no. 3 (Fall 2003): 663, 669, 678.

61. Afary, *Sexual Politics*, 370.

62. Abdullahi A. Al-Naim, "Re-affirming Secularism for Islamic Societies," *New Perspectives Quarterly* 20, no. 3 (July 2003): 39.

63. This conclusion sustains the main argument of Aran Keshavarzian and Anthony Gill, "State Building and Religious Resources: An Institutional Theory of Church-State Relations in Iran and Mexico," *Politics and Society* 27, no. 3 (September 1999): 431–465.

64. Keddie, *Modern Iran*, chapter 1.

65. This is the general assessment in Hamid Algar, *Religion and State in Iran, 1785–1906: The Role of the Ulama in the Qajar Period* (Berkeley: University of California Press, 1969).

66. Ibid., 148.

67. Ibid., chapter 8.

68. Keddie, *Modern Iran*, 54.

69. Algar, *Religion and State*, 171.

70. Ahmad Ashraf, "Bazaar-Mosque Alliance: The Social Basis of Revolts and Revolutions," *International Journal of Politics, Culture and Society* 1, no. 4 (Summer 1988): 538–567. "The politics of the bazaar was intermingled with the politics of informal campaign for candidates of the highest office in the Shii hierocracy" (542).

71. Azar Tabari, "Shi'i Clergy in Iranian Politics," in Nikki Keddie, ed., *Religion and Politics in Iran* (New Haven, CT: Yale University Press, 1983), 55.

72. Algar, *Religion and State*, 246.

73. Shahrough Akhavi, *Religion and Politics in Contemporary Iran: Clergy-State Relations in the Pahlavi Period* (Albany: State University of New York Press, 1980), 29.

74. Ibid., 59.

75. Roy Mottahedeh, *The Mantle of the Prophet: Religion and Politics in Iran* (New York: Pantheon, 1985), 234.

76. Akhavi, *Religion and Politics*, 129.

77. Homa Omid, *Islam and the Post-Revolutionary State in Iran* (New York: St. Martin's Press, 1994), 21.

78. "The *Shias* are expected to part willingly with one-fourth of their surplus worldly goods, *zakat*, and one-fifth of their surplus liquid cash, *khoms*, each year, to meet the needs of the poor and the needy; not those of the state and government. So the religious dues are paid to a religious leader of one's choice and never find their ways to the coffers of the state" (ibid., 141).

79. Akhavi, *Religion and Politics*, 141.

80. "It is obvious that from the beginning the prevalence of politics over religion was in Khomeini's mind" (Olivier Roy, "The Crisis of Religious Legitimacy in Iran," *Middle East Journal* 53, no. 2 [Spring 1999]: 205).

81. Saïd Amir Arjomand, *After Khomeini: Iran Under His Successors* (New York: Oxford University Press, 2009), 174–176.

82. Wilfried Buchta, *Who Rules Iran? The Structure of Power in the Islamic Republic* (Washington, DC: Washington Institute for Near East Policy, 2000), 54 and 55n.

83. Omid, *Islam*, 33, citing Ervand Abrahamian, *Iran Between Two Revolutions* (Princeton, NJ: Princeton University Press, 1982), 433.

84. Nikki Keddie, introduction to *Religion and Politics in Iran* (New Haven, CT: Yale University Press, 1983), 17.

85. Katajun Amirpur, "The Future of Iran's Reform Movement," in Amirpur and Walter Posch, eds., *Iranian Challenges*, Chaillot Paper 89 (Paris: European Union Institute for Security Studies, 2006), 29–40, declares, without specifying a source, that "unofficial estimates" put 80 percent of the Iranian economy in the hands of the "clerical conservative establishment."

86. Elliot Hen-Tov and Nathan Gonzales, "The Militarization of Post-Khomeini Iran: Praetorianism 2.0," *Washington Quarterly* 34, no. 1 (Winter 2011): 252.

87. Ibid., 53, quoting Babak Rahimi, "The Role of the Revolutionary Guards and Basij Militia in Iran's 'Electoral Coup,'" *Terrorism Monitor* 7, no. 21 (July 17, 2009).

88. Brumberg, "Dissonant Politics."

89. Omid, *Islam*, 20.

90. Zonis, *Political Elite*, 315.

91. Richard Bulliet, *Conversion to Islam in the Middle Period: An Essay in Quantitative History* (Cambridge, MA: Harvard University Press, 1979).

92. Golnar Mehran, "Iran: A Shi'ite Curriculum to Serve the Islamic State," in Eleanor Abdella Doumato and Gregory Starrett, eds., *Teaching Islam: Textbooks and Religion in the Middle East* (Boulder, CO: Lynne Rienner, 2007), 56.

93. Ibid., 64.

94. Omid, *Islam*, 157. Chapter 8 treats the efforts of the regime to reshape the political culture.

95. Mehran, "Iran: A Shi'ite Curriculum," 58.

96. Ibid., 62.

97. Ibid., 59.

98. Fariba Adelkhah, *Being Modern in Iran*, trans. Jonathan Derrick (New York: Columbia University Press, 2000), chapter 6.

99. Thierry Michel, *Iran: Veiled Appearances* (Brooklyn, NY: First Run/Icarus Films, 2002), DVD.

100. Fariba Adelkhah, "Le ramadan comme négociation entre le public et le privé: le cas de la République d'Iran," in Fariba Adelkhah and François Georgeon, eds., *Ramadan et politique* (Paris: CNRS, 2000).

101. Richard Tapper, ed., *The New Iranian Cinema: Politics, Representation and Identity* (London: I. B. Taurus, 2004). For the actual documentary, see Ziba Mir-Hosseini, *Divorce Iranian Style* (New York: Women Make Movies, 1998).

102. Adelkhah, *Being Modern*, 133.

103. Günes Murat Tezcür, Taghi Azadarmaki, Mehri Bahar, and Hooshang Nayebi, "Support for Democracy in Iran," *Political Research Quarterly* 65, no. 2 (2012): 245.

104. Pippa Norris and Ronald Inglehart, *Sacred and Secular: Religion and Politics Worldwide* (Cambridge, UK: Cambridge University Press, 2004), 226.

105. Ibid., 239.

106. Tezcür et al., "Support for Democracy in Iran," 246.

107. Note that 74 percent of the Saudi respondents to the World Values Survey done in 2003 said they were "best described" as Muslims; 12 percent chose "Saudi," and 10 percent said they were "Arab." Only 1 percent of Egyptians invoked their Arab ethnicity.

108. M. Reza Behnam, *Cultural Foundations of Iranian Politics* (Salt Lake City: University of Utah Press, 1986).

109. Zonis, *The Political Elite.*

110. Adelkhah, *Being Modern*, chapter 2.

111. Bill, "Cultural Underpinnings," 27.

112. Adelkhah, *Being Modern*, 178.

113. Tezcür et al., "Support for Democracy in Iran," 245.

114. Pardis Mahdavi, *Passionate Uprisings: Iran's Sexual Revolution* (Stanford, CA: Stanford University Press, 2009).

115. Delphine Minoui, "L'Iran des réformes: la société face au pouvoir," *Politique étrangère* 67, no. 1 (January–March 2002): 114, asserts that the regime "has not succeeded in infusing its population, the majority of which is young, with its political-religious ideology."

Chapter 6

1. King Fahd took the title after Khalid's death in 1982 (R. Hrair Dekmejian, "The Rise of Political Islamism in Saudi Arabia," *Middle East Journal* 48, no. 4 [Autumn 1994]: 627).

2. Gwenn Okruhlik, "State Power, Religious Privilege, and Myths About Political Reform," in Mohammed Ayoob and Hasan Kosebalaban, eds., *Religion and Politics in Saudi Arabia: Wahhabism and the State* (Boulder, CO: Lynne Rienner, 2009), 91.

3. Hamadi Redissi, *Le Pacte de Najd: Ou comment l'islam sectaire est devenu Islam* [The pact of Najd: Or how sectarian Islam has become Islam] (Paris: Seuil, 2007).

4. John R. Bradley, *Saudi Arabia Exposed: Inside a Kingdom in Crisis* (New York: Palgrave Macmillan, 2005), 99.

5. Fouad Ibrahim, *The Shiis of Saudi Arabia* (London: Saqi, 2006), 58.

6. *Ibn*, sometimes written *bin*, means "son of." One could write the name of the current king with multiple iterations of the term *ibn*, back to the founder of the kingdom. The founder of the third Saudi state, Abd al-Aziz ibn Abd al-Wahhab ibn [etc.], became known as Ibn Saud, even though his father was Abd al-Wahhab, not Saud. Some writers call him Abd al-Aziz, and some refer to him as "Ibn Saud."

7. Madawi Al-Rasheed, *A History of Saudi Arabia* (Cambridge, UK: Cambridge University Press, 2002), 61.

8. Ann Lesch, private communication.

9. William Ochsenwald, "The Annexation of the Hijaz," in Mohammed Ayoob and Hasan Kosebalaban, eds., *Religion and Politics in Saudi Arabia: Wahhabism and the State* (Boulder, CO: Lynne Rienner, 2009), 75ff. See also Bradley, *Saudi Arabia Exposed*, 13.

10. Ibrahim, *The Shiis.*

11. F. Gregory Gause III, "Official Wahhabism and the Sanctioning of Saudi-US Relations," in Mohammed Ayoob and Hasan Kosebalaban, eds., *Religion and Politics in Saudi Arabia: Wahhabism and the State* (Boulder, CO: Lynne Rienner, 2009), 142.

12. Michaela Prokop, "The War of Ideas: Education in Saudi Arabia," in Paul Aarts and Gerd Nonneman, eds., *Saudi Arabia in the Balance: Political Economy, Society, Foreign Affairs* (New York: New York University Press, 2005), 63, asserts that only 6

percent of the "economically active" women were in the formal labor force. Nora Alarifi Pharaon, "Saudi Women and the Muslim State in the Twenty-First Century," *Sex Roles* 51, no. 5–6 (September 2004): 359, puts women at 7 percent of the wage-earning force in 1990. To put those numbers in perspective: Only some 20 percent of Saudi citizens, or about 36 percent of the working-age population, are members of the formal workforce (Tim Niblock, *Saudi Arabia: Power, Legitimacy and Survival* [London: Routledge, 2006], 119).

13. Bradley, *Saudi Arabia Exposed*, 169–179, develops this theme in a number of ways with regard to the condition of women. A still more recent account reports that "now mixed workplaces in private businesses are not even cause for comment" (Frank E. Vogel, "Saudi Arabia: Public, Civil and Individual Shari'a in Law and Politics," in Robert W. Hefner, ed., *Shari'a Politics: Islamic Law and Society in the Modern World* [Bloomington: Indiana University Press, 2011], 83).

14. The celebration occurred one hundred lunar years (hijra dating) after the conquest of Riyadh in 1902.

15. Al-Rasheed, *A History of Saudi Arabia*, 214.

16. Alexei Vassiliev, *The History of Saudi Arabia* (New York: New York University Press, 2000), 439.

17. Joseph Nevo, "Religion and National Identity in Saudi Arabia," *Middle Eastern Studies* 34, no. 3 (July 1998): 35.

18. Khalid S. Al-Dakhil, "Wahhabism as an Ideology of State Formation," in Mohammed Ayoob and Hasan Kosebalaban, eds., *Religion and Politics in Saudi Arabia* (Boulder, CO: Lynne Rienner, 2009), 24–27. Some elements of the Islamist movement that stirred Saudi Arabia in the 1980s and 1990s subscribed to this sort of interpretation of Wahhabism. Those who objected to the Islamist interpretations insisted that Wahhabism had always been about ritual and proper conduct, not political matters (Stéphane Lacroix, *Awakening Islam: The Politics of Religious Dissent in Contemporary Saudi Arabia*, tr. George Holoch [Cambridge, MA: Harvard University Press, 2011], 86).

19. John Voll, "The Impact of the Wahhabi Tradition," in Mohammed Ayoob and Hasan Kosebalaban, eds., *Religion and Politics in Saudi Arabia: Wahhabism and the State* (Boulder, CO: Lynne Rienner, 2009), 151–153.

20. Sayyid Qutb, *Milestones*, rev. trans. (Indianapolis: American Trust Publications, 1990).

21. Madawi Al-Rasheed, *Contesting the Saudi State: Islamic Voices from a New Generation* (Cambridge, UK: Cambridge University Press, 2007), 71.

22. Lacroix, *Awakening Islam*, 179–181.

23. Mansoor Jassem Alshamsi, *Islam and Political Reform in Saudi Arabia: The Quest for Political Change and Reform* (New York: Routledge, 2011), 7; Vassiliev, *History of Saudi Arabia*, 466.

24. Niblock, *Saudi Arabia*, 108.

25. Lacroix, *Awakening Islam*, 186.

26. Ibid., 187.

27. Ibid., 198.

28. Ibid., conclusion.

29. Stéphane Lacroix, "Between Islamists and Liberals: Saudi Arabia's New 'Islamo-Liberal' Reformists," *Middle East Journal* 58, no. 3 (Summer 2004): 345–365.

30. U.S. Central Intelligence Agency, "Middle East: Saudi Arabia," in *The World Factbook,* last updated January 7, 2013, www.cia.gov/library/publications/the-world-factbook/geos/sa.htmlCIA. The figures were for the year 2009.

31. Andrew Hammon, "Maintaining Saudi Arabia's *Cordon Sanitaire* in the Arab Media," in Madawi Al-Rasheed, ed., *Kingdom Without Borders: Saudi Arabia's Political, Religious and Media Frontiers* (New York: Columbia University Press, 2008).

32. See Vogel, "Saudi Arabia," for a much more thorough analysis.

33. This and the following paragraph depend heavily on Vassiliev, *History of Saudi Arabia.*

34. Ibid., 90, reports that five sons and "numerous grandsons" became "renowned ulama."

35. See Al-Rasheed, *History,* 49–52, for an extended discussion of the mutawwaun. She writes: "Such religious specialists had existed in almost every town and oasis in Najd even before the reform movement had gathered momentum in the eighteenth century."

36. Ibid., 108.

37. Ibid., 76.

38. Ibid., 79.

39. Vassiliev, *History of Saudi Arabia,* 479.

40. Ibid., 430.

41. Al-Rasheed, *History,* 75–80.

42. Vassiliev, *History of Saudi Arabia,* 367.

43. Joseph A. Kechichian, *Succession in Saudi Arabia* (New York: Palgrave, 2001), 142.

44. Ibid.

45. Guido Steinberg, "The Wahhabi Ulama and the Saudi State: 1745 to the Present," in Paul Aarts and Gerd Nonneman, eds., *Saudi Arabia in the Balance: Political Economy, Society, Foreign Affairs* (New York: New York University Press, 2005), 22–24.

46. Al-Rasheed, *History,* 90.

47. Lacroix, *Awakening Islam,* 24.

48. Vassiliev, *History of Saudi Arabia,* 325.

49. See Roel Meijer, "The 'Cycle of Contention' and the Limits of Terrorism in Saudi Arabia," in Paul Aarts and Gerd Nonneman, eds., *Saudi Arabia in the Balance: Political Economy, Society, Foreign Affairs* (New York: New York University Press, 2005), on the Saudi suppression of violence in 2003–2004.

50. Vogel, "Saudi Arabia," in Robert W. Hefner, ed., *Shari'a Politics: Islamic Law and Society in the Modern World* (Bloomington: Indiana University Press, 2011).

51. Lacroix, *Awakening Islam,* 210.

52. Jonathan Fox, *A World Survey of Religion and the State* (New York: Cambridge University Press, 2008), 63, says that the GIR index takes a number of factors into account: "role of religion in the state . . . ; whether the government generally restricts some or all religions; whether the government restricts the religious practices of minority religions; whether the government regulates the majority religion or all religions; and whether the government legislates religion." Saudi Arabia scores 77.56; Iran 66.59; Egypt 62.92; Turkey 47.21; and Israel 36.84 (numbers from ibid., 219, table 1).

53. Mansoor Moaddel and Stuart A. Karabenick, "The Saudi Public Speaks: Religion, Gender, and Politics," *International Journal of Middle East Studies* 38, no. 1 (February 2006), 85.

54. World Values Survey, 1990–2005, online analysis. Variable F111 in the integrated version. The Saudi questionnaire prescribes that respondents be asked to respond in terms of importance, from "very important" to "not important" (V166). The Egyptian questionnaire puts the question in terms of answers ranging from strong agreement to strong disagreement (V177).

55. World Values Survey, online analysis. Saudi data from 2003.

56. Abu Dhabi Gallup Center, "Progress and Tradition in the Gulf Cooperation Council States," May 2011. The interviews were conducted in 2009 and 2010.

57. Sam Souryal, "The Religionization of a Society: The Continuing Application of Shariah Law in Saudi Arabia," *Journal for the Scientific Study of Religion* 26, no. 4 (1987): 429–449.

58. Bradley, *Saudi Arabia Exposed,* chapter 7.

59. Remke Kruk, "Harry Potter in the Gulf: Contemporary Islam and the Occult," *British Journal of Middle Eastern Studies* 32, no. 1 (May 2005): 52.

60. Ibid., 64.

61. Vassiliev, *History of Saudi Arabia,* 457.

62. Bradley, *Saudi Arabia Exposed,* 120.

63. Vassiliev, *History of Saudi Arabia,* 458.

64. Lacroix, *Awakening Islam,* chapter 3, speaks of a "sacrificed generation" among those drawn into the Islamist movement, which suffered a sharp reduction in resources (such as scholarships, teaching positions) put at its disposal by the regime.

65. Ibid., 129.

66. Bradley, *Saudi Arabia Exposed,* 177.

67. Ibid., 173.

68. Abu Dhabi Gallup Center, "Progress and Tradition in the Gulf Cooperation Council States," May 2011. The question was this: "Using a five-point scale, where 5 means strongly agree and 1 means strongly disagree, how much do you agree or disagree with the following statements? You may use any number between 1 and 5 to make your rating. 'I would not object to a person of a different religious faith moving next door.'" The percentages for "strongly agree" were 18 percent for Saudi Arabia, 39 percent for the median of the Arab League, 67 percent for Egypt, and 76 percent for Lebanon.

69. Moaddel and Karabenick, "The Saudi Public Speaks."

70. Jaime Kucinskas, "A Research Note on Islam and Gender Egalitarianism: An Examination of Egyptian and Saudi Arabian Youth Attitudes," *Journal for the Scientific Study of Religion* 49, no. 4 (2010): 766.

71. Michaela Prokop, "The War of Ideas," 62n17.

72. Vassiliev, *History of Saudi Arabia,* 310, writes: "According to al-Zirili, there were about 50 rural schools with 2,000 pupils, 90 primary schools with 13,000 pupils and 10 secondary schools with 600 pupils in the kingdom in 1950. Thus the total number of pupils was 15,600." He also says Philby, who "was often inclined to exaggerate," put the total at 55,000 in 1952.

73. Andrys Onsman, "It Is Better to Light a Candle than to Ban the Darkness: Government-Led Academic Development in Saudi Arabian Universities," *Higher Education* 62, no. 4 (October 2011): 521.

74. Mamoun Fandy, "Enriched Islam: The Muslim Crisis of Education," *Survival* 49, no. 2 (Summer 2007), 86.

75. Mounira I. Jamjoom, "Female Islamic Studies Teachers in Saudi Arabia: A Phenomenological Study," *Teaching and Teacher Education* 26 (2000): 555.

76. Al-Rasheed, *History of Saudi Arabia*, 191.

77. Ibid., 195.

78. See Hammon, "Maintaining Saudi Arabia's *Cordon Sanitaire*," for a general account of media access.

79. Nevo, "Religion and National Identity," 41.

Chapter 7

1. See Zachary Lockman, *Contending Visions of the Middle East: The History and Politics of Orientalism* (Cambridge, UK: Cambridge University Press, 2004), for a judicious discussion of the debate about Orientalism.

2. See Olivier Roy, *La Sainte Ignorance: Le Temps de la Religion Sans Culture* (Paris: Seuil, 2008), translated as *Holy Ignorance: When Religion and Culture Part Ways* (New York: Columbia University Press, 2010), for the critique of efforts to lift religion from its cultural habitat.

3. John C. Green, *The Faith Factor: How Religion Influences American Elections* (Westport, CT: Praeger, 2007).

4. Elizabeth Shakman Hurd, *The Politics of Secularism in International Relations* (Princeton, NJ: Princeton University Press, 2008), 12, writes: "Secularism refers to a public settlement of the relationship between politics and religion."

5. See Mark Lilla, *The Stillborn God* (New York: Alfred A. Knopf, 2007), for a superb discussion of Hobbes and those who have wrestled with this problem since he wrote.

6. Hurd, *Politics of Secularism*, 26ff.

7. Charles E. Lindblom, *The Intelligence of Democracy: Decision Making Through Mutual Adjustment* (New York: Free Press, 1965).

8. Samuel P. Huntington, *Political Order in Changing Societies* (New Haven, CT: Yale University Press, 1967), chapter 2.

9. Ibid., chapter 1.

10. Ronald Inglehart and Christian Weizel, *Modernization, Cultural Change, and Democracy: The Human Development Sequence* (Cambridge, UK: Cambridge University Press, 2005).

11. Dale Eickelman and James Piscatori, *Muslim Politics* (Princeton, NJ: Princeton University Press, 1996).

12. World Values Survey, G015, "Which of the following best describes you?" Online computation. Surveys of Egypt and Iran in 2000; Israel and Turkey in 2001; Saudi Arabia in 2003; United States in 1999. See Table 5.3 in this book.

13. World Values Survey, WVS 9062000, G006, "How proud are you of your nationality?" Surveys of Egypt and Iran in 2000; Israel and Turkey in 2001; Saudi Arabia in 2003.

14. World Values Survey, "Which of the following best describes you?"

15. Baruch Kimmerling, *The Invention and Decline of Israeliness: State, Society, and the Military* (Berkeley: University of California Press, 2001).

16. Ibid., 39–40. For a detailed discussion of Israeli historiography of the period, see Sylvain Cypel, *Walled: Israeli Society at an Impasse* (New York: Other Press, 2006), chapter 1.

17. The terms are those of Fouad Ajami, *The Arab Predicament: Arab Political Thought and Practice Since 1967* (Cambridge: Cambridge University Press, 1981).

18. Fouad Ajami, *The Vanished Imam: Musa al-Sadr and the Shi'a of Lebanon* (Ithaca, NY: Cornell University Press, 1986).

19. Huntington, *Political Order*, chapter 3.

20. Ali Bardakoğlu, "'Moderate Perception of Islam' and the Turkish Model of the Diyanet: The President's Statement," *Journal of Muslim Minority Affairs* 24, no. 2 (October 2004): 369.

21. Jonathan Fox, *A World Survey of Religion and the State* (New York: Cambridge University Press, 2008), 108.

22. Ibid, 103.

Glossary

aliya (pl. *aliyot*). "Ascension" to Israel. Ingathering of Jews. Often used to designate a particular period of immigration, as, for example, the "second aliya," which brought many of the country's founders to Palestine.

Anatolia. Peninsula containing the Asian provinces of modern Turkey.

Ashkenazi (pl. *Askenazim*). Israelis of European origin.

ayatollah. Literally, "sign of God." Title assigned to Iranian ulama who have achieved a high level of religious learning.

Bahais. Religious group founded by Bahaullah in nineteenth-century Iran. He was a follower of the Bab, who scandalized ulama by claiming to be the gate to the Hidden Imam. Iran regards Bahais as heretics.

bazaaris. Merchants. The bazaar is the central market in an Iranian city.

cadi (qadi). Judge. One who applies the law of Islam, the sharia.

Coptic Christians. One of the earliest Christian communities, host to some of the earliest Christian monasticism, distinguished in part by their attachment to the Monophysite position on the nature of Christ.

Dar al-Ifta. Office of the mufti, source of religious opinions called fatwas.

Dar al-Islam. The "house of Islam," or that territory governed by Muslims.

dati. Orthodox Jews. Those who follow most Jewish traditions and support Zionism.

devshirme. A levy imposed by the Ottoman Empire on the Christian provinces, by which young Christian boys were inducted into the imperial service. Converted to Islam and educated as soldiers and bureaucrats, they became "slaves" of the sultan.

dhikr. Routine by which Sufis (Muslim mystics) commune with God. A dhikr may include chanting the names of God, singing, dancing, or other acts.

dhimmi. Protected minority of the Ottoman Empire. "Religions of the book," such as Christianity and Judaism, enjoyed *dhimmi* status.

état laïque. French term for a secular state.

faqih (pl. *fuqaha*). Jurisprudent. One who practices fiqh, which is the science of law.

fatwa. A religious opinion.

fiqh. Jurisprudence. The science of law.

gazi (ghazi). Raider on behalf of the faith; holy warrior.

hadith (pl. *ahadith*). Saying or tradition attributed to the Prophet, known to subsequent generations by oral transmission and then in written compilations produced by legal scholars.

hajj. Pilgrimage to Mecca. One of the five pillars of Islam.

halakha. Jewish religious law.

haredim. Ultraorthodox Jews, many of whom reject the legitimacy of the state of Israel.

hijab (hejab). Scarf covering the head and shoulders. Some Muslims insist women must wear one when they are in a public place.

hijra. The movement of the fledgling Muslim community from Mecca to Yathrib (which became Medina, the city of the Prophet) in 622 CE. That is the starting point for the traditional Muslim calendar.

hojatoleslam. A title accorded to graduates of theological seminaries.

ijtihad. Interpretation of the sharia by qualified jurists. Legitimate at certain times and under certain conditions, according to some schools of thought.

imam. Prayer leader. Also, in the Shii tradition, one of the legitimate line of successors to the Prophet.

Islamist. A person or group who argues for the political relevance of Islam. In general, one who seeks the modern implementation of the sharia, or at least parts of it.

jahiliyya. Ignorance. Hence, the age before the coming of Islam. Also applied by some radicals (Qutb, Bin Laden) to the contemporary age.

javanmard. An Iranian conception of the ideal man.

jihad. Effort, striving on behalf of one's faith. May include the legitimate use of violence under some circumstances.

kahal (kehilla). Traditional Jewish community in the Diaspora.

kashrut. Jewish dietary rules.

kibbutz (pl. *kibbutzim*). An egalitarian community in Israel originally dedicated to agricultural production on the basis of rotating responsibilities linked to the Labor settlement movement.

Knesset. The Israeli parliament, a single-house legislature that exercises full sovereignty.

kufr. Nonbeliever, heretic.

laïcité. French term meaning secularism of a rather extreme form.

laïque. French term for secular. Thoroughly separate from religion.

madrasa (medrese). Higher-level school for Islamic learning.

Majlis. Parliament in Iran.

marja-e taqlid. Shii cleric regarded by his peers as a model worthy of emulation.

marja-e taqlid matlaq. Shii cleric regarded by his peers as the sole model of emulation in his generation.

maslahat. Public interest. Muslim jurists may seek to set aside provisions of the sharia to accommodate such interests.

masorti. "Traditional" Jews. Tend to observe generally accepted traditions as well as customs from Middle Eastern and North African settings that do not figure in Ashkenazi Orthodoxy (dati).

millet. A non-Muslim religious community enjoying some autonomy and protection (*dhimmi* status) in the Ottoman Empire.

Mizrachi (pl. *Mizrachim*). Israeli Jews of Middle Eastern and North African origin. (Also the name of an early Orthodox political movement that became the National Religious Party.) Such immigrants are also called Sephardim (as opposed to Ashkenazim) and Oriental (as opposed to Western) Jews.

mufti. A high religious official, source of religious opinions.

mujtahid. A Muslim jurist who engages in ijtihad, that is, exercises some independent judgment in interpreting the sharia.

mullah. Common word for a cleric in Iran. *Ulama* is a more formal (Arabic) term for the clerical class.

NGO. Nongovernmental organization, national or international.

niqab. An extreme form of modest dress in which women cover themselves head to toe. A veil may cover all but the eyes.

Orientalism. The study of the Middle East and North Africa as it developed in Europe in the nineteenth and early twentieth centuries. Marked by an emphasis on language and the analysis of texts.

Pahlavi. Family name taken by Reza Khan when he took the throne in Iran in 1925. His son Muhammad Reza ruled as king until the revolution of 1978–1979.

Qajar. Ruling family in Iran from the late eighteenth until the early twentieth century.

Quran (Qur'an). Holy scripture of Islam. Also spelled Coran or Koran.

sadr al-ulama. Cleric appointed by the monarch in an effort to control the ulama in Iran.

Safavids. Ruling family of Iran from 1501 until the early eighteenth century.

salafi (salafiyya). Pious ancestors and, by extension, modern Muslims who seek to follow the path of the pious ancestors.

sharia (shari'a). The law constructed by Muslim scholars working from the Quran and the sunna of the Prophet in the centuries after his death.

shaykh. A "white head," a leader, a tribal chief, or a mystic thought to have special abilities to commune with God.

Shaykh al-Azhar. Government-appointed head of Al-Azhar Mosque and University in Egypt. Usually regarded as the principal religious authority in the country.

Shaykh al-Islam. Principal religious authority in the Ottoman Empire.

Shia (Shi'a). The "party of Ali," those who supported him as the legitimate heir of Muhammad and who regard his descendants as the rightful rulers of early Islam. Muslims who are not Sunni or Khariji.

Shii (Shi'i) (pl. Shi'a). One who belongs to the "party of Ali." Also an adjective referring to that which pertains to the Shia. Also written "Shiite."

Sufi. A Muslim mystic, one who seeks spiritual purity in ways that go beyond adherence to the sharia.

sunna. What was done in the time of the Prophet. Initially known by oral transmission and by tradition. Later known principally through the hadith literature, which recorded acts and sayings of the Prophet and his companions.

Sunni. A mainstream Muslim, non-Shia. They constitute more than 90 percent of all Muslims in the world. Also an adjective used for those things pertaining to Sunnis and Sunnism.

tariqat (*tariqa* in Arabic; *tarikat* in Turkish). Sufi orders or brotherhoods, headed by a shaykh and often named from a founding shaykh.

tekkes. Meeting places of the Sufi brotherhoods in Turkey.

Twelvers. One strain of Shii Islam; a strain that predominates in Islam. Ismailis are Seveners. Zaidis are Fivers. Twelvers believe that the twelfth in a line of designated successors to the Prophet disappeared in the ninth century and will reappear someday.

ulama (ulema) (sing. *alim*). Scholars of Islam. Includes people who act in various religious capacities—preachers, prayer leaders, teachers—some much more scholarly than others.

umma. The community of Muslim believers.

velayat-e faqih. Persian for "rule of the supreme jurisprudent." A theory put forth by Ayatollah Khomeini and implemented in the Iranian constitution.

Wahhabi. A school of puritanical Islam that came to dominate in Saudi Arabia. Looks to Ibn Abd al-Wahhab, an eighteenth-century scholar, as its founding authority.

waqf (pl. *awqaf*). Pious foundation for the support of Islamic institutions. *Vaqf* (*evqaf*) is the Turkish form. The concept seems to date from the twelfth century. Most governments have taken over the pious foundations.

yeshiva. Ultraorthodox school for training pupils in the religious tradition. Little emphasis on modern subjects.

Yishuv. The Jewish community in Palestine before 1948, when it declared its independence as the state of Israel.

Bibliography

General

Ahmed, Leila. *Women and Gender in Islam*. New Haven, CT: Yale University Press, 1992.

Ajami, Fouad. *The Vanished Imam: Musa al-Sadr and the Shi'a of Lebanon*. Ithaca, NY: Cornell University Press, 1986.

Almond, Gabriel A., and Sidney Verba, eds. *The Civic Culture: Political Attitudes and Democracy in Five Nations*. Princeton, NJ: Princeton University Press, 1963.

———. *The Civic Culture Revisited*. Newbury Park, CA: Sage Publications, 1989.

Anderson, Benedict. *Imagined Communities: Reflections on the Origin and Spread of Nationalism*, rev. ed. London: Verso, 1991.

Antonius, George. *The Arab Awakening: The Story of the Arab National Movement*. New York: G. P. Putnam's Sons, 1946.

Arkoun, Mohammed. *Humanisme et islam: combats et propositions*. Paris: Vrin, 2005.

———. "Positivisme et tradition dans une perspective islamique: Le cas du kémalisme." *Diogène* 127 (July–September 1984).

———. *Rethinking Islam*, ed. and trans. Robert D. Lee. Boulder, CO: Westview, 1994.

Asad, Talal. *Formations of the Secular: Christianity, Islam, Modernity*. Stanford, CA: Stanford University Press, 2003.

Audi, Robert. *Religious Commitment and Secular Reason*. Cambridge, UK: Cambridge University Press, 2000.

Ayoob, Mohammed. *The Many Faces of Political Islam: Religion and Politics in the Muslim World*. Ann Arbor: University of Michigan Press, 2008.

Azmeh, Aziz al-. *Muslim Kingship: Power and the Sacred in Muslim, Christian and Pagan Polities*. London: I. B. Tauris, 1995.

Banfield, Edward C. *The Moral Basis of a Backward Society*. New York: Free Press, 1958.

Barbier, Maurice. *La Laïcité*. Paris: Editions L'Harmattan, 1995.

Barnett, Michael N. *Dialogues in Arab Politics*. New York: Columbia University Press, 1998.

Bates, Robert H. *Prosperity and Violence: The Political Economy of Development.* New York: Norton, 2001.

Baudoin, Jean, and Philippe Portier, eds. *La laïcité, une valeur d'aujourd'hui? Contestations et négociations du modèle français.* Paris: Presses universitaires de France, 2001.

Bayat, Asef. *Making Islam Democratic: Social Movements and the Post-Islamist Turn.* Stanford, CA: Stanford University Press, 2007.

Bedouelle, Greg, and Jean-Paul Costa. *Les laïcités à la française.* Paris: Presses universitaires de France, 1998.

Bencheikh, Saheif. *Marianne et le prophète: l'Islam dans la France laïque.* Paris: Bernard Grasset, 1998.

Berger, Peter. *The Sacred Canopy: Elements of a Sociological Theory of Religion.* Garden City, NY: Doubleday, 1967.

Binder, Leonard. "The Crisis of Political Development," in Leonard Binder et al., *Crises and Sequences in Political Development.* Princeton, NJ: Princeton University Press, 1971.

Brown, Nathan J. "Shari'a and State in the Modern Muslim Middle East." *International Journal of Middle East Studies* 29, no. 3 (August 1997): 359–376.

Burgat, François. *Face to Face with Political Islam.* London: I. B. Tauris, 2003, trans. from the French, *Islamisme en face.* Paris: Editions La Découverte, 1996.

Carter, Stephen. *The Culture of Disbelief.* New York: Basic Books, 1993.

Casanova, José. *Public Religions in the Modern World.* Chicago: University of Chicago Press, 1994.

Cesari, Jocelyne. *Musulmans et républicaines; les jeunes, l'islam, et la France.* Paris: Editions Complexe, 1998.

Chadwick, Owen. *The Secularization of the European Mind in the Nineteenth Century.* Cambridge, UK: Cambridge University Press, 1975.

Chatterjee, Partha. *Nationalist Thought and the Colonial World.* London: Zed, 1986.

Cook, Steven A. *Ruling but Not Governing: The Military and Political Development in Egypt, Algeria, and Turkey.* Baltimore: Johns Hopkins University Press, 2007.

———. *The Struggle for Egypt: From Nasser to Tahrir Square.* Oxford: Oxford University Press, 2012.

Coq, Guy. *Laïcité et République: Le lien nécessaire.* Paris: Editions du Félin, 1995.

Demerath, N. J. III. "Religious Capital and Capital Religions: Cross-Cultural and Non-Legal Factors in the Separation of Church and State." *Daedalus* 120, no. 3 (Summer 1991): 21–40.

Dobbelaere, Karel. "The Secularization of Society? Some Methodological Suggestions," in Jeffrey K. Hadden and Anson Shupe, eds., *Religion and the Political Order.* Vol. 3, *Secularization and Fundamentalism Reconsidered.* New York: Paragon House, 1986.

Doumato, Eleanor Abdella, and Gregory Starrett. *Teaching Islam: Textbooks and Religion in the Middle East.* Boulder, CO: Lynne Rienner, 2007.

Durkheim, Emile. "The Elementary Forms of Religious Life," in W. S. F. Pickering, ed., *Durkheim on Religion.* Atlanta: Scholars Press, 1994.

Eickelman, Dale F., and James Piscatori. *Muslim Politics.* Princeton, NJ: Princeton University Press, 1996.

Eisenach, Eldon J. *The Next Religious Establishment: National Identity and Political Theology in Post-Protestant America.* Lanham, MD: Rowman & Littlefield, 2000.

Ertman, Thomas. *Birth of the Leviathan: Building State and Regimes in Medieval and Early Modern Europe.* Cambridge, UK: Cambridge University Press, 1997.

Etienne, Bruno. *La France et l'islam.* Paris: Hachette, 1989.

Evans, Martin, and John Phillips. *Algeria: Anger of the Dispossessed.* New Haven, CT: Yale University Press, 2007.

Fortin, Ernest L. *Human Rights, Virtue and the Common Good: Untimely Meditations on Religion and Politics.* Edited by J. Brian Benested. Lanham, MD: Rowman & Littlefield, 1996.

Fox, Jonathan. *A World Survey of Religion and the State.* New York: Cambridge University Press, 2008.

Gauchet, Marcel. *The Disenchantment of the World: A Political History of Religion.* Translated by Oscar Burge. Princeton, NJ: Princeton University Press, 1997.

———. *La religion dans la démocratie.* Paris: Gallimard, 1998.

Gibson, William. *The Church of England, 1688–1832: Unity and Accord.* London: Routledge, 2001.

Green, John C. *The Faith Factor: How Religion Influences American Elections.* Westport, CT: Praeger, 2007.

Hadden, Jeffrey K. "Desacralizing Secularization Theory," in Hadden and Anson Shupe, eds., *Religion and the Political Order.* Vol. 3, *Secularization and Fundamentalism Reconsidered.* New York: Paragon House, 1986.

Haim, Sylvia, ed. *Arab Nationalism: An Anthology.* Berkeley: University of California Press, 1964.

Halpern, Manfred. *The Politics of Social Change in the Middle East and North Africa.* Princeton, NJ: Princeton University Press, 1963.

Hanson, Eric O. *Religion and Politics in the International System Today.* Cambridge, UK: Cambridge University Press, 2006.

Harris, Frederick C. "Something Within: Religion as a Mobilizer of African-American Political Activism." *Journal of Politics* 56, no. 1 (February 1994): 42–68.

Hefner, Robert W. *Civil Islam: Muslims and Democratization in Indonesia.* Princeton, NJ: Princeton University Press, 2000.

———, ed. *Shari'a Politics: Islamic Law and Society in the Modern World.* Bloomington: Indiana University Press, 2011.

Hefner, Robert W., and Mohammad Qasim Zaman, eds. *Schooling Islam: The Culture and Politics of Modern Muslim Education.* Princeton, NJ: Princeton University Press, 2007.

Henry, Clement M., and Robert Springborg. *Globalization and the Politics of Development in the Middle East,* 2nd ed. Cambridge, UK: Cambridge University Press, 2010.

Hodgson, Marshall. *The Venture of Islam.* Vol. 1, *The Classical Age of Islam.* Chicago: University of Chicago Press, 1961.

Huntington, Samuel P. *American Politics: The Promise of Disharmony.* Cambridge, MA: Belknap Press, 1981.

———. *The Clash of Civilizations and the Remaking of World Culture.* New York: Simon & Schuster, 1996.

Hurd, Elizabeth Shakman. *The Politics of Secularism in International Relations.* Princeton, NJ: Princeton University Press, 2008.

Inglehart, Ronald. *Modernization and Postmodernization: Cultural, Economic, and Political Change in 43 Societies.* Princeton, NJ: Princeton University Press, 1997.

Inglehart, Ronald, and Christian Weizel. *Modernization, Cultural Change, and Democracy: The Human Development Sequence.* Cambridge, UK: Cambridge University Press, 2005.

Kalyvas, Stathis N. "Democracy and Religious Politics." *Comparative Political Studies* 31, no. 3 (June 1998): 292–230.

Kaufman, Peter Iver. *Redeeming Politics.* Princeton, NJ: Princeton University Press, 1990.

Keddie, Nikki. *An Islamic Response to Imperialism: Political and Religious Writings of Sayyid Jamal al-Din "al-Afghani."* Berkeley: University of California Press, 1983.

Kedourie, Elie. *Afghani and Abduh: An Essay on Religious Unbelief and Political Activism in Islam.* New York: Humanities Press, 1966.

———. *Democracy and Arab Political Culture.* Washington, DC: Washington Institute for Near East Policy, 1991.

———. *Nationalism.* London: Hutchinson, 1960.

Kepel, Gilles, *Jihad: Expansion et déclin de l'islamisme.* Paris: Gallimard, 2000.

———. *Jihad: The Trail of Political Islam.* Translated by Anthony F. Roberts. Cambridge, MA: Harvard University Press, 2002.

Kerr, Malcolm. *Islamic Reform: The Political and Legal Theories of Muhammad Abduh and Rashid Rida.* Berkeley: University of California Press, 1966.

———. *The Arab Cold War.* London: Oxford University Press, 1967.

Kopstein, Jeffrey, and Sven Steinmo, eds. *Growing Apart?: America and Europe in the Twenty-First Century.* Cambridge, UK: Cambridge University Press, 2008.

Lamchichi, Abderrahim. *Islam et musulmans de France.* Paris: L'Harmattan, 1999.

Lee, Robert D. *Overcoming Tradition and Modernity: The Search for Islamic Authenticity.* Boulder, CO: Westview Press, 1997.

Leege, David C. "Toward a Mental Measure of Religiosity in Research on Religion and Politics," in Ted G. Jelen, ed., *Religion and Political Behavior in the United States.* New York: Praeger, 1989.

Lewis, Bernard, ed. and trans. *Islam from the Prophet Muhammad to the Capture of Constantinople.* Vol. 1, *Politics and War.* New York: Harper, 1974.

Lilla, Mark. *The Stillborn God.* New York: Alfred A. Knopf, 2007.

Lindblom, Charles E. *The Intelligence of Democracy: Decision Making Through Mutual Adjustment.* New York: Free Press, 1965.

Lockman, Zachary. *Contending Visions of the Middle East: The History and Politics of Orientalism.* Cambridge, UK: Cambridge University Press, 2004.

Margalit, Avishai. "Sectarianism." *Dissent* 55, no. 1 (Winter 2008): 37–46.

Martin, David. *A General Theory of Secularization.* Oxford, UK: Blackwell, 1978.

Martinez, Luis. *La guerre civile en Algérie, 1990–1998.* Paris: Editions Karthala, 1998.

Nasr, Seyyed Vali Reza. *Islamic Leviathan: Islam and the Making of State Power.* Oxford, UK: Oxford University Press, 2001.

Nicholls, David. *God and Government in an "Age of Reason."* London: Routledge, 1995.

Norris, Pippa, and Ronald Inglehart. *Sacred and Secular: Religion and Politics Worldwide.* Cambridge, UK: Cambridge University Press, 2004.

Norton, Augustus Richard, ed. *Civil Society in the Middle East,* 2 vols. Leiden, Netherlands: Brill, 1995–1996.

Owen, Roger. *The Rise and Fall of Arab Presidents for Life.* Cambridge, MA: Harvard University Press, 2012.

Pecora, Vincent P. *Secularization and Cultural Criticism: Religion, Nation, and Modernity*. Chicago: University of Chicago Press, 2006.

Pratt, Nicola. *Democracy and Authoritarianism in the Arab World*. Boulder, CO: Lynne Rienner, 2007.

Rodinson, Maxime. *Mohammed*. Translated by Anne Carter. New York: Viking, 1974.

Roy, Olivier. *La Sainte Ignorance: Le Temps de la Religion Sans Culture*. Paris: Seuil, 2008. Translated as "Holy Ignorance: When Religion and Culture Part Ways." New York: Columbia University Press, 2010.

Said, Edward. *Orientalism*. New York: Pantheon Books, 1978.

Scott, David, and Charles Hirschkind, eds. *Power of the Secular Modern: Talal Asad and His Interlocutors*. Stanford, CA: Stanford University Press, 2006.

Shaban, M. A. *Islamic History: A New Interpretation*, 2 vols. Cambridge, UK: Cambridge University Press, 1976.

Smidt, Corwin. "Religion and Civic Engagement: A Comparative Analysis." *Annals of the American Academy of Political and Social Science* 565 (September 1999): 176–192.

Smith, Donald Eugene. *Religion and Political Development*. Boston: Little, Brown, 1970.

Smith, Steven B. *Spinoza, Liberalism, and the Question of Jewish Identity*. New Haven, CT: Yale University Press, 1997.

Spinner-Halev, Jeff. *Surviving Diversity: Religion and Democratic Citizenship*. Baltimore: Johns Hopkins University Press, 2000.

Tepe, Sultan. "Moderation of Religious Parties: Electoral Constraints, Ideological Commitments, and the Democratic Capacities of Religious Parties in Israel and Turkey," *Political Science Quarterly* 65, no. 3 (September 2012): 467–485.

Tessler, Mark. *Public Opinion in the Middle East*. Bloomington: Indiana University Press, 2011.

Tessler, Mark, and Jodi Nachtwey. "Religion and International Conflict: An Individual-Level Analysis," in Mark Tessler, ed., *Area Studies and Social Science: Strategies for Understanding Middle East Politics*. Bloomington: Indiana University Press, 1999.

Waldner, David. *State Building and Late Development*. Ithaca, NY: Cornell University Press, 1998.

Weber, Max. *The Protestant Ethic and the Spirit of Capitalism*. Translated by Talcott Parsons. London: Routledge, 1992.

Willaime, Jean-Paul. "Unification européenne et religions," in Jean Baudoin and Philippe Portier, eds., *La laïcité, une valeur d'aujourd'hui? Contestations et négociations du modèle français*. Paris: Presses universitaires de France, 2001.

Wolfart, Johannes C. *Religion, Government and Political Culture in Early Modern Germany: Lindau, 1520–1628*. New York: Palgrave, 2002.

Wuthnow, Robert. *Communities of Discourse: Ideology and Social Structure in the Enlightenment, and European Socialism*. Cambridge, MA: Harvard University Press, 1989.

Egypt

Abed-Kotob, Sana. "The Accommodationists Speak: Goals and Strategies of the Muslim Brotherhood of Egypt." *International Journal of Middle East Studies* 27 (August 1995): 321–339.

Al-Ali, Nadje. *Secularism, Gender and the State in the Middle East.* Cambridge, UK: Cambridge University Press, 2000.

Amin, Galal. *Egypt in the Era of Hosni Mubarak, 1981–2011.* Cairo: American University in Cairo Press, 2011.

Ben Néfissa, Sarah. "Citoyenneté et participation en Egypte: l'Action vertueuse selon la Gami'iyya Shari'iyya." *Monde Arabe Maghreb Machrek* 167 (January–March 2000): 14–24.

Berger, Maurits S. "Apostasy and Public Policy in Contemporary Egypt: An Evaluation of Recent Cases from Egypt's Highest Courts." *Human Rights Quarterly* 25 (2003): 720–740.

Blaydes, Lisa, and Safinaz El Tarouty. "Women's Electoral Participation in Egypt: The Implications of Gender for Voter Recruitment and Mobilization." *Middle East Journal* 63, no. 3 (Summer 2009): 364–380.

Bowie, Robert R. *Suez, 1956.* New York: Oxford University Press, 1974.

Brown, Jonathan. "Salafis and Sufis in Egypt." Washington, DC: Carnegie Endowment for International Peace, December 2011.

Brown, Nathan J. "When Victory Becomes an Option: Egypt's Muslim Brotherhood Confronts Success." Washington, DC: Carnegie Endowment for International Peace, January 2012.

Cook, Bradley J. "Islam and Egyptian Higher Education: Student Attitudes." *Comparative Education Review* 45, no. 3 (August 2001): 379–409.

Crecelius, Daniel. "The Course of Secularization in Modern Egypt," in John L. Esposito, ed., *Islam and Development.* Syracuse, NY: Syracuse University Press, 1980.

———. "The Ulama and the State in Modern Egypt." PhD dissertation, Princeton University, May 1967.

Dupret, Baudouin. "Justice égyptienne, moralité publique et pouvoir politique." *Monde Arabe Maghreb Machrek* 167 (January–March 2000): 25–31.

Fandy, Mamoun. "Egypt's Islamic Group: Regional Revenge?" *Middle East Journal* 48, no. 4 (Autumn 1994): 611–625.

Faour, Muhammad. "Religious Education and Pluralism in Egypt and Tunisia." Washington, DC: Carnegie Endowment for International Peace, August 2012.

Faraj, Muhammad Abd al-Salam. *The Neglected Duty: The Creed of Sadat's Assassins and the Creed of the Islamic Resurgence in the Middle East.* Edited and translated by Johannes J. G. Jansen. New York: Macmillan, 1986.

Ferrié, Jean-Noël, and Saâida Radi. "Consensus national et identité morale: le sida comme analyseur de la société égyptienne." *Maghreb Machrek* 167 (January–March 2000): 6–13.

Gershoni, Israel, and James P. Jankowski. *Redefining the Egyptian Nation, 1930–1945.* Cambridge, UK: Cambridge University Press, 1995.

Guazzone, Laura. "Les Frères musulman en Egypte (1990–2011): entre néo-autoritarisme, réformisme et islamisme." *Maghreb Machrek* 207 (Spring 2011): 127–144.

Haawwa, Saeed. *The Muslim Brotherhood.* Translated by Abdul Karim Shaikh. Kuwait: Al Faysal Islamic Press, 1985.

Hatina, Meir. "On the Margins of Consensus: The Call to Separate Religion and State in Modern Egypt." *Middle Eastern Studies* 36, no. 1 (January 2000): 35–67.

Hirschkind, Charles. "The Ethics of Listening: Cassette-Sermon Audition in Contemporary Egypt." *American Ethnologist* 28, no. 3 (August 2001): 623–649.

Hirschl, Ran. "Constitutional Courts vs. Religious Fundamentalism: Three Middle Eastern Tales." *Texas Law Review* 82, no. 7 (June 2004): 1819–1870.

Ibrahim, Saad Eddin. *Egypt, Islam and Democracy: Critical Essays*. Cairo: American University in Cairo, 1996.

Jabarti, Abd al-Rahman al-. *Napoleon in Egypt: Al-Jabartī's Chronicle of the First Seven Months of the French Occupation, 1798*. Translated by Shmuel Moreh. Princeton, NJ: M. Wiener, 1993.

Johansen, Baber. "Apostasy as Objective and Depersonalized Fact: Two Recent Egyptian Court Judgments." *Social Research* 70, no. 3 (Fall 2003): 687–710.

Khatab, Sayed. "Al-Hudaybi's Influence on the Development of Islamist Movements in Egypt." *Muslim World* 91, no. 3–4 (Fall 2001): 451–479.

Levy, Guenter. "Nasserism and Islam: A Revolution in Search of Ideology," in Donald Eugene Smith, ed., *Religion and Political Modernization*. New Haven, CT: Yale University Press, 1974, 280, quoting from P. J. Vatkiotis.

Lindsey, Ursula. "Freedom and Reform at Egypt's Universities." Washington, DC: Carnegie Endowment for International Peace, September 2012.

Mahmood, Saba. "Feminist Theory, Embodiment, and the Docile Agent: Some Reflections on the Egyptian Islamic Revival." *Cultural Anthropology* 16, no. 2 (May 2001): 202–236.

Mitchell, Richard P. *The Society of Muslim Brothers*. New York: Oxford University Press, 1993.

Osman, Tarek. *Egypt on the Brink: From the Rise of Nasser to the Fall of Mubarak*, rev. ed. New Haven, CT: Yale University Press, 2010.

Qutb, Sayyid. *A Child from the Village*. Edited and translated by John Calvert and William Shepard. Syracuse, NY: Syracuse University Press, 2004.

———. *Milestones*, rev. trans. Indianapolis: American Trust Publications, 1990.

Saif, Ibrahim, and Muhammad Abu Rumman. "The Economic Agenda of the Islamist Parties." Washington, DC: Carnegie Endowment for International Peace, May 2012.

Sedra, Paul. "Class Cleavages and Ethnic Conflict: Coptic Christian Communities in Modern Egypt." *Islam and Christian-Muslim Relations* 10, no. 2 (July 1999): 219–235.

Shahin, Emad El-Din. "Political Islam in Egypt." CEPS Working Document 266, Center for European Policy Studies, Brussels, May 2007.

Shehata, Samer, and Joshua Stacher. "The Brotherhood Goes to Parliament." *Middle East Report* 36, no. 240 (Fall 2006).

Shepard, William E. "Muhammad Sa'id al-'Ashmawi and the Application of the Shari'a in Egypt." *International Journal of Middle East Studies* 28, no. 1 (February 1996): 39–58.

———. "Sayyid Qutb's Doctrine of Jāhiliyya." *International Journal of Middle East Studies* 35, no. 4 (November 2003): 521–545.

Skovgaard-Petersen, Jakob. *Defining Islam for the Egyptian State: Muftis and Fatwas of the Dār al-Iftā*. Leiden, Netherlands: Brill, 1997.

Smith, Charles D. "The Egyptian Copts: Nationalism, Ethnicity, and Definition of Identity for a Religious Minority," in Maya Shatzmiller, ed., *Nationalism and Minority Identities in Islamic Societies*. Montreal: McGill-Queen's University Press, 2005.

Starrett, Gregory. *Putting Islam to Work: Education, Politics and Religious Transformation in Egypt*. Berkeley: University of California Press, 1998.

Sullivan, Denis J., and Sana Abed-Kotob. *Islam in Contemporary Egypt: Civil Society vs. the State.* Boulder, CO: Lynne Rienner, 1999.

Van Doorn-Harder, Pieternella. "Copts: Fully Egyptian, but for a Tattoo?" in Maya Shatzmiller, ed., *Nationalism and Minority Identities in Islamic Societies.* Montreal: McGill-Queen's University Press, 2005.

Zeghal, Malika. *Gardiens de l'Islam: Les oulémas d'Al Azhar dans l'Egypte contemporaine.* Paris: Fondation nationale des sciences politiques, 1996.

Zeidan, David. "The Copts—Equal, Protected or Persecuted? The Impact of Islamization on Muslim-Christian Relations in Modern Egypt." *Islam and Christian-Muslim Relations* 10, no. 1 (March 1999): 53–67.

Israel

Arian, Asher. *The Second Republic: Politics in Israel.* Chatham, NJ: Chatham House, 1998.

Avishai, Bernard. *The Tragedy of Zionism: Revolution and Democracy in the Land of Israel.* New York: Farrar, Straus and Giroux, 1985.

Bar-Lev, Mordechai. "Politicization and Depoliticization of Jewish Religious Education in Israel." *Religious Education* 86, no. 4 (Fall 1991): 608–618.

Ben Zadok, Efraim. "State-Religion Relations in Israel: The Subtle Issue Underlying the Rabin Assassination," in Efraim Karsh, ed., *Israeli Politics and Society Since 1948: Problems of Collective Identity.* London: Frank Cass, 2002.

Bick, Etta. "A Party in Decline: Shas in Israel's 2003 Elections." *Israel Affairs* 10, no. 4 (Summer 2004): 98–129.

Cohen-Almagor, Raphael. "Vigilant Jewish Fundamentalism: From the JDL to Kach (or 'Shalom Jews, Shalom Dogs')." *Terrorism and Political Violence* 4, no. 1 (Spring 1992): 44–66.

Dominguez, Virginia. *People as Subject, People as Object: Selfhood and Peoplehood in Contemporary Israel.* Madison: University of Wisconsin Press, 1989.

Dowty, Alan. *The Jewish State: A Century Later.* Berkeley: University of California Press, 1998.

Edelman, Martin. "A Portion of Animosity: The Politics of the Disestablishment of Religion in Israel." *Israel Studies* 5, no. 1 (Spring 2000): 204–227.

Fox, Jonathan, and Jonathan Rynhold. "A Jewish and Democratic State? Comparing Government Involvement in Religion in Israel with Other Democracies." *Totalitarian Movements and Political Religions* 9, no. 4 (December 2008): 507–531.

Gross, Zehavit. "State-Religious Education in Israel: Between Religion and Modernity." *Prospects* 33, no. 2 (June 2003): 149–164.

Harrison, Jo-Ann. "School Ceremonies for Yitzhak Rabin: Social Construction of Civil Religion in Israeli Schools." *Israel Studies* 6, no. 3 (Fall 2001): 113–134.

Hirschl, Ran. "Constitutional Courts vs. Religious Fundamentalism: Three Middle Eastern Tales." *Texas Law Review* 82, no. 7 (June 2004): 1819–1870.

Isaac, Rael Jean. *Israel Divided: Ideological Politics in the Jewish State.* Baltimore: Johns Hopkins University Press, 1976.

Kimmerling, Baruch. *The Invention and Decline of Israeliness: State, Society, and the Military.* Berkeley: University of California Press, 2001.

Leibowitz, Yeshayahu. *Judaism, Human Values, and the Jewish State.* Edited by Eliezer Goldman. Cambridge, MA: Harvard University Press, 1992.

Lerner, Hanna. "Democracy, Constitutionalism, and Identity: The Anomaly of the Israeli Case." *Constellations* 11, no. 2 (June 2004): 237–257.

Liebman, Charles S., and Eliezer Don-Yehiya. *Religion and Politics in Israel.* Bloomington: Indiana University Press, 1984.

Liebman, Charles S., and Elihu Katz, eds. *The Jewishness of Israelis: Responses to the Guttman Report.* Albany: State University of New York Press, 1997.

Lockard, Joe. "Israeli Utopianism Today: Interview with Adi Ophir." *Tikkun* 19, no. 6 (November–December 2004): 18–21.

Mirsky, Yehudah. "Inner Life of Religious Zionism." *New Leader* 78, no. 9 (December 4, 1995): 10–14.

Neuberger, [Ralph] Benyamin. *Religion and Democracy in Israel.* Translated by Deborah Lemmer. Jerusalem: Floersheimer Institute for Policy Studies, 1997.

Nyroos, Lari. "Religeopolitics: Dissident Geopolitics and the 'Fundamentalism' of Hamas and Kach." *Geopolitics* 6, no. 3 (Winter 2001): 135–157.

Raday, Frances. "Women's Rights: Dichotomy Between Religion and Secularism in Israel." *Israel Affairs* 11, no. 1 (January 2005): 78–94.

Ravitzky, Aviezer. "Is a Halakhic State Possible? The Paradox of Jewish Theocracy." *Israel Affairs* 11, no. 1 (January 2005): 137–164.

Sacks, Jonathan. *One People? Tradition, Modernity, and Jewish Unity.* London: Littman Library of Jewish Civilisation, 1993.

Segev, Tom. *1949: The First Israelis.* Translated by Arlen Neal Weinstein. New York: Free Press, 1986.

Shafir, Gershon, and Yoav Peled. *Being Israeli: The Dynamics of Multiple Citizenship.* Cambridge, UK: Cambridge University Press, 2002.

Sharkansky, Ira. "Assessing Israel." *Shofar: An Interdisciplinary Journal of Jewish Studies* 18, no. 2 (Winter 2000): 1–18.

Sprinzak, Ehud. "Violence and Catastrophe in the Theology of Rabbi Meir Kahane: The Ideologization of Mimetic Desire." *Terrorism and Political Violence* 3, no. 3 (Autumn 1991): 48–70.

Weissbrod, Lilly. "Shas: An Ethnic Religious Party." *Israel Affairs* 9, no. 4 (Summer 2003): 79–104.

Zucker, Norman L. *The Coming Crisis in Israel: Private Faith and Public Policy.* Cambridge, MA: MIT Press, 1973.

Turkey

Ahmad, Feroz. *Turkey: The Quest for Identity.* Oxford, UK: Oneworld Publications, 2003.

Aral, Berdal. "Dispensing with Tradition? Turkish Politics and International Society During the Özal Decade, 1983–93." *Middle Eastern Studies* 37, no. 1 (January 2001): 72–88.

Arat, Yeşim. *Rethinking Islam and Liberal Democracy: Islamist Women in Turkish Politics.* Albany: State University of New York Press, 2005.

———. "Women's Rights and Islam in Turkish Politics: The Civil Code Amendment." *Middle East Journal* 64, no. 2 (Spring 2010): 235–251.

Aydintaşbaş, Asli. "Murder on the Bosporus." *Middle East Quarterly* 7, no. 2 (June 2000): 15–22.

Bardakoğlu, Ali. "'Moderate Perception of Islam' and the Turkish Model of the Diyanet: The President's Statement." *Journal of Muslim Minority Affairs* 24, no. 2 (October 2004).

Barkey, Henry J. "The Struggles of a 'Strong' State." *Journal of International Affairs* 54, no. 1 (Fall 2000): 87–105.

Çinar, Alev. *Modernity, Islam, and Secularism in Turkey: Bodies, Places, and Time.* Minneapolis: University of Minnesota Press, 2005.

Daği, Ihsan D. "Transformation of Islamic Political Identity in Turkey: Rethinking the West and Westernization." *Turkish Studies* 6, no. 1 (March 2005): 21–37.

Demiralp, Seda. "The Odd Tango of the Islamic Right and Kurdish Left in Turkey: A Peripheral Alliance to Redesign the Centre?" *Middle Eastern Studies* 48, no. 2 (March 2012): 287–302.

Deringil, Selim. "The Invention of Tradition as Public Image in the Late Ottoman Empire, 1808 to 1908." *Comparative Studies in Society and History* 35, no. 1 (January 1993): 3–29.

———. "'There Is No Compulsion in Religion': On Conversion and Apostasy in the Late Ottoman Empire: 1839–1856." *Comparative Studies in Society and History* 42, no. 3 (July 2000): 547–575.

Duran, Burhanettin. "Approaching the Kurdish Question via *Adil duzen*: An Islamist Formula of the Welfare Party for Ethnic Coexistence." *Journal of Muslim Minority Affairs* 18, no. 1 (April 1998): 111–128.

Ergul, F. Asli. "The Ottoman Identity: Turkish, Muslim or Rum?" *Middle Eastern Studies* 48, no. 4 (July 2012): 629–645.

Erman, Tahire, and Emrah Göker. "Alevi Politics in Contemporary Turkey." *Middle Eastern Studies* 36, no. 4 (October 2000): 99–118.

Gaborieau, Marco, Alexandre Popovic, and Thierry Zarcone, eds. *Naqshbandis: cheminements et situation actuelle d'un ordre mystique musulman . . . : actes de la table ronde de Sèvres . . . 24 mai . . . 1985.* Istanbul: Isis Yayimcilik Ltd., 1990.

Göle, Nilüfer. *The Forbidden Modern: Civilization and Veiling.* Ann Arbor: University of Michigan Press, 1996.

———. "Snapshots of Islamic Modernities." *Daedalus* 129, no. 1 (Winter 2000): 91–117.

Gülalp, Haldun. "Enlightenment by Fiat: Secularization and Democracy in Turkey." *Middle Eastern Studies* 41, no. 3 (May 2005).

———. "Globalization and Political Islam: the Social Bases of Turkey's Welfare Party." *International Journal of Middle East Studies* 33, no. 3 (August 2001): 433–448.

———. "Whatever Happened to Secularization? The Multiple Islams of Turkey." *South Atlantic Quarterly* 102, no. 2–3 (Spring–Summer 2003): 381–395.

Gülen, Fethullah. *Advocate of Dialogue.* Fairfax, VA: The Fountain, 2000.

Herman, Rainer. "Political Islam in Secular Turkey." *Islam and Christian-Muslim Relations* 14, no. 3 (July 2003): 265–276.

Houston, Christopher. "Civilizing Islam, Islamist Civilizing? Turkey's Islamist Movement and the Problem of Ethnic Difference." *Thesis Eleven*, no. 58 (August 1999): 83–98.

———. "Profane Intuitions: Kurdish Diaspora in the Turkish City." *Australian Journal of Anthropology* 12, no. 1 (April 2001): 15–31.

Kalaycioğlu, Ersin. "The Mystery of the Türban: Participation or Revolt." *Turkish Studies* 6, no. 2 (June 2005): 233–251.

Kaya, Ibrahim. "Modernity and Veiled Women." *European Journal of Social Theory* 3, no. 2 (May 2000): 195–214.

Kinzer, Stephen. *Crescent and Star: Turkey Between Two Worlds.* New York: Farrar, Straus and Giroux, 2001.

Kosebalaban, Hasan. "The Impact of Globalization on Islamic Political Identity: The Case of Turkey." *World Affairs* 168, no. 1 (Summer 2005): 27–37.

Kushner, David. "Self-Perception and Identity in Contemporary Turkey." *Journal of Contemporary History* 32, no. 2 (April 1997): 219–233.

Lewis, Bernard. *The Emergence of Modern Turkey.* London: Oxford University Press, 1961.

Mardin, Şerif. "The Just and the Unjust." *Daedalus* 120, no. 3 (Summer 1991): 113–129.

———. *Religion and Social Change in Modern Turkey: The Case of Bediüzzaman Said Nursi.* Albany: State University of New York Press, 1989.

———. "Turkish Islamic Exceptionalism Yesterday and Today: Continuity, Rupture and Reconstruction in Operational Codes." *Turkish Studies* 6, no. 2 (June 2005).

Mason, Whit. "The Future of Political Islam in Turkey." *World Policy Journal* 17, no. 2 (Summer 2000): 56–67.

Moaddel, Mansoor. *Islamic Modernism, Nationalism, and Fundamentalism: Episode and Discourse.* Chicago: University of Chicago Press, 2005.

Olsson, Tord, Elizabeth Ozdalga, and Catharina Randvere, eds. *Alevi Identity.* Istanbul: Swedish Research Institute in Istanbul, 1998.

Öniş, Ziya. "The Political Economy of Islamic Resurgence." *Third World Quarterly* 18, no. 4 (December 1997): 743–766.

Pamuk, Orhan. *Istanbul: Memories and the City.* Translated by Maureen Freely. New York: Random House, 2006.

Payaslyoğlu, Arif, and Ahmet Içduygu. "Awareness of and Support for Human Rights Among Turkish University Students." *Human Rights Quarterly* 21, no. 2 (May 1999): 513–534.

Pierini, Marc, with Markus Mayr. "Press Freedom in Turkey." Washington, DC: Carnegie Endowment for International Peace, January 2013.

Rahme, Joseph G. "Namik Kemal's Constitutional Ottomanism and Non-Muslims." *Islam and Christian-Muslim Relations* 10, no. 1 (1999): 23–39.

Rouleau, Eric. "Ce pouvoir si pesant des militaires turcs." *Le monde diplomatique* (September 2000): 8–9.

Sakallioğlu, Ümit Cizre. "Parameters and Strategies of Islam-State Interaction in Republican Turkey." *International Journal of Middle East Studies* 28, no. 2 (May 1996): 231–251.

Silverstein, Brian. "Islam and Modernity in Turkey: Power, Tradition and Historicity in the European Provinces of the Muslim World." *Anthropological Quarterly* 76, no. 3 (Summer 2003): 497–517.

Şimşek, Sefa. "New Social Movements in Turkey since 1980." *Turkish Studies* 5, no. 2 (Summer 2004): 111–139.

Sørensen, Bo Ærenlund. "The Ankara Consensus: Islamists, Kemalists, and Why Turkey's Nationalism Remains Overlooked," *Middle Eastern Studies* 48, no. 4 (June 2012): 613–627.

Tank, Pinar. "Political Islam in Turkey: A State of Controlled Secularity." *Turkish Studies* 6, no. 1 (March 2005): 3–19.

Turam, Berna. *Between Islam and the State.* Stanford, CA: Stanford University Press, 2007.

Vahide, Şükran. *Islam in Modern Turkey: An Intellectual Biography of Bediuzzaman Said Nursi.* Albany: State University of New York Press, 2005.

Ward, Robert E., and Dankwart Rustow, eds. *Political Modernization in Japan and Turkey*. Princeton, NJ: Princeton University Press, 1964.

Waxman, Dov. "Islam and Turkish National Identity: A Reappraisal." *Turkish Yearbook of International Relations* 30 (2000): 1–22.

White, Jenny. *Islamist Mobilization in Turkey: A Study in Vernacular Politics*. Seattle: University of Washington Press, 2002.

———. "State Feminism, Modernization and the Turkish Republican Woman." *NWSA Journal* 15, no. 3 (Fall 2003): 145–159.

Yavuz, M. Hakan. "Cleansing Islam from the Public Sphere." *Journal of International Affairs* 54, no. 1 (Fall 2000): 21–42.

———. *Islamic Political Identity in Turkey*. New York: Oxford University Press, 2003.

———. *Secularism and Muslim Democracy in Turkey*. Cambridge, UK: Cambridge University Press, 2009.

Iran

Abdo, Geneive. "Re-Thinking the Islamic Republic: A 'Conversation' with Ayatollah Hossein 'Ali Montazeri." *Middle East Journal* 55, no. 1 (Winter 2001): 9–22.

Abrahamian, Ervand. *Iran Between Two Revolutions*. Princeton, NJ: Princeton University Press, 1982.

———. *Khomeinism: Essays on the Islamic Republic*. Berkeley: University of California Press, 1993.

Adelkhah, Fariba. *Being Modern in Iran*. Translated by Jonathan Derrick. New York: Columbia University Press, 2000.

———. "Le ramadan comme négociation entre le public et le privé: le cas de la République d'Iran," in Fariba Adelkhah and François Georgeon, eds., *Ramadan and politique*. Paris: CNRS, 2000.

Afary, Janet. *Sexual Politics in Modern Iran*. New York: Cambridge University Press, 2009.

Ahmad, Jalal Al-i. *Occidentosis: A Plague from the West*. Translated by R. Campbell and edited by Hamid Algar. Berkeley, CA: Mizan Press, 1984.

Akhavi, Shahrough. *Religion and Politics in Contemporary Iran: Clergy-State Relations in the Pahlavi Period*. Albany: State University of New York Press, 1980.

Algar, Hamid. *Religion and State in Iran, 1785–1906: The Role of the Ulama in the Qajar Period*. Berkeley: University of California Press, 1969.

Alinejad, Mahmoud. "Coming to Terms with Modernity: Iranian Intellectuals and the Emerging Public Sphere." *Islam and Christian-Muslim Relations* 13, no. 1 (January 2002): 25–47.

Amirpur, Katajun. "The Future of Iran's Reform Movement," in Katajun Amirpur and Walter Posch, eds., *Iranian Challenges*, Chaillot Paper 89. Paris: European Union Institute for Security Studies, 2006.

Arjomand, Saïd Amir. *After Khomeini: Iran Under His Successors*. New York: Oxford University Press, 2009.

———. "The Rise and Fall of President Khatami and the Reform Movement in Iran." *Constellations* 12, no. 4 (December 2005): 502–520.

———. *The Turban for the Crown: The Islamic Revolution in Iran*. New York: Oxford University Press, 1988.

Ashraf, Ahmad. "Bazaar-Mosque Alliance: The Social Basis of Revolts and Revolutions." *International Journal of Politics, Culture and Society* 1, no. 4 (Summer 1988): 538–567.

Ashraf, Ahmad, and Ali Banuazizi. "Iran's Tortuous Path Toward 'Islamic Liberalism.'" *International Journal of Politics, Culture and Society* 15, no. 2 (Winter 2001): 237–256.

Bahramitash, Roksana. "Islamic Fundamentalism and Women's Economic Role: The Case of Iran." *International Journal of Politics, Culture and Society* 16, no. 4 (Summer 2003): 551–568.

Banuazizi, Ali. "Faltering Legitimacy: The Ruling Clerics and Civil Society in Contemporary Iran." *International Journal of Politics, Culture and Society* 8, no. 4 (Summer 1995): 237–256.

Berkey, Jonathan. *The Formation of Islam: Religion and Society in the Near East, 600–1800.* Cambridge, UK: Cambridge University Press, 2004.

Bill, James A. "The Cultural Underpinnings of Politics: Iran and the United States." *Mediterranean Quarterly* 17, no. 1 (Winter 2006): 22–33.

———. *The Politics of Iran: Groups, Classes and Modernization.* Columbus, OH: Merrill, 1972.

Brumberg, Daniel. "Dissonant Politics in Iran and Indonesia." *Political Science Quarterly* 116, no. 1 (2001): 381–411.

———. *Reinventing Khomeini: The Struggle for Reform in Iran.* Chicago: University of Chicago Press, 2001.

Buchta, Wilfried. *Who Rules Iran? The Structure of Power in the Islamic Republic.* Washington, DC: Washington Institute for Near East Policy, 2000.

Bulliet, Richard. *Conversion to Islam in the Middle Period: An Essay in Quantitative History.* Cambridge, MA: Harvard University Press, 1979.

Choksy, Jamsheed K. "Tehran Politics: Are the Mullahs Losing Their Grip?" *World Affairs* 175, no. 1 (May–June 2012).

Dabashi, Hamid. "The End of Islamic Ideology." *Social Research* 67, no. 2 (Summer 2000): 475–518.

———. *Iran: A People Interrupted.* New York: New Press, 2007.

———. *The Theology of Discontent: The Ideological Foundations of the Islamic Revolution in Iran.* New York: New York University Press, 1993.

Ehteshami, Anoushiravan, and Mahjoob Zweiri. *Iran and the Rise of Its Neoconservatives: The Politics of Tehran's Silent Revolution.* London: I. B. Tauris, 2007.

Eshkevari, Hasan Yusefi. *Islam and Democracy in Iran: Eshkevari and the Quest for Reform.* Edited by Ziba Mir-Hosseini and Richard Tapper. London: I. B. Tauris, 2006.

Friedl, Erika. *Children of Deh Koh.* Syracuse, NY: Syracuse University Press, 1997.

Gheissari, Ali, and Vali Nasr. "The Conservative Consolidation in Iran." *Survival* 47, no. 2 (Summer 2005): 175–190.

Hen-Tov, Elliot, and Nathan Gonzales. "The Militarization of Post-Khomeini Iran: Praetorianism 2.0." *Washington Quarterly* 34, no. 1 (Winter 2011): 245–259.

Ibn Khaldun. *The Muqaddima: An Introduction to History.* Translated by Franz Rosenthal. Princeton, NJ: Princeton University Press, 1967.

Jahanbaksh, Forough. "Religious and Political Discourse in Iran: Moving Toward Post-Fundamentalism." *Brown Journal of World Affairs* 9, no. 2 (Winter–Spring 2003): 243–254.

Kadivar, Mohsen. "An Introduction to the Public and Private Debate in Islam." *Social Research* 70, no. 3 (Fall 2003): 659–680.

Keddie, Nikki R. *Modern Iran: Roots and Results of Revolution.* New Haven, CT: Yale University Press, 2003.

Keshavarzian, Aran and Anthony Gill. "State Building and Religious Resources: An Institutional Theory of Church-State Relations in Iran and Mexico." *Politics and Society* 27, no. 3 (September 1999): 431–465.

Khomeini, Ruhollah. *Islam and Revolution: Writings and Declarations of Imam Khomeini*. Translated by Hamid Algar. Berkeley, CA: Mizan Press, 1981.

Kian, Azadeh. "Women and Politics in Post-Islamist Iran: The Gender Conscious Drive to Change." *British Journal of Middle Eastern Studies* 24, no. 1 (May 1997): 75–96.

Mahdavi, Pardis. *Passionate Uprisings: Iran's Sexual Revolution*. Stanford, CA: Stanford University Press, 2009.

Mayer, Ann Elizabeth. "The Islamic Law as a Cure for Political Law: The Withering of an Islamist Illusion." *Mediterranean Politics* 7, no. 3 (Autumn 2002): 117–142.

Mehran, Golnar. "Iran: A Shi'ite Curriculum to Serve the Islamic State," in Eleanor Abdella Doumato and Gregory Starrett, eds., *Teaching Islam: Textbooks and Religion in the Middle East*. Boulder, CO: Lynne Rienner, 2007.

Minoui, Delphine. "L'Iran des réformes: la société face au pouvoir." *Politique étrangère* 67, no. 1 (January–March 2002): 103–114.

Mir-Hosseini, Ziba. "The Conservative-Reformist Conflict over Women's Rights in Iran." *International Journal of Politics, Culture and Society* 16, no. 1 (Fall 2002): 37–53.

———. "Divorce Iranian Style," in Richard Tapper, ed., *The New Iranian Cinema: Politics, Representation and Identity*. London: I. B. Tauris, 2004.

Mottahedeh, Roy. *The Mantle of the Prophet: Religion and Politics in Iran*. New York: Pantheon, 1985.

Nafisi, Azar. *Reading Lolita in Tehran: A Memoir in Books*. New York: Random House, 2003.

Naim, Abdullahi A. Al-. "Re-affirming Secularism for Islamic Societies." *New Perspectives Quarterly* 20, no. 3 (Summer 2003): 36–45.

Omid, Homa. *Islam and the Post-Revolutionary State in Iran*. New York: St. Martin's Press, 1994.

———. "Theocracy or Democracy? The Critics of 'Westoxification' and the Politics of Fundamentalism in Iran." *Third World Quarterly* 13, no. 4 (December 1992): 675–690.

Osanloo, Arzoo. *The Politics of Women's Rights in Iran*. Princeton, NJ: Princeton University Press, 2009.

Paul, Ludwig. "'Iranian Nation' and Iranian-Islamic Revolutionary Ideology." *Die Welt des Islams* 39, no. 2 (July 1999): 183–217.

Roy, Olivier. "The Crisis of Religious Legitimacy in Iran." *Middle East Journal* 53, no. 2 (Spring 1999): 201–216.

Samii, A. William. "Iran's Guardians Council as an Obstacle to Democracy." *Middle East Journal* 55, no. 4 (Autumn 2001): 644–663.

Schirazi, Asghar. *The Constitution of Iran: Politics and the State in the Islamic Republic*. Translated by John O'Kane. London: I. B. Tauris, 1997.

Shaditalab, Jaleh. "Islamization and Gender in Iran: Is the Glass Half Full or Half Empty?" *Signs* 32, no. 1 (Autumn 2006): 14–21.

Shariati, Ali. *Marxism and Other Western Fallacies: An Islamic Critique*. Berkeley, CA: Mizan Press, 1980.

———. *On the Sociology of Islam: Lectures*. Berkeley, CA: Mizan Press, 1979.

———. *Red Shi'ism*. Houston: Free Islamic Literatures, 1980.

Tabari, Azar. "Shi'i Clergy in Iranian Politics," in Nikki Keddie, ed., *Religion and Politics in Iran*. New Haven, CT: Yale University Press, 1983.

Tabari, Keyvan. "The Rule of Law and the Politics of Reform in Post-Revolutionary Iran." *International Sociology* 18, no. 1 (March 2003): 96–113.

Takeyh, Ray. *Guardians of the Revolution: Iran and the World in the Age of the Ayatollahs*. Oxford, UK: Oxford University Press, 2009.

Tezcür, Günes Murat, Taghi Azadarmaki, Mehri Bahar, and Hooshang Nayebi. "Support for Democracy in Iran." *Political Research Quarterly* 65, no. 2 (2012): 235–247.

Thaler, David E., et al. *Mullahs, Guards, and Bonyads: An Exploration of Iranian Leadership Dynamics*. Santa Monica, CA: Rand Corporation, 2010.

Vahdat, Farzin. *God and Juggernaut: Iran's Intellectual Encounter with Modernity*. Syracuse, NY: Syracuse University Press, 2002.

Watt, W. Montgomery. "The Significance of the Early States of Imami Shi'ism," in Nikki R. Keddie, ed., *Religion and Politics in Iran: Shi'ism from Quietism to Revolution*. New Haven, CT: Yale University Press, 1983.

Zimmt, Raz. "Iran's 2008 Parliamentary Elections: A Triumph of the System." *Middle East Review of International Affairs* 12, no. 2 (June 2008).

Zonis, Marvin. *The Political Elite of Iran*. Princeton, NJ: Princeton University Press, 1971.

Saudi Arabia

Aarts, Paul, and Gerd Nonneman, eds. *Saudi Arabia in the Balance: Political Economy, Society, Foreign Affairs*. New York: New York University Press, 2005.

Al-Atawneh, Muhammad. "Is Saudi Arabia a Theocracy? Religion and Governance in Contemporary Saudi Arabia." *Middle Eastern Studies* 45, no. 5 (September 2009): 721–737.

Al-Hariri, Rafeda. "Islam's Point of View on Women's Education in Saudi Arabia." *Comparative Education* 23, no. 1 (1987): 51–57.

Al-Rasheed, Madawi. *Contesting the Saudi State: Islamic Voices from a New Generation*. Cambridge, UK: Cambridge University Press, 2007.

———. *A History of Saudi Arabia*. Cambridge, UK: Cambridge University Press, 2002.

———, ed. *Kingdom Without Borders: Saudi Arabia's Political, Religious, and Media Frontiers*. New York: Columbia University Press, 2008.

Ayoob, Mohammed, and Hasan Kosebalaban, eds. *Religion and Politics in Saudi Arabia: Wahhabism and the State*. Boulder, CO: Lynne Rienner, 2009.

Bagader, Abubaker. *La jeunesse Saoudienne: Identité, mutations, défis, enjeux et perspectives à l'aube du XXIe siècle*. Translated by Abdelmagid Guelmami. Paris: L'Harmattan, 2000.

Baskan, Birol, and Steven Wright. "Seeds of Change: Comparing State-Religion Relations in Qatar and Saudi Arabia." *Arab Studies Quarterly* 33, no. 2 (Spring 2011): 97–111.

Bradley, John R. *Saudi Arabia Exposed: Inside a Kingdom in Crisis*. New York: Palgrave Macmillan, 2005.

Dekmejian, R. Hrair. "The Rise of Political Islamism in Saudi Arabia." *Middle East Journal* 48, no. 4 (Autumn 1994): 627–643.

Fandy, Mamoun. "Enriched Islam: The Muslim Crisis of Education." *Survival* 49, no. 2 (Summer 2007): 77–98.

———. *Saudi Arabia and the Politics of Dissent*. New York: St. Martin's, 1999.

Gallagher, Eugene B., and C. Maureen Searle. "Health Services and the Political Culture of Saudi Arabia." *Social Science & Medicine* 21, no. 3 (1985): 251–262.

Ibrahim, Fouad. *The Shiis of Saudi Arabia.* London: Saqi, 2006.

Jamjoom, Mounira I. "Female Islamic Studies Teachers in Saudi Arabia: A Phenomenological Study." *Teaching and Teacher Education* 26 (2000): 547–558.

Kechichian, Joseph A. "The Role of the Ulama in the Politics of an Islamic State: The Case of Saudi Arabia." *International Journal of Middle East Studies* 18, no. 1 (February 1986): 53–71.

———. *Succession in Saudi Arabia.* New York: Palgrave, 2001.

Kruk, Remke. "Harry Potter in the Gulf: Contemporary Islam and the Occult." *British Journal of Middle Eastern Studies* 32, no. 1 (May 2005): 47–73.

Kucinskas, Jaime. "A Research Note on Islam and Gender Egalitarianism: An Examination of Egyptian and Saudi Arabian Youth Attitudes." *Journal for the Scientific Study of Religion* 49, no. 4 (2010): 761–770.

Lacroix, Stéphane. "Between Islamists and Liberals: Saudi Arabia's New 'Islamo-Liberal' Reformists." *Middle East Journal* 58, no. 3 (Summer 2004): 345–365.

———. *Les islamistes saoudiens: une insurrection manquée.* Paris: PUF, 2010. Translated by George Holoch as *Awakening Islam: The Politics of Religious Dissent in Contemporary Saudi Arabia.* Cambridge, MA: Harvard University Press, 2011.

Moaddel, Mansoor, and Stuart A. Karabenick. "Religious Fundamentalism among Young Muslims in Egypt and Saudi Arabia." *Social Forces* 86, no. 4 (June 2008): 1676–1710.

———. "The Saudi Public Speaks: Religion, Gender, and Politics." *International Journal of Middle East Studies* 38, no. 1 (February 2006): 79–108.

Nevo, Joseph. "Religion and National Identity in Saudi Arabia." *Middle Eastern Studies* 34, no. 3 (July 1998): 34–53.

Niblock, Tim. *Saudi Arabia: Power, Legitimacy and Survival.* London: Routledge, 2006.

Onsman, Andrys. "It Is Better to Light a Candle than to Ban the Darkness: Government-Led Academic Development in Saudi Arabian Universities." *Higher Education* 62, no. 4 (October 2011): 519–532.

Pharaon, Nora Alarifi. "Saudi Women and the Muslim State in the Twenty-First Century." *Sex Roles* 51, no. 5–6 (September 2004): 349–366.

Redissi, Hamadi. *Le Pacte de Najd: Ou comment l'islam sectaire est devenu Islam.* Paris: Seuil, 2007.

Rougier, Bernard, ed. *Qu'est-ce que le salafisme?* Paris: Presses universitaires de France, 2008.

Souryal, Sam. "The Religionization of a Society: The Continuing Application of Shariah Law in Saudi Arabia." *Journal for the Scientific Study of Religion* 26, no. 4 (1987): 429–449.

Vassiliev, Alexei. *The History of Saudi Arabia.* New York: New York University Press, 2000.

Vidyasagar, Girija, and David M. Rea. "Saudi Women Doctors: Gender and Careers Within Wahhabic Islam and a 'Westernised' Work Culture." *Women's Studies International Forum* 27 (2004): 261–280.

Index

Abbasid caliphate, 49
Abd al-Aziz (Ibn Saud), King, 222, 228, 241, 256
Abd al-Nasir, Gamal, President. *see* Nasir, Gamal Abd-al
Abd ul-Baha, 196
Abdu, Muhammad, 18, 49, 50–51
Abdülhamid II (Ottoman sultan), 130, 149, 169, 263
Abdullah ibn Abd al-Aziz, King, 222, 256, 257
Abu Bakr, 3, 174
Abu Zayd, Nasr Hamid, 66, 74
Academy of Islamic Research, 56, 61
Adelkhah, Fariba, 210, 214, 215
Afghani, Jamal al-Din al-, 18, 41, 43, 51, 70, 169
Afghanistan, Soviet occupation, 234
Afghans, 176, 195
African Americans, 21, 28
Agudat Israel party
  and education, 116
  in the Knesset, 96, 113
  origins of, 79
  and settlement of Palestine, 93, 97
  and status quo agreement, 88–89, 94, 96, 103–104, 105, 107
  and the Supreme Court, 111
Ahl al-Hadith, 234
Ahmad, Jalal Al-e, 178, 181, 200, 267
Ahmadinejad, Mahmoud
  elected, 217, 218
  as Holocaust denier, 188
  as populist, 188
  power, limited, 186, 188
  as principlist, 182, 189

reelected, 171, 187, 264
  in Revolutionary Guard, 204
Ahmadiyya, 65
Ahmed, Leila, 71
AIDS, 74
Akhavi, Shahbrough, 198, 199–200
Akhbaris, 195
AKP (Justice and Development Party), Turkey, 139
  attains majority in Parliament, 134, 147, 154–155, 167, 279
  and the European Union, 135
  rural supporters, 135
  and women's rights, 163
Alevis, 135–136, 147, 150, 162, 289, 290
Alexandria, 40
Algar, Hamid, 144, 197
Algeria, 25, 223, 274–275
Ali, Muhammad
  creates Islamic hierarchy, 76
  destabilizing influence, 75
  dynasty ends, 43
  as foreign ruler, 41, 77
  invades Saudi Arabia, 270
  meaning of Islam, for him, 49
  modernization, 38, 40, 42, 59–60, 70, 71
  takes power, 23, 221
Ali ibn Husayn, 223
Alids, 173–175
Altinoglu, Ebrin, 162
American Civil Liberties Union (ACLU), 259
American Jews, 112
American Revolution, 49, 221
Amir, Yigal, 100, 118
Anatolia, 7, 130–131, 135, 141, 151, 176

Index

CPSIA information can be obtained
at www.ICGtesting.com
Printed in the USA
BVOW08s2152090117
473054BV00001B/33/P